HUMAN GROWTH AND DEVELOPMENT IN CHILDREN AND YOUNG PEOPLE

Theoretical and Practice Perspectives

Edited by
Jonathan Parker and Sara Ashencaen Crabtree

T0369903

P

First published in Great Britain in 2020 by

Policy Press
University of Bristol
1-9 Old Park Hill
Bristol
BS2 8BB
UK
t: +44 (0)117 954 5940
pp-info@bristol.ac.uk
www.policypress.co.uk

North America office:
Policy Press
c/o The University of Chicago Press
1427 East 60th Street
Chicago, IL 60637, USA
t: +1 773 702 7700
f: +1 773-702-9756
sales@press.uchicago.edu
www.press.uchicago.edu

British Library Cataloguing in Publication Data
A catalogue record for this book is available from the British Library

Library of Congress Cataloging-in-Publication Data
A catalog record for this book has been requested

ISBN 978-1-4473-3742-3 paperback
ISBN 978-1-4473-3743-0 ePdf
ISBN 978-1-4473-3744-7 ePub

The right of Jonathan Parker and Sara Ashencaen Crabtree to be identified as editors of this work has been asserted by them in accordance with the Copyright, Designs and Patents Act 1988.

Cover design by blu inc
Front cover image: Stocksy/Ruth Black

Printed and bound by CPI Group (UK) Ltd, Croydon, CR0 4YY

Contents

Contents

List of figures and tables

Figures

Tables

Notes on contributors

Sara Ashencaen Crabtree is Professor of Social and Cultural Diversity and co-convenor of the Women's Academic Network at Bournemouth University. She is the author of the first European book on *Islam and Social Work* (2008).

Stephen Briggs is Professor of Social Work and Director of the Centre for Social Work Research at the University of East London, UK.

Lisa Bunting is Senior Lecturer in Social Work at Queen's University Belfast, researching in the impact of childhood adversity across the life-course.

Christine Cocker is Senior Lecturer in Social Work at the University of East Anglia. She completed her social work training in New Zealand in the 1980s. Christine researches and writes about social work and sexuality, and social work with looked-after children.

Stephen Cowden is Assistant Professor of Social Work and Course Director for the MA Social Work at Coventry University. His research looks at the impact of religious fundamentalism on social policy and social work in the UK.

Jo Finch is Reader in Social Work at the University of East London. She is Programme Leader for the Professional Doctorate in Social Work, and Deputy Director of the Centre for Social Work Research.

Nick Frost is Emeritus Professor of Social Work at Leeds Beckett University. He practised as a social worker for 15 years before commencing an academic career and is co-editor of *The Routledge Handbook of Global Child Welfare* (with Pat Dolan, Routledge, 2018).

Deborah Hadwin is Senior Lecturer in Social Work at De Montfort University and is a PhD student at Coventry researching local authority responses to unaccompanied refugee minors as they reach adulthood. Prior to entering academia, she worked in local authorities for 18 years, seven of those as a manager working with unaccompanied refugee minors.

Richard Heslop teaches Criminology at Bournemouth University and the Open University in the UK. He served for 28 years as a police officer in West Yorkshire Police before joining academia.

Sally Lee is Lecturer in Social Work at Bournemouth University with especial interest and expertise in adult services.

Wilfred McSherry is Professor in Nursing at the Department of Nursing, School of Health and Social Care, Staffordshire University/University Hospitals of North Midlands NHS Trust. He is also Part-time Professor at VID University College, Norway and a founding and executive member of the British Association for the Study of Spirituality (http://www.basspirituality.org.uk/).

Atle Ødegård is Professor at Molde University College. He is trained as a clinical psychologist and gained his PhD on inter-professional collaboration in child mental health care at the University of Oslo.

Louise Oliver is Lecturer in Social Work at Bournemouth University and a social worker in children and families practice.

Jonathan Parker is Professor of Society and Social Welfare at Bournemouth University. He is author of the best-selling book *Social Work Practice* (Sage, 2017).

Margarete Parrish is Senior Lecturer in Social Work at Bournemouth University. Her research interests include adaptation following trauma. She is author of *Social Work Perspectives on Human Behaviour* (Open University Press, 2014).

Alison Rodriguez is a health psychologist and Lecturer in Child and Family Health at the University of Leeds.

Siv E.N. Sæbjørnsen is Associate Professor at Molde University College in Norway. She is a social educator and completed her PhD on inter-professional collaboration and service-user involvement in adolescent child welfare cases at Molde University College.

Gabriele Schäfer is Professor in the School of Social Work at the University of Applied Sciences in Bremen/Germany. She is trained as a psychologist and family therapist and has worked in several therapeutic institutions in Auckland, New Zealand.

Gurnam Singh is Honorary Associate Professor of Sociology, University of Warwick and Visiting Professor of Social Work, University of Chester. In 2009, he was awarded a National Teaching Fellowship from the UK Higher Education Academy for his contribution to higher education.

Joanna Smith is Associate Professor in Child Nursing at the University of Leeds.

Sue Taplin is Lecturer in Social Work at the University of Leeds. Sue is registered as a social worker with practice and research experience in palliative care and inter-professional practice education.

Melanie Watts is Senior Lecturer in Social Work at Leeds Beckett University. She has been involved in social work education since 2006, before which she was a children and families social worker.

Elisabeth Willumsen is Professor in Social Work at the University of Stavangar, Norway. Her PhD is in public health on inter-professional collaboration in residential child care. She publishes in collaborative work, co-creation and social innovation in health and welfare services.

Acknowledgements

This book would not have been possible without the past contributions, patience and kindness of our teachers and guides, our social work and other professional colleagues over the years and, most of all, those people with whom we have worked as social workers. Our thanks go to you all. In relation to compiling the current volume, we would like to give special thanks to Catherine Gray, who first discussed the idea with us in the early spring of 2016 and worked alongside us encouragingly as we strived to bring our authors together. We would also like to thank Helen Carter, the marvellous development editor, who brought us expertly and swiftly to the production stage, passing us into the capable hands of production editor, Leonie Drake. Of course, our gratitude must also go to the authors of chapters who put up with our demands and requests, often in the face of very tight timescales, with good humour and fortitude. There are always too many people to thank personally in a project like this and for this we humbly apologise. You are remembered; without you all, this book would not have been possible.

Introduction

Jonathan Parker and Sara Ashencaen Crabtree

This edited book forms the first volume of a two-book set that provides comprehensive and analytical coverage of theories and models of human growth and development as they apply to contemporary professional social work practice with children and young people. While it is somewhat artificial to separate the life course in this way, this unique two-volume set allows us to focus on the issues that you, as social workers, will face and to introduce some of the knowledge base that will be important when practising as a social worker with children and young people. It also allows for greater depth and reflects many of the teams or agencies in which you may undertake your practice education or placement or may eventually take a job once qualified. However, being mindful of the 'whole family' approach indicates that wherever you practise you should make yourself familiar with adult development as well.

We have chosen to offer a two-volume set for a number of reasons:

- While social work necessarily views life through a whole family/eco-systemic approach, in practice, social workers focus on working with children and families or adults, and indeed on specific elements within those age ranges. Therefore, having the time to focus more deeply on the issues affecting children and young people in one dedicated volume allows us to contextualise and be specific at the same time.
- The original interest and research considered the development of children in bio-physical and psychological ways, while adults were (falsely) dismissed as static – grown and developed; some acknowledgement of this original emphasis is important. This is partly because many other professionals with whom social workers practise are also informed by these models and we share common understandings and challenges as a result. More importantly, many of the people we work with who use social work services believe this and draw (the wrong) conclusions of what might be wrong with them or with those they care for.
- The range of variation across the life span is great and it helps if broad parameters are set from which these theories and models can be discussed. This allows us to focus on early stages of development, growth through childhood, differences and potential for change, adolescence and the transitional period towards adulthood. We also focus on specific issues such as loss and bereavement, attachment, neglect and abuse, at various life points.
- Contemporary social contexts place people within chronological 'boxes' and it is helpful for you as a social worker to navigate your way through popular and professional knowledge in order to understand, explain and work within those areas.

As a student of social work, this textbook will equip you with the tools to understand what might be going on in situations in which you find yourself and to comprehend why others might be thinking or acting in certain ways. This might be other professionals with whom you have contact or it might be those people who use your services. You will be able to appreciate the theories that help you understand events and experiences in specific circumstances and to be able to apply your developing knowledge to practice settings.

In this volume, chapter authors draw on models and theories from major psychological and sociological schools of thought which are approached critically in each chapter, challenging normative approaches that suggest that development is linear or follows particular patterns in every child and young person. Psychoanalytic models, learning theories, biological development and cognitive developmental theories are explained and discussed within an integrated framework that understands the influence of the socio-cultural worlds inhabited by people at all stages in their lives. Ethno-cultural interpretations of normal and abnormal growth and development will be considered as forming an essential background for culturally competent and sensitive professional practice.

Who should use this textbook?

The main audiences for this book are:

- social work students who are beginning a career and starting their learning of complex social, political and psychological concepts that influence practice;
- social workers who are returning to post-qualifying study or who want to refresh their knowledge.

Thus, the emphasis throughout the book concerns social work examples and specifics.

However, other students of early childhood studies, teaching, police studies or nursing may also benefit from reading it. To ensure that the book fits into the multidisciplinary world in which social workers and others practise, we have included a range of professions in writing these chapters, which gives you a much wider perspective and helps you to make connections that will help throughout education and practice.

How to use this textbook

This textbook seeks to enhance your learning as part of your introductory social work course, and we have introduced examples of real-world practice throughout the chapters to help you reflect on what you are learning and to see the relevance of the theory in the practice of social work. Alongside providing you with an initial appreciation of the knowledge that is needed within social work practice, this reflective element will give you a critical and questioning sense in which no single explanatory theory or model is considered to be complete; the sense that the lives of children and young people are fluid, unique and set within a wider context.

Chapter pedagogy

Each chapter opens with a list of clear *objectives*, allowing you to see what you will be covering. These can also be used as a revision list when going back over the material and also making connections with key elements of knowledge for your social work degree. Throughout each chapter are *case studies with critical questions*, encouraging you to apply the theory you are learning in a real-world context. *Reflection points* are also placed within each chapter, giving you the opportunity to revisit the material being discussed and apply this to your own experiences. The chapters then close with three or four core *reflective questions* designed to embed the learning you have undertaken during the chapter, followed by some annotated suggestions for *further reading* around the chapter topics.

A note on terminology

While this book focuses predominantly on social work, it is important, in the current world of practice, not to isolate social work from its context. Therefore, we have embedded the discussion in a range of what we refer to as 'human service professions'. This is a term that has been used in the US often to refer to social workers and cognate disciplines. However, it seems to us to be an appropriate one to use at times in this book. This is because the core focus of our work is with humans and it helps us to recognise that other professional groups, such as nurses, doctors, teachers and police officers, also have this emphasis. It also adds a value dimension and one that does not preclude other professionals with whom we work. So, while we refer predominantly to social workers, we may also use human service professional. Also, we may at times use terms such as practitioner or professional practice in ways that expand the network of people we are referring to, while keeping that emphasis on social work.

Textbook outline

There are three parts to the book which build together to form a whole. The primary focus will be on social workers; however, other human service professionals (those people working with people directly on a daily basis) will be considered. The complex multidisciplinary settings in which social work takes place and the vast array of professionals working with people mean that we will also draw on expertise, thinking and practice from other professions such as nursing, health visiting, police, psychology and education. This should help you to make connections across disciplines and prepare you for real-world practice.

As mentioned, the book is presented in three parts:

- Part I: Introducing the theory
- Part II: Specific developmental issues
- Part III: Professional practice

Part I explores theories and models through associated history, research, socio-cultural variables and critical challenges and includes case studies and research in each chapter. Part II also takes a life-course approach throughout childhood and youth, although the focus may emphasise certain ages, periods and socio-cultural factors alongside structural, cultural and psychological impacts.

Part II discusses how the concepts raised in Part I relate to common issues and events in human life, including physical and emotional development as a child and young person within a family and in developing external relationships, losses in childhood and youth, crime and criminality, the impact of cultural and structural factors, and transitions towards adulthood. Parts I and II also include a reflective element to encourage students to examine their own life positions and pathways through the lifespan using the models and theories considered.

In Part III, authors take a human service profession, predominantly social work, perspective, drawing on the theoretical models and factor explored earlier, and consider how these might exert and impact on people using human services, organisations and those professionals themselves. The advantages and disadvantages of the model and theories will be identified and an approach that focuses on the person will be emphasised. It must be remembered, however, that each author comes from their own particular school of thought, and there are many of these. It is, therefore, important that you are exposed to different ways of thinking and able to argue from these positions and assess what you think and, therefore, determine your own position and thinking. The reflection points in the chapters will help you do this, as will the reflective questions at the end of each chapter.

Detailed overview of this textbook

Part I: Introducing the theory

The chapters in Part I cover the fluidity of the line between childhood and youth and moving into adulthood. While each chapter stands alone, each includes common elements reflecting the history and development of the theories and models, some of the key thinkers or theories and the place within contemporary practice, and does so taking a critical perspective.

Chapter 1 offers an introduction to the traditional approaches to a child and young person's development. We chart the influence of bio-medical and evolutionary approaches recognising the centrality of understanding about physical growth and complications within it. However, we identify the challenges faced by children and young people in terms of environmental and ecological influences and describe the growth of behavioural psychology and learning theories. These 'traditional' approaches are subjected to an initial critique taken up in subsequent chapters and especially in Chapter 6.

Following on from this, **Chapter 2** introduces psychoanalytic theories. From the initial thinking of Freud in the latter part of the 19th century and its refinement in the early part of the 20th century, psychoanalytic theory has added profoundly to our understanding of human growth and development and the importance of childhood and youth in forming our thinking patterns and growth. This is evidenced by the continuing recognition of Freud's theories and the ubiquity of Erikson's stage approach to human growth and development. This chapter offers an historical overview of the advances made by and importance of key psychoanalytic thinkers in respect of human growth and development and sets out central concepts. A contemporary understanding and analysis of the contribution of psychoanalytic thought is provided for the human service professions.

Chapter 3 concerns the place of cognitive theories building on the social learning theories introduced in Chapter 1 and psychoanalytic theories in Chapter 2. These theories build alternative understandings which consider the importance of internal schema, and the impact on the emotions of children and young people, in affecting behaviour. This chapter introduces readers to some core theories and thinkers, the development of their ideas and the beginning appreciation of synergies with other models. The advantages and limitations are drawn out for the modern-day human service professional working in a multicultural environment.

Following from the discussions of the cognitive aspects of human growth and development in children and young people, **Chapter 4** will consider emotional development specifically and its importance in personality development. The impact of emotions on aspects of development and the impact of developmental stage and context on emotional development represent the focus of this chapter.

The preceding chapters are drawn together in **Chapter 5**, which deals with critical perspectives on human growth and development. The ways in which the world is experienced in multiple ways and dependent on a range of social and structural positions, alongside the influence of individual social actors on the world around them and the world on their development, is examined and questioned through sociological theories. These are seen within a wider ecological context in which individual experiences and characteristics are part of the mix influencing growth and development for individuals.

The re-emergence of spiritual and existential aspects of our human selves has added another dimension to consider in the holistic development of children and young people. We move to consider the moral, spiritual and existential development of children and young people in **Chapter 6**. These concepts have often been associated exclusively with religion and, to a large extent, erroneously avoided as a result. However, in cultural terms, the belief systems and faiths of children, young people and their families and communities represent important reference points in growth and development, sometimes marked by physical and/or psycho-social ritual, and religion cannot be avoided. Equally so, spirituality and the things that people find most meaningful in life are powerful forces endorsing or questioning 'right' development within particular social contexts and in terms of the individual's sense of place within his or her world.

Part II: Specific developmental issues

The second part of the book introduces specific issues commonly considered in traditional discussions of human growth and development. Each chapter critically questions the application of the models and understandings.

A common but flexible format means that each chapter includes an introduction and overview of the specific model being introduced, central theorists and approaches, and critique of the model and applications in a complex human context in which differences, diversity and multiple perspectives abound.

Chapter 7 considers the socio-historical development of research concerning attachment and bonding, the gendered, context-embedded aspects of Bowlby's and Ainsworth's early discussions and the revisiting of understanding as social contexts develop and change.

Chapter 8 builds on Chapter 7, examining the development and importance of relationships for development and what those relationships may mean. It also includes a discussion of developing sexuality and sexual awareness and the place of that in individual, cultural and social lives.

Relationship development and social mores have a great impact on the ways in which norms are established and rules governing social behaviour are accepted. Relationships with peers and within families exert a significant impact on the social development and behaviour of individuals, the opportunities they get in society and their subsequent development. We explore this in **Chapter 9**, focusing on studies concerning life course and criminal behaviour and suggesting that the ways in which people learn to behave are, as we saw in Chapters 1 and 5, much more complex than we might initially think.

Chapter 10 looks at children and young people's experiences of loss and bereavement, including both the external significant losses of siblings, parents, relatives and friends and internal losses of their own abilities, health and at times their own impending death. The profound and often lasting influence of loss and bereavement is explored in the context of the growth and development of children and young people as people learning to negotiate the social world.

Finally in this section, in **Chapter 11**, the fluid, culturally determined and elusive context of transition from young personhood to young adulthood will be debated and critiqued in a multicultural contemporary society, focusing on Muslims and using cultural interpretations of gender normativity and constructions of childhood to adulthood status. The importance of development milestones and achievements for successfully moving into adulthood will be examined and differences that are influenced by culture and context considered.

Part III: Professional practice

Part III more overtly introduces the professional contexts in which practice takes place. Each chapter discusses the models and theories of relevance to professional practice and the key theorists associated with them, and discusses ways forward in using knowledge of human growth and development within the specific area of focus.

Chapter 12 considers the potential impact of abuse and neglect on a child and young person's development. Insights from contemporary neuropsychology are explored and critiqued as a socio-cultural construction with assumed power influencing potential for change and development in the minds of human service professionals.

Chapter 13 considers the situation when children and young people can no longer live within their family, recognising that the success of subsequent care arrangements can be dependent on the ways in which children and young people have developed and grown and dealt with changes throughout their lives, as well as understanding the developmental needs of offering substitute care. Ways in which practitioners can help children and young people make sense of life changes and take advantage of substitute care offered will be explored and critiqued and application of attachment theories are made here, making connections with Chapter 7.

In **Chapter 14**, the social historical contexts of working with physical and learning disabilities in children and young people are described and critiqued as socially constructed and leading to valorised assumptions of how children and young people with disabilities and their families should behave and interact with wider society. Concepts of social role valorisation and the campaign *Nothing About Us Without Us* will be introduced and the meanings and applications of the critique explored for professional practice in these areas.

The ways in which children and young people experience the world and are affected by losses and change is explored as a context in which mental health problems may arise in **Chapter 15**. The ways in which different concepts of mental health are understood and applied in a human professional context are critiqued from the perspective of a nurse academic adding a different direction from that covered in earlier chapters in the book.

Chapter 16 explores the experiences of children and young people seeking asylum or made refugees, something of increasing importance and significance within the contemporary world and something that exerts a profound influence on development.

Each chapter and section of this book lays the foundations for further study of aspects of children and young people's growth and development. They also provide the building blocks that presage transitions in these stages or on this journey of development. These aspects are continued in the companion volume, which takes adult development as its focus.

PART I

Introducing the theory

This first part of the book introduces you to core elements of theory that relate to children and young people. It is important to follow this introduction before looking at specific social work fields of practice in the later chapters. This is because the theories will often act as a guide to your own understanding as a social worker and also as a template to the ways in which other professionals work and organise their services. So, in fact, theories provide a context which helps you negotiate your way around the complex area of social work with children and young people and the various professionals with whom you will come into contact.

Given this part of the volume concerns the theories helping to explain aspects of growth and development, the application to practice may not seem immediately obvious. The examples, case studies and reflective questions are designed to help you make those links. However, it is important that you reflect on your understandings, positions and perspectives to make these theories real for you.

It is also the case that there will be some repetition of theories and models in later chapters where these are applied to the areas in which social workers practise. This is intentional and necessary, for two reasons in particular. The first is that different people as individuals and people in different professions often have different perspectives or approaches to theories and it is important you become used to this and able to critique from your point of view. The second reason is that application will differ slightly from area to area of practice.

The terms 'mental health' and 'psychosocial problems' will be used interchangeably, unless otherwise specified. The term 'children and young people' refers to individuals aged between 0 and 18 years, unless otherwise specified.

Part I objective

- develop an understanding of the history and development of core theories and models used in contemporary social work practice.

9

1

Traditional approaches to human growth and development

Jonathan Parker

Introduction

The field of human growth and development is central to informed and 'best' practice in all the human service or helping professions. It is, however, a diverse and somewhat contested area of study including many theoretical, ideological and practice-focused positions. These paradigms have shifted in acceptability and importance through history, often associated with parallel shifts in the social and political climate of societies. As a social work student in the 1980s, I was taught by a psychologist who first of all presented Mary Sheridan's (1960) growth charts, concerning physical development, before enlightening us with psychosocial, behavioural and cognitive understandings. Social development was little to be seen and the impact of structural conditions was largely ignored despite its prominence within social work thinking and education at the time. This chapter will introduce traditional approaches to human growth and development in children, outlining key tenets from biophysical and learning theories.

Chapter objectives

- provide an overview of biophysical aspects of human growth and development and an introduction to social learning theories in the context of children and young people;

- introduce and critique some key thinkers and theorists;

- explore how biophysical models of human growth and development and social learning theories may still be relevant to and important in professional practice today;

- apply these models and theories to real-world examples and practice.

Background and context

The physical development of a child or young person, the stages in which this takes place and the instinctual behaviours of babies, toddlers and growing children fall within the realm of biophysical development. The biophysical realm has enjoyed a privileged place within thinking about human growth and development. This is understandable, to a large extent, as it sits within a positivist natural science tradition which purports to deal with objective facts, with rights and wrongs and with the quantifiable and verifiable. Indeed, it is closely linked to medical science and, therefore, has enjoyed a lofty status. It is unlikely that anyone would challenge the importance of genetic inheritance in determining some aspects of our physical growth and capabilities or, indeed, to an extent, personality and behaviour (Beckett and Taylor, 2019).

There are many examples of our belief in biogenetic connections between blood relatives. An example might be of twins separated early in life and being brought up in different families and places but having similar interests, beliefs, physical characteristics, illnesses and looks throughout life. However, it is equally unlikely that those working in human service professions would suggest taking Richard Dawkins' (1976) arguments to their logical extreme and state we are nothing but our genetic and physiological inheritance and, by which, our whole lives are determined. If we did accept such a premise, it would obviate any need to adapt social structures and policies to effect positive changes or to help people because it would all be considered to be predetermined and nothing could be done about it. Walker (2017) suggests that biological and physical models of human development remain useful but must be integrated with others to avoid such problems. This is something we will return to in this chapter as we consider the role of environment and social learning alongside physical development.

> **REFLECTION POINT 1.1**
>
> Think about a baby that you know or have known. Consider their needs, vulnerabilities and the ways in which they interact with different people – for instance, their parents or close family, doctors and nurses. If you have known the baby for some time, catalogue some of the changes you have seen in its young life. You will no doubt identify that while physical growth may be evident, it is dependent on its environment or context and, indeed, that physical development cannot be disaggregated from other forms of development, such as the emotional and social aspects of life. Consider your thoughts as you read through the following section.

The first two years of human life are noted for the rapid development in skills, abilities and growth. Newborn babies have some instinctual reflexes necessary for survival, such as rooting and suckling for nourishment. However, the capacity for physical dexterity and the development of gross motor skills and later fine motor skills takes time and interaction with the environment around them, and especially the people populating that environment. Physical growth, weight gain and brain growth are profound within these initial years of life but profoundly influenced by a much wider social world.

Differences in early growth and development result from a mix of genetics, temperament and emotional, social and structural factors. However, the monitoring that takes place by health professionals relies on percentile charts, the UK growth charts, that are based on norms (mean averages taken from large numbers of babies and young children in a certain context). The charts measure weight, length and head circumference and provide an indication of normal growth or potential problems. If these charts are accepted without question, they can lead to normative understandings that may suggest a baby or young child is assumed not to be developing appropriately. There are gender and ethnic differences that are recognised and the Department for Education (2007) importantly recognised that all children develop differently. We will now turn to an overview of biophysical development and a consideration of the importance of social learning theories as a start to understanding integrated approaches to human growth and development.

Key theories and thinkers

Biological theories posit that both individual and shared patterns are based on inherent templates laid down in the genes, and these control hormones in the body and patterns of growth. Gesell (1928) identified that genes determine the sequence of maturation through twin studies. Later, this patterning and thinking around genetic dispositions helped Bowlby (1969) to develop his theories concerning maternal attachment (expanded to include other attachment figures since that time; see Chapter 7 of Part II for an introduction to attachment theory).

One of the first thinkers that we might associate with biological and physical development theories is Charles Darwin, the 19th-century evolutionary scientist. There is a connection between physical development and genetic inheritance and theories of evolution.

Darwin wrote his famous *Origin of the Species* in 1859, describing the ways in which animals adapted to environmental challenges. The evolutionary approach to human development has lent itself to key theories in biology-based theories of child development that also include more nuanced and inclusive understandings (Martin and Fabes, 2009) – we will see the links with behavioural or social learning later in the chapter.

Theories based on evolutionary psychology and biology have been heavily criticised, in no small part owing to their association with the development of the eugenics movement under Darwin's cousin Galton (Gillham, 2001) and the development of Herbert Spencer's Social Darwinism (a term deriving from Spencer's earlier concept of the 'survival of the fittest'). The latter has been associated with unpalatable right–wing ideology, although Spencer himself was concerned with individual happiness – not transgressing the rights of others (Hossain and Mustari, 2012).

The eugenics movement believed they were making an important contribution to national strength by encouraging birth from certain people and groups and discouraging it from others so that the 'bloodline' would be stronger and purer. While we may see healthy, intelligent children and young people as a positive, it begs many questions as to what happens to those who are not so classified, how they are treated and who determines what is health, intelligence or strength. Despite these unfortunate associations, it is important to know a little about evolutionary approaches to growth and development in childhood.

Bjorkland (2016) understands evolutionary child development in terms of equipping the child for survival, through language acquisition and communication, play and aggression games, and overcoming inhibition to adapt to and survive in 'dangerous' environments. Ethological theories add the value of visual cues and their interpretation for eliciting particular responses. For instance, a newborn baby is extremely vulnerable but provides verbal and aural cues to its parents for attention, food and comfort. The big eyes and plump faces of babies are attractive to parents and likely to draw attention, while crying behaviour will be rewarded with food or comfort. It is easy, perhaps, to see how these ethological models gave birth to Bowlby's (1951) beginning theories of attachment (which is covered in detail in Chapter 7 of Part II). More recently, there has been an increased focus on the relationship of brain development to behaviour and thinking in child development (Beddoe and Joy, 2017; Wastell and White, 2017; Chapter 12 of Part III in this volume). The experiences children have in their early years help to hardwire patterns and connections which influence the ways in which they respond to the world around them.

An overview of biophysical development

At the earliest points of development, the human genome contains a template for each individual's protein construction. It provides the code for the building blocks of that individual that determines physical characteristics and some diseases. In the biophysical model, the individual's genetic make-up is responsible for determining personality, behaviour and intelligence (DeHart et al, 2000; Keenan and Evans, 2009). In strictly determinist terms, we may suggest that self-styled 'militant atheist' evolutionary scientist Richard Dawkins (1976) takes forward this thinking. However, this suggestion of linear determinism is challenged and most proponents of this model accept a complex interplay between genetics and the environment (see Walker, 2017).

Early biological development moves through a germinal stage, after conception and when the fertilised egg implants in the uterine wall, with rapid organ and body development in the subsequent six weeks or so (embryonic stage), to the complex elaboration of physical structures, organs and brain in the foetal stage until birth. However, environmental factors influence this developmental process.

We know much more today about the ways in which nutrition, alcohol, substance use and smoking affects early development but also where the mother lives, who she lives with, poverty and employment are all influential. We can see that health professionals and social workers need to take a holistic approach to understand needs, which demands listening to other professionals and their knowledge as well as considering one's own perspectives (Sudbery and Whittaker, 2018; Beckett and Taylor, 2019).

During the first two years of life, from infancy to toddlerhood, children's growth in height and weight and the development of motor skills tends to be quite rapid. It is at this stage that percentile charts, like the ones introduced earlier in this chapter, may be of some use. However, it must be remembered that they are contextual and any norms are taken from a particular population sample and may not always apply to everyone (McCartney and Phillips, 2008). Environment and behavioural patterns are central to this physical development. For instance, adequate sleep and stimulation through talking and play promote development and brain growth in which neurons start to make connections with one another and establish patterns of behaviour and response. Infant brains are plastic (they have the ability to grow and adapt) and the environment in which children are exposed to influences which connections are made and which may be lost. It must be remembered, however, that change and development can still occur after this early period (Abbott and Burkitt, 2015).

The development of the senses and their use is dependent on the quality of relationships that children have at this stage. Children move from predominantly reflex actions to more conscious, deliberate behaviour. Both gross motor skills (head and body control, crawling, standing and walking) and fine motor skills (the ability to manipulate, reach for and grasp single objects) are refined during the first two years or so, and bowel and bladder control is usually achieved by about the age of three (often earlier, sometimes later). Again, it is important for people working with others to understand biophysical development markers as general and certainly not as prescriptive. They may help us to understand or to identify where there might be a need, but they should not be seen as truths that can be rigidly applied.

In early childhood, growth is slower but children begin to lose their baby-like appearance and to develop in muscular strength. By about the age of five years, Western children have developed between 75 and 90 per cent of brain capacity, although the brain develops at different rates at different stages. Important to children's development is the prefrontal cortex, which is associated with more complex cognitive and regulatory behaviours, including making plans and carrying them out, developing inhibitory responses that prevent certain, unhelpful behaviours, and developing a working memory that helps in problem solving. Knowledge of such development is important, as negative experiences such as abuse can change children's responses and create unwanted developmental connections such as anger and impulse control problems (Pollack and Sinha, 2002). These responses might be transferred to everyday situations as a result of 'experience-dependent plasticity', which refers to adapting and learning to recreate certain behaviours in other circumstances. This is somewhat similar to aspects of social learning theory and is addressed later in this chapter and in Chapter 3 in this volume.

Constructive brain development is important in establishing other physical behaviours, such as running, jumping, catching, throwing and climbing. In turn, this helps to refine the fine motor skills, such as drawing and dressing, as coordination improves – although these can also be culturally determined, so it is important to remember not to apply the knowledge rigidly when working with children who are different. While nutrition and sleep are important to good development, this does not necessarily mean that a child who does not meet these indicators is not getting a good diet, sufficient food or enough sleep (Abbott and Burkitt, 2015).

In late childhood, physical growth slows even further but the brain continues to develop and motor skills improve. At this stage, the influence of environmental factors is easier to see in respect of body growth and musculature development, but also in terms of problem solving, planning and language use. It is at this stage that bone growth is laid, which will be important in later life. Children tend, in Western societies, to develop in independence and, despite our risk-averse society, late childhood is a time when accidents become more common.

Adolescence is a time of development which shows the interactions of biology and environment in stark relief (Abernethy et al, 2018). We will consider some of these when we look at social learning theory later in this chapter, but it is a time when risk-taking behaviours increase, such as smoking, drinking alcohol, experimenting with sex or becoming involved in crime (Walker, 2017). However, it is still a time of growth in biophysical terms. The prefrontal cortex, concerned with planning and organisational behaviours, and the limbic regions of the brain, which are central to the control or regulation of emotional behaviour and sexual expression, develop. Brain development links with hormonal changes and can exert a significant impact on behaviour. For instance, increase in testosterone in boys underlies the growth of the amygdala, which is associated with fear and anger.

Puberty is an important time in the growth of children and young people in many cultures, as shown by the many rites of passage associated with this age. This is not surprising in biophysical terms, as it is a time of great change in which sexual maturation occurs. The changes are influenced by sex, religiosity, ethnicity, nutrition and structural factors, such as health care and education, but the physical growth taking place is something that needs to be considered when working with adolescents (Abernethy et al, 2018).

REFLECTION POINT 1.2

Why do you think an understanding of biophysical models of growth and development in children and young people is important for you as a social worker?

It may be that you identify the importance of working with other professionals – perhaps especially those in health care, where such models have direct application. You may also recognise that it is useful to be well-versed in a range of theories and models as this highlights the reputation of your profession and may help to build rapport with others. Of course, you may also consider it important to know these models because you want to take a critical approach to them and to introduce social and environmental aspects which come within the purview of social workers. Some of these alternative or additional approaches are considered in the following section.

Towards alternatives: systems and behaviour

If we take an integrated approach to understanding growth and development in children and young people, we can see that biophysical theories must be positioned within a systemic context. Systems thinking was first identified in relation to biology by von Bertalanffy in the 1920s and posits an interactive view that would suggest genetic predispositions in a child or young person are triggered, halted or modified by social and environmental factors (Drack et al, 2007; Haight and Taylor, 2013). For instance, a mother's pre-birth nutritional intake, substance use and general health will all have an impact on the development of the unborn child and the child post-birth. While this is clear, it opens the way for blame to be levelled against an individual mother for her behaviour during pregnancy and her responsibility for the growth and development of her child. This is open to political use and abuse, and does not pay due attention to structural impacts on behaviour and lifestyle. In times of austerity, this approach can be very useful to governments and organisations wanting to save money through social policies that promote individual responsibility regardless of means (see Chapter 5 in this volume for more discussion of this issue).

The 'nature' debate had its critics early on in its history, especially from those social and psychological thinkers who saw the influence of learning, as a social and interactive being, as centrally important to the development of behavioural characteristics (O'Brien, 2016). Early behavioural psychologists challenged a strict deterministic approach to biophysical development theories, however, and seemed to introduce new forms of determinism in terms of the inexorable impact of a child's living context. In learning theory or behaviourism, the environment takes centre stage, advancing on the mediating effect to which we have drawn attention when describing biophysical development. Behaviour, in these earlier models, is defined as those actions that are seen or empirically verifiable, of people acting in response to, within, on, or as part of their wider social environment. Later models introduced a cognitive element (see Chapter 3 in this volume for more details on cognitive theories) and indicated that behaviour is also the product of our thoughts and deliberations about how we ought to act in particular situations and under particular circumstances (Parker, 2017) – something that children and young people adopt within their families and living groups as survival strategies early in life.

Social learning theories and development

Behavioural or social learning theories (SLTs) refer to the ways in which our experiences of and interactions with our environment increase, decrease or maintain certain behaviours because of the responses those interactions evoke. SLTs involve altering the triggers to and/or consequences of behaviours – those things that provoke a reaction or happen as a result of one's actions. These models seek to understand human behaviour in its social context. A basic presupposition is that change and development depend on our experiences and context. Increasingly, however, it is seen that human agency, the decision-making capacity of an individual child or young person, can be important in effecting alternative responses and reactions and thereby changing the impact of circumstances and the behavioural reactions to them (Sheldon and Macdonald, 2009).

There are a number of theories that have developed to explain the ways in which children and young people learn to behave. Over the years, there have been bitter divisions between behavioural psychologists drawing on a combination of Watson's (1924) stimulus response approach or Skinner's (1976) operant conditioning principles, and those favouring the cognitive schools (see Chapter 3 in this volume for more details on cognitive theories). In this chapter, we focus on three SLTs that reflect different paradigms and approaches but are seen to inform one another in practical applications:

- respondent or classical conditioning;
- operant or instrumental conditioning;
- modelling, imitative or vicarious learning (*or* social learning theory).

Respondent or classical conditioning

Respondent or classical conditioning developed from Pavlov's famous study of dogs' reactions to stimuli associated with anticipation of food (Pavlov, 1927). Important practical development of the applications began, however, with Watson's research into learning and conditioning (Watson, 1924). The theory suggests that an automatic or unconditioned response may be repeated if the trigger provoking it, or stimulus, is paired with another event or stimulus. This 'conditioned stimulus' or trigger event may also be paired with another event to produce the original response and so on. Taken to its logical conclusion, it could offer a very complex view of how behaviours develop and are associated with environment triggers. One of the key criticisms of this model lies in its complexity, as it takes a detailed and very skilled analysis to identify actual triggers provoking behaviours and reactions (Parker, 2017).

The model in simple terms suggests:

- An unconditioned stimulus (S1) – an event occurring within one's living situation – provokes an unconditioned response (UR1) or particular behaviour. For instance, think of a five-year-old child who has an injection at the doctor's surgery. It is likely that this will provoke a reaction expressing pain, perhaps crying and some minor distress. The child reacts to the situation rather than understanding, as the parent will, that this vaccination will protect them.
- An unconditioned stimulus (S1) paired with a different stimulus or trigger (S2) elicits the unconditioned response (UR1) and a conditioned response (CR1) – the same reaction to the paired stimulus as in the first bullet-point. Thinking of the previous example, it may be the case that the same child displays distress and anxiety when visiting the doctor for their next vaccination. This is because the injection (unconditioned stimulus) becomes associated with visiting the doctor and both begin to produce the same response of crying and distress (the original response to the pain of the needle – the unconditioned response – becomes a conditioned response when visiting the doctor).
- The conditioned stimulus (S2) produces a conditioned response (CR1) – the next time the child is taken to the doctor (now a conditioned stimulus) regardless of the reason for the visit, they cry and show distress, refusing to go (the conditioned response).

Behaviours are prompted or learned by association with a certain event or stimulus. The same response may occur when the initial prompt is associated with a second event or stimulus. This model is known as respondent conditioning or associative learning because the behaviour is considered to be a response to the initial stimulus or event.

If the conditioned stimulus is repeated over time without the corresponding appearance of the unconditioned stimulus or trigger, it eventually disappears (see Figure 1.1). Having said this, however, it must be noted that well-established phobic responses do become very resistant to change or, as it is termed in this theory, to classical extinction. This is why fears learned in childhood and youth can continue to exert an impact into adult life and indicates why we should be mindful of dealing with them as early as we can.

Respondent learning theory has been helpful in explaining the development of fear reactions or phobic responses (Watson and Rayner, 1920; Sheldon, 1982, 1995; Hudson and Macdonald, 1986; Sheldon and Macdonald, 2009; Parker, 2017). However, if, on the other hand, a person learns through experience that

Figure 1.1: Classical extinction

Conditioned stimulus - - - - - - - - - - - - - - - - - Conditioned response
(CS1)   (CR1)

The response eventually disappears
without being paired with the
unconditioned stimulus (CS1)

there is no reliable connection between a stimulus event initiated by them or by others and a behaviour, this can lead to apathy and a lack of motivation – a type of 'why bother?' approach. The works of Seligman (1975) on the concept of 'learned helplessness', and Lefcourt (1976) and Rotter et al (1972) are useful here. Where people are prevented from assuming control over events in their lives because they have learned from experience they have no such influence, a behavioural approach can help to re-establish some sort of order and predictability. It teaches and fosters a reassertion of control over the environment. In this sense, the behavioural approach using respondent conditioning seeks to empower people and increase their choices in living. Furthermore, it is not restrictive and dogmatic in the kinds of behaviour it seeks to teach. However, in respect of understanding human growth and development in children and young people, learned helplessness can help social workers recognise problems of motivation and behaviour arising from life events and the need for positive experiences to replace those which seem to have no effect. A second model can help here.

Operant or instrumental conditioning

Rather than learning how to behave because of specific environmental triggers provoking a response, operant learning theory states that behaviours are learned and repeated because of the consequences immediately following their expression: what happens as a result of the child or young person's behaviour rather than what leads to it. The strength, frequency and type of these consequences greatly influence any future expression of that behaviour. In respondent conditioning, it is the initial stimulus that leads to the expression of the behaviour; however, in operant conditioning, it is the consequences of the behaviour that *reinforce* it or make it more likely to happen again in the future.

While it is the case that specific stimuli do not automatically elicit operant behaviours, events and social contexts remain important as they provide cues for the kinds of behaviour that are appropriate for them. These cues are referred to as antecedent stimuli (see Figure 1.2). Social cues can often indicate to a person when reinforcement may be available for the expression of a particular form of behaviour and so the child or young person learns a repertoire of behaviour that allows them to achieve reinforcing consequences in certain contexts. If social workers

Figure 1.2: Operant learning theory

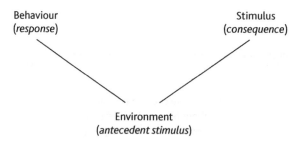

20

can learn what signals or cues precede particular behaviours, their interventions can be aimed at modifying these if they are not helpful to that young person.

Various elements of operant conditioning

In order to describe operant conditioning more fully, it is necessary to consider some of the components that make up the theory, such as:

- types of reinforcement – there are different types of consequence that are considered to maintain behaviours;
- schedules of reinforcement – this refers to how these behavioural consequences are delivered in the real world;
- punishment – this refers to the controversial subject of negative consequences deliberately activated following certain behaviours;
- the shaping and moulding of behaviour; and
- fading.

The various types of reinforcement or consequences which make a young person's behaviour more likely to happen in the future include:

- positive reinforcement
- negative reinforcement
- conditioned reinforcers
- generalised reinforcers
- extinction

Some explanation of these different types is helpful to understand why a child or young person may behave in the ways they do and how their behaviour may be adapted. **Positive reinforcement** is the term used for a consequence which increases the frequency and likelihood of future behaviour; it is therefore said to strengthen behaviour. An example may help. Whenever 15-year-old Jermain helps his mother by tidying his bedroom, emptying the rubbish and vacuuming the carpets, she gives him extra spending money so he can go and watch his favourite football team. The positive reinforcement is to be given the money he needs and it makes these domestic behaviours much more likely to happen in future.

Negative reinforcement, on the other hand, refers to the removal of an unpleasant consequence when one behaves in a certain way or performs a certain action. For instance, when a young person is praised by teachers for being helpful, this is likely to be appreciated and lead to them acting in similar ways in the future (positive reinforcement). The same young person who worked through a study period and lunchtime to tidy the library at school was told they didn't have homework that day. The removal of the 'unpleasant consequence' (the homework) may again strengthen that young person's helpful behaviour (negative reinforcement).

The term **extinction** is used to refer to the withholding of positive reinforcement for behaviours, which tends to discourage their repetition. If, for example, the teacher who praised the pupil begins to offer no word of thanks and ceases to allow the young person not to do homework, it is likely that the young person will soon withdraw from helping.

Any consequence that is regularly associated with the reinforcement of behaviour eventually acquires an independent reinforcement value of its own. This consequence is known as a **conditioned reinforcer**. This can become generalised to other circumstances when the conditioned reinforcer strengthens several types of behaviour in several situations. This demonstrates just how complex learning behaviour actually is and unravelling it takes a great deal of skill. Indeed, consequences that reinforce the behaviour of one child might be the trigger, or antecedent, of behaviour for another young person. However, for the purposes of your learning, it is important to note how behaviours can be learned by children and young people.

An example will illustrate some of the complexity. Think of a young male who has started shoplifting because he has no money and his school friends have been teasing him that he does not have the right clothes or trainers. At first, he was pleased he now had the clothes that all his friends had but he also felt good because he 'had got away with it' and more so his school friends were giving him a great deal of attention because of what he was doing. Eventually, the attention and feelings acted as conditioned reinforcers that made his shoplifting more likely to continue. Over time, it may be that seeking the attention of his peers is generalised to other behaviours which could increase further his antisocial behaviour (see Chapter 9 in Part II of this volume for further discussion of the influence of friends on crime and criminal behaviour).

Learning occurs through reinforcement and there are many different ways in which behaviour can be reinforced. In behavioural psychology, these are referred to as schedules of reinforcement and include continuous reinforcement, where the child learns that the desirable consequence happens every time they behave in a certain way, which may be weakened by its frequency. An example of this may be a young person being allowed to watch a favourite television programme if they tidy their room when asked, while growing out of the TV programme would mean this was no longer reinforcing. However, a much stronger way of reinforcing behaviour is known as fixed ratio reinforcement. This suggests that when a young person received the desired consequence a certain number of times but did not know exactly when they would receive it, this is likely to be embedded into their learning because they are anticipating gaining their 'reward' at some point. This type of learned behaviour is associated with gambling, which is something for social workers practising with adolescents to consider given its prevalence (Calado et al, 2017).

Knowing about reinforcement schedules is important when studying models and methods in your social work learning, but a full review is outside the scope of this chapter. (For more information, see Sheldon and Macdonald, 2009.)

However, recognising that environmental cues and responses reinforce aspects of learning in children and adolescents is central to understanding their development and growth as young people.

Punishment represents a controversial aspect of social learning theory, but is something that we need to cover as important to your learning as social workers. It is fundamental to say that it does not necessarily imply retribution or punitive measures as understood in popular terms. There are two types of punishment that are a little confusing in themselves. Indeed, it is so-called 'positive punishment' that relates to something unpleasant being done to a child or young person generally to stop a specific behaviour. The psychological language used here can be off-putting since you are unlikely to see anything positive in something unpleasant or hurtful being done to someone. However, it is important to know the term as you may read about it in some texts. This kind of punishment is meant to stop behaviour. It can be seen in the parent who hits a child to prevent them doing something the parent considers wrong or 'naughty'. However, not only does it go against the value base that you are learning in social work, but it is also seen to be ineffective in changing and shaping behaviour. Indeed, it can lead to a child or young person seeking ways of getting out of punishment that involve yet more behaviours that the parent may wish to stop or to a suppression of all behaviours, including the pro-social ones, because of a fear of being punished. As the child grows into adolescence, they may seek revenge on those doing the punishing. It may also have the effect of teaching the punished adolescent that this is the way to behave towards younger people or towards those with less power or ability to stop such punishment. So, it reflects a problematic and unnecessary form of interacting and seeking to change behavioural learning.

Where perhaps you may see the concept of 'punishment', in terms used by behavioural psychology, as having more of a place in family life and parenting is in negative punishment. This is negative in the removal of a consequence or 'positive reinforcement' if the child or young person behaves in an undesirable way. Of course, as a social worker, you are being taught to be constantly reflective and would be asking in these circumstances who it is and why a certain behaviour would be considered undesirable.

Modelling or imitative learning

A further way in which children and young people learn to behave is found in modelling and mimicking the behaviour of others. Many of the ways in which we all learn to act have been developed in this way – through imitation or the observation of what others do in specific situations. A negative example of this way of learning and developing as a young person is particularly pertinent to social work. This can be seen in Case Study 1.1.

CASE STUDY 1.1

Jermaine was nine years old. He lived with his mother and father and his sister, Chantal. After crying at school and having bruises on her arm, Chantal had complained to her teacher that Jermaine was hitting her. This continued over three weeks and the teacher contacted social workers because of her concerns. The social worker who visited learned that Jermaine's father, Roland, had been physically violent to Sally-Ann, Jermaine's mother, for a number of years, but his parents believed this was kept out of sight of the children. Recently, however, Jermaine had seen his father being violent to Sally-Ann and when told to help around the house by his older sister Chantal he had started hitting her and telling her she had "better shut up if she knows what's good for her". These were things that Sally-Ann had experienced from Roland and when Jermaine started behaving in this way she had asked Roland to leave.

Questions

1. Why do you think Jermaine may have copied his father's abusive behaviour?
2. Do you think role models are an important source of learning how we behave?
3. Identify some of your influences and role models and think why they became so special to you.

Discussion

It is likely that Jermaine saw his father Roland as an important figure in his life and someone he thought portrayed what a man 'ought to be'. Roland may have acted as a role model and, thinking of descriptions of learning through modelling, Jermaine perceived that Roland got positive 'rewards' as a result of his behaviour.

As a social worker, you would, of course, wish to alter the learned behaviour seen in Case Study 1.1. However, it is important here to become familiar with some of the ways in which children and young people learn their behavioural patterns. The concept of modelling – sometimes also known as vicarious leaning because it concerns watching and copying the behaviour of another – has a number of elements. Sheldon (1995), a long-term advocate for behavioural social work, identifies a range of steps in the development of modelling behaviour that comprise the identification of behaviours, dividing the behaviour into component parts and practising the behaviour until it is practised fluently. Some of the elements can be seen in Case Study 1.2.

CASE STUDY 1.2

Markus watches Zeb in the classroom and notes that when he pinches the boy next to him or takes a pencil or book from him, everyone, except that boy, laughs and giggles (*observation of behaviour*). Markus believes, after watching Zeb, that he waits until classmates are watching and the teacher has turned attention to something or someone else. He plays to those watching (*opinion forming*). Zeb gets a lot of attention and enjoys the laughs and giggles of his classmates (*evaluation*). Markus tries this behaviour himself as he values the attention of his classmates and wants more of it (*behaviour reproduction*).

Questions

1. Think of times you have copied the behaviour of another person and note down why you think you did so.
2. What was in it for you?
3. What do you think might help Markus to temper his mimicry of Zeb?

Discussion

There are a number of components necessary for modelling to be successful in developing or adapting behaviour (see Parker, 2017). Primarily, it is necessary for the model to be attractive to and highly valued by the young person observing it. It is much more likely to be copied if the behaviour is rewarded and we know that rewards are individually appreciated. There is usually some similarity between the person who is being modelled and the person copying the behaviour for it to work.

In respect of Markus, you may have thought that his need or wish for attention is entirely understandable. We all need positive feedback from others and this is very reinforcing to us all. Therefore, you may wish to consider how he might gain this positive appreciation without doing things that may get him into trouble at school – perhaps praise from his teacher or being given an important role or responsibility within the class.

The success of modelling is dependent on the degree to which it creates or strengthens feelings of self-efficacy. Self-efficacy is a concept developed by psychologist Albert Bandura and concerns the belief a person has that they are able to perform the actions that are necessary to successfully achieve an outcome (Bandura, 1977; Parker, 2006). There are two types of expectation associated with this model: outcome expectations and efficacy expectations. The former refers to the knowledge or belief that if you behave in a certain way, it will produce certain results; the latter refers to self-belief in one's capability to produce the necessary behaviours.

Consider the example of 14-year-olds Jadwiga and her friend Magda, who were part of a local youth football team. Both girls knew what they needed to do in order to play according to an agreed plan (outcome expectations) – Jadwiga to stay on the wing, while Magda would feed long passes of the ball for Jadwiga or the other wing to chase. However, while Magda believed she was skilled at long passes and was confident that she could do this, Jadwiga was unsure that she could run fast enough to get the ball (efficacy expectations). Children and young people with high self-efficacy are likely to try harder if they do not achieve their goal or target on the first attempt. The most powerful means of increasing self-efficacy is through successful accomplishment or performance and children and young people learn this through their experiences in families and schools, and with their friends. In Jadwiga's case, her self-efficacy beliefs had been shaken through two games in which she had missed most of the balls passed to her. However, the football coach, Belinda, had told her she was a good footballer and just had a run of bad luck – that she could do it. This helped Jadwiga to try and believe that, with effort, she could get the ball.

In all social learning theories, it is now recognised that our cognitions, thought processes and perceptions act as mediators between what happens in the environment, with both trigger events and situations, and consequent behavioural outcomes.

In modelling, reinforcement can be anticipated and mediated through one's thought processes. As we will see in Chapter 3, it is not surprising that cognitive and cognitive-behavioural learning theories follow logically from modelling or imitative learning. The interpretation and evaluation of social situations are likely to differ from child to child and from young person to young person. This, in turn, is likely to lead to different emotional and behavioural responses. Sometimes, these responses can be so negative and entrenched that emotional disorders can result. These are covered in Chapter 3 and are outside the scope of the current chapter.

Conclusion

Making it real: applications to practice

Funded by the World Bank, Fernald et al (2017) use the stages of biological and physiological development to measure children's growth and development to make cross-cultural comparisons and to feed into important social and health policy processes, to complement and aid diagnosis and treatment decisions and to do so in verifiable and reliable ways. Used uncritically, these approaches would impose a normative perspective; however, there needs to be a degree of criticality to recognise social and structural factors that have an often profound mediating influence on the growth and development of children and young people (Fowler and Farrell, 2017). On their own, they fail to include the psychological and emotional aspects of what makes us human; therefore, they cannot be accepted on their own (Gibson and Gibson, 2016; Sudbery and Whittaker, 2018).

Beckett and Taylor (2019) refer to the important argument of nature versus nurture to explore how important bio-physiological theories are today. Importantly, they recognise that these debates are inherently political as they determine funding, resource and social acceptability. There are, therefore, many vested interests involved.

Reflective questions

1 How useful are theories of biological and physical development in understanding children and young people's behaviour?

2 What are some of the problems with relying only on biological and physical development theories and what might help you to overcome these difficulties?

3 How might structural and cultural factors influence the ways in which children and young people develop both physically and socially?

Further reading

- Graham, M. (2011) Changing paradigms and conditions of childhood: Implications for the social professions and social work, *British Journal of Social Work*, 41(8): 1532–1547. Graham's article will help you develop a critical perspective that demonstrates the importance of diversity, context and change. This is important for you as social workers and will help you challenge static approaches to children and young people's development.

- Keenan, T. and Evans, S. (2009) *An Introduction to Child Development* (2nd edn). London: Sage.
  This book provides an expanded introduction to the traditional theories and models designed to explain growth and development in children. It will help you develop an in-depth understanding of these approaches.

- Walker, J. (2017) *Social Work and Human Development* (5th edn). London: Sage.
  Walker's book provides a useful overview and introduction to human growth and development theories used in social work. It is a generic text and so does not solely relate these to children and young people. It provides a useful array of models and theories to further your understanding.

References

Abbott, E. and Burkitt, E. (2015) *Child Development and the Brain*. Bristol: Policy Press.

Abernethy, B., Kippers, V., Hanrahan, S.J., Pandy, M.G., McManus, A.M. and MacKinnion, L. (2018) *Biophysical Foundations of Human Movement* (3rd edn). Champaign, IL: Human Kinetics.

Bandura, A. (1977) Self-efficacy: Toward a unifying theory of behavioral change, *Psychological Review*, 84(2), 191–215.

Beckett, C. and Taylor, H. (2019) *Human Growth and Development* (4th edn). London: Sage.

Beddoe, E. and Joy, E. (2017) Questioning the uncritical acceptance of neuroscience in child and family policy and practice: A review of challenges to the current doxa, *Aotearoa New Zealand Social Work Review*, 29(1): 65–76.

Bjorkland, D.F. (2016) Incorporating development into evolutionary psychology: Evolved probabilistic cognitive mechanisms, *Evolutionary Psychology*, 14(4). Available from: https://doi.org/10.1177/1474704916670166

Bowlby, J. (1951) *Maternal Care and Mental Health*. Geneva: World Health Organization Monograph Series, No. 2, 19–52 and 107–127.

Bowlby, J. (1969) *Attachment and Loss*, Vol. 1: *Attachment*. New York, NY: Basic Books.

Calado, F., Alexandre, J. and Griffiths, M.D. (2017) Prevalence of adolescent problem gambling: A systematic review, *Journal of Gambling Studies*, 32(2): 397–424.

Darwin, C. (1859) *On the Origin of the Species – by Means of Natural Selection*. London: John Murray.

Dawkins, R. (1976) *The Selfish Gene*. Oxford: Oxford University Press.

DeHart, G.B., Sroufe, L.A. and Cooper, R.G. (2000) *Child Development: Its Nature and Course* (4th edn). New York, NY: McGraw-Hill.

Department for Education (2007) What is the research evidence on writing? DFE-RR238. Available from: https://assets.publishing.service.gov.uk/government/uploads/system/uploads/attachment_data/file/183399/DFE-RR238.pdf

Drack, M., Apfalter, W. and Pouvreau, D. (2007) On the making of a system theory of life: Paul A Weiss and Ludwig von Bertanlanffy's conceptual connection, *Quarterly Review of Biology*, 82(4): 349–373.

Fernald, L.C.H., Prado, E., Kariger, P. and Raikes, A. (2017) A toolkit for measuring early childhood development in low- and middle-income countries prepared for the Strategic Impact Evaluation Fund, the World Bank. Available from: http://documents.worldbank.org/curated/en/384681513101293811/text/WB-SIEF-ECD-MEASUREMENT-TOOLKIT.txt

Fowler, P.J. and Farrell, A.F. (2017) Housing and child well being: Implications for research, policy and practice. *American Journal of Community Psychology*, 60: 1–2, 3–8.

Gesell, A. (1928) *Infancy and Human Growth*. New York, NY: Macmillan.

Gibson, A. and Gibson, N. (2016) *Human Growth, Behaviour and Development: Essential theory and application in social work*. London: Sage.

Gillham, N.W. (2001) Sir Francis Galton and the birth of eugenics, *Annual Review of Genetics*, 35: 83–101.

Haight, W.L. and Taylor, E.H. (2013) *Human Behaviour for Social Work Practice: A Developmental Ecological Framework* (2nd edn). Chicago, IL: Lyceum Books.

Hossain, D.M. and Mustari, S. (2012) A critical analysis of Herbert Spencer's theory of evolution, *Postmodern Openings*, 3(2): 55–66.

Hudson, B. and Macdonald, G. (1986) *Behavioural Social Work: An introduction*. London: Palgrave.

Keenan, T. and Evans, S. (2009) *An Introduction to Child Development* (2nd edn). London: Sage.

Lefcourt, H.M. (1976) Locus of control and the response to aversive events, *Canadian Psychological Review/Psychologie canadienne*, 17(3): 202–209.

Martin, C.L. and Fabes, R. (2009) *Discovering Child Development* (2nd edn). Boston, MA: Houghton Mifflin.

McCartney, K. and Phillips, D. (eds) (2008) *The Blackwell Handbook of Early Childhood Development*. Oxford: Blackwell.

O'Brien, E.Z. (2016) *Psychology for Social Work: A Comprehensive Guide to Human Growth and Development*. London: Palgrave Macmillan.

Parker, J. (2006) Developing perceptions of competence during practice learning, *British Journal of Social Work*, 36(6): 1017–1036.

Parker, J. (2017) *Social Work Practice* (5th edn). London: Sage.

Pavlov, I.P. (1927) *Conditioned Reflexes: An Investigation of the Physiological Activity of the Cerebral Cortex*. Oxford: Oxford University Press.

Pollack, S.D. and Sinha, P. (2002) Effects of early experience on children's recognition of facial displays of emotion, *Developmental Psychology*, 36: 784–791.

Rotter, J.B., Chance, J.E. and Phares, E.J. (1972) *Applications of a Social Learning Theory of Personality*. New York, NY: Holt, Rinehart & Winston.

Seligman, M.E.P. (1975) *Helplessness: On Depression, Development and Death*. New York, NY: W.H. Freeman and Co.

Sheldon, B. (1982) *Behaviour Modification: Theory, Practice and Philosophy*. London: Tavistock.

Sheldon, B. (1995) *Cognitive Behavioural Therapy: Research, Practice and Philosophy*. London: Routledge.

Sheldon, B. and Macdonald, G. (2009) *A Textbook of Social Work*. London: Routledge.

Sheridan M.D. (1960) *The Developmental Progress of Infants and Young Children*. London: HMSO.

Skinner, B.F. (1976) *About Behaviorism*. New York, NY: Vintage.

Sudbery, J. and Whittaker, A. (2018) *Human Growth and Development: An Introduction for Social Workers* (2nd edn). London: Routledge.

Walker, J. (2017) *Social Work and Human Development* (5th edn). London: Sage.

Wastell, D. and White, S. (2017) *Blinded by Science: The Social Implications of Epigenetics and Neuroscience*. Bristol: Policy Press.

Watson, J.B. (1924) *Behaviorism*. New York, NY: People's Institute Publishing Co.

Watson, J.B. and Rayner, R. (1920) Conditioned emotional reaction, *Journal of Experimental Psychology*, 3(1): 1–14.

2

Psychoanalytic approaches

Stephen Briggs

Introduction

Psychoanalysis takes a distinctive approach to understanding human development through being organised around the concept of the unconscious. Freud's formulation that most of what occurs in the human mind, including thought processes, memories and motivations, is not known but affects behaviour is both widely known and yet still controversial. Psychoanalysis excites strong feelings, for and against, and is subject to myth–making, including that psychoanalysis has not changed or developed in the 80 years since Freud's death. Contemporary psychoanalytic approaches are characterised by rich, varied and evolving theoretical frameworks and practice.

Psychoanalytic theories of development make a powerful contribution to understanding the most difficult and disturbing aspects of being human, including destructiveness, sexuality and conflict, alongside ways of understanding some of the beauties of life, such as loving relations. Contemporary psychoanalysis provides a social and developmental approach, with a strong emphasis on emotional and relational factors, although its focus on drives and instincts shares connections with biophysical approaches.

Psychoanalytic theories are complex and apply a distinctive method for generating knowledge and you will need to persevere to understand them. Don't worry if at first you find them difficult; this is to be expected. This chapter introduces both theoretical concepts and the processes through which they are formulated, stemming initially from how psychoanalytic therapeutic work is practised. I begin with an overview of the characteristics of psychoanalytic approaches to development and growth, followed by a discussion of the contribution of key theorists. I then explore some key concepts and processes. Finally, I apply these to professional social work practice.

Chapter objectives

- provide an overview of current psychoanalytic approaches to development;

31

- explore developmental theory and processes for selected key concepts;
- understand and discuss applications for professional social work practice.

Background and context

Psychoanalysis is a thriving discipline internationally; it uses an effective therapeutic method to bring about change and growth and the reduction of serious mental ill health in individuals, including depression (Fonagy et al, 2015) and borderline personality disorder (Bateman and Fonagy, 2009), and serious risks, including self-harm and suicide (Guthrie et al, 2001; Clarkin et al, 2007). Countering earlier myths suggesting there are few benefits to psychoanalytic therapies, systematic reviews of randomised controlled trials (a highly regarded experimental research design) show that both short-term and longer-term psychoanalytical therapies improve outcomes for mental health conditions (Abbass et al, 2014; Fonagy, 2015). Psychoanalytic therapies have also demonstrated an advantage over other approaches where benefits have been found to be longer lasting (Fonagy et al, 2015).

In addition to a clinical method, psychoanalysis provides a theory of human development, which coheres around the core and distinguishing concept of the unconscious. Freud's discoveries and theorisations of unconscious mental life have become widely known, albeit often distorted and sometimes dismissed (for example, the unconscious is frequently referred to as 'subconscious'). Organising mental life and human relations around the principle of the unconscious has advantages and disadvantages. It enables access to, and understanding of, the irrational and disturbing aspects of human behaviour and relationships, but it can also be extremely challenging, especially when confronted with the complex ways in which theory describes these inevitably elusive phenomena. Focusing on the unconscious tells us we do not know the content of our own minds. This can be an affront to the notion that people are rational beings; indeed, having within us a mixture of sexual and destructive desires and phantasies, despite the best efforts of socialisation, can be difficult to face and accept. It is not surprising, therefore, that psychoanalysis is a controversial discipline, as well as one that is difficult to understand.

Freud's pessimism, aphoristically expressed in the phrase that psychoanalysis aimed to change neurotic misery into 'ordinary human unhappiness', makes for a hard sell in current contexts that prefer instant gratification and happiness. Facing the sources of mental pain and human destructiveness are central to psychoanalytic thinking and the therapeutic method; it is also important to add that Freud and other theorists, including Jacques Lacan (1960), Donald Winnicott (1971), Hanna Segal (1991) and Anne Alvarez (1992), have explored sources of creativity and joy.

To engage with the rich potential of psychoanalysis as providing a clinical treatment for mental ill health, a source of understanding of human development, society and culture, and a useful approach for professionals in the human services, including social work, it is important to gain an understanding not only of theoretical concepts, but also of the distinctive methods and processes through which psychoanalytic knowledge is generated: 'Psychoanalytic thinking is not easily contained in a linear argument; premises leading to conclusions. It is a particular way of thinking ... so comprehension does not arrive like a light being switched on, it grows slowly – often irritatingly slowly' (Hinshelwood, 1994, p 3).

Within the discipline of psychoanalysis, learning about theory is accompanied by learning about process. The requirement that analysts and therapists have their own analysis enables self-understanding and familiarity with the process of linking theory to experience. This is perhaps not something that most social workers will undertake, but it is worth knowing something about it as part of your development; and it is useful to understand how other professions may learn and work.

A conundrum is how to describe concepts, ideas and experiences that are remote from consciousness. Freud's method, which has been subsequently followed and adapted, involved the patient saying whatever came to mind – 'free association' – and the analyst taking up a reflective, observational approach: a particular way of listening, understanding and responding with '"free floating attention", being "lost" in the analytic process as the musician is at his instrument' (Meltzer, 1967, p. xi), and then surfacing to think, wonder and put into words what has been understood. Clinical accounts therefore involved a detailed narrative of what the patient said in the session, the emotional qualities of these accounts and the process of making sense of these through generating and/or applying theory.

Theory development, then, involves the retrospective construction of earlier experiences from the material of the analytic situation. Melanie Klein, in particular, developed the approach to produce detailed, complex accounts of infancy from clinical work with children. Klein was not alone in this: there were others, including Freud and Winnicott, 'indeed virtually all analysts are very free in constructing hypothetical accounts of the mental development of infants' (Spillius, 2007, p 57). Freud agonised over the method, especially in relation to its scientific status: 'I always envy the physicists and mathematicians who can stand on firm ground', he wrote, 'I hover so to speak in the air'. He reflected that his case studies 'read like novellas, and that they, so to speak, lack the serious stamp of science' (Gay, 1988, p 89). However, he added – and this is crucial – that it was 'the nature of the subject, rather than my predilection, that is responsible for the result' (Gay, 1988, p 89).

As psychoanalysis could not have developed knowledge of the inner world by direct observation alone, the theories thus developed have to be judged not as to whether the concepts (for example, the Oedipus complex – a famous psychoanalytic concept[1]) 'exist', but rather whether the features that lead to this categorisation from clinical material from one patient are identifiable in other patients, and whether the concept has clinical usefulness (Rustin, 2007). It is perhaps a limitation, though by no means a reason to ignore or refute the findings from psychoanalysis, that it is difficult to confirm or falsify concepts by the criterion of direct observation. Falsifiability, as the famous philosopher of science, Karl Popper, would argue, constitutes the main criteria of scientific theories. However, some psychoanalytic concepts have been triangulated by recent work in psychology and neuroscience. For example, Melanie Klein, controversially at the time, suggested very young babies were capable of relating to others, supporting her theory with some observations.

Rather than exaggerating the capacity of babies to relate to other people, current knowledge suggests that Klein underestimated this. It is now recognised that the infant is oriented towards relationships from birth, and it is in the context of this emotional environment in primary relationships that the infant develops. Stern (2002) described how the 'dance' of mother and child interactions introduce the child to the intersubjective world of others. (Throughout, I use the term 'mother' to refer to a person in a primary caring role of any gender; when I am referring specifically to the person who is the biological mother, I try to make that clear.) For instance, the way in which a parent figure coos over a child and plays by vocalising, smiling, tickling and so forth produces responses that emulate, adapt and evoke further responses from the parent figure. Malloch and Trevarthen (2009) identify that the musical rhythms of communication between a mother and her baby in the first months guide the child into the world of meanings, intentions and knowing. Together, mothers and infants are understood to make sense of each other through the rhythm and synchronicity of their exchanges.

Sometimes, it can appear as though psychoanalysis is associated solely with Freud and hence located in the past. Marion Bower has commented that, in social work, much of the teaching of psychoanalysis is out of date, while over recent years in psychoanalysis 'there has been an explosive development in theory and practice applications' (2005, p 4). These include theory developed from psychotherapy with children who have been abused or have been in care, adolescents at risk, offenders and people with drug and alcohol problems. Thus, some commentators will claim psychoanalytic thought is no longer relevant in social work, whereas, in actual fact, social work has not kept pace with developments.

Psychotherapeutic work with many of these groups involves understanding fragile, vulnerable individuals. This has had a far-reaching effect on the theory

---

[1] This refers to Freud's taking the Greek myth of Oedipus to be a cornerstone in individual childhood development, in which the infant's desire for the opposite sex parent and competition with the same sex parent (and vice versa) creates a passionate – and bloody – set of 'phantasies'. The 'Oedipus complex' has a number of significant aspects and variations, which when placed in a 'modern' context, has a continuing relevance for understanding development.

and techniques used in practice, alongside how they develop. Social changes in the way that authority is considered, expectations in relationships, more open approaches to sexuality and gender, and how communications and friendships take place in the era of online and social media also feed into transformations in psychoanalytic practice. Psychotherapy has developed over time to become more intersubjective and relational – less about uncovering the repressed past, and more about working through the complexities of relationships, suffused by unconscious processes, integrating parts of the personality to achieve a sense of freedom in oneself, freedom from the painful constraints of defences built to protect the self from debilitating anxieties and freedom to engage in relationships in a more alive and fulfilling way. White (2007, p 203) describes the current shift in psychoanalysis as being towards 'process models of mind and self in constant evolution' that 'explode any lingering notions, of "normal" (ideal) states to be achieved through psychoanalytic psychotherapy', as exciting, in opening up the possibilities for new thinking about subjectivity and intersubjectivity. Thus, the psychoanalytic process is now characterised as 'a dynamic exchange between two engaged subjects in which new and unexpected configurations and developments may emerge' (White, 2007, p 203).

These ideas have been taken up in psychosocial studies (Frosh, 2010; Hollway and Jefferson, 2013). The dynamics of racism have been discussed (Davids, 2011); while the movement from 'doer and done to' relationships towards recognition (Benjamin, 2018) has implications for political as well as personal and therapeutic relationships (Hoggett, 2016). These changes make psychoanalytic thought continually relevant to social work practice, as they concern the ways in which children and young people negotiate and take part in relationships in the social environment. In a sense, although Freud is no longer with us, these developments free up the possibility to re-evaluate his achievements, which have contemporary relevance: his exploration of the unconscious and 'the contradictions inherent in adult sexuality and the dangerous subject of child sexuality, the intricacies of gender acquisition, the drives which transmute our animal nature, the perilous regions of transference and transference love, and the problem of human destructiveness' (White, 2007, p 1).

Theories and theorists

It is important to examine some of the key thinkers who have been involved in developing psychoanalytic thought over the years. This will give you, as a social worker, a solid foundation from which to judge the relevance of these theories and to apply them. Innovative ideas have led to psychoanalysts adopting different positions where differences in theoretical emphasis tend to be organised as schools. Post-war British psychoanalysis is divided into two camps: those following Freud's daughter, Anna (1895–1982); and those following Melanie Klein (1888–1960). A third group, led by Donald Winnicott (1896–1971), became known as the Independents.

Klein's significance is as an innovative if divisive figure, especially regarding her theories of infant development and method of child analysis. Her work has been further elaborated by post-Kleinians, including Wilfred Bion (1897–1979), Hanna Segal (1918–2011) and Herbert Rosenfeld (1910–86), through work with highly disturbed narcissistic and psychotic patients. In North America, post-war emphasis on ego-psychology, followed by Heinz Kohut's (1977) psychology of the self and narcissism, contrasted with the object relations theories of Klein, Winnicott and others. Object relations theory views development as influenced primarily through relationship with significant others, initially caregivers, and the internalisation of aspects of these relationships. 'Object' refers, therefore, not to inanimate entities, but to the experience of significant others.

Heading into the 21st century, as psychoanalysis globalised, Kleinian approaches spread through North and South America and Europe. Spin-off developments drawing on psychoanalysis are also plentiful: attachment theory, developed by Bowlby in the UK, but influential globally, is a pivotal example. Winnicott, Lacan (1901–81) and Bion are widely considered to be the most significant figures influencing 21st-century psychoanalysis (Green, 2005; White, 2007). Although there are significant differences in their thinking, some commonalities of approach can be found. They each take a deeply intersubjective approach to development. Lacan (1960) conceptualised the child's development in relation to the desires and language of the Other. Bion developed a theory of the dynamics of the mother–infant relationship, which he called the container-contained, and its implications for thinking. Winnicott's (1964) view that 'there is no such thing as an infant' meant: 'If you set out to describe a baby you will find that you are describing a baby and someone. A baby cannot exist alone, but is essentially part of a relationship' (Winnicott, 1964, p 88).

Some of these ideas are shown in Case Study 2.1.

CASE STUDY 2.1

Lizzie, who is 17, complains about being at school. She says she has lost all interest in studying and can't wait to leave. She has a tense relationship with her mother, and she complains her father, who lives separately, does not have enough time for her. She says she is bored, and wants to work and earn money. She experiences her peers as immature and says she is much happier in the company of older people. She spends much of her time in therapy talking about boyfriends, who are always much older than she is. She says that she expects older boyfriends to be able to look after her better than boyfriends of her own age. In these relationships an initial enthusiasm with extravagant hopes is quickly turned to bitter disappointment and disillusionment, when she feels her boyfriend has let her down. Unperturbed, and defiant, she continues to search for another, who will not disappoint her.

Questions

1. How might past events contribute to Lizzie's current feelings, thoughts and behaviour?
2. How might psychoanalytic thinking help explain Lizzie's states of mind?
3. How might these theories and understandings be helpful in planning how to work with her?

Discussion

The interpersonal realm is where the individual's identity, experiences and environment interconnect and develop ways of responding that may be based on one's own interpretations of the other person as well as ourselves.

A second similarity between the three seminal thinkers (Winnicott, Bion and Lacan), emphasised by White (2007), is that in their work there develops a movement towards greater openness of conceptualising subjectivity, in comparison with the more structural approaches of their predecessors – notably, Freud's model of id, ego and superego. Clearly, the thinking of Winnicott, Bion and Lacan, while innovative in many respects, constitutes developments of Freud (and Klein) rather than a totally new departure.

Strands of developments in contemporary practice include Independent analysts' configuration of the therapeutic relationship as a creative shared venture. Ogden (1994) and Benjamin (2018) conceptualise an analytic third, which is a creation formed through therapeutic interaction. Benjamin's work refocuses thinking about gender, difference and power in transcending exploitative 'doer and done to' relatedness. Post-Kleinians, through work with severely disturbed patients, have greatly enhanced understanding of destructive relatedness and parts of the personality, including envy, narcissism, rage, violence and suicide, and their associated defensive organisations (Meltzer, 1992; Steiner, 1994; Britton, 1998). Feminist psychoanalysts Julia Kristeva (1993) and Luce Irigaray (1977) have taken up Lacanian theorising of the generation of the subject, or 'subjectification'.

In the following discussion, I explore some selected theories, processes and concepts to illustrate how these theorists work with and use psychoanalytic theories to understand development. These include Klein's concepts of the paranoid schizoid and depressive positions, Winnicott's 'holding', Bion's container–contained and Lacanian ideas of subjectification.

REFLECTION POINT 2.1

What are your thoughts on reading this chapter? Reflect on your experiences to date of learning about psychoanalytic approaches – what do you recall now? And what psychoanalytic ideas have you encountered as part of our culture (e.g. 'Freudian slip')?

Psychoanalytic development

Routinely, accounts of development are organised according to phases: conception, babyhood, early childhood, school-aged childhood, adolescence and early adulthood, and adulthood. This is true, for example, of two excellent sources: Hindle and Smith (1999) and Waddell (2002). Organising development in phases provides a clear framework; development occurs in time. The rapid growth and change of the human child and the effects of extended dependency on adults are apparent when thinking about development organised in this way. However, both traditional and contemporary psychoanalytic thinking about development includes key elements that transcend linear descriptions, which reflects what we see in everyday life.

REFLECTION POINT 2.2

How do you think psychoanalytic thinking can help you in contemporary social work practice? You may not have thought that such in-depth psychosocial models of understanding the ways in which children and young people develop can be of use to social workers in busy situations that call for immediate practical support. However, if you think about the relationships that are necessary when working with people, however immediate the situation, one needs to be aware of our anxieties, impulses and desires and the defences we use to protect ourselves and to make feelings more acceptable to us.

A central tenet of psychoanalytic thinking is that past experiences influence the present in ways that are not available to consciousness (for instance, relationships with key figures in our lives and, especially, how important aspects of these relationships were perceived and internalised to become transferable to present relationships). The concept of transference that stems from this is one of the cornerstones of psychoanalytic thinking. Freud quickly realised it was of huge assistance in the therapeutic process, enabling indirect access to unconscious expectations of self and others in relationships. Current thinking proposes that aspects of early relations, internalised via mediations and modifications by the infant's perceptions of situations – which Klein called 'phantasies' – permeate all aspects of current relationships. Stern et al (1998) state that formative early experiences form dynamic templates, and these are activated in present relationships (Lyons-Ruth, 1999). For example, an early experience of uncertain reactions from a parent figure may result in anxieties when confronted by all people in authority positions.

Margot Waddell (2002), from a post-Kleinian perspective, discusses the complex relationship between phases of development and states of mind that are experienced at any point in time. Earlier developmental phases are experienced in the present, especially when circumstances evoke the emotions of these earlier experiences. Some developmental experiences have a crucial impact on later experiences, especially when the developmental issues have not been resolved or adequately worked through at the time. The example of a child or young person's feelings of anxiety when meeting an authority figure, if prior experience indicates such meetings are unpredictable, also works here. However, alongside this, there is constant movement between different states of mind. Klein described two distinct ways of relating to oneself and others that persist throughout life. In the paranoid schizoid position is a preoccupation with the self's survival, in dealing with pains and anxieties by attempting to keep unpleasant feelings at bay. The depressive position is a more mature state of concern for others, in which generosity and a sense of guilt about the effects of one's aggression mingle with concern for the self. This can be persistent over time – a very early, infantile state of mind repeating the emotional issues that babies contend with at that stage. Again, the anxious child or young person may develop survival techniques based on rejection and immediate aggression so they control the situation.

Bion elaborated the implication that development consists of oscillation between positions – as a constantly fluctuating field. He thought the emotional work needed for developmental progress is always accompanied by anxiety and internal disruption, so that emotional growth inevitably involves a sense of turbulence. Anxieties about the disrupting effects of change and development are experienced as 'catastrophic', resulting in a regressive pull and fear of change. However, if they can be borne, the benefits of the developmental achievement, and a change in internal organisation and relatedness to others, can occur (Bion, 1970). The child or young person who controls anxiety-provoking situations by acting aggressively may also oscillate between extreme anxiety and aggression, or indeed replace both reactions with others to negotiate their pathway through problematic encounters. Therefore, there is interdependence between paranoid schizoid and depressive functioning. Bion used the notation PS ↔ D (paranoid schizoid ↔ depressive) to indicate this two-way process; there is 'movement through each position in turn as part of a continuous, lifelong, cyclical development' (Britton, 1998, p 69). The 'reverse' process of movement from depressive to paranoid schizoid functioning occurs in times of intense change. Paranoid schizoid relating defends the individual against the complex, ambivalent feelings of the depressive position; while paranoid schizoid functioning can be useful in generating the energy to effect internal reorganisation to achieve transitions (Britton, 1998, p 81).

Klein used the term 'position' to indicate a constellation of feelings, especially anxieties, defences aiming to deal with these and ways of perceiving the world, or object relatedness. Initially, she conceived these as core to development in infancy. In the paranoid schizoid position, the primary anxiety is persecutory (hence 'paranoid'); the infant feels that discomforts are threats, as revealed by Miller: 'the pains of stomach ache must be felt as dangerous onslaughts by an enemy within' (1999, p 36). Bad feelings are threats to the self and survival, and they are defended against by projecting them into others and splitting the object into an all good and all bad (hence the schizoid). It is as though the infant relates to two mothers: one is the beneficent provider of all good things; the other is perceived as the cause of all bad, frustrating and hateful feelings, and the infant projects all bad, hateful feelings into this mother. Think of your own childhood knowledge of folk tales and fairy stories: you will note examples of these positions in literature – for example, the story of Little Red Riding Hood. The infant thus creates two universes: an ideal state and one characterised by terror and persecution. Increasingly, the illusion of these two worlds is challenged by the infant's perceptions of reality as the infant makes the developmental step towards becoming more integrated.

In the depressive position, the realisation that the 'good' and the 'bad' mothers are the same person gives rise to a sense of guilt that expelling bad feelings into the (bad) mother risks damaging the 'good' mother. Depressive position relating involves an awareness of guilt, and a desire to make reparation for the damage that has been done, in phantasy, by aggression towards the object. It includes an increased sense of separateness, and that the love of mother is shared with others – including powerful others, like father and siblings. This can be difficult to tolerate and, if overwhelmed, the infant retreats to the paranoid schizoid position. Parent–infant relating helps to create the possibility to tolerate separateness. For example, Winnicott (1971) described the baby and play, where the baby can play in the presence of another and the creative possibilities of a space to play are enabled.

Weaning – whether from breast to bottle, or bottle to cup – is thought to be an important process in the infant's emotional work in attaining the depressive position (Wittenberg, 2013, p 44). The capacity to relinquish and bear loss entails a deep struggle between despair and grief, arousing depressed, miserable feelings, rage and hate, which may be difficult for the self and others to bear, together with the desire to evade and resort to the defences of the paranoid schizoid position: splitting, projection, denial and idealisation. Weaning can lead to a flattening of feeling, a wish to seek out and return to an idealised state, expressed, for example, by the idea of not having to work or worry; or it can bring a sense of new opportunities – to try a whole new range of interesting foods – and the sense of balance and satisfaction that comes from recognition of integration and somehow managing developmental challenges. If you have younger brothers or sisters or, indeed, if you are a parent or know someone who has young children, you will no doubt be able to identify some of these developments and changes.

The attainment of the depressive position in infancy is a critical phase in development. The cluster of experiences (including how the (m)other is perceived in this process, the defences that are employed, whether loss is felt to be modulated by mourning, separation bearable, the sense of guilt tolerable, destructiveness reparable) lays down a prototype for future developmental conflicts. Furthermore, how later losses are related and responded to will connect with earlier experiences, which are constantly in the process of modification in development. Children use symbolic play to work through experience and relatedness. In adolescence, there is an intense process of reorganising early experiences in the contexts of the changed body, cognitive capacities and changes in relation to adults, especially in the context of being more separate.

Infant–carer relationships

How infant relationships with parental figures help to manage feelings and states of mind are described by two views of the mother–infant relationship: Winnicott's concept of holding and Bion's container-contained relationship. Together with Lacan's ideas of becoming a subject, these conceptualisations of infant–carer relationships provide frameworks for relational processes that are present throughout life in personal, therapeutic and other professional relationships. They provide important ways of understanding relationship development for social workers, since they offer explanations of how those relationships develop, work or become derailed.

Holding

Winnicott's concept of holding is deceptively simple, but is a profound way of seeing babies' early development in the context of their fragility and vulnerability. Winnicott thought of holding as the mother providing the infant with a sense of continuity of being (Winnicott, 1965). Ogden (2004) grasps Winnicott's meaning when he describes the mother, through 'primary maternal preoccupation', being able to enter the sense of time of the infant's world and protecting the baby from the intrusions of adult time, of calendar time, hours and days and diurnality. This function is so vital because the baby needs to be protected from the intrusion of the 'unbearable otherness' (Ogden, 2004, p 1351) of adult time; it also 'provides a setting ... for the infant to experience spontaneous movement and become the owner of the sensations that are appropriate to this early phase of life' (Winnicott, 1965, p 303).

The infant can therefore become actively involved in their own developmental processes rather than be subject to the continuity-shattering demands of adult time. Gradually, over time, the baby is subject to a process of disillusionment as the mother's holding is reduced. As the infant becomes able to tolerate frustration, and feels more separate from mother, there arises a potential space for creativity between them (Winnicott, 1971). In the hands of current theorists Ogden (1994) and Benjamin (2018), Winnicott's concepts have been developed to provide new thinking about the potential space, between illusion and disillusion, which creates a new, 'third' understanding. Thus, the infant grows from close holding to a sense of attached release.

Container-contained

Bion had a 'penchant for using words in a way that invents them anew' (Ogden, 2004, p 1349). His concept of container-contained, which has become extremely influential in psychoanalytic theory and practice, describes a way of processing emotions, with the effect that something untamed, unnamed and unbearable becomes manageable and known within language – or contained. A critical part of this is the mother's availability for her baby's emotional experiences, through what Bion described as her 'reverie' (Bion, 1962). Like Winnicott, Bion describes how the mother makes herself available for the baby's emotional experiences, through taking in their communications of all kinds.

Reverie works because the mother conceives that infant communications of all kinds have meaning and need understanding, and because she is aware of how precarious is baby's capacity to manage their own states of feeling. The infant's early mental life is dominated by the need to take in, through feeding and the mother's holding and containing, and the need to expel, or project, unwanted and unbearable feelings and sensations. Klein (1959) described the processes of introjection and projection occurring from the start of life. Bion (1962) developed her concept of projective identification and placed it at the centre of the process of early, preverbal relatedness. Infants communicate by stirring up feelings in the other and projecting feelings into the (m)other. The container-contained relationship therefore involves the baby as an active partner, initiating interactions through projective identification to which the mother responds through her reverie. The outcome of the mother returning feelings in more tolerable form, with names, contributes to the internalisation of emotional experience. The baby takes in the named experience, together with the mother's containing capacity. Learning experiences become a prototype for emotional learning that becomes the basis for all future experiences, but which can be modified by later experiences of containment – that is, the containing function of the (m)other and the capacity for new learning from experience.

What happens if the mother is unable to provide reverie, if her anxieties prevent her from bearing the intensity of the infant's communications? Two aspects of this have been identified. Bion (1967) wrote about the first aspect – when the mother blocks (namely, does not take in) the emotionality of the infant's communication so that the infant then receives back an intensification of the original feeling, as a 'nameless dread' (p 117). The second aspect is where the mother's uncontained feelings are projected into the infant (Williams, 1997), leading to the infant being filled up to overflowing with these feelings, refusing to take in, including feeding, or withdrawing from relating to others. Difficulties in feeding, thinking and learning are possible consequences of disturbance of the container-contained relationship. Difficulties in the container-contained relationship disturb the process of the development of a secure internal world, compromising the capacity to relate to others, be separate, think about experiences and process anxiety. When these disturbances persist, defences develop with the aim of protecting the baby from painful experiences, but at the potential cost of reducing the capacity to develop and relate to others.

Subjectification (or subjectivation)

Lacan conceptualised a mirror stage, occurring between 6 and 18 months, as a first step in the infant developing internal psychic separation from the Other. The three domains of experience are the imaginary, the real and the symbolic. The imaginary is a narcissistic identification with an ideal, an imaginary illusory structure. The real represents raw experience which can never be known directly, and is approached through symbolic functioning; symbolisation occurs through the child's entry into language, through the 'paternal metaphor', 'the Name (No) of the Father'. In essence, the elements combine 'as structural moments constitutive of subjectivity in complex and mutually independent ways' (White, 2007, p 204). Recent Lacanians have written about these processes as subjectification (or subjectivation), or becoming a subject. Kristeva (1993) and Irigaray (1977) have made significant contributions to subjectification in terms of gendered identity. However, it is the application of the idea of subjectification to adolescence that provides a way of illustrating this thinking.

Raymond Cahn (1998) and Perret-Catipovic and Ladame (1998) discuss the process of becoming a subject as involving the adolescent in an internal struggle and social process, to differentiate self from other, inside from outside and new from familiar, and to achieve ownership of one's own thoughts. This requires giving meaning to experiences, symbolisation and reflection, and takes place in a reflective 'space' that is open to interrogation (Cahn, 1998, p 11). There is correspondence here with Bion's process of container-contained, through which emotional experiences are named and transformed through thinking, and Winnicott's 'holding', which supports the continuity of being and becoming over time.

Therefore, adolescents develop characteristic ways of relating to new experiences, primarily in relationships. Some adolescents may relate newness back to the familiar or already known, while others are open to the unknown. Preference for the familiar and known leads to repetitive or mechanical ways of relating (see also Case Study 2.1), while a privileging of newness over the familiar may lead to a manic search for excitement. Between these two extremes are oscillating moments of openness and closure. Owning one's thoughts, drives and the adult sexual body and symbolisation, one achieves freedom from power of another or imposition of that power. Adolescents confront the many and powerful obstacles to appropriating their own thoughts, wishes and desires (Cahn, 1998); and failure to develop the capacity for subjecthood may 'lure him/her into a closed ideology or delusion, alienating or imprisoning him/her and distorting his/her world' (Cahn, 1998, p 159).

Recent applications of subjectification address the influence of online and social media on identity. The nature of virtual space and how it is used by young people change the notion of intimacy by moving the boundaries between private and public domains. Gozlan (2013) contrasts the notion of 'extimacy', the process of sharing the intimate with others (Tisseron, 2011), with her own term 'dis-intimacy', where the adolescent loses ownership of the intimate so that it no longer belongs to them. Here, Gozlan considers how adolescents who are vulnerable and need to seek affirmation may in virtual space lose possession of parts of themselves, through sharing with others and suffering a loss which is difficult, if not impossible, to mourn.

Applications in practice

Psychoanalytic thinking has been applied for many years in professional contexts, including nursing, social work and criminal justice (such as probation work). Winnicott's ideas of holding and the facilitating environment have made a significant contribution to social work. Bower (2005) demonstrates the application of contemporary psychoanalytic thinking to social work practice. Training of professionals in the Tavistock Clinic and the inclusion of the infant observation method in social work training also make significant contributions. The *Journal of Social Work Practice* (which has the strapline 'psychotherapeutic approaches in health, welfare and the community') focuses on the generation of psychoanalytically informed theory and practice in social work and cognate professions.

Bower (2005) points out that professionals usually need help when faced with the more difficult, disturbed aspects of their clients, patients and service-users' behaviour and attitudes to help (for example, those who repeatedly appear to put themselves at risk of harm, are 'hostile, suspicious, critical or uncooperative' or 'reject or spoil potentially helpful interventions' [Bower, 2005, p 3]). The interplay of conflicts that occur in development – thinking here particularly of Bion's discussion of catastrophic anxieties and the fluctuations between paranoid schizoid and depressive positions – and the impact of earlier development on later life provides a useful framework for making sense of and hence guiding approaches and interventions. In addition, psychoanalytic approaches help us to understand the emotional impact of the work that may leave social workers feeling 'confused, fragmented, inadequate, despairing or enraged' (Bower, 2005, p 4). The concept of countertransference is vital here. Psychoanalytic thinking uses this term in several ways. Firstly, it refers to the feelings raised within the therapist relating to their own difficulties, prejudices and blind spots, and their expectations of self and other in relationships. In this sense, countertransference is an impediment to self-awareness. In a second sense, countertransference refers to what is projected into the therapist/professional by the patient/service-user. If these can be thought about, through reverie, they can be informative of the other's states of mind and lead to understanding. There are also situations where the professional is 'nudged' by projections to enact the countertransference – to act in ways that are not professional when boundaries can become blurred or broken.

REFLECTION POINT 2.3

Think of the concepts of transference, countertransference and projection. They can be quite complex concepts to understand, so spend a little time trying to think of examples from your own life and/or social work practice that help you to explain them.

Ferguson (2017) emphasises the important contribution of psychoanalytic approaches to the capacity for reflective practice, in particular noting that we defend against anxieties generated by the analysis. Professionals need to be able to sit with uncertainty, powerful feelings and impulses, and treat them seriously (Briggs, 2017). Knowledge of concepts like container–contained and holding can help professionals think about the processes that are involved, but the capacities to work effectively with these processes are developed through learning from experience – through, for example, supervision with a psychoanalytic professional, personal therapy or undertaking a psychoanalytically informed infant or child observation. Observing a baby in the home settings, weekly for an hour, over the baby's first year of life or part of this, provides a powerful learning experience regarding infantile states of mind, the impact of these on the observer and what is needed to be able to stay with and process these feelings. This surveillance exposes the observer to a 'maelstrom of feelings', facilitating 'the development of capacities essential for psychotherapeutic work' (Urwin and Sternberg, 2012, p 3). The interplay among observation, reflection and using one's own feelings and thoughts to aid understanding are described in Case Study 2.2.

CASE STUDY 2.2

Tom, 14 years old, had come into care when, after his parents separated, his mother left him, his two older brothers and his younger sister. I started to work with him when he was placed with his father and his father's new partner. Tom's siblings seemed to settle but Tom frequently went missing from home and school. He would say very little when sitting with me in a room, and I spent most of my time with him outside the home. I saw him most frequently when collecting him from the police station, where he was taken after his frequent running-away episodes. He could not – or would not – tell me anything about his reasons for running away, nor how he felt about his home life or the changes in his life, including the quite sudden loss of his mother and his equally sudden reunion with his father. He was always ready for me when I called at the house and he seemed to look forward to my visiting him. Of course, Tom's running away caused considerable inter-agency anxiety and tension. Frequent inter-agency meetings were held and these discussions were fraught and conflictual, as participants divided into two camps. One group argued that Tom should be removed from home – he was, after all, on a Care Order – and placed in a secure setting. The other group thought that this would not provide a workable solution as surely Tom would continue to run away from wherever he was placed, and he had not indicated to me that he wished to leave his father's home; thus anxieties about Tom generated splits in the professional group.

On one of my visits to Tom, he started to talk about the park we were just passing in my car. He really liked the park, he said. I offered to stop and walk in the park, and he agreed. We walked for a few minutes through the park, which was more a woodland than a city park, and Tom suggested we played hide and seek – he would hide and I would try to find him. Immediately, I had anxious images of losing him and having to call the police to report him missing; I saw tabloid headlines: 'Social worker, playing hide and seek, loses child who has run away from home 80 times in past month'. However, some other, less anxious thoughts emerged and, without consciously formulating why, I began to feel the game might be a good idea. So I said, OK, as long as he agreed to some boundaries. I pointed out the limits of the game: the road to the left, the line of trees ahead and so on. He nodded in agreement, smiling, and took off. He was really hard to find. I was sweating and anxious when I at last found him. As soon as I got close he popped out, eyes shining with delight: 'that was great,' he said. I was struck by the strength of his feeling, and as this mingled with my relief at locating him, I suddenly realised it was not that he wanted to run away, but that he wanted to be looked for and found, and this was why he ran away. As we drove back to the house, I said some of this to him and also talked about his estrangement from his mother. He ran away less after this episode; his rather fragile father therefore began to feel less rejected by him and their relationship improved.

Questions
1. What do you think might be happening for Tom in this case study?
2. How might psychoanalytic thinking help you to understand his situation?
3. Consider some of the ways in which you have learned to cope with difficult and traumatic events and ask yourself how this might affect how you practise as a social worker in situations such as these.

Discussion
The beauty of the choice of hide and seek is its relevance to Tom's predicament, of loss and disruption; playing the game creates a new understanding of his behaviour – running away – which it is subsequently possible to put into words. This adaptation to his predicament provides holding and the process of reflecting on feelings stirred up in me has a containing possibility. Thus, it helps make more bearable and nameable his current losses. The episode is possible because Tom clearly has a positive feeling for the relationship with me – and he wants to be found. Nothing in my work with him had suggested a sadistic wish to inflict humiliation on me; had this been the case, the episode would not have been possible. As it was, he made me work hard to find him and to bear considerable anxiety, to have an emotional experience of Tom's feelings about his own situation. In this sense, I interpreted that his projected sense of being lost and his wishes to be found, made active by running away (of which he was originally the passive recipient, being left), was perhaps to gain mastery of this predicament, perhaps to gain some relief, probably to process his experiences and facilitate his development.

Conclusion

In this chapter, I have discussed psychoanalytic theories and theorists, exploring some key concepts in detail and linked these with the processes through which psychoanalytically informed work takes place. This is based on taking a particular kind of reflective stance to facilitate understanding, to look beneath the surface to approach unconscious aspects of relationships, emotionality and motivations. It requires approaching oneself and others as defended and partially aware subjects. I have emphasised that psychoanalysis is a living, evolving discipline in which new thinking and changing priorities contribute to ensuring it is relevant to current priorities. Although the concepts and processes involved in psychoanalytically-informed practice and understanding of development are complex, they provide a framework for understanding, in particular, some of the most disturbed and disturbing aspects of development. As such, it is important for social workers to be aware of and apply these concepts as they assess and work with families, children and young people.

Reflective questions

1 To what extent do you think an understanding of psychoanalytic concepts is important to contemporary social work?

2 How might you use and develop your understanding of psychoanalytic thinking for social work practice further?

3 What cultural issues are important to bear in mind when approaching a situation using psychoanalytic thought?

Further reading

Use your library database to access the *Journal of Social Work Practice*, which will give you a range of up-to-date research and conceptual articles on the use of psychoanalytic thought in social work practice.

• Bower, M. and Solomon, R. (eds) (2017) *What Social Workers Need to Know: A Psychoanalytic Approach*. Abingdon: Routledge.
This book, edited by two social workers with extensive experience in practice, offers a comprehensive introduction to many of the issues that arise in psychoanalytic practice. It offers the interested reader a greater depth to explore the practice ramifications of these theories and models.

- Brandell, J.R. (ed.) (2014) *The Essentials of Clinical Social Work.* Thousand Oaks, CA: Sage. This book, although written and abridged for the US market, presents modalities of clinical practice that are useful for those readers interested in developing specialist social work practice, particularly in psychoanalytic practice.

References

Abbass, A.A., Kisely, S.R., Town, J.M., Leichsenring, F., Driessen, E., De Maat, S., et al (2014) Short-term psychodynamic psychotherapies for common mental disorders, *Cochrane Database of Systematic Reviews*, Issue 7, Art. No. CD004687, DOI: 10.1002/14651858.CD004687.pub4.

Alvarez, A. (1992) *Live Company*. London: Routledge.

Bateman, A. and Fonagy, P. (2009) Randomized controlled trial of outpatient mentalization-based treatment versus structured clinical management for borderline personality disorder, *American Journal of Psychiatry*, 166(12): 1355–1364.

Benjamin, J. (2018) *Beyond Doer and Done to: Recognition Theory, Intersubjectivity and the Third*, London: Routledge.

Bion, W. (1962) *Learning from Experience*. London: Maresfield.

Bion, W. (1967) *Second Thoughts*. London: Maresfield.

Bion, W. (1970) *Attention and Interpretation*. London: Maresfield.

Bower, M. (2005) Psychoanalytic theories for social work practice. In M. Bower (ed.), *Psychoanalytic Theory for Social Work Practice: Thinking under Fire*. London: Routledge.

Briggs, S. (2017) Working with troubled adolescents: Observation as a key skill for practitioners. In H. Hingley-Jones, C. Parkinson and L. Allain (eds), *Observation in Health and Social Care: Applications for Learning, Research and Practice with Children and Adults*. London: Jessica Kingsley.

Britton, R. (1998) *Belief and Imagination: Explorations in Psychoanalysis*. London: Routledge.

Cahn, R. (1998) The process of becoming-a-subject in adolescence. In M. Perret-Catipovic and F. Ladame (eds), *Adolescence and Psychoanalysis: The Story and the History*. London: Karnac Books.

Clarkin, J., Levy, K., Lenzenweger, M. and Kernberg, O. (2007) Evaluating three treatments for borderline personality disorder: A multiwave study, *American Journal of Psychiatry*, 164(6): 922–928.

Davids, F. (2011) *Internal Racism: A Psychoanalytic Approach to Race and Difference*. Basingstoke: Palgrave.

Ferguson, H. (2017) How social workers reflect in action and when and why they don't: The possibilities and limits to reflective practice in social work, *Social Work Education*, 37(4): 415–427.

Fonagy, P. (2015) The effectiveness of psychodynamic psychotherapies: An update, *World Psychiatry*, 14(2): 137–150.

Fonagy, P., Rost, F., Carlyle, J., McPherson, S., Thomas, R., Fearon, P. et al (2015) Pragmatic randomized controlled trial of long-term psychoanalytic psychotherapy for treatment-resistant depression: The Tavistock Adult Depression Study (TADS), *World Psychiatry*, 14(3): 312–321.

Frosh, S. (2010) *Psychoanalysis outside the Clinic: Interventions in Psychosocial Studies.* London: Palgrave.

Gay, P. (1988) *Freud, a Life for Our Time.* London: Dent and Son.

Gozlan, A. (2013) The virtual machine: A dis-intimacy at work, *Recherches en psychanalyse*, 16(2): 196–205.

Green, A. (2005) *Key Ideas for a Contemporary Psychoanalysis.* London: Routledge.

Guthrie, E., Kapur, N., Mackway-Jones, K., Chew-Graham, C., Moorey, J., Mendel, E. et al (2001) Randomised controlled trial of brief psychological intervention after deliberate self-poisoning, *British Medical Journal*, 323(7305): 1–5.

Hindle, D. and Smith, M. (eds) (1999) *Personality Development: A Psychoanalytic Perspective.* London: Routledge.

Hinshelwood, R. (1994) *Clinical Klein.* London: Routledge.

Hoggett, P. (2016) *Politics, Identity and Emotion.* London: Routledge.

Hollway, W. and Jefferson, T. (2013) *Doing Qualitative Research Differently.* London: Sage.

Irigaray, L. (1977) *This Sex which Is Not One.* New York, NY: Cornell University Press.

Klein, M. (1959) Our adult world and its roots in infancy. In M. Klein (1988) *Envy and Gratitude and Other Works 1946–1963.* London: Virago.

Kohut, H. (1977) *The Restoration of the Self.* New York, NY: International Universities Press.

Kristeva, J. (1993) *New Maladies of the Soul.* New York, NY: Columbia University Press.

Lacan, J. (1960) The subversion of the subject and the dialectic of desire in the Freudian unconscious. In A. Sheridan (trans.) (2001) *Écrits: A Selection.* London and New York, NY: Routledge Classics.

Lyons-Ruth, K. (1999) The two-person unconscious: Intersubjective dialogue, enactive relational representation, and the emergence of new forms of relational organization, *Psychoanalytic Inquiry*, 19(4): 576–617.

Malloch, S. and Trevarthen, C. (2009) *Communicative Musicality: Exploring the Basis of Human Companionship.* Oxford: Oxford University Press.

Meltzer, D. (1967) *The Psychoanalytic Process.* Perthshire: Clunie Press.

Meltzer, D. (1992) *The Claustrum: An Investigation of Claustrophobic Phenomena.* Perthshire: Clunie Press.

Miller, L. (1999) Babyhood: Becoming a person in the family. In D. Hindle and M. Smith (eds), *Personality Development: A Psychoanalytic Perspective.* London: Routledge.

Ogden, T. (1994) *Subjects of Analysis.* London: Karnac Books.

Ogden, T. (2004) On holding and containing, being and dreaming, *International Journal of Psychoanalysis*, 85(6): 1349–1364.

Perret-Catipovic, M. and Ladame, F. (1998) *Adolescence and Psychoanalysis: The Story and the History*. London: Karnac Books.

Rustin, M. (2007) How do psychoanalysts know what they know? In L. Braddock and M. Lacewing (eds), *The Academic Face of Psychoanalysis: Papers in Philosophy, the Humanities and the British Clinical Tradition*. London: Routledge.

Segal, H. (1991) *Dream, Phantasy and Art*. London: Routledge.

Spillius, E. (2007) Developments in Kleinian thought: Overview and personal view. In E. Spillius, P. Roth and R. Rusbridger (eds) *Encounters with Melanie Klein: Selected Papers of Elizabeth Spillius*. London: Routledge/International Library of Psychoanalysis.

Steiner, J. (1994) *Psychic Retreats*. London: Routledge.

Stern, D. (2002) *The First Relationship: Infant and Mother*. Cambridge, MA: Harvard University Press.

Stern, D.N., Saner, L., Nahum, J., Harrison, A., Lyons-Ruth, K., Morgan, A. et al (1998) Non-interpretive mechanisms in psychoanalytic therapy: The 'something more' than interpretation, *International Journal of Psycho-Analysis*, 79(5): 903–921.

Tisseron, S. (2011) Les nouveaux réseaux sociaux sur internet, *Psychotropes*, 17(2): 99–118.

Urwin, C. and Sternberg, J. (eds) (2012) *Infant Observation and Research: Emotional Processes in Everyday Lives*. London: Karnac Books.

Waddell, M. (2002) *Inside Lives: Psychoanalysis and the Growth of the Personality* (2nd edn). London: Duckworth.

White, J. (2007) *Generation: Preoccupations and Conflicts in Contemporary Psychoanalysis*. London: Routledge.

Williams, G. (1997) *Internal Landscapes and Foreign Bodies*. London: Duckworth.

Winnicott, D. (1965) Primary maternal preoccupation. In D. Winnicott *The Maturational Processes and the Facilitating Environment*. London: Karnac Books.

Winnicott, D. (1964) *The Child, the Family and the Outside World*. London: Penguin.

Winnicott, D. (1971) *Playing and Reality*. London: Penguin.

Wittenberg, I. (2013) *Experiencing Endings and Beginnings*. London: Karnac Books.

3

Cognitive theories and cognitive development

Margarete Parrish

Introduction

Cognitive development and cognition are fundamentally associated with how and what people think and believe, and how those thoughts and beliefs may change and develop over time and across circumstances. In respect of children and young people, this concerns, especially, the ways in which those thoughts and beliefs develop and the effect of environmental influences and interpretations of those interactions on those thoughts and beliefs. Cognitive factors are implicated in developing different understandings, alternative explanations and solutions to life problems. When a child or young person is growing, cognitive development is particularly important for helping professionals, including social workers, to understand their lives, thinking, behaviours and emotions. This is especially the case regarding the ways in which they interpret their difficulties (and no doubt also the ways in which social workers interpret them).

While much of cognition is conscious or intentional, much also occurs outside the realm of conscious awareness as we have seen when considering psychoanalytic approaches in Chapter 2. This chapter will also address topics relating to the processes of acquiring, retaining and interpreting information and excavating some of those hidden cognitions that can be so important in devising alternative ways of thinking. However, unlike its psychoanalytic predecessors' emphasis on the unconscious drives and conflicts (described in more detail in Chapter 2), cognitive theories tend to be more focused on the present here-and-now, especially as they relate to thoughts, beliefs and how people interpret the world around them. Especially when working with children and young people, social workers often apply aspects of developmental awareness in their understanding and responses to children experiencing challenges involving unfamiliar emotions and experiences.

Chapter objectives

- provide an overview of key contributors to cognitive theories relating to children and young people, such as Piaget, Vygotsky, Kelly, and more generically, such as Bandura, Seligman, Ellis and Beck;

- debate the key concepts associated with cognitive theories – accommodation and assimilation, self-efficacy, learned helplessness, 'A–B–C' principle;

- make links between cognitive theory and current social work practice with children and young people.

History and development of the theories and models

From the early 20th century, cognitive theories have played a major role in influencing the ways in which professionals (including social workers), theorists and academics have understood and assessed people's circumstances and difficulties. Behavioural theorists, social workers and other professionals, as we have seen in Chapter 1, have sometimes contributed alongside their more cognitively focused counterparts, and thus cognitive and behavioural theories are often considered in tandem – hence the term cognitive-behavioural. However, we will be focusing in this chapter on cognitive theories, in particular what we might term social learning theory. The term places emphasis on the social, the interactive, as this is what makes these theories important and for social workers the relational aspects are core to what we do.

Key thinkers and theorists

This section presents an overview of some of the key cognitive thinkers and theorists. Most theoretical concepts in cognitive approaches to human development were originated in respect of children and young people. However, the models have been increasingly applied to adults across the life course and, so, in Chapter 2 in the companion volume, we shall rehearse some of the theoretical material given its relevance to both areas of growth and development.

Jean Piaget

The work of Swiss researcher Jean Piaget (1896–1980) is often viewed as the earliest contribution to understanding childhood cognitive development, although, as we argue in Chapter 2 in the companion volume, his work is relevant to growth and development across the life course. During that same year, Piaget also studied psychology under the guidance of Carl Jung and Eugen

Bleuler in Zurich, where his interest in abnormal psychology, psychiatry and psychodynamic thought deepened. He was well versed in contemporary thinking at the time and well positioned to develop his own approaches. After pursuing further studies at the Sorbonne in Paris, Piaget contributed to the development of standardised reasoning tests in the laboratory of Alfred Binet in Paris. Variations in the measures of intelligence and error in reasoning further deepened Piaget's interest in understanding how children learn and the logic of their conclusions (Vourlekis, 2009). His interest in children's moral reasoning has become a classic of psychological and psycho-social thought throughout the West.

While Piaget viewed intelligence as an evolving process that serves the individual's adaptations to the world around them, he did not equate children's factual knowledge with intelligence or understanding. His theory was essentially epistemological, and thus focused on how children come to know what they know (Shute and Slee, 2015). He based some of his early work on his naturalistic observations of his own three children during their infancies, with the objective of understanding how they explored the world around them.

REFLECTION POINT 3.1

Consider the ways in which Piaget developed his thinking from observations of the world around him and especially of his own children. Do you think that such modes of theory development would have credibility today? Consider the ethical issues involved and also consider what we might not be researching in respect of children and young people's development that could add to our knowledge.

Piaget's theory of how children's cognition develops, and how moral development occurs, provided a fundamental basis of subsequent cognitive and child development theories. Despite his historical prominence in the area of child development, developmental psychology and education, Piaget regarded himself as a genetic epistemologist, which he defined as the study of the development of abstract thought on the basis of a biological or innate environment.

Piaget's contributions challenged the existing premise that children's thoughts and understanding followed the same patterns as those of adults. Historically, adults have often presumed that children were not attending to adult discussions that they did not (or were not meant to) understand. Far from considering children to be miniature adults, Piaget considered children to be naturally curious explorers and experimenters, with clear intentions to interpret their observations and experiences in an increasingly systematic and (at least to themselves) logical way. This adds an important perspective to social workers when practising with children and young people. It demands that we do not interpret a child's meaning of the world from our own perspective, but that we search out how they, themselves, are constructing and approaching the world around them; that we listen to the child or young person.

Piaget proposed that children's learning is essentially experiential; it occurs when they actively construct their own cognitive realities and understandings of their environment. Hence, Piaget's concepts are sometimes referred to as constructivism. He regarded development as an ongoing, dynamic process stemming from the ability to adapt thinking and form new ideas in response to the demands of a changing environment. His theory reflects the emergence of meaning stemming from the active process of interactions with the physical, social and emotional environment (Shute and Slee, 2015). In your social work education, much of your learning is experiential and adaptive and it is helpful to consider how these ways of developing may influence some of the children and young people you come into contact with during your practice.

Piaget's cognitive stages represent an essential reorganisation of how a child 'knows' the world. He considered these stages to be universal or applicable to all children, regardless of culture or environment – a point that has since been contested (Robinson, 2007). His stages are epigenetic, meaning that progression from one stage to the next necessitates both physical and mental maturation through the previous stage. Achieving the previous stage is a prerequisite for progression to the next, although the rate at which children move may vary according to individual abilities and environment. Piaget believed that children consistently reached the same cognitive conclusions and developed their thinking along essentially similar routes, regardless of their circumstances. He identified four factors that influenced the developmental process:

- physical maturation of the brain, resulting in new capacities;
- experiences that resulted in developing knowledge;
- social transmission of knowledge (education);
- equilibration or equilibrium.

Piaget regarded these factors as being mutually interactive. For example, while the brain's physical maturation is necessary for cognitive development, it is not sufficient without opportunities to undergo experiences that reinforce that development. Likewise, experiences typically strengthen the social transmission of knowledge, and vice versa. Finally, the interactions among maturation, experiences and social transmission of knowledge are underpinned through 'equilibration', or the capacity for establishing balance.

According to Piaget, knowledge results from the simultaneous and corresponding mental processes he called 'assimilation and accommodation'. Assimilation involves the way in which new information is absorbed into the existing intellectual organisation. Accommodation refers to the modifications required to deal with the new material. According to Piaget, 'there is no accommodation without assimilation' (1970, p 8).

Intrigued by his observations of children of similar ages making similar errors in reasoning, Piaget questioned whether these errors actually reflected age/developmental patterns of intellectual development. He consequently proposed a universal sequence of four stages of cognitive development: (1) sensorimotor; (2) preoperational thought; (3) concrete operations; and (4) formal operations. According to Piaget, the four stages provide an invariant sequence of intellectual development, meaning that they necessarily occur in the same order for all children, and that progression to the next stage necessitates having successfully completed the previous stage.

REFLECTION POINT 3.2

Think of some of the ways in which Piaget's assumption that these stages are immutable and universal may be challenged. What might this mean for your own practice and learning and how might you ensure you keep a critical and reflective approach to these?

Piaget's theory has been criticised on account of both his methodology and his concept of the sequencing of children's stages of learning. His methodology has been criticised on account of its reliance on interviews, and the possibilities of subjective interpretation of interviews with children and the bias this could represent. His premise that stages are universal among children has raised questions related to individual differences and the role of environment. Likewise, Piaget's lack of attention to the roles played by parents and carers within the children's lives has also been a subject of critical debate (Shute and Slee, 2015). Nonetheless, Piaget remains a pivotal contributor to the study of children's cognitive development, with particular emphasis on the active process of children's acquisition of knowledge.

Lev Vygotsky

At the same time that Piaget was developing his understandings, the Russian psychologist Lev Vygotsky (1896–1934) was working on his own cognitive and constructivist theories. A combination of his tragically young death and political suppression during the Stalinist era, alongside the lack of sufficient translations, delayed his work becoming familiar to most Western readers until the 1970s (Passer et al, 2009). However, Vygotsky's work provides a fascinating combination of Marxist ideas of tensions involving the larger society with psychological concepts of developmental processes. These concepts are important in furthering our understanding of the ways in which environment, conflict and experience shape children's development.

Vygotsky argued that cognition is a social function because of the interactions of learning and social activities, which are shaped by environment and culture. In that sense, his approach was very contextual in its emphasis. Joravsky (1979, p 260) quotes Vygotsky as saying, "the brain is not a hotel for a series of conditioned reflexes dropping in". His concept of the zone of proximal development refers to the combined influences of culture and context on how children learn through their associations with (or 'proximity' to) others. While distinguishing between what children can do independently and what they can do with help, Vygotsky emphasised the cooperative endeavours ('joint collaboration') involved in that exchange as an essential component of learning to solve problems (Shute and Slee, 2015).

Because of his emphasis on how children's cognitive development is based on interactions with those around them, Vygotsky's framework is considered dialectical (Shute and Slee, 2015), something which is very influential in Marxist thought. His theory incorporates the importance of language as well as imitation as an indicator of a child's readiness to undertake new tasks and behaviours. According to Vygotsky, children's interactions with their surrounding culture and social environment (such as family and more capable siblings and peers) are essential aspects of their intellectual development (Luria, 2004). His ideas were later appreciated for their importance to both clinical and educational psychology. When compared with Piaget's theory, Vygotsky emphasised the collaborative process of children's learning, involving relationships with peers as well as adults, as essential factors in cognitive development more than the interpretation of other environmental factors and stimuli.

George Kelly

The American psychologist George Kelly (1905–66) is considered by some to be the 'father' of cognitive clinical psychology. Kelly's work is generally used when working with adults, but it also has relevance to child development. Kelly suggests that people function as though they were individual 'research scientists', perpetually engaged in anticipating and predicting future outcomes and then testing these in the real world through their behaviours. His main work, personal construct theory, proposed that in the course of daily life, people are engaged in the process of constructing explanatory theories and testing their hypotheses against reality, and then revising those hypotheses according to their predictive accuracy (Kelly, 1963). Thus, people routinely experiment with their own personal constructs for purposes of interpreting, predicting and managing their environment, much like the development of research hypotheses or theory building. From this theoretical framework, Kelly proposed that people form 'core' binary personal constructs, such as 'good vs. bad', 'intelligent vs. stupid' and 'safe vs. dangerous'. From such basic constructs, people assess their environment in ways that contribute to reliable anticipations and predictions of what they think should/will happen in diverse circumstances (Ewen, 2010). So the child may anticipate that touching a hot fire will cause pain and therefore develop a construct of safe vs. dangerous in respect of hot things.

According to Kelly's perspective, individuals are ideally capable of revising their constructs as a means of adapting to testing and experience. While Kelly's personal construct theory is not necessarily viewed specifically as a child development theory, it has nonetheless influenced ideas about children's cognitive development. Kelly argued that children had the capacity to test and anticipate in reliable and productive ways, starting from infancy (for example, 'if I cry, someone will come and feed me'). He proposed that parenting extremes (such as overindulgence, inconsistency and maltreatment) were potentially detrimental to children's otherwise healthy development of personal constructs (Kelly, 1963). For instance, if a child or young person learns to cry, complain or moan until they get their own way – rather like the character of the over-indulged Dudley Dursley, Harry Potter's cousin – a personal construct of entitlement at all times may develop for that child, which would not be helpful as they grow.

Albert Bandura

Albert Bandura's (1925–present) innovative research was originally referred to as social cognitive theory. Bandura challenged Skinnerian behaviourism that suggests one needs to control the external environment in order to modify behaviour. His major contribution was to the areas of social learning theory and self-efficacy.

Social learning theory uses the concept of modelling behaviour, which is discussed in Chapter 1 in this volume. It is worth rehearsing and building on those concepts here as observing different models of behaviour provides children and young people with a frame of reference for anticipating consequences and making judgements of worth (evaluations) about them. Bandura's concept of learning through observation suggested that people's behaviour changes through the replication or interpretation and then replication or adaptation of observing others' behaviour ('models'). By imitating the model's behaviour (including speech, dress and so on), people can expand upon their existing cognitive and behavioural repertoires. By observing and replicating behaviours, they may learn to smoke, to use correct (or incorrect) grammar, dance or where to get a tattoo. Unlike traditional behaviourist ideas from respondent or operant schools of thought, social learning necessitates the individual having paid attention, constructing, interpreting and remembering mental representations of what they observed, and being able to retrieve them for future reference in order to replicate what they observed (Bandura, 1969).

> **REFLECTION POINT 3.3**
>
> Consider a situation when you were a child where you may have been influenced by the behaviour of another and reflect whether this was helpful to your development or otherwise.
>
> Consider a situation where a child may copy an adult's behaviour in a social learning situation – could this be considered a positive or a negative?

Social learning theory emphasises the contextual influences on people's behaviour, with particular attention to environmental influences (as we see in Case Study 3.1). An important aspect of social learning theory is its capacity to explain both why behaviour develops as well as ways in which behaviour can be changed by altering environmental influences. The emphasis on observing and the vicarious reinforcement that results from those observations expanded the scope of social learning theory's applicability to children's cognitive development considerably (Bandura and Walters, 1963).

Bandura's contributions to cognitive studies include his attention to how people's self-appraisal amounted to a belief system about themselves. Bandura (1977, 1986) introduced the term self-efficacy to refer to individuals' perceptions of their own capacity to succeed at a given task or effort. According to Bandura, self-efficacy entails beliefs about the self that can shape behaviour by influencing willingness to try new behaviours. High self-efficacy entails a sense and expectation of competence, and a capacity to envision succeeding at a given task (Vourlekis, 2009). It can also determine the level of persistence or willingness to tolerate frustration when a person is willing or able to devote time and effort to practising unfamiliar or difficult tasks. People with higher levels of self-efficacy are more likely to take on challenges that others might avoid, because they are more likely to see challenges as surmountable, rather than overwhelming. This can result in a self-fulfilling prophecy.

Bandura's studies of aggression and how children learn to replicate aggressive behaviours have proven valuable for practice with children and their families, especially when violence occurs. By demonstrating how children's exposure to violence is significantly linked with replicating violence, Bandura has contributed immensely to the appreciation of observational learning in the transmission of aggression.

CASE STUDY 3.1

Genie is 14 years old, and is in her first romantic relationship with Don, age 16. She is very infatuated with him and her parents are worried that the relationship seems to be progressing rather quickly for a girl of her age. Genie's parents like Don, but are mindful that he is quite a bit more mature than Genie.

Genie has informed her older sister (age 17) that she plans to get a tattoo of Don's name on her left forearm. She is not informing her parents of her plan. If they object, she plans to point out that they both have each other's names tattooed on their backs (where they are not readily visible to others) as a rationale. Her parents had their tattoos done in celebration of their tenth anniversary of being together.

Questions

1. What are some implications of Genie's developmental age on her decision making?

2. How would social learning theory apply to Genie's perspective on getting a tattoo?

Discussion

Genie is still, of course, a minor. However, she is able increasingly to make her own decisions and this can, at her age, bring her into some degree of conflict with those responsible for her – her parents. Using social learning theory may, however, also offer a clue to some of her deep beliefs in her parents as role models, especially in respect of their tattoos and her interpretation of their positive relationship. Understanding this can help in negotiating this situation.

Martin Seligman

Often considered alongside Bandura's concepts of self-efficacy which we will consider later, Martin Seligman (1942–present) is associated with promoting what is referred to as 'positive psychology'. He is also credited with introducing the concept of 'learned helplessness', which is outlined briefly in Chapter 1 and can be seen in Case Study 3.2. In Seligman's landmark (1979) study, dogs were exposed to an electrical shock as they tried to cross a room. They came to perceive the pain inflicted by the electrical shock as being unavoidable and resigned themselves to its inevitability – even after it was discontinued. Even in other settings, the dogs appeared apathetic and passive, seeming always to expect punishment regardless of their behaviour (Seligman, 1979). Seligman's contributions to the understanding of 'learned helplessness' is particularly relevant to the understanding of how some interpretations and expectations become 'foregone conclusions' or 'self-fulfilling prophecies', especially when linked with negative outcomes.

REFLECTION POINT 3.4

Can you think of any time when, as a child or young person, you have felt that whatever you do you will not be able to influence the outcome of a situation? If so, note this down, how it made you feel and what helped you move on from this position.

Seligman, whose early studies were influenced by his admiration for Aaron Beck, has gone on to develop what he refers to as 'positive psychology', focusing on the characteristic strengths that contribute to resilience and well-being (Peterson and Seligman, 2004). The factors he emphasises are typically subjective to each individual, but include positive emotions, meaning found through an awareness of something bigger than one's self and achievement that is accomplished regardless of material rewards. Seligman has highlighted concepts of well-being that include wisdom, humanity, courage and temperance as alternatives to the deficits that are often used to assess people's problems. He is also very much associated with the empowerment perspective, which emphasises working with people's strengths, rather than focusing on pathologies (Seligman, 2002).

CASE STUDY 3.2

Simon (age 6) lives with his mother Liz (age 26) in rather chaotic circumstances. Liz is a lone parent; Simon's birth father's identity is unknown. They have slept rough on occasion, but for the past year, have drifted among various friends' and relations' homes, sleeping on sofas much of the time. In recent weeks, they have been housed by the council, but Liz is struggling to maintain positive relationships with her neighbours and her landlord. They may be required to relocate again soon, which would be the third major move during the past year for her and Simon.

Liz began exhibiting signs of schizophrenia at age 16. When she doesn't take the prescribed medicines, Liz tends to become quite paranoid. An example of this is her insistence that they must only eat certain foods, preferably those that are white. She has various beliefs about red meat and other colours of food giving her warnings about their being unsafe to eat. Along with her psychotic features, Liz typically has some very eccentric but strong religious ideas, including hearing arguments between angels and demons regarding everyday decisions. During psychotic episodes, these ideas tend to become more intense. Liz has recently become convinced that she should only call Simon by the name 'Peter'. She insists that everyone else, including his teachers and doctors, must also call him Peter. Simon expresses a real preference for being called Simon, but he is content to be called Peter if that makes Liz happy. In many ways, Simon functions as Liz's carer, sometimes missing school in order to keep an eye on her when she is particularly fragile.

Simon appears small for his age, and his GP has commented on his being thin. He pays very close attention to Liz. His attendance at primary school is irregular, about which his teacher has raised concerns. Simon's spoken vocabulary is advanced for his age; although clearly bright, Simon still struggles with reading on the level of most of his classmates. When asked, Simon states that he is 'useless' at school, and that the other children tease him for being small and shy.

During your interview, you notice that he sucks his thumb when his mother becomes agitated, or when he is uncertain of what he is expected to be doing. Liz complains that he has recently started wetting the bed during the night, and she is clearly impatient with him about this.

Questions

Using a cognitive framework, please consider the following:

1. What would your primary concerns for Simon be?
2. What cognitive development factors would you consider noteworthy for Simon?

3. What social learning factors would you consider noteworthy in relation to Simon's cognitive development? How would learned helplessness apply to your consideration of Simon?

Discussion

First of all, you are likely to be concerned for Simon's overall development and this being seemingly held back. He seems to be acting in ways that show his distress and his concern for his mother. You may also be thinking of possible safeguarding issues. However, you are likely also to have noted that he is very protective of his mother and has demonstrated a degree of learned helplessness in his self-deprecating comments to you about his school work and efficacy. This perhaps gives you an inroad into helping him find alternative interpretation of his current situation, especially given his intelligence.

Albert Ellis

Two of the names most commonly associated with the combined influence of cognitive-behavioural approaches to mental health difficulties, particularly depression, in the 20th century are Albert Ellis and Aaron Beck. Both are North American psychologists, and their work shares many common premises. It is important to note this background as it indicates certain beliefs and thoughts in itself, such as a focus on the individual and their responsibility for certain ways of being.

Albert Ellis (1913–2007) trained in psychology at Columbia University. Originally, he trained in the psychoanalytic tradition, but then Ellis departed from psychoanalytic practice during the 1950s and came to refer to himself as a 'rational psychologist'. This indicates a departure from his roots and suggests a more 'scientific' approach in the sense that it is more empirical. Ellis's development of rational-emotive therapy (RET) represents a crucial application of cognitive theory, with his emphasis on irrational thinking as the source of much unnecessary suffering. His rational-emotive therapy is based on the premise that negative emotions and problematic relationship patterns arise from inaccurate interpretations of experiences, rather than from the experiences per se (Passer et al, 2009). Ellis is particularly associated with the concepts of the 'A–B–C principle of problematic beliefs'. Ellis used this concept to explain how flawed interpretations of Antecedents (or Activating Events) influenced problematic Behaviours or Beliefs, thus leading to negative or distressing Consequences.

Aaron Beck

Regarded by some as the 'father of cognitive therapy', Aaron Beck (1921–present) trained as a psychiatrist and psychoanalyst. Similar to Ellis, he also became disenchanted with the psychoanalytic approach and began focusing more intently on people's conscious belief systems, rather than their unconscious conflicts – so again, he looked more to the Anglo-Saxon belief in empirical approaches, those that can be verified experimentally. From his work with cognitive behavioural processes, Beck came to consider that dysfunctional thinking resulted in problematic behaviours, and that underlying beliefs were the source of dysfunctional thinking. According to Beck, changes in symptoms result from changes in thinking (Fenichel, 2000). Beck is renowned for addressing the cognitive aspects and measurement of depression, an important aspect of cognitive theory.

Place within contemporary human service practice

Bandura's concept of self-efficacy is essential for working with people in ways that facilitate positive change. By applying concepts of existing strengths and self-efficacy, workers can enhance a person's self-efficacy through encouraging them to perceive themselves as being competent and capable of new, more effective behaviours. This has direct relevance to anti-oppressive practice, as does the concept of 'learned helplessness'. Social learning theory has been effectively applied in work with families experiencing difficulties across a variety of settings, particularly involving children with behavioural problems (Kilpatrick and Holland, 2009; Chavis, 2012).

High self-efficacy is typically linked with an expectation of competence, and the ability to envision succeeding at a given task (Vourlekis, 2009). It can also influence an individual's level of persistence or willingness to tolerate frustration in order to master unfamiliar or difficult tasks. Higher levels of self-efficacy are associated with greater willingness to take on challenges that others might avoid, because of a greater likelihood of seeing challenges as surmountable, rather than overwhelming. This can result in a positive self-fulfilling prophecy. An example could be a child who has experienced success in learning to ride a bicycle might feel more inclined to teach a younger sibling to ride a bicycle than one who lacked confidence in their own ability to succeed. Similarly, adolescents who perceive themselves as successful with academic tasks are potentially more likely to attempt additional academic challenges than their classmates who lack confidence in their own academic capacities.

Within Bandura's model, the role of mentoring is sometimes emphasised as a means of providing children and adolescents with pro-social examples of behaviour. On a positive level, mentoring can provide positive alternatives to difficult situations. Whereas a child may have come from a family background where problems were not discussed, but corporal punishment was delivered for any infringement of rules, regardless of circumstances, then a mentor could provide a means of learning more effective, verbal ways of solving problems without resorting to physical violence.

Seligman's theory of learned helplessness has important implications for working with people across the life cycle. For children who have come to perceive themselves as being incapable of succeeding at school, the expectation of failure, regardless of effort or practice, can prove a powerful disincentive, sometimes amounting to a self-fulfilling prophecy. Likewise, for children consistently compared critically to a sibling, the messages may become equated with self-perceptions of inadequacy or failure. For people in violent relationships, a childhood history of family violence and/or previous partnerships involving violence can also relate to the theory of learned helplessness. When people have come to perceive themselves as being effectively destined to be in punitive, unhealthy relationships, their expectations of partners may also amount to self-fulfilling prophecies – that is, they may see themselves as somehow deserving nothing better than an abusive relationship. Learned helplessness is a crucial concept linked with understanding ways in which people come to regard themselves as lacking the capacity to change or improve their circumstances.

Ellis's A-B-C principle is particularly applicable to working with people following trauma or struggling with difficulties linked with consequences of problematic behaviours (including, but not limited to, substance use). It provides a readily applicable, non-threatening way of challenging ways in which people interpret their circumstances and experiences, along with modes of reinterpreting material in ways that can lead to modifying behaviour – producing more positive outcomes. The primary objective of applying Ellis's A-B-C principle is to help people link their expectations, their behaviour and its consequences in ways that create different, more positive outcomes.

Helping people to understand the role of antecedents typically entails looking at those factors that trigger or exacerbate problematic behaviours. Those triggers may be expectations of positive or negative consequences. For example, a child may think that, because they have seen their parents engage in violent behaviour, hitting their siblings is acceptable behaviour. When the problematic *behaviour* (that is, hitting their siblings) occurs, and the consequences include the aggressive child being punished or excluded, then one of the possible outcomes could also include implementing an A-B-C approach to reconsidering the sequence of events. This would include helping the child to consider that the original antecedent of having observed parental violence was problematic. With that reinterpretation of events in place, then the child's behaviour of hitting the siblings is more likely to be understood as being problematic than if the sequence was not addressed. The negative consequences of hitting, along with the potentially positive consequences of more pro-social problem solving, are then more likely to be comprehensible for a child. Even in cases where a child perceives their problematic behaviour as having been triggered or provoked by others, Ellis's A-B-C model provides a means of reinterpreting the consequences of responding to that provocation.

Conclusion

Critical perspectives and thinking

While many working in the helping professions rely heavily on cognitive and behavioural approaches, this does not mean that those approaches are not subject to criticism. One of the main criticisms levelled at Piaget's work is its cultural and gender bias. Application of Piaget's work with children from different cultural backgrounds or languages can pose considerable challenges. More recent research has expanded upon his concepts in order to address more of the complexities and variations in children's learning styles.

While cognitive behavioural therapy (CBT) provides a very popular and well-supported approach to helping people with an array of problems, it also represents a more structured and complex approach than is often acknowledged. CBT is generally applicable as a relatively short-term intervention, and is often congruent with collaborative, person-centred approaches. It is, however, primarily focused on here-and-now concerns, rather than being focused on underlying problems that may be contributing to the person's difficulties. CBT is generally focused on individual work, rather than on social or environmental factors (elements such as oppression, racism, discrimination or poverty), which may play essential roles in people's difficulties.

Thus, while cognitive theories have certainly contributed to an important range of thoughts and approaches, the phrase 'necessary but not sufficient' may be relevant to their evaluation as an effective methodology. Professionals are encouraged to be careful and critical in their analysis of the application of cognitive theories, just as they would be with any other approach to the intricacies of working with people with complex needs.

Reflective questions

1 What are some ways in which Bandura's social learning theory, and concepts of self-efficacy, might be applied to children who experience bullying in the playground?

2 What are some ways in which concepts of learned helplessness could be applied to children who struggle with schoolwork (such as being scolded at school for not reading fluently)?

3 How would Ellis's A-B-C principle apply to a child who has witnessed family violence at home, and has behaved aggressively toward classmates at school?

Further reading

- Bandura, A. (1986) *Social Foundations of Thought and Action*. Englewood Cliffs, NJ: Prentice-Hall.
  In this book, Bandura sets out his theory of self-efficacy and the belief systems which underpin motivations for actions and behaviours. While this work relates to adults in the main, it is also useful for children and young people.

- Parrish, M. 2014. *Social Work Perspectives on Human Behaviour* (2nd edn). Maidenhead: McGraw-Hill.
  In this book, I cover many aspects of social and behavioural development in people. Cognitive learning theory forms a major plank within this work.

- Shute, R. and Slee, P. 2015. *Child Development: Theories and Critical Perspectives* (2nd edn). Hove: Routledge.
  This volume provides a general introduction to child development theories, of which cognitive theories are dealt with in clear terms.

References

Bandura, A. (1969) *Principles of Behaviour Modification*. New York, NY: Holt, Rinehart & Winston.

Bandura, A. (1977) Self-efficacy: Toward a unifying theory of behaviour change, *Psychological Review*, 84(2): 191–215.

Bandura, A. (1986) *Social Foundations of Thought and Action*. Englewood Cliffs, NJ: Prentice-Hall.

Bandura, A. and Walters, R.H. (1963) *Social Learning and Personality Development*. New York: Holt, Rinehart & Winston.

Chavis, A. (2012) Social learning theory and behavioural therapy: Considering human behaviors within the social and cultural context of individuals and families, *Journal of Human Behavior in the Social Environment*, 22(1): 54–64.

Ewen, R. (2010) *An Introduction to Theories of Personality* (7th edn). London: Psychology Press/Taylor & Francis.

Fenichel, M. (2000) New concepts in practice: on therapy – a dialogue with Aaron T. Beck and Albert Ellis. American Psychological Association 108th Convention. Current Topics in Psychology. Available from: http://www.fenichel.com/Beck-Ellis.shtml

Joravsky, D. (1979) Scientists as servants, *New York Review of Books*, 28 June, p 260.

Kelly, G. (1963) *A Theory of Personality: The Psychology of Personal Constructs*. New York, NY: Norton.

Kilpatrick, A. and Holland, T. (2009) *Working with Families: An Integrative Model by Level of Need* (5th edn). Boston, MA: Pearson.

Luria, A. (2004) Vygotsky, Lev. In R. Gregory (ed.), *The Oxford Companion to the Mind* (2nd edn). Oxford: Oxford University Press.

Passer, M., Smith, R., Holt, N., Brenner, A., Sutherland, K. and Vliek, M. (2009) *Psychology: The Science of Mind and Behaviour* (3rd edn). Boston, MA: McGraw-Hill.

Peterson, C. and Seligman, M.E.P. (2004) *Character Strengths and Virtues.* Oxford: Oxford University Press.

Piaget, J. (1970) *Science of Education and the Psychology of the Child,* New York: Viking.

Robinson, L. (2007) *Cross-Cultural Child Development for Social Workers: An Introduction.* Basingstoke: Palgrave.

Seligman, M.E.P. (1979) *Helplessness: On Depression, Development and Death.* San Francisco, CA: Freeman.

Seligman, M.E.P. (2002) *Authentic Happiness.* New York, NY: Free Press.

Shute, R. and Slee, P. (2015) *Child Development: Theories and Critical Perspectives* (2nd edn). Hove: Routledge.

Vourlekis, B. (2009) Cognitive theory for social work practice. In R. Greene (ed.), *Human Behavior Theory and Social Work Practice* (3rd edn). New York, NY: Aldine Transaction, pp 133–163.

4

Social construction and emotional development

Jo Finch

Introduction

This chapter begins with a brief discussion about the social construction of childhood itself – a useful starting point, as we will be exploring a wide range of ideas here. It explores children and young people's personality and emotional development and also considers the connecting issue of identity formation and development. It then takes a critical and psychosocial perspective to the exploration of these issues, going beyond narrow individualistic psychological theories to consider the impact of the environment on such development. The chapter also discusses the disconnect between social policy concerning children and young people and the realities of their emotional development. The example of a recent UK policy, Prevent, will be used to explore this further. Finally, the chapter considers the implications of such theories for professional practice in the human services.

Chapter objectives

- discuss how childhood is socially constructed and the implications of this for practitioners;

- examine personality and whether it is fixed;

- explore what is meant by emotional development and identity;

- discuss whether social policy reflects the realities of children's emotional development.

The social construction of childhood

The social construction of childhood is one that is not static. Ariès (1962), in his historical research into children's lives, claimed that the notion of childhood is socially constructed. Indeed, in medieval times, children were considered to be small adults and accordingly were not given any special status or privileges as a result of being young. Ariès (1962) contends further that notions of special status, or a need for protection, or any notions that children have distinct needs has slowly evolved over time. His (1962) work has been criticised on a number of grounds, but the important point he makes, and one that has significant implications for social workers, is that childhood is not a universal experience: it is more complex than just a linear and unproblematic biological phase that all children pass through in a similar ways.

James and James (2004) argue further that childhood is therefore very much shaped by cultural, historical and political contexts, as well as by the dynamic process between an individual child and how adults behave towards them. For instance, it is easily recognisable that children born into a brutal conflict situation, where child soldiers were the norm, would have a different world view from children brought up in loving, caring environments where they were protected from all forms of perceived harm. The importance of a psychosocial approach to the study of childhood is therefore raised, as such approaches recognise the interplay between the child's internal world and the external world.

The historical shift from the idea of children as small adults to children with distinct needs, including a need for protection, became firmly established, both legally and socially in the UK, in the Victorian times. During this period, the rapid growth of industrialisation, with the move from a rural to a more urban society and new forms of work, meant that poor children were more visible, and were used as cheap labour (Simpson and Connor, 2011). The idea that children needed special protection grew, initially in the workplace, together with the acceptance that government should more readily intervene to protect and safeguard the lives of the populace. Therefore, the Victorian era saw the introduction of what can be considered to be the first piece of child welfare legislation – the 1833 Factory Act – where it was recognised, for the first time, that a 'child', albeit it the context of an employee, had a distinct need for protection (Payne, 2005).

The 1833 Factory Act was followed by a range of other protective laws. Compulsory schooling was introduced in 1870; this further developed the idea of children having distinct needs – not simply being small adults (Spicker, 2014). This was followed two years later with the 1872 Infants Life Protection Act, which recognised children as being more than just the 'chattels' (property) of the father (Dickens, 2010): in other words, they had legal rights. It is important to recognise, however, that such shifts in how we view children, and the accompanying legislation that protects their distinct needs and, indeed, rights, has not been universal or global.

The point of highlighting the ever-shifting, changing, socially constructed notion of childhood is an important one for this chapter, as theories of child development are also to some extent constructions of a particular society. Indeed, early research on child development, and also early theorisation of children's emotional, social and developmental needs in the UK, developed rapidly in the post-First World War and pre-Second World War eras, often in response to concern about the adverse impact of loss and separation. Other external factors also played a part, including the growth of social sciences and the idea that children have distinct mental health needs (the work of Anna Freud and later psychotherapists and attachment theorists pushed this idea further). This is an important point to recognise, not least in our direct professional work with children and families with diverse origins. In other words, multiple factors contribute to notions of childhood, adulthood and the so-called 'norms' of children's development and connected issues around safeguarding. Case Study 4.1 provides a discussion point about so-called norms of child development.

CASE STUDY 4.1

A primary school has raised concerns with social services that one of their pupils, Adeola, an eight-year-old girl of African origin, is travelling to and from school on her own. It takes her about 20 minutes to walk to school and there are several busy roads to cross. However, one of these busy roads does have a pedestrian crossing. According to the school, the parents have commented to them that it is 'normal' for eight-year-olds to walk to school unaccompanied and they do not feel the child is at risk.

Questions

1. What are your views about the appropriate age a child can walk to school on their own?
2. What age did you walk to school on your own?
3. What is informing your thinking about whether this issue is a safeguarding concern or a matter of parental choice?

Discussion

This case study raises the point about how norms of what is considered safe (or not safe) activities for children to undertake at particular ages may change over time in a particular country.

Criticism aside, this is not to say that biophysical and determinist psychological child development theories have no place in professional practice: clearly, they are important to professionals who work or have contact with children and young people. As highlighted in Chapter 1, however, there is an obvious need for professionals to refrain from uncritical application of traditional theories – not least because they are theories that have developed in the West and can, too often, though not always, claim universality rather than recognise diversity. How we understand children and young people's personality and emotional development, therefore, is inevitably a construction of a particular culture and legal, economic and political system, and as James and James (2004) contest, this is subject to constant change (as Case Study 4.1 demonstrates).

This chapter will go on to argue that social policy often fails to take account of children's developmental and emotional needs, and much psychological theory fails to take into account important structural and sociological factors that may shape societies' responses to children. This perspective is of vital importance in today's globalised world. The discussion begins with a consideration of what is personality — a concept that is often used by a wide range of professionals without question. However, as a starting point, it is useful to review your understanding by reading Case Study 4.2.

CASE STUDY 4.2

Sajid was a 12-year-old British boy born to second-generation migrant parents who originally came from Pakistan. His family were Muslim by culture, but rarely attended the Mosque. At home, Sajid's family spoke English as a first language and appeared to non-Muslim friends to be 'quite Westernised'. Sajid's Muslim peers at school considered him with suspicion, while non-Muslim peers called him 'terrorist' and 'ISIS-lover'.

Questions

1. Why do you think these different perspectives of Sajid developed?
2. How does an understanding of the context/environment in which Sajid lives and the notion of social construction help social workers here?
3. How might you work alongside other professionals in working with Sajid?

Discussion

Sajid's 'Westernised' family life and perspective may have led his Muslim peers to consider him to be somewhat removed from and antithetical to his Muslim roots and they have therefore showed a lack of trust towards him. On the other hand, his non-Muslim peers may have been picking up popular stereotypes and applying them to him simply on the basis of his colour and ethnic and religious background. Understanding how people, including both Sajid and his peers at school, develop within a historical, social and political context and how interactions help to form our approach to the world around us can be helpful to social workers and other professionals working with people. This understanding offers a fluid and changeable approach that doesn't view the child or young person as fixed in belief and behaviour, but rather as open to further development and change. It is also important in illuminating the influence of the surrounding world in which children and young people live.

The concept of personality

The concept or notion of personality has received much attention from the psychology community. Indeed, the term 'personality' is one we may often take for granted, without thinking about what it might mean in practice. A helpful definition is 'the combination of characteristics or qualities that form an individual's distinctive character' (*English Oxford Living Dictionary*, no date). A further definition is offered by Weinberg and Gould, who argue that personality represents: 'The characteristics or blend of characteristics that make a person unique' (1999, p 46). Both of these definitions can be considered ideographic (subjective and individual), in that they assume that individual personality traits are inherently unique and cannot be shared by other people. This approach contrasts to nomothetic perspectives (generalisations or what is shared with others), which see a range of personality traits or behaviours as potentially comparable, or common, across human beings. For example, when we make statements such as 'all teenagers are moody and self-centred', this is a nomothetic perspective.

Debates about the development of personality often centre around whether personality in a human is fixed and is biological in origin – that is, an argument of nature over nurture, or whether certain events or experiences shape personality in a developing child. In other words, the argument is that personality is nurtured, rather than inherent or fixed, whatever the circumstances in which a child is brought up. Therefore, explanations for differences in personality, which may in fact relate to specific behaviours – or indeed what influences personality – can be psychological, biological or sociological. Freud, for example, argued that early childhood experiences shaped the eventual adult (2003). Personality in later adult life, therefore, was shaped by inherent psychological factors that he considered instinctual, and how these instincts were shaped, met and responded to (or not) by the caregivers.

This view contrasts with Eysenck, a prominent psychologist who proposed in 1967 that there were distinct, universally applicable 'personality types'. This, for Eysenck, was based on an individual's biology (nervous system). He claimed, therefore, that there are two dimensions to personality: introvert/extrovert and neuroticism/stability. For many, this view of fixed personality, universally applied, is difficult now to accept: surely, human beings are much more complicated and diverse? Yet, it is worth contemplating how prevalent and dominant psychology as a discipline has been in pursuing the idea of personality as biological in nature, which continues to this day.

Modern applications of such approaches can be seen, perhaps, by the growing appeal of neuroscience and epigenetics, and the often misused image of a brain of a child who has lived with trauma and neglect compared with the image of a 'normal' child's brain. In this image, the neglected child's brain is much smaller than that of the other child. The image has been heavily used within many professional training courses and, indeed, was significantly reported in the press (see, for example, Tanner, 2017; Downey, 2018). It was originally published in a paper by Perry and Pollard, which claimed that neglect by US parents had adversely impacted their children's 'physical growth and organisation of the brain' (1997, p 4). It was later revealed that the smaller brain was that of a young child who lived in a Romanian orphanage and had experienced severe sensory, physical and emotional deprivation. This is not to overestimate the point, but professionals must be cautious about the evidence base on which such strong assertions are made and accepted without question. Wastell and White (2017), therefore, argue strongly that all professionals should be attuned to the reductionist (and unproven) claims of neuroscience and epigenetics.

There is also significant research that proves that human brains have plasticity (known as neuroplasticity) – meaning the brain can modify its neural connections or rewire itself. This is essential for development from infancy through to adulthood and allows brains to recover from injury. Importantly, in terms of professions working with children, the impact of early childhood trauma on the brain (if this is proven) can therefore be overcome. Yet, like Eysenck, some theories, or images, persist over the years, with little in the way of critique. Again, in order for practitioners to remain impartial and limit the impact of their personal and professional beliefs, such universal and bold claims must be critically reflected upon.

Discussions about personality almost inevitably lead on to socially constructed notions of what are 'good' or 'bad' personality traits or behaviours. Of course, what are considered to be 'good' traits in adults may not be considered 'good' in children or young people. There are also differences in how certain personality traits or behaviours are viewed among women or men, or indeed girls or boys, within different social classes, as well as across diverse racial and ethnic groups. This raises the issue of discrimination, therefore, and the unconscious bias we all hold about what are 'good', 'bad', acceptable or unacceptable personality traits – all of which may show themselves through particular behaviours. A prominent example of this relates to the importance of adult-to-adult eye contact in Western culture, when, in other cultures, eye contact with an elder can be viewed as being rude and disrespectful. All professionals working with children and young people are therefore required to understand how prejudice, discrimination and oppression occur, who is at risk of discrimination and how to reflect on their own biases and values, which may serve to discriminate against at-risk and already structurally disadvantaged groups even further. For instance, if you come from a family in which values creating independence in children and young people you might find this acts as a lens through which families who are more protective and involved in looking after children are judged. This point is therefore worth considering as you work through the questions in Reflection Point 4.1.

REFLECTION POINT 4.1
- What personality traits are considered useful, or are valued, in your profession?
- What personality traits are valued more for girls than boys and vice versa?
- What personality traits are valued in your family and community?
- Do you believe that personality is fixed or that it can change and adapt?
- What do you think are the greatest influences on personality?

Keep your thoughts and refer back to them as you consider Case Study 4.3 later in the chapter.

Personality development

In terms of exploring personality development in children and young people, it is clear that, for many professionals, a holistic approach is required. This includes the extent to which children's personality development may be shaped by the environment they live in (the social context), which may include their immediate family, the local community and wider society. It also includes a biological approach which explores physiological maturation processes – for example, individual temperament, and children and young people's developing understanding of themselves as both individuals and as part of the social world (that is, their identity).

Personality development in children and young people, therefore, needs to be viewed not as nature versus nurture, but as the continuous, dynamic interactions among the social, biological and representational (that is, self-identity) aspects. As indicated by the questions in Reflection Point 4.1, certain behaviours, traits and personality types (if, indeed, there are such things) can be valued differently in different settings and when displayed by different people. In point of fact, we often ascribe personality traits to entire nations of people! (Many of us will recall jokes about people from different parts of the UK, such as 'an Englishman, an Irish man and a Scotsman walk into a bar ...'.) This is not to say, however, that personality is not important, but rather that we need to view it as part of a child or young person's continually developing identity, continued emotional development and maturation. In other words, personality in children should be viewed as not fixed, but fluid.

CASE STUDY 4.3

Hanna, a 16-year-old Romanian girl, lived with her parents and siblings in a large Scottish city. Her parents were Christian evangelicals and required Hanna and her younger brother and sister to attend church services every week and to pray together each night. Hanna considered herself a Christian, but had started having doubts about the way in which her parents conducted their religious lives and the insistence that the children follow. She began to refuse to attend church, Bible study and prayer evenings.

Questions

1. Think back to the questions contained in Reflection Point 4.1 and use them to explore your understanding of and approach to Hanna's situation.
2. How might your own beliefs (religious or not) influence your practice with Hanna and family?
3. Who else may be important to work with in helping in this situation?

> **Discussion**
>
> As a social worker or professional working with children and young people, you need to be aware of the influences on your thinking of your own understanding of who you are and how and why you think or act the way you do: this will have a great impact on those you work with. For instance, in Hanna's case, you may be influenced by your own experiences of or thoughts towards religion. You may think this is how things are or you may believe that situations change and can be adapted. These thoughts will influence you as a social worker and it is important to be aware of and reflect on them.
>
> Taking a social constructionist approach would see Hanna's actions and thoughts as a unique response to the social world she occupies – one that is shaped and influenced by her interactions with it and with the people close to her.
>
> Confidentiality is a central concern in social work and seeking the individual's permission to share anything with others is imperative. However, it may be that Hanna would like others to be involved in a problem-solving group (see Chapter 4 in the companion volume). This may include key figures from her church or school, for example.

Emotional development

Green (2017) argues that a major criticism of developmental psychology is how it has shaped popular beliefs about what is a good childhood without being questioned, for example, or, indeed, what can be considered normal or abnormal childhood behaviours. Traditional lifespan and developmental psychological theories propose that all humans will pass through distinct developmental stages (including emotional, social, cognitive and physical development) that are universally applied. Freud, for example, argued that children go through five distinct psycho-sexual stages of development at particular ages (oral, anal, phallic, latency and genital). Piaget, as we have seen in Chapter 3, argued that children go through distinct stages of emotional development and, most importantly, that their thinking differs from that of adults. Within such approaches, the social context is seen as less important than biology and genetics. For example, a child who won't sit still, finds it difficult to concentrate and takes a great deal of attention from their teachers may be considered to be hyperactive – to have a condition such as attention deficit hyperactivity disorder (ADHD). This may be the case, but alternative understandings are also possible. Without a comprehensive understanding of the child's social world, such approaches remain limited.

A sociological perspective, on the other hand, would argue that a child's social, emotional and cognitive development are not the result of biology, or indeed personality or genetics, but rather result from socialisation and the impact of other social structures (namely, families and other societal institutions). All of these theories, however, can be criticised for depicting a child as passive in these socialisation and developmental processes. Kitzinger (1997), for example, argues that there is a danger in depicting children as empty vessels who are moulded by external factors and bring nothing of themselves to their development. Perhaps, more importantly, the socially constructed notion in many Western contexts of childhood innocence, passivity and asexuality can also be unhelpful in some circumstances. These constructs suggest that children and young people should act in certain prescribed ways which immediately suggest that any deviance from these norms is seen in a negative light, dismissing cultural variants, experiential differences and so on.

Criticisms aside, it is important for social workers to have a broad idea of the twists and turns of children's emotional development, not least to avoid stereotyping or undertaking oppressive work (imposing one's professional beliefs without including individuals and their situation and needs) with children and young people, but also to identify where there may be concerns about a child's mental health, for example. Professionals will also be in a better position to support parents in helping them understand their children's emotional developmental norms in the ecological context in which they live. To that end, professionals do need to have an understanding of the ages at which infants, children and young people can express various emotions and begin to self-regulate according to the customs and values of the environment.

For lifespan psychologists, the focus on emotional development is likely to cut across several areas of development, namely: cognitive development (how we learn to think, our thought processes and how we deal with problems); personal development (how we develop our sense of self, our emotions and our feelings); and social development (such as relationships with others).

It is important to think about emotional development more broadly, not least to understand what is meant by this wide-ranging, rather catch-all, term. Emotional development can include:

- how a child exhibits their basic emotions, such as anger, fear, sadness;
- the development of what Berk refers to as 'self-conscious emotions' (2009, p 406) – second-order emotions like embarrassment, guilt and envy;
- emotional self-regulation – for example, the ability of a child to manage their internal emotional states and, linked to this, the development of emotional display rules.

Emotional display rules refer to how children learn to communicate their emotional states and we can see here where societal notions of what is or is not acceptable behaviour come strongly to the fore (for example, in Victorian times, children were very much expected to be seen, but not heard). Children also need to learn how to understand and respond to others (the development of sympathy and empathy). However, Berk (2009) also raises the issue of individual temperament within emotional development, which links back to the notion of personality. The concept of identity adds to our understanding here, and it is to this that we now turn.

Identity

'Identity' is another popular concept used without question by professionals. However, like many ideas, it is often contested within psychological and social work literature. A useful and helpful definition of identity can be found in the dictionary and includes:

- the distinguishing character or personality of an individual;
- the relation established by psychological identification;
- the condition of being the same with something described or asserted;
- sameness of essential or generic character in different instances;
- sameness in all that constitutes the objective reality of a thing.
  (Merriam–Webster, no date)

Children and young people are therefore engaged in a constant process of identity formation, which means constructing and developing a clear understanding of who they are (Trawick-Smith, 2010). It is important to question, however, in what ways identity is different from personality. Identity refers to someone's sense of self, who they are and which specific traditions or values they share. Identity, therefore, can be personal, social or cultural, as suggested by the previous definition. Thus, in a psychological sense, it refers to questions about who we are or what it means to be you. It can include our gender, class and ethnic identities, to name but a few. In a sociological sense, this might be rephrased as: who are we in the context of a particular community or environment? Of course, this takes us into philosophical territory – beliefs about what it means to be a person, a child or a young person – which is beyond the scope of this chapter. However, consider the continuation of Hanna's story (from Case Study 4.3) in Case Study 4.4.

CASE STUDY 4.4

As Hanna attended college, she developed close friendships with a number of people – some who shared her religious beliefs and some who did not. However, she also began questioning aspects of her developing sexuality – something that made her anxious and, at times, ashamed. She came to the conclusion that she was asexual and non-binary, changing her preferred pronoun to 'they'. Hanna's parents believed this was part of growing up and were not concerned by it. Hanna's friends thought they had 'discovered' their identity and who they were.

Questions
1. Do children and young people have an established sense of self and identity?
2. How does your profession conceptualise identity in children and young people?

3. How does an understanding of social and emotional development help you as a social worker to understand Hanna's situation?

Discussion

In Hanna's case, we can see that personality and identity are constantly changing and may change again in the future. As a social worker, you will need to balance respect for a young person's identity with an appreciation that this may develop, without being patronising. This is no mean feat, but understanding some of the theories and models developed to explain social, emotional and personality development can help.

It is important to note that identity is always evolving: it is not final and it continues to develop and change throughout the lifespan. However, identity is a difficult concept for professionals to grasp. It has many nuanced meanings which intersect with other concepts, such as personality. Identity as a concept, however, does take for granted the interaction of the social and the personal.

Let us now examine the aforementioned issues of personality and emotional development and identity formation and development from a critical and psychosocial perspective.

Assessing children and young people's needs

In the area of social work, many assessment processes can be said to be psychosocial in origin, and so take account of individuals within the context of their family and wider community. Some other professions may not take into consideration as fully the centrality of psychosocial work factors. The Framework for the Assessment of Children in Need and their Families (FACNF), for example, followed by social workers, and the Children's Assessment Framework (CAF), a shorter version of the FACNF which can be undertaken by other professionals, adopt an approach that requires an assessment of the individual (in this case, the child) very much in the context of their environment.

REFLECTION POINT 4.2

- To what extent are social work assessments psychosocial in origin?
- What are the underlying assumptions and theoretical perspectives that inform the assessment model/tool?

The FACNF was developed in 2000 and, as the guidance states, the approach is rooted in child development theory, ecological in approach and child centred (Department of Health, 2000). The assessment approach involves three areas of focus: dimensions of a child's developmental needs; dimensions of parenting capacity and family; and environmental factors. The following areas are included as part of the assessment of a child's developmental needs:

- health
- education
- emotional and behavioural development
- identity
- family and social relationships
- social presentation
- self-care

While undertaking an assessment of this type, the aim is to consider the extent to which a child may be in need or, indeed, at risk of suffering significant harm (see Chapter 12). We can still see the significance of emotional and behavioural development and the associated norms, as well as the importance of identity. The CAF, which can be completed by a range of professionals, not only social workers, has a similar focus on emotional and behavioural development and identity. However, the FACNF offers useful guidance about particular areas of emotional development – namely, the focus on the extent to which a child demonstrates appropriate feelings and actions to parents or caregivers and others beyond the family. The quality of a child's early attachments are also to be explored as part of the assessment: 'their characteristics or temperament, adaptation to change, response to stress and degree of appropriate self-control' (Department of Health, 2000, p 18).

In terms of identity, the guidance suggests social workers focus on assessing:

- the child's growing sense of self as a separate and valued person;
- the child's view of self and abilities, self-image and self-esteem;
- the child's sense of themselves in terms of age, religion, age, gender, sexuality and disability;
- feelings of belonging and acceptance by family, peer group and wider society, including other cultural groups. (Adapted from Department of Health, 2000, p 19)

Theories around early attachments and the importance of these in later life are not discussed in this chapter. For fuller accounts, see Chapter 7 in Part II of this volume and Chapter 6 in Part II of the companion volume.

Social policy and children's emotional development

As we have seen, a wide range of theories attempt to understand children's personalities and the interplay of emotional development and identify formation, the interconnections between the self and other, nature and nurture, and the impact of globalisation (see Chapter 16). There is also a recognition of the importance of being critical of Western theories that imply universality. Given this, it is not surprising that social policy, in its broadest sense, does not always take effective account of children's developmental needs. As stated at the outset of this chapter, if we accept that childhood is a socially constructed notion, then dominant notions about childhood will inevitably shape, and in turn be shaped by, legal and political systems. It is useful at this point to use an example from contemporary social policy in England and Wales to ground some of these theories and to show why they have relevance to our understanding as social workers.

An obvious example of shaping by legal and political systems concerns global differences regarding the age at which a child or young person is deemed to be criminally responsible (that is, the age at which a child can be arrested or charged with a crime). In England and Wales, for example, this age is ten years old, and if children are prosecuted they are dealt with by youth courts (Muncie, 2015). In Scotland, the age of criminal responsibility is eight years old, although a child must be 12 before they can be criminally prosecuted in a court (this would only be for very serious crimes) (McAra and McVie, 2010). In Sweden, however, the relevant age is 15 years old, in Germany, 14, and in Portugal, 16 (Papadodimitraki, 2016a, 2016b, 2016c). This variation demonstrates contrasting societal constructs of responsibility and how age is viewed, as well as differences in approaches to children's offending behaviour. Indeed, at what age we view children as 'adults' is also socially constructed. In the UK, 18 years of age is when one legally becomes an adult, but, of course, developmentally or socially, this may not actually be the case for some years. Mortimer and Moen (2016) argue that as economic conditions and differences in perspectives regarding post-age-16 education have both changed, for example, 'adulthood' may come later for the current generation than for previous ones. Indeed, until as recently as the early 1970s, leaving school at the age of 15 to enter the workplace would have been the norm in the UK.

We now turn to an example of the fluid socially constructed aspects of childhood using one contested aspect of current policy.

Prevent

The policy known as Prevent will be explored here to highlight how the ambiguities and socially constructed nature of childhood (and therefore the concepts of personality, emotional development and identity) may be at odds with government policy and practice. Prevent is one strand of the UK's overall counter-terrorism policy, known as CONTEST (Finch and McKendrick, 2019). Prevent aims to: identify those at risk of radicalisation and extremism; assess the nature and extent of that risk; and 'develop the most appropriate support plan for the individuals concerned, to "safeguard" children and adults being drawn into terrorism by intervening early before illegality occurs' (HM Government, 2014).

The Counter Terrorism and Security Act was passed in July 2015. This Act made it a requirement for a wide range of specified professions, including social workers, teachers, early years practitioners, librarians, nurses and prisons officers, to work within the Prevent agenda. Such professionals are required, therefore, to be alert to issues of radicalisation and extremism and to report (or manage) any concerns about these. In the Prevent policy pronouncements, it is clear that such professional activity in this realm should be regarded as safeguarding work (McKendrick and Finch, 2016).

Prevent has been subject to a wide range of criticism since its introduction in 2003 and full implementation some years later. These include, but are not limited to, concerns that the policy serves only to increase mistrust and suspicion on an already discriminated-against Muslim community (Awan, 2012) and that it legitimises surveillance on 'suspect' (Kundani, 2015) communities. Coppock and McGovern (2014) have argued that de-radicalisation programmes are based on individualistic psychological models that do not take adequate account of the wider economic and social contexts. Furthermore, McKendrick and Finch (2017) argue that Prevent does not take into account the realities of children and adolescent development. Indeed, the government's own policy documents about the possible signs of young people being radicalised, such as growing beards in adolescence or wearing more traditional forms of Islamic dress, does not allow for their growing need to develop their own sense of selfhood and identity – be it religious, cultural or, indeed, a rejection of familial values. Green's argument is relevant here in her concerns about developmental psychologists' view of children as 'mini adults under construction' (2017, p 39) who do not possess adequate decision-making skills and are simply moulded by biology or the environment – both of which perspectives are essentially paternalistic. The image of the vulnerable child being groomed by radicalisers is therefore a simplistic notion which ignores a young person's agency and, indeed, the turbulence of adolescence.

Let us now consider the implications of these theories for your social work practice.

Implications for professionals

It can be quite bewildering for many professionals to be faced with so many different competing theories about things we may initially take for granted – for example, personality, emotional development and identity.

For professionals who often work in environments which require evidenced, informed approaches and have to undertake a wide range of assessments of children and young people, how to utilise and balance both grand theories with post-modern constructs can be challenging. An atheoretical approach, however, runs the risk of relying on common-sense arguments – some of which, as we saw in the example of the brain-imaging scan picture, have little basis in evidence. It is therefore incumbent upon all professionals working with children and young people to understand the range of constructs and perspectives surrounding personality and emotional development, as well as the important issue of identity. Professionals need to be clear about the range of meanings ascribed to each term, and reflect on deeply held assumptions and beliefs they may unconsciously hold about these terms.

The case studies in this chapter have aimed to help you apply some of the competing theories. Knowledge of theories, however, is needed in a range of discrete tasks, as well as professional skills, including:

- assessment;
- promoting well-being;
- safeguarding;
- developing working relationships with children and young people;
- challenging stereotypical, so-called common-sense and oppressive practice or beliefs others may hold about children and young people.

Conclusion

As illustrated in this chapter, numerous theories claim universality in respect of children and young people's emotional development, many of which might be deemed 'grand narratives'. Other theories, however, stress the socially constructed nature of emotional development, and indeed the very notion of childhood. These perspectives may have more in common with post-modern constructs, and important, difficult and critically debated concepts, such as personality, resilience and identity, are further raised within such theories.

Returning to this chapter's overall objectives, it can be argued that personality or temperament is not fixed; rather, it is a product of an ever-changing interplay among the biological, the environment and the political. Emotional development in children and young people relates to the expression and understanding of first- and second-order emotional states, self-regulation and conforming (or not) to the norms of a particular community or society. Identity is much more than temperament or personality, but focuses on a broader understanding of selfhood, values and belonging. It is important for professionals to take a critical perspective with social policy directives, which will inevitably be based on particular constructions or notions of childhood and adolescence.

Reflective questions

1 How will the theories considered in this chapter exert an impact on your professional practice as a social worker?

2 How will this learning change your understanding of some of the children or young people you work with?

Further reading

- Dowling, M. (2014) *Young Children's Personal, Social and Emotional Development* (4th edn). London: Sage.

  As an early-years practitioner, Dowling's work is also relevant to developing your understanding of children's emotional development. Early-years workers and social workers share a great deal of knowledge. As a social worker, however, you may want to extend your thinking beyond this focus and widen it to adolescents and transitions too. Nonetheless, this book provides useful information.

- Green, L. (2017) *Understanding the Life Course: Sociological and Psychological Perspectives* (2nd edn). Cambridge: Polity Press.

  Green's book provides a wide-ranging introduction to life-course theories which form part of the many approaches to growth and development in children and young people.

- James, A. and James, A.L. (2004) *Constructing Childhood: Theory, Policy and Social Practice*. Basingstoke: Palgrave Macmillan.

  This book is a little old now, but it is unsurpassed as a rigorous theorisation of childhood using sociological and anthropological approaches. For students who want to engage in real depth with this subject, this is a good place to start.

References

Ariès, P. (1962) *Centuries of Childhood*. London: Jonathan Cape.

Awan, I. (2012) 'I'm a Muslim not an extremist': How the Prevent strategy has constructed a 'suspect' community, *Politics & Policy*, 40(6): 1158–1185.

Berk, L. (2009) *Child Development* (8th edn). Boston, MA: Pearson Education Inc.

Coppock, V. and McGovern, M. (2014) 'Dangerous Minds?' Deconstructing Counter-Terrorism Discourse, Radicalisation and the 'Psychological Vulnerability' of Muslim Children and Young People in Britain, *Children and Society*, 28(3): 242-256.

Department of Health (2000) *Framework for the Assessment of Children in Need and Their Families*. London: The Stationery Office.

Dickens, J. (2010) *Social Work and Social Policy: An Introduction*. London: Routledge.

Downey, A. (2018) SPOT THE DIFFERENCE: Scans reveal the shocking impact extreme neglect has on toddlers' brains. *The Sun*. Available from: https://www.thesun.co.uk/fabulous/4825334/brain-sizes-different-children-emotional-abuse-study/

English Oxford Living Dictionary (no date) Personality. Available from: https://en.oxforddictionaries.com/definition/personality

Eysenck, H.J. (1967) *The Biological Basis of Personality*. Springfield, IL: Thomas.

Finch, J. and McKendrick, D. (2019) Securitising social work: Counter terrorism, extremism and radicalisation. In S. Webb (ed.), *Routledge Handbook of Critical Social Work*. London: Routledge.

Freud, S. (2003) *Beyond the Pleasure Principle and Other Writings.* London: Penguin Modern Classics.

Green, L. (2017) *Understanding the Life Course: Sociological and Psychological Perspectives* (2nd edn). Cambridge: Polity Press.

HM Government (2014) *Prevent* duty guidance: a consultation. Available from: http://www.gov.uk/government/uploads/system/uploads/attachment_data/file/388934/45584_Prevent_duty_guidance-a_consultation_Web_Accessible.pdf

James, A. and James, A.L. (2004) *Constructing Childhood: Theory, Policy and Social Practice.* Basingstoke: Palgrave Macmillan.

Kitzinger, J. (1997) Who are you kidding? Children, power and the struggle against sexual abuse. In A. James and A. Proust (eds), *Constructing and Re-Constructing Children.* London: Routledge.

Kundani, A. (2015) *The Muslims are coming: Islamophobia, extremism and the domestic war on terror,* New York, NY: Verso.

McAra, L. and McVie, S. (2010) Youth crime and justice in Scotland. In H. Croall, G. Mooney and M. Munir (eds), *Criminal Justice in Scotland.* Abingdon: Willan Publishing.

McKendrick, D. and Finch, J. (2016) Under heavy manners: Social work, radicalisation, troubled families and non-linear war, *British Journal of Social Work,* 47(2): 308–324.

McKendrick, D. and Finch, J. (2017) Downpressor man: Securitsation, safeguarding and social work, *Critical and Radical Social Work,* 5(3): 287–300.

Merriam-Webster online Dictionary (no date) Meaning of Identity. Available from: https://www.merriam-webster.com/dictionary/identity

Mortimer, J.T. and Moen, P. (2016) The changing social construction of age and the life course: Precarious identity and enactment of 'early' and 'encore' stages of adulthood. In M.J. Shanahanm, J.T. Mortimer and M. Kirkpatrick Johnson (eds), *Handbook of the Life Course* (Vol. 2). Cham, Switzerland: Springer.

Muncie, J. (2015) *Youth and Crime* (4th edn). London: Sage.

Papadodimitraki, J. (2016a) Minimum age of criminal responsibility (MACR) – comparative analysis international profile – Germany, Centre for Youth and Criminal Justice. Available from: https://cycj.org.uk/wp-content/uploads/2016/03/MACR-International-Profile-Germany.pdf

Papadodimitraki, J. (2016b) Minimum age of criminal responsibility (MACR) – comparative analysis international profile – Portugal, Centre for Youth and Criminal Justice. Available from: https://cycj.org.uk/wp-content/uploads/2016/03/MACR-International-Profile-Portugal.pdf

Papadodimitraki, J. (2016c) Minimum age of criminal responsibility (MACR) – comparative analysis international profile – Sweden, Centre for Youth and Criminal Justice. Available from: https://cycj.org.uk/wp-content/uploads/2016/03/MACR-International-Profile-Sweden.pdf

Payne, M. (2005) *The Origins of Social Work: Continuity and Change.* Basingstoke: Palgrave.

Perry, B. and Pollard, R. (1997) Altered brain development following global neglect in early childhood. Society for Neuroscience: Proceedings from Annual Meeting, New Orleans. Available from: https://childtrauma.org/wp-content/uploads/2013/12/PerryPollard_SocNeuro.pdf

Simpson, G. and Connor, S. (2011) *Social Policy for Social Welfare Professionals*. Bristol: Policy Press.

Spicker, P. (2014) *Social Policy: Theory and Practice* (3rd edn). Bristol: Policy Press.

Tanner, C. (2017) A tale of two toddler brain scans: One shows the shocking impact caused by abuse and the other reveals the difference love can make – but can you tell which is which? *The Mail Online*. Available from: https://www.dailymail.co.uk/health/article-5043215/Brain-scans-toddlers-reveal-impact-childhood-neglect.html

Trawick-Smith, J. (2010) *Early Childhood Development: A Multicultural Perspective* (5th edn). Harlow: Pearson Education.

Wastell, D. and White, S. (2017) *Blinded by Science: The Social Implications of Epigenetics and Neuroscience*. Bristol: Policy Press.

Weinberg, R. S. and Gould, D. (1999) *Foundations of Sport and Exercise Psychology* (2nd edn). Champaign, IL: Human Kinetics.

5

Critical perspectives

Jonathan Parker

Introduction

Theoretical perspectives can often appear hermetically sealed off from the world of experience. The consequences can skew the value of theories and theorising for understanding the social world for the helping professions. This may lead us to accept, uncritically, the axioms set out in certain theories or, at the other end of the spectrum, to reject entirely the use of traditional development theories in social work. The previous chapters in Part I have outlined some of the traditional approaches to human growth and development in children and young people. In this chapter, we will take a critical approach, emphasising the centrality of observing and questioning at all times. This does not mean, necessarily, the dismissal or replacement of other ways of understanding these issues, but rather the addition of a transformatory perspective. In Chapter 5 in Part I of the companion volume, we explore some of the major changes in adulthood that affect growth and development. You may wish to read this chapter and reflect on how those adult changes may have an impact on the ways in which children and young people develop and how they might be affected by changes occurring in family members.

Chapter objectives

- critically review some of the accepted paradigms in human growth and development in children and young people;

- examine approaches that emphasise the social, structural and agentic as important in human growth and development;

- provide alternative perspectives to help social workers negotiate the thorny paths of theoretically informed practice.

Background and context

This chapter brings together the preceding introductory theoretical chapters specifically relating to children and young people. An ecological model of development will be introduced, which is then explored sociologically and critically. The ways in which the world is experienced by children and young people are multifarious. They include multiple perspectives and are dependent on a range of personal, social, cultural and structural positions. The influence of individuals and groups of social actors on the world around them and the corresponding influence of the world on their development creates a range of opportunities for developing understandings and growing as human beings in context. This is equally true for young people as for adults. These influences will be examined and questioned in this chapter.

The malleability and cultural specificity of models and theories of human growth and development will also be discussed. A critical perspective will be offered as a way of ensuring that models and theories are not applied in a prescriptive way, but are seen within a wider ecological context in which individual experiences and characteristics are part of the mix influencing individual growth and development. We will consider aspects of gender power relations, ethnicity, stereotyping and discrimination and the potential impact of intersecting social characteristics on the ways in which children and young people experience and grow in the world. This will set the scene for Part II of this book, in which the models, theories and understandings will be applied to the social world.

Before we consider the theories and models that add a critical edge to our understanding of human growth and development, we need to identify what we mean when talking about critical perspectives. In popular parlance, the term 'critical' is often used to convey a negative appreciation of something, as Shaw (2005) notes in respect of social work. For instance, one might be critical of the way a tennis player has performed during an important match, meaning that she or he has not played as well as they expected or wanted, or they have not demonstrated the specific process and expertise associated with the 'science' of tennis. However, we are using the term here in a more technical sense to refer to a sceptical, analytic or questioning approach taken to the theories and models, rather than simple acceptance. This is highly important in all professions working with people, and especially within social work, as it is the person-in-context who forms the focus of concern (Germain, 1981; Gitterman et al, 2013). Ferguson (2008) explores the importance of critical best practice as a means of questioning and reflecting within the specific organisational context in which social work is practised. This approach recognises that social work, along with other human service professions, is mandated and legitimated by the state and that regulation and control has increased. However, the critical practitioner's role is to negotiate a route through this that is creative and inspirational, rather than instrumental and bureaucratic.

Fook (2016) also suggests that social work, having come from a social and community-based background, does have a critical perspective and an important emphasis on social justice and identifying discourses of power at work throughout society. However, she integrates the structural and political element of social work with the need for a personalised individual approach to people in need. In seeing the interplay between these elements, Fook leads us to recognise the centrality of developing critical reflection and questioning what we do, why we do it and how we do it. This is crucial in developing an approach to our social work practice that takes nothing for granted. If we were simply to assume something, we would be likely to miss important aspects in the lives of those with whom we are working.

You will no doubt hear the term 'critical' or criticality' used also in respect of your studies, and while this relates to academic endeavour, it also has clear practice-related value (Rutter and Brown, 2015). It means, as previously noted, that what is said, seen, assumed or interpreted is subject to rigorous questioning and reflexivity to ensure that you are not missing something important to those people you are working with. As such, it is an integral part of working in an anti-oppressive manner – something that is central to good social work, health care and human service practice (Thompson, 2016).

REFLECTION POINT 5.1

Think for a moment of ways in which you are developing criticality. This might be in your academic work, where tutors encourage an analytic approach. It might also be in the ways in which you understand social work practice. This may involve political, organisational and personal aspects. Throughout this chapter, consider your own approach and understanding to being and becoming a critical practitioner and check this against the discussion while deliberating on your own development as a social worker and critiquing the discussion itself.

In this chapter, therefore, we are not using a critical position to distance ourselves from practices we do not like or approve of, but we are being mindful of the context in which we practice and questioning, challenging, reflecting and acting creatively to achieve the goals of our service-users. Social work and other cognate professions demand criticality – even more so in times of service reduction and austerity (Parker and Ashencaen Crabtree, 2018).

History and development of the theories and models

Models of human growth and development have focused on the traditional models developed in established settings and for recognised professions. These include, primarily, the bio-medical and genetic fields, psychology and evolutionary schools (for more information on these, see Chapters 1 and 2). We must also note that these have been developed and have gained acceptance within Western schools of thought and are therefore contextual and limited.

We have seen that biophysical approaches to human growth and development can tell us much about brain growth in children, how a child or young person grows in height and weight, and how they develop gross and fine motor movements. However, we need to include contextual and environmental factors to help explain this evolvement further. For instance, a child who lacks adequate food or emotional support is unlikely to progress through their expected milestones in the same ways as another child who is well-nourished and resides in a loving environment. Within these extremes, of course, there are many nuances, and historically accepted thoughts and ways of rearing children and young people have changed.

An example may help us here. We now accept that breastfeeding is positive for the growth, development and health of babies, while in the 1960s many mothers were encouraged to turn to formula milk (Henderson et al, 2000; Grummer-Strawn and Shealy, 2009). Some of these ideas stemmed from genuine, albeit erroneous, belief in technological, medical progress, but the role of business and global capital can also exert an influence. As beliefs shifted in favour of a return to breastfeeding in the Global North, there was still a push to encourage the use of formula milk in many low-income countries, despite knowing the benefits of the former and the problems associated with the latter (World Health Organization, 2002). So, while improvements in the health and development of children in some areas rose, the actions of large global corporate enterprises exacerbated problems in others, reflecting what we may see as evidence of coloniality – more powerful former colonising nations exploiting less powerful countries for their resources and for financial gain.

There were also class-based differences in children's growth and development in those high-income countries that promoted healthy lifestyles. The cost of adequate nutrition for both parents and children and young people has meant many low-income or unemployed families have been driven into buying cheaper alternatives, often including processed, high salt and high sugar foods. The benefit system penalises those on low or with no income and thereby increases the chances of ill-health and delayed growth and development. After the passing of the 2012 Welfare Reform Act in the UK, the Universal Credit benefits system has been introduced. This replaced many different and complex benefits with a single payment, but payments in arrears and paying housing benefit directly to families rather than landlords has increased the potential for debt, housing arrears and homelessness (see Centre for Social Justice, 2009; Alston, 2018).

Alongside biophysical models of development, there have been social learning theories which demonstrate the importance of our interactions with the environment and the expectations we create in order to negotiate daily life. If we know we can influence the environment around us and can gain from it some of the things we need to flourish, we are more likely to engage in the behaviours that are necessary to achieve those gains. If, on the other hand, we rarely see anything positive come from our actions, we may engage in behaviours that are not necessarily pro-social and may, in fact, be negative – we may act in a way consistent with 'learned helplessness' (described in Chapter 1). As we have seen in Chapters 1 and 3, in terms of child development, positive experiences may encourage learning and being prepared to stretch one's capacity for engaging with new opportunities as one's self-efficacy increases. The child who is praised, assisted and listened to will feel more confident and sure in their interactions with the wider world. The child who is constantly put down, who never sees a benefit from acting in a particular way, may give up engaging with the social world and may develop new behaviours that are counterproductive and dangerous to their development.

Psychoanalytic theories, as Briggs states in Chapter 2, consider the ways in which children and young people's unconscious motivations, thoughts and experiences influence behaviour and development. This demonstrates the importance of the context in which people live and the interpersonal relationships that have surrounded them. Again, not everything can be understood by reference to suppressed memories or unconscious motivations or drives, but these theories add to the panoply of understandings available.

These approaches to the growth and development of children and young people have jostled for position over time. Popularity of each has depended on what social and political discourses have been in vogue and the promotion of one or other approach often rests on the specific preferences of individuals – themselves influenced by their own upbringing, experiences and interpretations of the world. These theories are, necessarily, of their time. A critical approach challenges the idea of fixed models seeing the world not in terms of immutable, objective truths that simply exist, but acknowledges the, albeit limited, value of each model when understood in context. The context includes not just the individual's immediate social world or the nexus of people and organisations around them, but also the social and structural milieu (see Thompson, 2016). The micro, mezzo and macro environments interact and influence the different ways in which children and young people will grow and develop. So, returning to the questions we suggested earlier, it is imperative for a critical practitioner to unpick the varied and interacting reasons why a child or young person may be developing or acting in certain ways and never to accept unquestioningly what has been stated as the underlying cause or reason. Case Study 5.1 may help to make this clearer.

CASE STUDY 5.1

15-year-old Sammi had a child, a boy, of three months. Sammi's mother had demanded she leave the house when she announced her pregnancy, saying that such 'disgusting behaviour' would be a bad influence on Sammi's younger sister and that she was not surprised at her becoming pregnant given how badly she had behaved throughout her life. She said her grandmother would have been appalled if she had been alive and would have found it difficult to show her face in the synagogue. Her mother said she was pleased she no longer attend *schul*.

Sammi was pleased to leave her mother and happy to be accommodated by social workers, arguing that her mother had never loved her and always criticised her. The situation in many ways seemed somewhat chaotic and distressing. Social workers and teachers were concerned about Sammi's sexual activity, her mother's attitude to her and the well-being of Sammi's son. These were all important issues, but what had not been addressed was the physical poverty in which Sammi and her mother had lived, the stress that this engendered in everyone and the seeking to escape through unwise relationships and activities, drinking and smoking, for both Sammi and her mother.

Questions
1. What do you think might be some of the important environmental influences on Sammi?
2. How do you think these factors and understandings might affect the ways in which you work with Sammi and her family?

Discussion
You may have some immediate thoughts about the situation depending on your own perspectives, upbringing and views of the world. It is important to recognise this and to critique why you are seeing the situation in the ways you do. For instance, if you are shocked at Sammi's behaviour, is this because of your own experiences, your beliefs or your family? If, on the other hand, you see this in structural terms with external social and political forces acting on both Sammi and her family, you should critique this. There are multiple ways of seeing all situations and as a social worker you need to be aware of all of them.

You also need to closely question what is happening. Why might Sammi's behaviour be so sexualised? Why might she be smoking and drinking when she has a new baby? What possible influences are there at the personal, family, community and social levels? The following section introduces some theories and models that may be helpful in developing your understanding.

Central theories important to a critical approach

Social theory and sociological thinking provide a range of tools for critically evaluating accepted approaches to human growth and development and offering alternative and often creative ways of seeing society and the individuals who are part of it. The relevant social theories include systems thinking, labelling, symbolic interactionism, social constructionism (see Chapter 4) and postmodern thought. While there is not sufficient space in this chapter to cover these theories in depth and they are covered elsewhere (see Teater, 2020; Dunk-West and Verity, 2014; Parker and Ashencaen Crabtree, 2018), these models help us to question what we see and experience and to form alternative ways of understanding the world and its developmental shibboleths. They offer ways of beginning to question and reflect, and to attune our understandings of children and young people rather than to see them through the lens of traditional models and approaches.

Systems thinking

Systems thinking developed from von Bertanlanffy's studies of biological systems in the 1920s (Drack et al, 2007; Parker, 2017). In essence, it suggested that we, as social beings, live in interacting systems that influence how we respond, what we think and how we behave. For instance, a family may include parents, children, pets and wider relatives. The ways in which families are constructed may influence what a child in a family believes about families and human relationships. The personality and characteristics of the child are also likely to have an influence on other members of the family and so the continual development of behaviours, beliefs and daily practice goes on. The model helps us to understand how each person may influence each other, but it has been accused of blaming victims of violence or abuse if it is thought that interpersonal interactions within the living system or family led to the violence or abuse. This is compounded further if structural pressures on people are ignored and the influences on behaviour are localised. So, we need to be cautious and critical of the use of systems thinking, but, of course, this is part of critical practice.

Labelling

Labels are important to who we are. By applying a label or name to something, we extend our control over the world around us. By 'labelling' something a chair, we know that we can sit on it. However, there is a more insidious form of labelling that imposes a value onto a person because of a characteristic or behaviour. At times, that person may assume the label and act accordingly (Parker and Ashencaen Crabtree, 2018). Case Study 5.2 explores this idea further.

CASE STUDY 5.2

Jane is 13 and lives with her mother and younger brother, Harry, in a disadvantaged area of Newtown. They are a white British family. Her mother is unemployed and the family have struggled financially since being moved on to Universal Credit. At school, Jane has been an average pupil academically and well behaved, but after failing a maths test some of her peers have begun calling her 'stupid' and 'thick, like all the others from your flats'. Her confidence has taken a knock and she has begun to believe that she is not good at schoolwork. She has decided not to bother trying at school or doing her homework because she is 'stupid' and it does not matter.

Questions
1. Why do you think Jane has stopped trying with her schoolwork?
2. How do you react to labels when they are applied to you?
3. Might there be times when labels are helpful?

Discussion
Jane was not only diminished by the label given by others, but she internalised and believed the label that was given to her. It created a meaning that she adopted and she altered her behaviour to fit (Lemert, 1967).

Symbolic interactionism

Symbolic interactionism stems from the 20th-century Chicago School, which produced some of the antecedents of radical approaches to social work. It is a complicated-sounding term that is simpler to understand. It focuses on the meanings of human-to-human communication. In this way, it shares similarities with systems thinking and to an extent labelling, but it allows for both the personalities of people communicating and the contexts in which they communicate, as this will influence meaning. Therefore, it can avoid ignoring structural influences: agency (the person) and structure (the macro environment) interact together to produce meaning. When we bring social constructionism into this mix of theories – the way in which we see the world is contingent on our continuing experiences of it – then we can see how different meanings and constructions of the social world become possible (Berger and Luckmann, 1966).

Postmodern thought

Postmodern theories, developed more recently, are contested. Taken to an extreme, they would seem to be permissive of anything and equalising the value of everything. However, they too have an importance in critical thinking because they allow us to focus on difference and to understand that values, behaviours and expectations may all be seen and evaluated in different ways. We do, of course, as social work professionals, need an anchor, and in social work we have the International Federation of Social Workers' (IFSW, 2014) definition of 'social work' which helps, alongside the legislation and policy in the country in which we practice.

These theoretical perspectives offer us different lenses to understand the experiences of children and young people. They assist the critical process because they help us to ask questions and not simply to accept traditional approaches – often construed as social diagnoses in a quasi-medical sense. They force us to seek alternatives and, crucially, to ask the children and young people we are working with, and their carers, how they understand the situation or experiences that have brought them to us.

We will now turn to three key domains of sociological thinking that can help us in expanding our comprehension of a young person's development. A class-based discourse would be appropriate in this section because the impacts of structural pressure and class have a great bearing on the ways in which children and young people develop (Parker, 2018). However, this is excellently covered elsewhere, so we will focus in this chapter on feminism, racism and disablism (Ioakimidis, 2013; Ferguson et al, 2018).

Feminism

Social movements are always multifaceted and we should really be talking about 'feminisms' as a plural noun so that it reflects the many different approaches that are taken. However, feminism, as an overarching concept, is important when we are considering growth and development in children and young people. This is because of the illumination of relations between the sexes (males and females) and the construction of gendered roles within society which starts before infancy, with expectations and plans for the, as yet, unborn child.

Assumptions that are made about what male children and female children and young people may like to do, play with or become when they grow up are predicated by a range of underlying assumptions. These assumptions may be internalised by the particular child or young person and accepted as reflecting what 'ought' to be in the world, and judging themselves against this standard. This underpins patriarchy, which refers to the continuing dominance of male privilege at overt and hidden levels in society. This in itself highlights some of the normative understandings that affect us all – whether hetero-normative understandings of developing sexuality, gender-normative occupations and toys, games or clothing. Consider the youngster who is increasingly unsure of their sexuality. While most young people go through a process of understanding who and what they are in terms of sexuality, being given a constant message that heterosexuality is the only legitimate way of growing up is likely to generate significant anxiety in someone who is unsure or realises more clearly they are gay or lesbian.

Sometimes the effects of normative thinking are more subtle. Think for a moment of the kinds of toys you were given or, indeed, wanted when you were younger. If you had been a different sex, would those toys have been considered appropriate for your gender? What we are seeing here is the pervasion of stereotypes that assume all boys like, want or should have toy A and all girls toy B – the 'pinkification' of boys and girls (Janes, 2014).

So, feminism illuminates the impacts of these stereotypes and challenges the notion that they are based on objective 'truths' rather than being promoted because of unspoken and uncritically accepted positions that are gendered and reinforce inequality between sexes. This is reinforced by patriarchy and can be used in misogynistic ways by those wishing to reinforce their privilege and dismissing gender equality in patronising and derogatory ways. These assumptions are often employed actively in more sinister ways to preserve the power imbalances and to maintain the ascendancy of boys.

Consider the recognition of 'crisis' in boys' education as achievements have plummeted compared to those of girls (Abraham, 2013; van Hek et al, 2016; Jakiela and Hares, 2019). This has resulted in a flurry of activity and the assessment systems of GCSE and A-level qualifications in the UK moving away from more coursework-based approaches to more formal examinations. Educational theorists recognise that boys are less likely to do well at coursework, but can 'cram' for examinations, whereas girls tend to do better in coursework-assessed work. If there had been a noticeable downturn in girls' achievements, we must ask whether this would have resulted in the same identification of a 'crisis' and a need to change the system. Education exerts an ongoing influence throughout life, as can be seen in Chapter 8 in Part II of the companion volume. For a critical approach to children and young people's development, feminism offers unique ways of asking questions and showing inequalities. We can also see this in terms of ethnicity.

Racism

Racism rests on the assumption of biological or cultural superiority of one group over another. This is based on a person's colour, or ethnic or national background, and can have a profound impact on the child or young person experiencing it. Thompson's (2016) critique of racism, using his PCS analysis, is illustrative. PCS stands for the ways in which personal discrimination, cultural and organisational discrimination and structural or societal discrimination all work together, as well as independently, to stigmatise and disadvantage people on the basis of their perceived inferiority (see also Ahmed et al, 2017).

Thompson's analysis also portrays the differences in which racism is expressed, which, again, can exert significant pressure on individuals to behave and develop in certain ways. An overt instance of racism may be seen in verbal taunts and abuse about a child or young person's characteristics. These may hurt and damage the confidence of the person on the receiving end or may provoke a defensive reaction that, because of subtler assumptions, is interpreted as characteristic of that person's group or culture. This reflects a more insidious form of racism in which assumptions about a person's characteristics remain unquestioned and guide other people's responses. They are part of the structural aspects of racism that are difficult to change because they lie below the surface.

A child who lives each day with a mindset that they are inferior, not tolerated or included because of their ethnicity and likely to engage in anti-social behaviours is likely to be affected by these experiences and their development to be affected as a result. So, it is important to ensure that children and young people's ethnic and cultural backgrounds are seen as of central importance and that questions about their development and growth should be considered with this in mind.

Of course, this does not mean that culture and ethnicity can be used as a convenient way for practitioners to avoid confronting issues of growth, development and behaviour. There have been instances when social workers have been accused of failing to question potentially and/or actually abusive behaviour by considering it to represent a cultural variant. Lord Laming brought this out during the inquiry into the death of Victoria Climbié in 2003. Victoria Climbié was an eight-year-old girl from the Ivory Coast who was being looked after by her great aunt and her boyfriend in London. After being convinced by the pastor of her church that Victoria had been possessed by the devil, the great aunt and boyfriend inflicted terrible and cruel acts on her, resulting in her death. Social workers, police and health services had been involved, but mistakes were made, sometimes because of a misplaced 'respect' for different cultures, and this resulted in no protective action being taken (Laming, 2003; Parker, 2017).

Abuse, stigmatisation and denying the rights of another can never be acceptable. Equally so, this must not be approached simply from a normative-cultural perspective, that is, one which assumes the prevailing culture and ethnicity is the norm and everything else is somewhat deviant to it. This is another insidious and embedded form of racism of which we need to be aware and to question critically at all times. Ashencaen Crabtree et al (2016) bring this out clearly in their analysis of reactions to the cases of Asian men grooming young women and girls.

Yip (2004) provides a helpful approach to guide social workers through this complex area, identifying some of the tensions between Eurocentric and traditional Asian perspectives and different approaches to the problems of living. He used an East–West binary to demonstrate these:

- responsibility versus rights;
- social norms versus equality;
- family versus individual;
- stability versus change;
- relation versus empowerment.

For Yip, the focus was more on a 'good outcome' for the person in their context, something that reflects Gitterman et al's (2013) ecological approach, rather than the application of an abstract concept of human rights. He gives the example of domestic violence and leaving a relationship for reasons of responsibility to one's children and to protect their development rather than as a means of individual empowerment and self-determination, which may be reflected in Western social work approaches (see also Hutchings and Taylor, 2007). This echoes Nussbaum's (2000) emphasis on capabilities, which must be context-specific and local, but can work with wider value positions.

Disablism

Disablism represents another form of discrimination and marginalisation of a group on the basis of the perceived worth of certain characteristics – in this case, ability or disability, whether that is physical and/or intellectual. As with racism and sexism, it is a form of discrimination that exists in a taken-for-granted way that there is a homogeneous majority group of non-disabled people who form the norm, and that anyone deviating from that position is prone to different and negative treatment on that basis alone.

The disability movement has been vocal in challenging this state of affairs and has shown that many of the 'impairments' faced by children and young people with disabilities are the result of our social, and built, environment rather than simply owing to a specific medical condition. This turns the tables on those who are 'non-disabled' to make changes and to ensure that children and young people with disabilities are not denied access to those aspects of social life that others enjoy. If this is not attended to, it is those considered able who are directly discriminating against those who are 'differently abled' by disabling them.

The social model of disability adds a corrective to the assumed and often unquestioned primacy of the medical model, just as psychosocial approaches, learning theories and a critical, questioning perspective do to biophysical models of development (Evans and Lee, 2020). However, children and young people with disabilities may have their growth and opportunities for development restricted and impaired because of the ways in which others treat them. We can, perhaps, ask the question about what we can do differently in order to highlight these concerns and to discover alternative approaches that do not unfairly discriminate against children and young people with disabilities. This might include looking at the physical environment in which activities take place, the pace at which they are run, sound, lighting and expectations that are set. Indeed, the key is to ask what can be changed, but also to be honest when it cannot be changed; critically challenging what is taken for granted does not mean replacing it with the notion that everyone is or wants to be the same.

REFLECTION POINT 5.2

Think of other social domains, areas and understandings (other than feminism, racism and disablism) that may be considered within a critical framework when acting as a social worker practising with children and young people. What do you need to bear in mind?

There are many aspects of contemporary life that could be identified, such as the rights and voices of children and young people, health status and conditions and, of course, class, poverty and employment opportunities. We can also see that there are many interconnections between these social conditions and also across the life course. For instance, a child or young person is materially and may also be psychologically affected by their parents' unemployment. So, a critical approach must question contexts in a wide manner.

Criticality, cultural relativism and the precarity of theories of development

Our critical approach to human growth and development concerns questioning and upturning traditional understandings, and seeking alternative ways of approaching the child and young person's world. This does not suggest that traditional approaches are wrong in principle and need to be replaced, but that they are partial and perhaps precarious, insecure platforms on which to base judgements about young people's lives. Theories and models are developed in a context and are more likely to address that context best. Contexts, however, change and develop over time and so must models and theories. Critical practitioners need to be aware of a range models and theories, including traditional ones, to be able to question and challenge when they do not fit or suggest a course of action that might be to a young person's detriment.

Critical approaches to development lend support to ecological models by recognising and giving place to the importance of context: to the family and friendship systems, the cultures and communities and wider social structures in which children and young people live. While its beginnings with the work of Germain (1973, 1981) focused more on immediate contexts and environments, this approach has allowed the structural to be acknowledged (Pardeck, 1988; Teater, 2014). Ahmed et al (2017) also see its use in enhancing culturally competent practice negotiating the spaces between different living systems and helping social workers to see people in these contexts and the difficulties they might have in moving across systems.

The concept of the person–in–environment, or the contexts in which young people live, is central to growth and development. We need to challenge preconceptions and what we have been told or read about a child, young person and/or their family and to see them in the multiple contexts in which they live, considering the impact of structure, interaction, and nurture at social, community, family and individual levels if we are to move towards critical best practice (Ferguson, 2008).

Negotiating the structural alongside the personal represents a tightrope act performed by social workers and other cognate professionals every day. It is easy to understand how practice has sometimes focused on individuals and their need to change, as this may be easier to influence and does allow an offloading of responsibility onto those individuals if positive outcomes are not achieved. So, a youngster who is struggling with school attendance and displaying behavioural difficulties may become the sole focus of attention, rather than also recognising the impoverishment of their neighbourhood, families and emotional lives or them being ignored by generations of politicians. The critical practitioner will recognise and take into account the intersectional aspects of the lives of children and young people, seeing that the young person's class, gender, ethnicity, sexuality, family background, neighbourhood and so on will exert strong influences on their development and growth (Hill Collins and Bilge, 2016; Parker and Ashencaen Crabtree, 2018).

Human rights and social justice are contested terms, but are central aspects of many helping professions, including social work (Fook, 2016; Parker and Ashencaen Crabtree, 2018). The protection of human rights and a focus on structural change and social justice are considered important to social well-being and represent foundational values in social work. Again, other professions include such values, but, according to Hugman (2010), it is the interpretation of them and enactment in social work that make them special (Hugman and Bowles, 2012). Banks (2006) compared 31 codes of ethics from different countries' national social work associations. While values and codes of ethics are not accepted without critique, she found three common elements running through them:

- The codes were represented by statements of values.
- They provided a framework for the application of 'good' practice in that country.
- Only South Africa included an oath to be taken by social workers; the other 30 countries simply expressed the moral qualities expected of social workers in their practice.

The IFSW 2014 statement and definition of social work provided a structure for individual countries to begin to develop their own codes as a 'variation on a theme' (see Parker, 2017; Parker and Ashencaen Crabtree, 2018). Four broad ethical principles, the first three drawing on traditional Western thought, with a wider focus on relational perspectives underpinning the fourth, underlay this statement:

- duty – to respect each person in themselves (a perspective drawn from the philosophy of Immanuel Kant);
- consequences – weighing up which acts promote the best outcomes (a Utilitarian approach adapted from Jeremy Bentham's thought);
- virtue – important moral qualities and characteristics (Aristotle);
- relationship – the worth of persons shown through social work relationships (a syncretic amalgamation of religious and philosophical thinking).

The definition and statement was criticised as reflecting the dominance of the Global North and being inherently 'Eurocentric'. For Hugman (2010), this represented a debate between universalism and cultural relativism. Interpretations of human worth, dignity, rights and social justice differ widely. Also, in so far as international social work values and ethics are constructed in a universalist way, they remain a form of professional imperialism. However, while some values might have universal acceptance if they can be interpreted in context and setting, we can avoid imperial imposition and floating relativism. The IFSW 2014 definition attempted to make this shift. The international statement was revised with a greater emphasis on authenticity and relativism within a context. It has reached greater agreement.

> Social work is a practice-based profession and an academic discipline that promotes social change and development, social cohesion, and the empowerment and liberation of people. Principles of social justice, human rights, collective responsibility and respect for diversities are central to social work. Underpinned by theories of social work, social sciences, humanities and indigenous knowledge, social work engages people and structures to address life challenges and enhance wellbeing.
>
> The above definition may be amplified at national and/or regional levels. (IFSW, 2014)

Critical perspectives within contemporary social work practice

Being a critical practitioner requires us to question and not accept traditional assessments of why children and young people may be developing in a certain way without questioning, challenging and seeking confirmatory or disconfirmatory evidence. In this, social workers, nurses, teachers and others working in the human services are faced with a dilemma. Social work professionals are generally employed and paid by an organisation, often a statutory or quasi-statutory one, to undertake a specific job. Sometimes the demands of that job, role or task are in conflict with the personal and professional perspectives and values of the individual worker. The question then arises: what should that individual do? It is easy to be idealistic when observing from a distance (or, indeed, writing in a volume such as this one), not so when faced with an immediate situation and many competing demands. However, if we very briefly consider the professional codes of ethics and international standards that underline social work and other helping professions, we must note that it is respect for the dignity and worth of the people with whom we are working that takes precedence. This means we must sometimes expect to be in conflict with those who employ us. It also means, however, that we must be prepared to challenge the theories and accepted knowledge base of our professions and seek localised, authentic approaches to our work.

In our work with children and young people, the decisions we make, based on our assessments, do not just affect us and our professional life – they will also have a profound and sometimes life-changing impact on these youngsters. We carry a heavy responsibility for the lives of people, but the decisions and actions we take may impact the rest of their lives. Therefore, it is a moral imperative that we question how decisions are made and assessments are completed, and critique the possible impact they may have on people's lives. If we do not, we may well fail them.

Conclusion

At the outset of this chapter, we suggested that some of the potential consequences of current theories of human growth and development can skew the value of theories and theorising for understanding the social world for social workers. We have critically examined some of the core theories related in this volume and the implications of these for practice. We have stressed the importance of wide-ranging understandings that do not exclude the influence of structural, environmental and contextual factors, as well as the importance of the individual in determining growth and development in children and young people.

Reflective questions

1 How can traditional theories of human growth and development be used when taking a critical approach?

2 Can contemporary professionals truly take a critical stance in their practice?

3 Can an ecological model of practice be used to develop critical social work?

Further reading

- Fook, J. (2016) *Social Work: A Critical Approach to Practice* (3rd edn). London: Sage.
  Jan Fook's approach is grounded in reflective practice that is so important to developing yourself as a professional – learning to question everything. She also discusses how the personally and critically reflective social worker also works in wider structures, and how social workers must negotiate the political and structural as well as the personal and interpersonal domains of life.

- Thompson, N. (2017) *Promoting Equality: Working with Difference and Diversity* (4th edn). Basingstoke: Palgrave.
  Neil Thompson provides a comprehensive approach to working with difference and diversity and the complexities and difficulties that abound in social work and elsewhere in seeking equality. The book deals with practice rather than focusing on children and young people, but it offers important insights.

- Ferguson, I., Ioakimidis, V. and Lavalette, M. (2018) *Global Social Work in a Political Context: Radical Perspectives*. Bristol: Policy Press.
  This book brings together a fundamental critique of how and under what conditions social work is practised. It provides a radical element to social work that some professionals shy away from because it creates tensions with employing bodies. However, this work illustrates how political structures exert such an influence on people's development that it is essential to develop your understanding and knowledge. It adds a wider context to the current chapter.

References

Abraham, J. (2013) *Divide and School: Gender and Class Dynamics in Comprehensive Education*. London: Routledge.

Ahmed, S.R., Amer, M.M. and Killawi, A. (2017) The ecosystems perspective in social work: Implications for culturally competent practice with American Muslims. *Journal of Religion and Spirituality in Social Work: Social Thought*, 36(1/2): 48–72.

Alston, P. (2018) Statement on visit to the United Kingdom, by Professor Philip Alston, United Nations Special Rapporteur on extreme poverty and human rights London, 16 November 2018. Available from: https://www.ohchr.org/Documents/Issues/Poverty/EOM_GB_16Nov2018.pdf

Ashencaen Crabtree, S., Hussein, F. and Spalek, B. (2016) *Islam and Social Work: Culturally Sensitive Practice in a Diverse World*. Bristol: Policy Press.

Banks, S. (2006) *Ethics and Values in Social Work* (3rd edn). Basingstoke: Macmillan.

Berger, P.L. and Luckmann, T. (1966) *The Social Construction of Reality: A Treatise in the Sociology of Knowledge*. London: Penguin.

Centre for Social Justice (2009) *Dynamic Benefits: Towards Welfare that Works*. London: Centre for Social Justice.

Drack, M., Apfalter, W. and Pouvreau, D. (2007) On the making of a system theory of life: Paul A Weiss and Ludwig von Bertanlanffy's conceptual connection, *Quarterly Review of Biology*, 82(4): 349–373.

Dunk-West, P. and Verity, F. (2014) *Sociological Social Work*. Aldershot: Ashgate.

Evans, E. and Lee, S. (2020) Social work and learning disability/difficulties (children, young people and adults). In J. Parker (ed.), *Introducing Social Work*. London: Sage.

Ferguson, H. (2008) The theory and practice of critical best practice in social work. In K. Jones, B. Cooper and H. Ferguson (eds), *Best Practice in Social Work: Critical Perspectives*. Basingstoke: Palgrave.

Ferguson, I., Ioakimidis, V. and Lavalette, M. (2018) *Global Social Work in a Political Context: Radical Perspectives*. Bristol. Policy Press.

Fook, J. (2016) *Social Work: A Critical Approach to Practice* (3rd edn). London: Sage.

Germain, C. (1973) An ecological perspective in casework, *Social Casework*, 54: 323–330.

Germain, C.B. (1981) The ecological approach to people-environment transactions, *Social Casework*, 62(6): 323–331.

Gitterman, A., Germain, C.B. and Knight, C. (2013) Ecological framework. *Encyclopaedia of Social Work*. National Association of Social Workers Press/Oxford University Press. Available from: https://oxfordre.com/socialwork/view/10.1093/acrefore/9780199975839.001.0001/acrefore-9780199975839-e-118

Grummer-Strawn, L.M. and Shealy, K.R. (2009) Progress in protecting, promoting, and supporting breastfeeding: 1984–2009, *Breastfeeding Medicine* 4(Suppl. 1): S31–S39.

Henderson, L., Kitzinger, J. and Green, J. (2000) Representing infant feeding: Content analysis of British media portrayals of bottle feeding and breast feeding, *British Medical Journal*, 321: 1196–1198.

Hill Collins, P. and Bilge, S. (2016) *Intersectionality*. Cambridge: Polity Press.

Hugman, R. (2010) *Understanding International Social Work: A Critical Analysis*. Basingstoke: Palgrave Macmillan.

Hugman, R. and Bowles, W. (2012) Social work values, ethics and professional regulation. In K. Lyons, T. Hokenstad, M. Pawar, N. Huegler and N. Hall (eds), *The Sage Handbook of International Social Work*. London: Sage.

Hutchings, A. and Taylor, I. (2007) Defining the profession? Exploring an international definition of social work in the China context, *International Journal of Social Welfare*, 16(4): 382–390.

IFSW (2014) Global definition of social work. Available from: http://ifsw.org/get-involved/global-definition-of-social-work/

Ioakimidis, V. (2013) Beyond the dichotomies of cultural and political relativism: Arguing the case for a social justice based 'global social work' definition, *Critical and Radical Social Work*, 1(2): 183–199.

Jakiela, P. and Hares, S. (2019) Mind the gap: 5 facts about the gender gap in education, Center for Global Development. Available from: https://www.cgdev.org/blog/mind-gap-5-facts-about-gender-gap-education

Janes, C. (2014) Sexism, pinkification and our daughters, *Huffington Post*. Available from: https://www.huffingtonpost.co.uk/2014/08/14/sexism-pinkification-and-our-daughters_n_7362792.html?guccounter=1&guce_referrer=aHR0cHM6Ly93d3cuZ29vZ2xlLmNvLnVrLw&guce_referrer_sig=AQAAAL85HY_dEvyojkDpOn3pIAgN_BXc0tfE9cphxYPUOXf6edICggczkblQUO7VGgv--DChk5Qh2eSkTVJkl7qDUOajnVxaeRPmqTInxNYJ4LMDgt1pn6ZDV8bAYjx_ICiIG0GAaeIEgw9iTFDSNkLHUd2Y9Yx0gURoB2t4PZmd5JPg

Laming, H. (2003) The Victoria Climbié Inquiry. CM 5730. Available from: https://assets.publishing.service.gov.uk/government/uploads/system/uploads/attachment_data/file/273183/5730.pdf

Lemert, E. (1967) *Human Deviance: Social Problems and Social Control*. Englewood Cliffs, NJ: Prentice-Hall.

Nussbaum, M. (2000) *Women and Human Development*. Cambridge: Cambridge University Press.

Pardeck, J.T. (1988) An ecological approach for social work practice, *Journal of Sociology & Social Welfare*, 15(2): 133–142.

Parker, J. (2017) *Social Work Practice* (5th edn). London: Sage.

Parker, J. (2018) Social work, precarity and sacrifice as radical action for hope, *International Journal of Social Work and Human Services Practice*, 6(2): 46–55.

Parker, J. and Ashencaen Crabtree, S. (2018) *Social Work with Disadvantaged and Marginalised People*. London: Sage.

Rutter, L. and Brown, K. (2015) *Critical Thinking and Professional Judgement in Social Work*. London: Sage.

Shaw, I. (2005) Practitioner research: Evidence or critique? *British Journal of Social Work*, 35(8): 1231–1248.

Teater, B. (2014) Social work practice from an ecological perspective. In C.W. LeCroy (ed.), *Case Studies in Social Work Practice* (3rd edn). Belmont, CA: Brooks/Cole.

Teater, B. (2020) *An Introduction to Applying Social Work Theories and Methods* (3rd edn). London: Open University Press.

Thompson, N. (2016) *Anti-Discriminatory Practice* (6th edn). London: Palgrave.

van Hek, M., Kraaykamp, G. and Maarten, H.J.W. (2016) Comparing the gender gap in educational attainment: The impact of emancipatory contexts in 33 cohorts in 33 countries. *Educational Research and Evaluation*, 22(5–6): 260–282.

World Health Organization (2002) *Infant and Young Child Nutrition: Global Strategy on Infant and Young Child Feeding*. Geneva: WHO.

Yip, K.-S. (2004) A Chinese cultural critique of the global qualifying standards for social work education, *Social Work Education*, 23(5): 597–612.

6

Moral, spiritual and existential development

Wilfred McSherry, Alison Rodriguez and Joanna Smith

Introduction

It is important that we appreciate the spiritual and existential aspects of our human selves. These concepts have often been, erroneously and detrimentally, associated exclusively with religion and frequently avoided when considering their influence on social and emotional development. However, in cultural terms, the belief systems and faiths of children, young people, their families and communities represent important reference points in growth and development that can be marked by physical and/or psycho-social ritual and religious practices. Equally, spirituality and the things that people find most meaningful in life are powerful forces endorsing or questioning what can be termed 'appropriate' development within particular social contexts and in terms of the individual's sense of place within their world.

This chapter explores how spirituality and belief systems are being 'rediscovered' along with their importance, relevance and influence to the lives of children and young people. A critical perspective will be taken that questions assumptions made about the moral, spiritual and existential development of children and young people.

Chapter objectives

- introduce human evolution and the key attributes of spirituality to rethink how they contribute to an understanding of children and young people's development;

- provide an account of developmental theories and their usefulness in explaining how children and young people develop spiritually, through cognitive and moral reasoning;

- evaluate factors in children and young people's environments that stimulate healthy development and growth.

Background and context

The complexity and uniqueness of spirituality as part of the human experience, and its relevance to the challenges of contemporary society, are widely recognised (Kim and Esquivel, 2011). Moral, spiritual and existential development in young children is influenced and nurtured primarily by the family ecosystem – family relationships, culture and beliefs – and external influences, such as schools, peers and the wider society (Bronfenbrenner, 1979). Moral, spiritual and existential development is likely to reflect how the child and young person responds, copes and develops resilience to meet life challenges, and to promote subjective well-being (Davis et al, 2003; Van Dyke and Elias, 2007). We will briefly review some evolutionary theory, which has been introduced in Chapter 1. We will examine its application and relevance to exploring key attributes of spirituality, and their relevance to children and young people's moral and spiritual development.

Human evolution is dependent on the survival and perpetuation of the human species; at a primordial level, this involves: having adequate nutrition (food) and hydration (water); a place of safety (home); human procreation (reproduction); and the fashioning of an environment(s) where children can be nurtured and mature (Maslow, 1943). Evolution also involves humanity having a sense of 'awe and wonder' at nature and creation; generating an awareness of something transcendent, bigger than humanity, yet intimately related to each person. Hay (2006) describes this sense of transcendence as 'something there' – a spirituality that existed long before formal religion emerged. He suggests this is 'hardwired' – by this, he means an integral part of our human physiological and biological structures (our DNA) and purports this dimension is present in all human beings. For Hay (2006), spirituality may be relevant to both religious and non-religious discourses.

The three constructs often associated with spirituality, 'genetics', 'biology', and 'religion' (Swinton, 2010), need to be considered with caution. A genetic and evolutionary origin of religiosity has emerged because of the association with specific chemicals and neural networks within the brain, suggesting that the development of religious beliefs is inherited (Kapogiannis et al, 2009). Swinton (2010) has postulated that the generic and biological constructs are reductionist and problematic because spirituality is diminished to a set of neurological and synaptic processes. This biological 'lens' to spirituality may be compromised if an individual's biological function is damaged or destroyed, as in the case of intellectual impairment or significant physical disability (Swinton, 2010). Consequently, considering a purely biological dimension to spirituality is not adequate if it is disconnected from other discourses or dimensions of the person. A closer analysis of our human evolution reveals that every human being can be constructed as a composite 'whole' holistic being; comprised of physical, psychological, social and spiritual dimensions (see Figure 6.1). We possess a physical body, consisting of cells, tissues, systems and processes, which require oxygen, food and water to sustain life. We experience and express a range of emotions, happiness and sadness. We have a 'mind' and intellect (psychology) that enables us to explore our world,

Figure 6.1: Dimension of 'whole' person

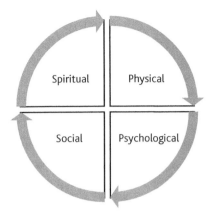

reflect, develop and be creative. Many people live and work within the context of a family and community, meaning they are connected socially, culturally and ethnically. Finally, every person (as Hay (2006) would suggest) possesses a spiritual dimension, which generates a sense of awe and wonder and the existential desire to invest in a life with meaning and purpose. Creating a sense of fulfilment for some people will be rooted within a religious tradition, while for others their spirituality will be based on non-religious values and beliefs.

A bio-psycho-social-spiritual model

Humans are 'bio-pyscho-social-spiritual' in nature and evolutionary in design. We do not operate and function in discrete dimensions – for example, our physical bodies are not detached from our psychological processes and our spiritual dimension is not fragmented from our physical and psychological dimensions. Equally, all our dimensions may be influenced and shaped by social environments, cultural norms and beliefs that are important to our group, community and identity. Therefore, to view the spiritual dimension as a separate and discrete one is a misrepresentation of what it means to be holistic and human. The spiritual dimension of humans has and will continue to influence and shape the moral and social development of children and young people in a profound but real way, as it is an integral part of our biology.

> **REFLECTION POINT 6.1**
>
> Consider your own views and beliefs. Why are these important to you and what do they do for you as a person? Also, consider how your beliefs concerning what is important to your life and how to behave may influence your social work practice. It is important to have an awareness of what gives life meaning to you so that you do not unconsciously place your values on the children and young people you are working with.

Defining spirituality

There is a lack of empirical research undertaken with children and young people that has explored the meaning of spirituality to them, resulting in the 'adult' evidence base being applied to them (McSherry and Jolley, 2009). This transferring of evidence makes inherent assumptions about spiritual development across childhood, its meaning and application to their lives and contexts. However, the key attributes of spirituality, highlighted next, are likely to have a relevance to children and young people.

Spirituality is a contested subject (Nash et al, 2015), with Paley (2008a, 2008b, 2009, 2010) highlighting that its meaning is created from a range of worldviews, perceptions and experiences, and differing contexts and experiences, which generates impassioned debates about its very existence and relevance for humanity. Puchalski et al defined spirituality, based on an international consensus conference on spirituality within healthcare, as: 'A dynamic and intrinsic aspect of humanity through which persons seek ultimate meaning, purpose, and transcendence, and experience relationship to self, family, others, community, society, nature, and the significant or sacred. Spirituality is expressed through beliefs, values, traditions, and practices' (2014, p 646).

This definition has relevance when applied to the moral and spiritual development of children and young people because of the core attributes underpinning it – namely, 'meaning and purpose', 'transcendence' and 'relationships' (see also Weathers et al, 2016).

The key attributes of spirituality have been defined by McSherry (2016) as follows:

- **Existentialism** – the way an individual derives and finds meaning, purpose and fulfillment in life (Weathers et al, 2016). Children, particularly when young, are naturally enquiring, with a 'spiritual' sense of wonder at their environment and the world around them.
- **Transcendence** relates to having a sense of something greater and beyond self, which could be God and/or aspects of life that enable the individual to transcend themselves or situations (Weathers et al, 2016). Many children and young people demonstrate tremendous resilience and courage while enduring some very difficult situations. They appear to have an inherent capacity to look beyond (transcend) the suffering, drawing on inner personal, emotional and spiritual resources to do this.
- **Connectedness** has been defined as 'a sense of relatedness to oneself, to others, to nature or the world, and to a Higher Power, God, or Supreme Being' (Weathers et al, 2016, p 83). The prominence of these relationships shifts throughout childhood and during transition to adulthood. Humans are social beings, with relationships an essential part of life and a significant and influential factor in the social and moral development of young adults (Pallini et al, 2014). Aspects of spirituality are common across the lifespan.

Spirituality is influenced by a number of intrinsic (arising from within the person) and extrinsic (arising from outside the person) factors (Puchalski et al, 2014), including:

- beliefs
- values
- traditions
- practices

The interplay between intrinsic and extrinsic factors adds to the complexity of spiritual development, which is shaped by tradition and history, language, culture, norms and practices, rituals and symbols. Therefore, to import a universal set of defining attributes of spirituality and suggest that these are relevant to every child and young person would be culturally insensitive, exposing a lack of awareness of the complexities and subtleties of the concept of spirituality and the diverse contexts in which it is developed. However, the core attributes can be considered and applied to the different developmental theories and stages of children and young people's growth. Smith and McSherry (2004) and McSherry and Smith (2007) provided examples of attributes of spirituality that could be displayed in children and young people and mapped them to the developmental stages of two seminal child development theories of Piaget (1952) and Erikson (1963). Read Case Study 6.1 and consider how children may express their inner-most thoughts.

CASE STUDY 6.1

A three-year-old, whose brother was terminally ill, was describing what happens when a person dies: "People who die go to prison". This little boy was an avid watcher of the A-team, where lots of "bad guys" were blown up as a matter of routine, and somehow end up in prison (Pfund, 2000, p 145).

During late infancy and toddlerhood, young children become fascinated with magic and mystery and may express themselves in elaborate thoughts. Children at this age may take meanings very literally and in the extract highlighted there appears to be a link between illness and death, with punishment and wrongdoing (Table 6.2). The age and developmental stage of the child and life context, a terminally-ill brother, are likely to determine how the child makes sense of their world, how they process information and what external factors may influence the processing of events, such as watching television. For children experiencing illness, or in this case life-threatening illness in a sibling, feelings and emotions will intensify, and may be difficult to express, resulting in frustration and distress. Supporting the child to express their feelings, often through the medium of play, is essential to help facilitate an understanding that illness is not due to the punishment of a wrongdoing, and as a way of expressing fears and fantasies.

Adapted from McSherry and Smith (2007) and Smith and McSherry (2004)

Questions
1. How and in what ways can families, peers, significant others and wider societies shape the spiritual development of children and young people?
2. Does the spiritual development of children and young people support their wider learning and well-being? Can you think of examples?
3. How might the spiritual development of children and young people be influenced by the range of professionals – teachers, nurses, doctors and social workers – they may meet and how might this influence your practice?

Discussion
Case Study 6.1 suggests that the age and developmental stage of the child and life context, a terminally ill brother, are likely to determine how the child makes sense of their world, how they process information and what external factors that may influence the processing of events such as watching TV. The spiritual and moral principles held by a young child may be deeply influenced by their parents and peers. These intrinsic forces may shape identity, beliefs, values, attitudes and behaviours and be influenced by cultural values and norms providing 'a lens through' which the child will view the world. But as a young person matures, these earlier beliefs and values may be reformed and reshaped by the time they reach adulthood. It is also recognised that our approach to children and young people may have an impact on their spiritual development.

The attributes of spirituality and intrinsic and extrinsic factors suggest that spirituality and moral development evolve synonymously – shaped and informed by culture, personal and religious beliefs, as well as a wide range of external, social and environmental situations. As the child grows, they encounter an increasing range of other influential people, such as teachers, religious leaders and peers. Increasingly, children are exposed to a wide range of factors that may inform their perceptions of the world through television, music and, in today's digital world, social media. Evolutionary processes are more than inherited physiological and biological DNA and include an evolutionary transmission in passing on traditions, beliefs, cultural values and identities.

Although evolutionary processes have occurred throughout human history and will continue to do so as long as humanity exists, the primary necessities of life have remained relatively constant. However, the landscape in which this evolution, and human needs, and spirituality and moral development, occurs has changed significantly for many because of industrialisation, globalisation (including digital communication systems), high economic growth and development. Ultimately, the child and young person's different and varied experiences of these changes will impact on their perception of spirituality and their moral compass – consciously or unconsciously.

Key theories and theorists

William James (1961) progressed our thinking about how religion could be related to the experiential aspects of spirituality. The association between spirituality and morality is long rooted in the belief that spiritual intentions influence our moral behaviour. This association is evidenced in early Christianity, where pastoral ethics highlight morally appropriate behaviour. These ethics, based on Judaism, Persian mystical religions and Jesus's teachings, advocate upholding the ten commandments, witnessing ritual practices and following the teachings of Jesus. Through following this 'spiritual development', St. Paul advocated that one would engender a 'new life', attitudes would change towards others and they would experience the virtues of love, peace, kindness, faithfulness and self-control (Galatians 5:22–23), humility, gentleness and patience (Ephesians 4:2). St. Paul compared the 'new life' with the 'previous' or 'other life', where vices such as anger, theft, slander, sexual immorality, greed and drunkenness were accepted as the norm (Ephesians 4:5). Spiritually religious writers have long debated how our sense of morality provides evidence of deeply-held beliefs and influences the relationships we have with others across our lifespans.

Al-Ghazali has been described as 'one of the most influential philosophers and thinkers on Islamic history' (Nofal, 1993, p 519). Teachings on virtue and ethics are central throughout his teachings and he argues that 783 verses detail pure morality and 748 verses detail applied morality in the Holy Qur'an (Rafiel, 2002). Al-Ghazali states that we all have an essence to our nature, but that this essence needs to be stimulated within us; this is enabled by individuals seeking or being given a spiritual leader and good companions to know or have a developed awareness of what behaviour types to conduct and avoid. This moral education guidance is of highest importance with regard to personal development and maturity, from the Islamic perspective (Alavi, 2010).

Similarly, Judaism concurs that the spiritual/moral intention precedes the behavioural outcome. The Hebrew Bible has numerous collections of behavioural laws to guide followers – for example, Leviticus 19. These laws are expressed in the Bible to both outline rituals, for example, the Sabbath and holidays, and to guide morality, such as judging fairly and helping others. The rabbinic tradition has followed, supplementing the rich literature of story and legend with an in-depth legal corpus focused on detailing the standards of good behaviour. This is handed down in families and communities in accordance with a tradition of right and wrong.

More recently, an understanding of spirituality has been substantiated by scholars in the field of counselling and psychology (Maslow, 1968; Witmer and Young, 1985). Similarly, a sense of purpose and meaning in life has been suggested as ingrained in the human condition (Edwards et al, 1974; Brallier, 1982; Canda, 1986; Elkins et al, 1988). Articulating children's spirituality and spiritual development remains a complex task, yet much of the discussion remains within the psychology of religion. Definitional debate around what spiritual development and the concept of spirituality itself means in childhood remain, and indeed if it can exist outside of a religious context. It has also been suggested that spiritual development comes to the fore only from the maturation point of adolescence or young adulthood (Irwin, 2002; Paloutzian, 2016). Critical thinkers have postulated that spirituality will relate to factors and experiences that shape child development, such as teachings from religious doctrines (Coles, 1991; Nye, 1999).

In using the term 'spiritual development' (Benson, 1997), we also assign a Piagetian sense of children progressing through stages of spiritual achievement as they physically mature (for more on Piaget's theories, see Chapter 3). According to Fowler (1981), cognitive development guides our complex faith structures. His position is based on his research with children, where he observed a relatedness between a child's stage of cognitive development and their increasing faith or development of increasing faith structures. Increasing faith structures were found to resonate with the cognitive processing of 'meaning making'. The theory is influenced by Piaget's model of cognitive development (for more on Piaget's theories, see Chapter 3), Erikson's theory of psychosocial development and Kohlberg's (1964) theory of moral development. The premise is that children develop the capacity to progress from concrete to abstract thinking as they mature. In addition, as children mature, their ability to cognitively process morally appropriate ways of being becomes increasingly apparent.

The stages of faith development, adapted by Thompson and Randall (1999, pp 98–99), from Fowler (1981) are as follows:

Stage 0 Undifferentiated (Primal) Faith (Infancy): The earliest faith is the basic trust and hope in the care of others. Undifferentiated faith experience of infancy is built upon secure attachments with significant caregivers.

Stage 1 Intuitive-Projective Faith (Preschool years): A preschooler's experience of faith is rooted in the young child's imagination, intuitive, and conceptual qualities. Faith is magical, imaginative, intuitive, and illogical, filled with fantasy and fascinated by stories of the power and omnipotence of God and the mysteries of birth and death. These stories are internalized in terms of the concerns of children of this age and may be much different from the meanings intended by their adult tutors.

Stage 2 Mythic-Literal Faith (Early school years): Faith is captured in the stories that children hear and tell about God, and the meanings that their literal but logical interpretations of these stories provide about human relations with the divine. Participation in the symbols and observances of the religious community also fosters initial appropriation of religious beliefs.

Stage 3 Synthetic-Conventional Faith (Late school years, early adolescence): Faith is encompassed in a fairly uncritical, tacit acceptance of the conventional religious values taught by others, centred on feelings of what is right and wrong, especially in interpersonal relationships.

Stage 4 Individuative-Reflective Faith (Late adolescence, early adult years): Faith is forged from personal reflection and experiences (sometimes entailing critical life transitions) that may cause the adolescent or adult to question prior assumptions and to reconstruct new and different beliefs and commitments that are more personally meaningful, individualized, and depend less on the guidance of authorities.

Stage 5 Conjunctive Faith (Adulthood): Faith confronts but also accepts the paradoxes and contradictions of religious life: the irrational mysteries of prayer and worship, but also the rational reflections of belief and values.

Stage 6 Universalizing Faith (Adulthood): Faith is grounded in comprehensive truths – concerning justice, love, and compassion – that may cause individuals to take unusual (sometimes radical) steps to live out their faith, such as selfless devotion to the poor (as with Mother Teresa) or non-violent (as with Gandhi) or even violent (as with Dietrich Bonhoeffer) resistance to political wrong.

A criticism of Fowler's stages of faith development is an emphasis on the need for intellect and the ability of the developing child to engage in life critically and retrospectively (reflectively). This approach does not seem inclusive, especially when applying the stages to children living with profound intellectual impairment, where the stages of faith development appear to have limited application (McSherry, 2001, p 36).

Fowler (2001) stated that the person's worldview was structured alongside the demands and influences of the cultural environment. However, Baxter (2006) highlights cultural specificity as an important criticism of Fowler's Faith Development Theory because conceptualisations occurred within the context of the late 20th century, a period of Western, Euro-American intellectual culture, and may not be applicable to non-Western contexts (Baxter, 2006). Indeed, Clore and Fitzgerald (2002) suggest that full development of faith as perceived by Fowler may occur only in more 'developed' cultures (p 98) and DeLaurentis (1985, p 78) suggests the theory is relevant only to 'the faith of the radical monotheist'. Broughton (1986) highlighted that more than 80 per cent of Fowler's respondents, whose transcripts were used to evolve his theory, were Christian. Therefore, it is possible that his theory may not be applicable to those who are from non-Christian or non-Western backgrounds.

To move our theoretical understanding into the 21st century and to explore the impact of current societal make-ups and challenges, we perhaps need to draw on the body of literature of postmodern psychology, which values different viewpoints, and which appreciates varied spiritual and moral discourses. There is a need to explore faith development in multicultural contexts (Keeley, 2010).

Drawing extensively on Fowler's (1981) stage theory of faith development, Helminiak (1987) postulated that general human development and spiritual development are inter-related. Helminiak's (1987) five-stage model of spiritual development is also a linear stage theory suggestive of children moving through stages of increasingly sophisticated thought processing and conceptualisations of spirituality, from concrete spiritual ideas to highly abstract thinking. The 'spiritual child movement' (Oser et al, 2006, p 968), however, is distinct from the traditional stage-structural cognitive-based theories, proposing that spiritual development is a more fluid phenomenon (Hart, 2010). It is argued that children can appreciate and understand much more than they can verbalise; as such, they are able to appreciate complex spiritual conceptions. Even young children can recognise the more advanced notions of injustice, suffering and compassion. Reflecting on his social ethnographic research, many hundreds of interviews with individual children, engaging them in discussion about spiritual experiences, Hart (2010) highlights how children enquire about existential topics and seemingly can engage in mystical thinking.

Much of our understanding and appreciation of human spirituality and spiritual development resides within theology and the psychology of religion. Scholars draw on Biblical references and stage theory to try and convey spiritual developmental processes. However, over time, we have come to realise that spiritual development is a complex process, highly individual and also built upon our experiences with others, our environments, cultural teachings and our appreciation of moral concepts.

Developing spiritually cognitive and moral reasoning

How to understand and research children's spirituality continues to challenge scholars (Boyatzis, 2012) and has been likened to 'trying to hold water in our hands' (Hart, 2003, p 8). However, we are moving towards more cohesive definitions and a collective conceptualisation of spiritual development (King, 2014). Drawing on a social-ecological framework arguably helps us to better understand that children's different and unique contexts can infer a number of factors influential in their religious and spiritual development (King, 2014). Boyatzis (2012) supports a socio-ecological view that draws on the work of Bronfenbrenner (1979) and his ecological model. The model suggests that children form relationships with a 'Higher Being or purpose prior to religious socialisation' (Boyatzis, 2012, p 153). Children can therefore be viewed as capable of cognitively processing associations between themselves and a divine entity/higher spiritual purpose, from early in their development (King et al, 2005).

Attachment theory, explored further in Chapter 7 of Part II, offers us a guiding scheme, here, of how the relationships/bonds we form from early infancy throughout childhood help to mould our spiritual identities (Bowlby et al, 1965). In collaboration with this theory, Hart (2003) suggests that spirituality is reached and searched for throughout development. However, it is still widely considered as something we relate to or appreciate once we have reached the 'top of the developmental ladder' (Hart, 2003, p 9). As such, many believe that spirituality is not something that is naturally implicit in children's thinking.

Piaget never explicitly made links to religious or spiritual development. However, from a Piagetian perspective, once in the formal operation period, it would be reasonable to infer that it is at this time that the child's relationship with a higher being and spiritual purpose begins. Cognitive development mediates our understanding of what is existent/happening between life and death/the Eternal. Piaget's (1952) theory of cognitive development as outlined in Chapter 3 helps us to understand some of its major claims. Intellectual development is proposed to be age-related. However, it has been well recognised that intellectual development is not necessarily age-determined (Mulqueen and Elias, 2000). The spiritual essence of intellectual development could possibly be what causes individual differences in terms of cognitive and spiritual development. As such, the spiritual component of our intellect can affect our own understandings of what or who we perceive to be our God or our higher purpose/meaning (Cartwright, 2001). If our spirituality is initially rooted in experience, then it is only something that can be explored or understood at an intellectual level. As already discussed, a possible critique of some of the classical developmental theories is an overemphasis on intellectual development and the need for the child to be reflective and self-aware. It could, therefore, be argued that an individual (child) can only appreciate their spirituality or spiritual needs once they have reached a stage or period of development where they can be reflective and self-aware (Love, 2002). Yet, even though (young) children are often perceived as developmentally immature, without sufficient intellectual capacity or maturity to express spiritual awareness, they demonstrate attributes associated with spiritual awareness, such as empathy, and connection with others and nature (McSherry and Smith, 2007; Hyde, 2008).

Exploring who we are and our purpose can be cognitively challenging for some children and young people, but this does not mean that the individual is without a spiritual belief system. Similarly, individuals may find it difficult to articulate the meaning and purpose of their spiritual beliefs to others, but this inability to offer a concrete objectiveness does not mean that person's Being in the world is not spiritual.

Table 6.1 summarises the theoretically aligned stage theories of Piaget, Erikson, Kohlberg and Fowler.

Spirituality and the moral development of children and young people are intimately related. It is not a simple case of nature versus nurture, but far more complex, involving socialisation, social learning, psychologically cognitive and developmental processes and the influence of culture and environment.

Table 6.1: Stages of cognitive, psychosocial, moral and spiritual development

Piaget's Cognitive development	Erikson's Psychosocial development	Kohlberg's Moral development	Fowler's Faith development
Sensorimotor period (birth to the acquisition of language)	Stage 1: Basic trust versus mistrust (birth–12/18 mths) Stage 2: Autonomy versus shame/doubt (18 mths –3 yrs)		Pre-stage: Undifferentiated faith (birth–18 mths)
Pre-operational period (2–6/7 yrs)	Stage 3: Initiative versus guilt (3–6 yrs)	Level 1: Preconventional (4–10 yrs) Stage 1: Punishment and obedience orientation Stage 2: Naïve instrumental hedonism	Stage 1: Intuitive projective faith (3–7 yrs)
Concrete operations period (7–11 yrs)	Stage 4: Industry versus inferiority (6–12 yrs)	Level 2: Conventional (10–13 yrs) Stage 3: Good boy/girl morality Stage 4: Authority-maintaining morality	Stage 2: Mythic-literal faith (6–12 yrs)
Formal operations period (11/12–adulthood)	Stage 5: Identity versus role confusion (adolescence) Stage 6: Intimacy versus isolation (young adulthood) Stage 7: Generativity versus stagnation (middle adulthood) Stage 8: Ego integrity versus despair (old age)	Level 3: Post conventional (late adolescence) Stage 5: Morality of contract, of individual rights and of democratically accepted law Stage 6: Morality of individual principles and conscience (adulthood)	Stage 3: Synthetic conventional faith (12–adulthood) Stage 4: Individuate-reflective faith (young adulthood and beyond) Stage 5: Conjunctive faith (middle adulthood and beyond) Stage 6: Universalising faith (adulthood, but very rare)

Environmental factors that stimulate development and growth

> **REFLECTION POINT 6.2**
>
> Having read the chapter so far, consider what understandings of spirituality are important for you as a social worker, or other professional practitioner, to be mindful of when working with children and young people.
>
> Note some ideas down and compare these to the discussion in the following section.

Spiritual development in children and young people can be viewed as an ongoing/continuous process that relates to the experiencing and questioning of the fundamental aspects of 'Being'. This process is concordant with relationship and identity formation, situatedness and purpose. Children's spiritual experiences and perceptions are understood to engender the spiritual, moral and existential paradoxes of what can be deduced as the most wonderful and most difficult aspects/experiences of human lives. Children can also be active agents in their own spiritual growth (Lerner, 2001). The dynamic interaction between ecological influences and personal agency suggests that both the individual and the culture to which they belong create their spiritual, moral and existential life story (Reker and Chamberlain, 2000). Consideration must be given to the role and impact played by education in forming and shaping the moral and spiritual values of the child.

Illness can have a significant impact on an individual's well-being, which can be ameliorated by drawing on spiritual experiences. These often focus on a search for meaning and purpose to make sense of physical and psychological changes, and are a resource to develop coping strategies (Clarke, 2013). When working with children and young people, there will be specific considerations and challenges in relation to how spirituality is embedded into care that must account for their developmental needs and family contexts, using age-appropriate language and activities to enhance spiritual care (Smith and McSherry, 2004). Health professionals will be working with both the child or young person and their family; the spiritual needs of the child/young person and family members may differ. Hospitalisation creates a new and often bewildering community for the child or young person, and their uniqueness and identity can be lost in the challenging context of sickness and ill health and in normalising spiritual care (Nash et al, 2015), Effective spiritual care includes:

- empowering children and young people to participate in choices and decisions about their care, and respecting their views;
- creating space and using activities to promote self-reflection and contemplation;
- developing effective relationships, built on rapport and trust, with children, young people and their families;

- if appropriate, facilitating existing religious connections for the child or young person respecting their faith tradition (Nash et al, 2015).

Patterns of understanding in children and young people are fluid; children's individual experiences, environment, including family environment, their intellectual capacities, and their emotional profiles, ethnic, cultural and religious backgrounds all contribute to how and when they come to fully understand the meanings of their Being. However, the developmental theories outlined overleaf fail to acknowledge the impact of life events on development – for example, chronic or life-limiting illness or the bereavement of close relatives. It is argued that a cognitively-aware child with a life-limiting illness will typically acquire a precocious understanding of illness and death beyond their chronological years and presumed developmental stage (Faulkner and Miell, 1993).

There are branches of developmental psychology that have an overt social realm and the work of Vygotsky (1978) challenged research that argued that cognitive development is a universal process. Vygotsky's work was focused on the individual, like Piaget's, but in contrast he realised that to acquire an understanding of child development, one needs to understand how and in what ways mental processes stem from and develop via social interactions and different contexts, and how mediating socio-cultural factors, particularly language, can affect development (Rowe and Westch, 2002). The social constructivist movement has also progressed this wider psychological debate, critiquing developmental psychology (see Burman, 2016). Social constructivists propose that development is advanced by children and young people sharing their experiences and interacting in their social environments. Children and young people are naturally reflexive, actively monitoring their proximal relationships and environments, and can be critical and creative, developing through the modification or rejection of norms against their experiences. As a result, we may find that children and young people with chronic or life-limiting conditions, or those who have faced bereavement, trauma or, indeed, have been extensively involved in caring roles, do not follow the predefined stages of cognitive development (Piaget, 1960). In addition, their understandings of their experiences may also not be aligned to their biological age or assumed level of cognitive development (Morss, 2002).

Debates about the spiritual and moral development in children and young people and the impact on the child's well-being are therefore not new. For example, in the United Kingdom, within the field of education, the National Curriculum Council (1993) developed a discussion paper entitled 'Spiritual and moral development' (Table 6.2). This discussion paper aimed to support schools to meet their challenges and responsibilities in the spiritual and moral development of children, which ultimately provides a foundation for adulthood and society in the future.

The aspects of spiritual and moral development outlined in Table 6.2 reinforce that spiritual and moral development of any child or young person is multifaceted, involving a dynamic interplay between many aspects of the person and their micro and macro living systems. This multifaceted dynamic interplay of social or cultural context, along with cognitive and psycho–social development, may be expressed in feelings, emotions and reactions to situations and events that occur in life. Life events may be positive, such as achieving a specific goal or target, or the birth of a sibling; or hugely challenging, with devastating impact, such as bullying or the loss of a parent, sibling or close friend. Existential aspects of life are also important because ultimately they provide a child and young person's sense of meaning and purpose in life.

Table 6.2: Aspects of spiritual and moral development

Beliefs	The development of personal beliefs, including religious beliefs; an appreciation that people have individual and shared beliefs on which they base their lives; a developing understanding of how beliefs contribute to personal identity.
A sense of awe, wonder and mystery	Being inspired by the natural world, mystery, or human achievement.
Experiencing feelings of transcendence	Feelings which may give rise to belief in the existence of a divine being, or the belief that one's inner resources provide the ability to rise above everyday experiences.
Search for meaning and purpose	Asking 'why me?' at times of hardship or suffering; reflecting on the origins and purpose of life; responding to challenging experiences of life such as beauty, suffering and death.
Self-knowledge	An awareness of oneself in terms of thoughts, feelings, emotions, responsibilities and experiences; a growing understanding and acceptance of individual identity; the development of self-respect.
Relationships	Recognising and valuing the worth of each individual; developing a sense of community; the ability to build relationships with others.
Creativity	Expressing innermost thoughts and feelings through, for example, art, music, literature and crafts; exercising the imagination, inspiration, intuition and insight.
Feelings and emotions	The sense of being moved by beauty or kindness; hurt by injustice or aggression; a growing awareness of when it is important to control emotions and feelings, and how to learn to use such feelings as a source of growth.
Behave morally as a point of principle	Knowledge of the codes and conventions of conduct agreed by society. Knowledge and understanding of the criteria put forward as a basis for making responsible judgements on moral issues, and apply moral principles, insights and reasoning.

Source: Adapted from National Curriculum Council (1993)

Children and young people want to explore, learn and expand their minds and should be facilitated to discuss and 'grapple' with the big questions about life and existence. Experiencing the beauty of creation may also inspire a sense of awe, wonder and transcendence, providing a deeper appreciation of the world, relationships and people. The notion of creativity seems fundamental to any discussion on spirituality and moral development, allowing children and young people to express thoughts and feeling through art, music and play, developing imagination to gain a deeper and richer understanding of themselves, relationships and their place in the world.

The ethos of the school and the way in which it helps children/young people to develop demonstrates a concern for their well-being, reflecting the values which the community intends to promote because such values determine behaviour (National Curriculum Council, 1993). Analysis of the attributes outlined in Table 6.1 associated with spiritual and moral development affirms that children and young people are unitary in nature, in that they do not function solely in discrete compartments – physical, psychological, social and spiritual. Spirituality and moral development are intimately linked with other dimensions of the person, such as culture, ethnicity and religious belief, since these have a dramatic impact on the person's own worldview, moral codes and beliefs, sense of self, identity, dignity and place in the world. Spirituality and moral development may influence and determine the values and attitudes they hold about the meaning and purpose in life. For some individuals, these may stem from a deep religious belief.

Children have spiritual capacities and experiences that influence their lives in enduring ways. However, spiritual awareness in children is often dismissed and sometimes labelled as pathology by adults who have no recipe or guidance for understanding children's spiritual needs. This dismissal or pathologisation can become a barrier for a child's spiritual growth and openness, as discussed in Case Study 6.2.

CASE STUDY 6.2

One of the findings from King et al's (2014) study that explored the meaning of spirituality for young people from diverse cultures related to the importance of 'living a moral life'. For example, one young person stated: 'Spirituality means how well, to me, you can follow a set of morals that everyone pretty much has in common, and how well you can live up to I guess good standards for moral settings. So that would be a kind of spirituality' (p 201).

The study identified that transcendence, fidelity and behaviour are important aspects of spirituality for young people (King et al, 2014), and this 'fits' with the development of morality of individual principles and conscience. Unsurprisingly, world challenges and tensions have resulted in an increased interest in one of the most enduring questions: How and why do some young people emerge through the turbulent period of adolescence well-adjusted with a moral compass that guides them into adulthood, whereas others follow a path of what can be considered deviant behaviours or delinquency?

Certainly, research suggests religiosity and/or spirituality may play a role in supporting a positive developmental trajectory, with young people who consider themselves religious or spiritual less likely to engage in delinquent behaviours and more likely to have a greater connection to society (Blakeney and Blakeney, 2006). Blakeney and Blakeney (2006) suggest that, rather than focusing on whether religiosity and/or spirituality are protective against delinquent behaviours (and therefore mutually exclusive), the emphasis should be on how religiosity and/or spirituality can help young people learn and develop.

Questions
1. What contextual factors might influence a child's moral development?
2. All children have a capacity for forming moral judgements; what can families, peers, significant others and wider societies do to promote positive moral development in children and young people?
3. Is it important to explore spiritual and religious development in children and young people? Do you think this is something we could/should measure?
4. Does fostering religious and/or spiritual beliefs in children and young people influence their moral development and make a positive difference in their lives?

Discussion
Research is important in identifying why developing moral and spiritual sensitivity in children and young people can help promote their future development as emotionally strong people. Paying attention to and valuing children and young people's spirituality, beliefs and cultures shows respect and ensures that they are affirmed. This can offset emotional difficulties and also lead young people into more pro-social ways of living, such as not engaging in alcohol or substance abuse or risky sexual behaviours. It may even divert them from criminality.

Much of the research on the cultural influences on spirituality and psychosocial outcomes (such as academic achievement, crime, drug or alcohol abuse) focuses on race, with race and ethnicity being used interchangeably (Mattis et al, 2006). Similarly, perspectives about spirituality differ, with some ethnic and culture communities making no distinction between the secular and spiritual, and others delineating spirituality as rooted in self-actualisation (Mattis et al, 2006). Poor conceptualisation of ethnicity, religion and spirituality has the potential for young people's experiences to be misconstrued as psychopathology; cultural contexts need to be considered when making a diagnostic judgement about a child's psychological well-being (Fukuyama and Sevig, 1999). For example, if a child from a Catholic Latin American culture claimed that they had a vision of the 'Virgin Mother of God', this would be acceptable and even revered by their cultural counterparts. Similarly, if a child of a voodoo community from the same geographical region claimed spiritual possession, then this would also be celebrated as an event marking a level of spiritual maturity or awareness. However, in many

Western contexts, this very same behaviour would be considered worrisome and the child may be labelled as 'delusional' or as having hallucinations. As such, it can be difficult for health and social care practitioners to delineate what is happening psychologically with children and young people, especially in increasing multicultural contexts. Any evaluation of a child's psychological well-being can be influenced by the professional's awareness of that child's context and the assumptions made about the norms of any manifesting behaviour (Johnson and Friedman, 2008).

The developing evidence base identifies that spirituality (most often deduced as expressed through religiosity) informs a wide variety of important psychological and social phenomena in children and young people:

- overall wellbeing (Markstrom, 1999);
- positive life attitude, satisfaction and hope for the future (Smith et al, 2003);
- altruism and service (Smith et al, 2003);
- access to internal and external developmental resources that attribute to risk reduction, well-being and thriving (Wagener and Malony, 2005);
- resiliency and coping (Benson, 1997);
- physical health (Wallace and Forman, 1998);
- positive identity formation (Youniss et al, 1999).

As a means to nurture spiritual growth in children, Hyde (2008) advocates the creation of spaces that foster trust, respect and safety, both at home and in school. Thompson and Randall (1999) also suggest ways to support spiritual growth in children, including:

- appreciating that the ways in which children understand religious issues and their understanding is likely to be aligned with their developmental maturation;
- assigning religious/spiritual roles to children that they can understand/embrace and that can also be recognised as meaningful by adults within the community;
- allowing children to be involved in spiritual/religious work that is both intergenerational and specific to their age and interests;
- fostering relationships based on trust, security, empathy and compassion, especially within the family, which nurture the child's growth and attachment;
- appreciating that every child's spiritual path is unique and rooted in their experiences and how they interpret these;
- providing human support for children during development, especially in periods of difficulty and crisis; it is in these times that familiar beliefs can be tested and children need support to work through their meaning-making;
- being open to talking about spiritual issues with children and exploring their beliefs with them. Children need to be encouraged to explore their spirituality without fear of being ridiculed or rejected.

Spiritual development, though a unique aspect of human development, cannot be separated from other elements of one's being (Bradford, 1995, p 72). A thorough understanding of a normative child and adolescent development and family life is also a necessary precursor to assessing, nurturing and treating concerns about atypical development or other pathologies. This same premise holds relevance in the area of normative faith and spiritual development (Dell and Josephson, 2006).

Conclusion

Although the notion of spirituality in children and young people is a complex interplay between cognitive development, experiences, and their micro and macro environments, children and young people have a capacity for developing a spiritual awareness and forming moral judgements. Available research suggests that spirituality has a powerful effect on life and is implicit in human psychosocial, cognitive and moral development. We have outlined that the literature available to date focuses extensively on the dynamics of religiosity in the lives of Christian and Jewish children (more so adolescents) in Western countries, with little consideration of the impact of spirituality for young people within other or no religious traditions, or in other parts of the world (Benson et al, 2010). The problems we incur with our knowledge to date are incumbent with the number of different definitions operationalised by studies, the varied theoretical nuances and the many studies that have not delineated religiosity from spirituality, not least in their tools of measurement. Further investigations are required that explore the subjective consciousness of spirituality in childhood and what different factors influence and shape children's spiritual realities.

We have provided an overview of the development theories and their usefulness in explaining how children and young people develop spiritually, through cognitive and moral reasoning. We have provided some insights into the factors that stimulate a healthy foundation for spiritual development and moral reasoning in children and young people. However, many questions remain regarding how spiritual developmental processes impact on growth and well-being in children and what aspects of spiritual development (for example, beliefs, practices, socialisation) are most predictive of different outcomes, particularly for those outside of Judeo–Christian traditions. The limited research we do have with children, however, suggests a positive association between spirituality and children's health, broader development and well-being. The characteristics attributed with developing a spiritual awareness, such as inner confidence, positive attitude and self-belief, are likely to contribute to a child or young person becoming resilient and having the ability to develop coping strategies at times of difficulty, but also a moral orientation towards ensuring a fair, just and equitable society.

This chapter will have stimulated you to think critically about how children and young people develop spiritually, through cognitive and moral reasoning.

Reflective questions

1 What is your understanding of the concept of spirituality and what role does this play in how you live your life?

2 How can professionals working with children and young people identify and support a child or young person who may be experiencing spiritual distress?

3 How can we label the spiritual norms and needs of children and young people?

4 How can we support children and young people to nurture spiritual reflection and thus development?

5 What are the threats to spirituality in children and young people, including loss, relocation and separation from their culture, death, personal or familial stress?

Further reading

• Fowler, J. (1981) *Stages of Faith*. San Francisco, CA: Harper & Row.
Fowler's work is a classic in its field. It covers the development of faith and spirituality across the human life span and so is wider than just children and young people. However, it is a good place to start should you wish to expand your knowledge of this key area of life.

• Nash, P., Darby, K. and Nash, S. (2015) *Spiritual Care with Sick Children and Young People*. London: Jessica Kingsley.
This book offers practice advice and insights for working with children and young people who are ill. While it focuses on health professionals and hospital chaplaincy workers, it has direct relevance to social workers who work in health settings and beyond because of its practical approach.

• Roehlkepartain, E.C., King, P.E. Wagener, P. and Benson, P.L. (eds) (2006) *The Handbook of Spiritual Development in Childhood and Adolescence*. Thousand Oaks, CA: Sage.
This book offers a comprehensive consideration of spiritual development in children and young people across many areas of theory and research. It offers, in the main, a developmental psychological approach, but is also rooted in social science.

References

Alavi, R.H. (2010) Al-Ghazali on moral education, *Journal of Moral Education*, 36(3): 309–319.

Baxter, P. (2006) From Ubuzungu to Ubuntu: Resources for pastoral counselling in a Bantu context. Unpublished PhD thesis, Kimmage Mission Institute of Theology and Culture, Milltown Institute, Dublin.

Benson, P. (1997) Spirituality and the adolescent journey, *Reclaiming Children and Youth: Journal of Emotional and Behavioral Problems*, 5(4): 206–209.

Benson, P.L., Roehlkepartain, E.C. and Rude, S.P. (2010) Spiritual development in childhood and adolescence: Toward a field of inquiry, *Applied Developmental Science*, 7(3): 205–213.

Blakeney, R.F. and Blakeney, C.D. (2006) Delinquency: A quest for moral and spiritual integrity? In E.C. Roehlkepartain, P.E. King, P. Wagener and P.L. Benson (eds), *The Handbook of Spiritual Development in Childhood and Adolescence*. Thousand Oaks, CA: Sage.

Bowlby, J., Fry, M., Ainsworth, M.D.S. and the World Health Organization (1965) *Child Care and the Growth of Love*. World Health Organization. Harmondsworth: Penguin Books.

Boyatzis, C.J. (2012) Spiritual development during childhood and adolescence. In L.J. Miller (ed.), *The Oxford Handbook of Psychology and Spirituality*. New York, NY: Oxford University Press.

Bradford, J. (1995). *Caring for the Whole Child: A Holistic Approach to Spirituality*. London: The Children's Society.

Brallier, L. (1982) *Transition and Transformation: Successfully Managing Stress*. Los Altos, CA.: National Nursing Review.

Bronfenbrenner, U. (1979) *The Ecology of Human Development: Experiences by Nature and Design*. Cambridge, MA: Harvard University Press.

Broughton, J. (1986) Political psychology of faith development theory. In C. Dykstra and S. Parks (eds), *Faith Development and Fowler*. Birmingham, AL: Religious Education.

Burman, E. (2016) *Deconstructing Developmental Psychology*. London: Taylor & Francis.

Canda, E.R. (1986) A conceptualization of spirituality for social work: Its issues and implications. Doctoral dissertation. The Ohio State University.

Cartwright, K.B. (2001) Cognitive developmental theory and spiritual development, *Journal of Adult Development*, 8(4): 213–220.

Clarke, J. (2013) *Spiritual Care in Everyday Nursing Practice: A New Approach*. Basingstoke: Palgrave Macmillan.

Clore, V. and Fitzgerald, J. (2002) Intentional faith: An alternative view of faith development, *Journal of Adult Development*, 9(2): 97–107.

Coles, R. (1991) *The Spiritual Life of Children*. Houghton: Mifflin Harcourt.

Davis, T.L., Kerr, B.A. and Kurplus, S.E.R. (2003) Meaning, purpose, and religiosity in at-risk youth: The relationship between anxiety and spirituality, *Journal of Psychology and Theology*, 31(4): 356–365.

DeLaurentis, H. (1985). Maturity of faith: An interdisciplinary clarification of the term. Unpublished thesis. Catholic University of America.

Dell, M.L. and Josephson, A.M. (2006) Working with spiritual issues of children, *Psychiatric Annals*, 36(3): 176–181.

Edwards, T.H., Mead, L.B., Palmer, P.J. and Simmons, J.P. (1974) *Spiritual Growth: An Empirical Exploration of Its Meaning, Sources, and Implications*. Washington, DC: Metropolitan Ecumenical Training Center.

Elkins, D., Hedstrom, L., Hughes, L., Leaf, J. and Saunders, C. (1988) Toward a humanistic phenomenological spirituality, *Journal of Humanistic Psychology*, 28(4): 5–18.

Ephesians 4:2 New International Version (NIV) Bible.

Ephesians 4:5 New International Version (NIV) Bible.

Erikson, E.H. (1963) *Childhood and Society* (2nd edn). New York, NY: W.W. Norton.

Faulkner, D. and Miell, D. (1993) Settling into school: The importance of early friendships for the development of children's social understanding and communicative competence, *International Journal of Early Years Education*, 1(1): 23–46.

Fowler, J. (1981) *Stages of Faith*. San Francisco, CA: Harper & Row.

Fowler, J.W. (2001) Faith development theory and the postmodern challenges, *International Journal for the Psychology of Religion*, 11(3): 159–172.

Fukuyama, M.A. and Sevig, T.D. (1999) *Integrating Spirituality into Multicultural Counseling* (Vol. 13). Thousand Oaks, CA: Sage.

Galations 5:22–23 New International Version (NIV) Bible.

Hart, T. (2003) *The Secret Spiritual World of Children*. Novato, CA: New World Library.

Hart, T. (2010) *The Secret Spiritual World of Children: The Breakthrough Discovery that Profoundly Alters Our Conventional View of Children's Mystical Experiences*. Novato, CA: New World Library.

Hay, D. (2006) *Something There: The Biology of the Human Spirit*. London: Darton, Longman & Todd.

Helminiak, D.A. (1987) *Spiritual Development: An Interdisciplinary Study*. Chicago, IL: Loyola Press.

Hyde, B. (2008) *Children and Spirituality: Searching for Meaning and Connectedness*. London: Jessica Kingsley.

Irwin, R.R. (2002) *Human Development and the Spiritual Life: How Consciousness Grows toward Transformation*. New York, NY: Springer.

James, W. (1961) *The Varieties of Religious Experience*. New York, NY: Collier Books.

Johnson, C.V. and Friedman, H.L. (2008) Enlightened or delusional? Differentiating religious, spiritual, and transpersonal experiences from psychopathology, *Journal of Humanistic Psychology*, 48(4): 505–527.

Kapogiannis, D., Barbey, A.K., Su, M., Zamboni, G., Krueger, F. and Grafman, J. (2009) Cognitive and neural foundations of religious belief, *Proceedings of the National Academy of Sciences of the United States of America*, 106(12): 4876–4881.

Keeley, R. (2010) Faith development and faith formation: More than just ages and stages, *Lifelong Faith*, 20–27.

Kim, S. and Esquivel, G.B. (2011) Adolescent spirituality and resilience: Theory research and educational practices, *Psychology in the Schools*, 48(7): 755–765.

King, M. (2014) The challenge of research into religion and spirituality, *Journal for the Study of Spirituality*, 4(2): 106–120.

King, P.E., Cantrell, M., Clark, J. and Abraam, M. (2005) *Key Informants of Spiritual Development: Emerging Issues in the Field of Spiritual Development.* Pasadena, CA: Fuller Theological Seminary.

King, P.E., Clardy, C.E. and Ramos, J.S. (2014) Adolescent spiritual exemplars: Exploring spirituality in the lives of diverse youth, *Journal of Adolescent Research*, 29(2): 186–212.

Kohlberg, L. (1964) Development of moral character and moral ideology. In M.L. Hoffman and L.W. Hoffman (eds), *Review of Child Development Research* (Vol. 1). New York, NY: Russell Sage Foundation.

Lerner, R.M. (2001) *Concepts and Theories of Human Development* (3rd edn). Mahwah, NJ: Psychology Press.

Leviticus 19. New International Version (NIV) Bible.

Love, P.G. (2002) Comparing spiritual development and cognitive development, *Journal of College Student Development*, 43(3): 357–373.

Markstrom, C.A. (1999) Religious involvement and adolescent psychosocial development, *Journal of Adolescence*, 22(2): 205–221.

Maslow, A.H. (1943) A theory of human motivation, *Psychological Review*, 50(4): 370–396.

Maslow, A. (1968) Some educational implications of the humanistic psychologies, *Harvard Educational Review*, 38(4): 685–696.

Mattis, J.S., Ahluwalia, M.K., Cowie, S.A.E. and Kirkland-Harris, A.M. (2006) Ethnicity, culture and spiritual development. In E.C. Roehlkepartain, P.E. King, P. Wagener and P.L. Benson (eds), *The Handbook of Spiritual Development in Childhood and Adolescence.* Thousand Oaks, CA: Sage.

McSherry, W. (2001) Spirituality and learning disabilities: Are they compatible?, *Learning Disability Practice*, 3(5): 35–39.

McSherry, W. (2016) Reintegrating spirituality and dignity in nursing and health care: A relational model of practice. In O. Tranvåg, O. Synnes and W. McSherry, W. (eds), *Stories of Dignity within Healthcare: Research, Narratives and Theories.* Keswick: M&K Publishing.

McSherry, W. and Jolley, S. (2009) Meeting the spiritual needs of children and families. In J. Price and P. McNeilly (eds), *Palliative Care for Children and Families – An Interdisciplinary Approach.* Basingstoke: Palgrave Macmillan.

McSherry, W. and Smith, J. (2007) How do children express spiritual needs?, *Paediatric Nursing*, 19(3): 17–20.

Morss, J. (2002) The several constructions of James, Jenks and Pratt: A contribution to the sociological development of childhood, *International Journal of Children's Rights*, 10(1): 39–54.

Mulqueen, J. and Elias, J.L. (2000) Understanding spiritual development through cognitive development, *Journal of Pastoral Counseling*, 35: 99–113.

Nash, P., Darby, K. and Nash, S. (2015) *Spiritual Care with Sick Children and Young People*. London: Jessica Kingsley.

National Curriculum Council (1993) Spiritual and moral development: A discussion paper. Available from: http://www.educationengland.org.uk/documents/ncc1993/smdev.html

Nofal, N. (1993) Al-Ghazali, prospects, *Quarterly Review of Comparative Education*, 23(3/4): 519–542.

Nye, R.M. (1999) Relational consciousness and the spiritual lives of children: Convergence with children's theory of mind. In K.H. Reich, F.K. Oser and W.G. Scarlett (eds), *Psychological Studies on Spiritual and Religious Development*, Vol. 2: *The Case of Religion*. Lengerich: Pabst.

Oser, F.K., Scarlett, W.G. and Bucher, A. (2006) Religious and spiritual development throughout the life span. In Richard M. Lerner (ed.), *Handbook of Child Psychology*, Vol. 1: *Theoretical Models of Human Development*. Hoboken, NJ: John Wiley & Sons.

Paley, J. (2008a) Spirituality and nursing: A reductionist approach, *Nursing Philosophy*, 9(1): 3–18.

Paley, J. (2008b) Spirituality and secularization: Nursing and the sociology of religion, *Journal of Clinical Nursing*, 17(2): 175–186.

Paley, J. (2009) Keep the NHS secular, *Nursing Standard*, 23(43): 26–27.

Paley, J. (2010) Spirituality and reductionism: Three replies, *Nursing Philosophy*, 11(3): 178–190.

Pallini, S., Baiocco, R., Schneider, B.H., Madigan, S. and Atkinson, L. (2014) Early child–parent attachment and peer relations: A meta-analysis of recent research, *Journal of Family Psychology*, 28(1): 118–123.

Paloutzian, R.F. (2016) *Invitation to the Psychology of Religion*. New York, NY: Guilford Press.

Pfund, R. (2000) Nurturing a child's spirituality, *Journal of Child Health Nursing*, 4(4): 143–148.

Piaget, J. (1952) *The Origins of Intelligence in Children*. London: Penguin; New York, NY: International Universities Press.

Piaget, J. (1960) Equilibration and development of logical structures. In J.M. Tanner and B. Inhelder (eds) (1969) *Discussions on Child Development*. New York, NY: International Press.

Puchalski, C.M., Vitillo, R., Hull, S.K. and Reller, N. (2014) Improving the spiritual dimension of whole person care: Reaching national and international consensus, *Journal of Palliative Medicine*, 17(6): 642–656.

Rafiel, B. (2002) Ideas of Muslim scholars of education and its foundations. In G.T. Reker and K. Chamberlain (eds) (2000) *Exploring Existential Meaning*. London: Sage.

Reker, G.T. and Chamberlain, K. (eds) (2000) *Exploring Existential Meaning*. London: Sage.

Rowe, S. and Westch, J. (2002) Vygotsky's model of cognitive development. In V. Goswami (ed.), *Blackwell Handbook of Childhood Cognitive Development*. Oxford: Blackwell.

Smith, C., Faris, R. and Regnerus, M. (2003) Mapping American adolescent subjective religiosity and attitudes of alienation toward religion: A research report, *Sociology of Religion*, 64(1): 111–133.

Smith, J. and McSherry, W. (2004) Spirituality and child development: A concept analysis, *Journal of Advanced Nursing*, 45(3): 307–315.

Swinton, J. (2010) The meanings of spirituality: A multi-perspective approach to 'the spiritual'. In W. McSherry and L. Ross (eds), *Spiritual Assessment in Health Care Practice*. Keswick: M&K Publishing.

Thompson, R.A. and Randall, B. (1999) A standard of living adequate for children's spiritual development. In A.B. Andrews and N. Kaufman (eds), *Implementing the U.N. Convention on the Rights of the Child: A Standard of Living Adequate for Development*. Westcott, Ct.: Praeger Publishers.

Van Dyke, C.J. and Elias, M.J. (2007) How forgiveness, purpose, and religiosity are related to the mental health and well-being of youth: A review of the literature, *Mental Health, Religion and Culture*, 10(4): 3595–3415.

Vygotsky, L.S. (1978) *Mind and Society: The Development of Higher Psychological Processes*. Cambridge, MA: Harvard University Press.

Wagener, L.M. and Malony, H.N. (2005) Spiritual and religious pathology in childhood. In E.C. Roehlkepartain, P.E. King, P. Wagener and P.L. Benson (eds), *The Handbook of Spiritual Development in Childhood and Adolescence*. Thousand Oaks, CA: Sage.

Wallace Jr., J.M. and Forman, T.A. (1998) Religion's role in promoting health and reducing risk among American youth, *Health Education & Behavior*, 25(6): 721–741.

Weathers, E., McCarthy, G. and Coffey, A. (2016) Concept analysis of spirituality: An evolutionary approach, *Nursing Forum*, 51(2): 79–96.

Witmer, J.M. and Young, M.E. (1985) The silent partner: Uses of imagery in counseling, *Journal of Counseling & Development*, 64(3): 187–190.

Youniss, J., McLellan, J.A. and Yates, M. (1999) Religion, community service and identity in American youth, *Journal of Adolescence*, 22(2): 243–253.

PART II

Specific developmental issues

This second part of the book introduces specific issues that are commonly considered in traditional discussions of human growth and development. However, these are focused on children and young people and make specific connections with social work practice so you can understand how knowledge and theory is applied. Each chapter will focus on one particular developmental area and question the application of the models and understandings, many of which we have introduced in Part I, and bring in a critical edge to the discussion. It is important that you grapple with critical questioning because you will come across a range of different interpretations from other social workers, other professionals and those people you work with. You need to develop confidence in knowing what you think, but also why.

Chapter authors come from different backgrounds in social work and the police and report on work in Germany, the UK and aspects of South East Asia, which is important as this provides you with opportunities to consider complexity and diversity in thinking and application of theories and models. Each chapter author will offer their own specific approach to the subject area and thus there will be some repetition where theories, models and understandings overlap. You should expect this and use it to make links across the various chapters in the book, although pointers will be made to help you within the chapters.

Part II objectives

- develop a critical understanding of some of the models and underpinning theories used in contemporary social work;

- how to apply complex and diverse theories and models to practice;

- how to analyse practice situations and best support children and young people in difficult circumstances, including crime, loss and bereavement;

- develop culturally appropriate ways of understanding, using and practising with theories and models in social work with children and young people.

Knowledge of the theoretical outlines provided in Part I will help you to read and understand the authors' approach to the field being discussed. The part opens with a consideration of attachment theory (included here rather than in Part I because of its particular focus on practice settings in social work and because it is employed so widely), which then leads directly into a discussion of the complexities of being a young person today, with its array of experiences and obstacles to negotiate, crime and criminality, loss and bereavement and negotiating transitions focusing on Muslim communities in the UK. All issues you will come into contact with as a student of social work.

These specific issues then lead us to Part III of the book, which concerns professional social work practice.

7

An introduction to the principles of attachment theory

Gabriele Schäfer

Introduction

Social connections with others are critical to the survival of our species (Reagan, 2011). According to Reagan (2011), it is not surprising that we come into this world biologically 'ready' to form relationships. She explains that if we assume normal gestation and prenatal development, all babies are born with a set of (unlearned) biological endowments that allow and facilitate relationship formation and social relationships. An important biological foundation is the attachment system. John Bowlby (1951, 1958, 1969, 1973, 1977, 1988, 1991) originally introduced the evolutionary concept of attachment. Bowlby's belief that attachment is a fundamental and integral part of human nature was influenced by a number of different theories and research.

Chapter objectives

- outline the development of attachment theories, including the work of John Bowlby, concerning the four phases of growth of attachment, and Mary Ainsworth's work on the Strange Situation Procedure;

- describe Reactive Attachment Disorder;

- explore the role of the child's temperament since there are complex interconnections between temperament and attachment processes.

The development of attachment theory

It is worth spending some time considering some of the central thinkers who developed attachment theory. In this section, we will focus on the initial research of John Bowlby.

Edward John Mostyn Bowlby was a British psychologist, psychiatrist and trained psychoanalyst who engaged in pioneering work in child development.

He developed attachment theory, which remains one of the most influential developmental theories. According to Bretherton (1992), the basic concepts that currently influence attachment theory have a long developmental history. Although Bowlby was influenced by psychoanalytic theory, he disagreed with the psychoanalytic assumption that infants' responses relate to their internal fantasy life rather than events in real life (Bretherton, 2009). As Bowlby developed his thinking, he examined case studies on disturbed children and those who offended and, together with other clinicians, he began to document the harmful effects of institutional foster care and other disruptions on family life (see Reagan, 2011). In 1951, he published his monograph for the World Health Organization, *Maternal Care and Mental Health*, in which he claimed that infants and young children should experience intimate and continuous relationship with their mother. This is perhaps something that would now be criticised for being so specific about gender, as we will see later. Since Bowlby stressed the importance of the mother–child relationship, his critics have claimed that the mother is usually seen as uncaring if the child is not closely attached. This may be viewed as evidently problematic and can lead to mother-blaming. However, the impact of his and other clinicians' research and observations showed the fundamental importance of the parent–child relationship and demonstrated that the quality of this relationship influenced the life of a person far beyond infancy. It is this parent–child or significant-adult-to-child relationship that we now emphasise (Reagan, 2011).

Apart from psychoanalysis, developmental psychology and clinical empirical studies on attachment processes, Bowlby was also influenced by ethological research and thought – the study of animal behaviour (Bretherton, 1992). In the 1950s, he learned about Konrad Lorenz's theorisation of 'imprinting', and was very impressed with this work. Imprinting is a characteristic of some birds and mammals and involves fast learning of recognition by the young, of a specific, or comparable, object (Bretherton, 2009). However, Bowlby did not apply the concept of imprinting in its entirety to human attachment.

At around the same time, Bowlby became interested in the research on affectional responses in monkeys, drawing on experiments where inanimate surrogate mothers were presented to rhesus monkey infants and their attachment processes were observed (Harlow, 1958). The research showed that infant monkeys preferred soft-clothed surrogate mothers who provided no food to hard-wire-covered surrogate mothers who offered food. This preference was especially accentuated when the infant monkeys were confronted with stressful situations (see Gerrig, 2015). Applied to human beings, this research suggested that close physical contact and felt security may be essential components of the parent–child relationship (Reagan, 2011). Through these ethological studies, Bowlby came to the innovative idea that mechanisms underlying an infant's emotional tie to the caregiver(s) were the result of evolutionary pressure (see Reagan, 2011).

Bowlby's clinical experience and careful analysis of different schools of thought, such as psychoanalysis, developmental psychology and ethology, led him to the understanding that, to grow up mentally healthy, 'the infant and young child should experience a warm, intimate, and continuous relationship with their mother (or permanent mother substitute) in which both find satisfaction and enjoyment' (Bowlby, 1951, p 13).

Children who form an attachment to an adult, especially the first six months of life, are more likely to survive (Lamb and Lewis, 2011, p 265). In the unfortunate case that there is no consistent caretaker over this critical period, the infant may not form an attachment. Bowlby (1969; see Kail and Cavanaugh, 2007 for an overview) outlines four phases of growth of attachment:

1. *Pre-attachment* (birth to six weeks): An infant's inborn signals, such as crying and cooing, elicit close proximity with their caregiver. Babies recognise a caregiver's voice and are comforted by parental behaviours such as holding the child or smiling at the child. Through these processes, the beginnings of attachment are forming.
2. *Attachment-in-the-making* (six weeks to eight months): During this stage, attachment is getting stronger and the infant responds differently to familiar caregivers than to strangers. Babies smile and laugh more often with their caregiver and when they get upset it is easier for their caregiver to comfort them.
3. *True attachment* (six to 18 months): By approximately seven or eight months, children have learned to recognise the attachment figures in their lives. Children generally would choose to be with their preferred attachment figures and experience separation anxiety in the caregiver's absence. Caregivers usually attempt to strengthen attachment patterns with their children by being receptive to their needs for attention and fulfilling basic needs.
4. *Formation of reciprocal attachment* (18 months on): Rapid cognitive and language growth facilitates the child's understanding of parental behaviours and attachment patterns. They recognise that they can initiate interactions by negotiating with their caregivers. They also cope better with separations because they have learned that parents will return. At this stage, parents can help a child to develop secure attachment by being present as much as they can and, of course, by continuing to meet the child's basic needs in a sensitive way.

In *Attachment* (1969), Bowlby began to address the problem raised by stressing the infant's connection to its mother. He recognised that the primary attachment was not always the mother, and he began to use the term 'mother-figure' instead. He perceived that the tie between a 'mother-figure' and her or his child was rooted in instinct (see Parkes, 2006). This notion retained a gendered perspective and can be seen as being influenced by the social position of males and females in society at that time, although it has led to serious criticism of both Bowlby and the concept of attachment.

Attachments as working models of self and others

Developmental psychologists have asked why the quality of early attachments is often stable over time and which parental behaviours determine the quality of attachment. It can be observed that if babies have dependable and caring parents, they usually develop trust. They learn that they can rely on the parents in times of stress or difficulty. In a longitudinal study, babies were more likely to develop secure attachments at 12 months of age when their parents responded quickly and sensitively to their infant at three months (Cox et al, 1992; Kail and Cavanaugh, 2007).

Bowlby (1982, 1988) emphasises that children try to make sense out of their experiences and in that process form models and ideas about who they are. Children also conclude who their parents are based on the way they react to them; so the person showing warmth and affection and dependability is sensed as the parent-figure.

According to Main and her colleagues (1985), a child's internal working model is developed in reaction to their experience of the results of their proximity-seeking behaviours. Accepting and nurturing caregivers who respond adequately to these proximity-seeking behaviours and offer access allow children to develop a secure attachment style, whereas caregivers who consistently deny the infant love and care will have a child with an avoidant attachment style (Main et al, 1985). If the caregiver inconsistently offers access, an ambivalent attachment style develops.

As children grow up, their internal working models continue to develop (Main et al, 1985). These internal working models become more complex when children get older because they have better understanding of themselves and others. This has consequences for peer relationships and school success. Research with grade-school students indicates that children who have developed negative self-representations receive lower grades as adolescents than those children with positive working models (Jacobson and Hofmann, 1997). According to Rudolph et al (1995), they also experience negative representations of peers and are frequently rather unpopular with them. Since these internal working models are so essential to us and all of our social interactions, Bowlby thinks they should be the main focus of every therapeutic process (Fremmer-Bombik, 2009).

Fremmer-Bombik (1987) reports that it is possible to work through negative childhood experiences – even with a history of severe parental rejection. She conducted a study with mothers who were able to react openly and reflectively to their negative experiences and were able to develop secure attachments with their children. An example may help here. A child who receives warmth, physical affection and verbal praise in the early years of life is likely to have a secure base from which they can develop and extend their understanding and experience of the world around them and not to feel too hurt when they receive negative reactions from others as they grow older. They have an established base to refer back to. However, if they had only received cold and not affectionate responses from their significant parent-figure in early life, they may not have the internalised confidence to see there are securities in life which can be fallen back on when needed.

Mary Ainsworth

Mary Dinsmore Ainsworth was a developmental psychologist who was known for her work in the development of attachment theory (see Bretherton, 1992). During their early careers, Bowlby and Ainsworth worked independently of each other. Nevertheless, they were both influenced by Freud and other psychoanalytic thinkers – in Bowlby's case, especially Melanie Klein (for more on Klein's approach, see Chapter 2 of Part I in this volume). Later, they worked more closely together and Mary Ainsworth's new methodology made it possible to empirically test some of Bowlby's ideas.

Ainsworth obtained a position at the East African Institute of Social Research at Kampala in Uganda. With help from this institute, she was able to observe the development of infant–mother attachment. She recruited 26 families with unweaned babies (aged one to 24 months) and observed these mothers with their infants every two weeks for two hours per visit over a period of up to nine months (see Bretherton, 1992). These visits were accompanied by an interpreter and took place in the mothers' living rooms. Ainsworth's research interest was the onset of proximity-promoting behaviours. Through the observation of the mothers and their children in their own living rooms, she noted carefully when the infant's signals and behaviours became directed towards their mother. The data from this project (Ainsworth, 1963, 1967) provided an interesting source for the study of individual differences in the quality of mother–infant interaction. So, what Ainsworth found was that mothers who were good informants and able to provide a lot of spontaneous detail were rated as highly sensitive compared to other mothers in the sample who seemed to be more imperceptive of the infant's signals. She delineated three infant attachment patterns:

1. Infants that were securely attached cried little and seemed content to explore in the presence of mother.
2. Infants who were insecurely attached cried often, even when their mothers held them. They also explored little.
3. Infants that were not yet attached showed no differential behaviour to their mothers.

Not surprisingly, secure attachment was significantly correlated with maternal sensitivity. Babies who had sensitive mothers tended to be securely attached. Infants who had less sensitive mothers were more likely to be insecurely attached. It was also observed that mothers who enjoyed breast-feeding their babies had babies who were securely attached. These findings prepared the way for her later studies.

However, there has been criticism of this position that different attachment patterns can be understood as equivalent adjustments to different parenting styles and constitute alternative developmental paths (Lamb et al, 1984). Studies indicated that mothers and in general caregivers can behave differently in different cultures and historical contexts within a given culture and society (Grossmann et al, 1985; Miyake et al, 1985; Sagi et al, 1985). This issue will be discussed in more detail later in this chapter, as it is important to note in our globalised and multicultural environments.

After returning from Africa, Ainsworth began the Baltimore project, which was strongly influenced by Bowlby's ideas (Bretherton, 2009). The study provided a naturalistic longitudinal field examination of the development of infant–mother attachment throughout the infant's first year of life. The main goals were to identify behaviours that may be classed together as attachment behaviours and to trace their development. The research also focused on individual differences in the development of attachment behaviour and the organisation of attachment. The research sample consisted of 26 white infant–mother pairs in intact middle-class families from metropolitan Baltimore, Maryland.

Ainsworth et al (1978) examined the narratives revealed in the studies and found that, during the first three months, characteristic mother–infant interaction patterns emerged. Separate data analyses resulted in separate articles on feeding situations (Ainsworth and Bell, 1969), mother–infant face-to-face interaction (Blehar et al, 1977), crying (Bell and Ainsworth, 1972), close bodily contact (Ainsworth et al, 1971), obedience (Stayton et al, 1973), approach behaviour (Tracy et al, 1976), affectionate contact (Tracy and Ainsworth, 1981), and infant greeting and following (Stayton and Ainsworth, 1973).

One of the main research findings referred to differences in how sensitively and readily mothers responded to their infant's needs and signals. Some mothers had problems feeding their infants, while others experienced no problems. Some mothers had problems reacting to their infant's signals, while others were able to adjust to their babies without effort. Babies who had mothers who experienced problems adjusting to them tended to choke, spit up and struggle. In face-to-face interactions between mothers and infants during the first six to 15 weeks, similar patterns were observed (Blehar et al, 1977). Mothers who showed playful behaviours with their infants had babies that responded with smiling, bouncing and vocalising. On the other hand, when mothers had unsmiling expressions in their faces, the responding interactions of their babies were brief and muted (Bretherton, 1992). Bell and Ainsworth reported significant variations in how many crying episodes a mother ignored and how long she let her baby cry. They concluded that 'an infant whose mother's responsiveness helps him to achieve his ends develops confidence in his own ability to control what happens to him' (Bell and Ainsworth, 1972, p 1188).

Patterns of maternal sensitivity in early infanthood were predictive of harmonious mother–infant interactions in later stages (Bell and Ainsworth, 1972). Also, babies with mothers who had provided close and tender holding in early infanthood sought less contact with their mothers later (Ainsworth et al, 1971). This indicates that secure attachments allow children to seek novel experiences and to expand their worlds.

The Strange Situation Procedure

Ainsworth and Wittig (1969) were interested in investigating the topic of individual attachment behaviour. In order to assess differences in attachment, they designed the *Strange Situation Procedure* by evoking an individual's reaction when encountering stressful situations and based on her earlier studies (Ainsworth, 1967; Ainsworth et al, 1978; Lohaus and Vierhaus, 2015). It was developed as a research tool rather than being something designed for diagnosis and practice.

It is highly likely that today the Strange Situation Procedure would be deemed unethical since it exposes children aged between 12 and 18 months to 'strange' or 'unfamiliar' people in an unfamiliar laboratory setting (Ainsworth et al, 1978). It is divided into eight episodes in which the child is separated and reunited with the caregiver. All episodes, apart from the first, last for three minutes and these episodes can be shortened if the child becomes too distressed. In the first episode, which lasts 30 seconds, the infant and their caregiver enter into a laboratory setting, with many toys. In the second episode, the caregiver and the child are left alone for three minutes. After this period, a person unknown to the infant comes into the room and tries to make contact with the child for three minutes (third episode). In the fourth episode, the caregiver leaves the child with the stranger for three minutes, then returns. This episode can end earlier if the child becomes stressed (for instance, starts to cry) (see Lohaus and Vierhaus, 2015). In the fifth episode, the caregiver comes back into the room and greets the child. If necessary, the child is comforted by the caregiver. The stranger leaves the room again. At the end of this period, the caregiver departs for a second time, leaving the child alone for three minutes (sixth episode). This phase is again completed earlier if the child is too distressed. In the seventh episode, it is the stranger who enters. If the child is upset, the stranger offers to comfort the infant. In this phase, the episode may also be interrupted if the infant shows signs of being too upset. In the eighth episode, the caregiver returns, and is instructed to comfort the child. The stranger leaves the room again.

REFLECTION POINT 7.1

What are your immediate thoughts about this study and why do you think it was conducted?

In this experiment, the stress of the infant is increased by increments. The observer can witness the infant's attachment behaviour both in the presence of and in the absence of the parent (Bretherton and Ainsworth, 1974). It is obvious that it is very questionable whether a scientific experiment or psychological assessment can justify putting infants in a potentially stressful situation. Ethical considerations considering the Strange Situation Procedure will be discussed further at the end of this chapter.

Differences in attachment patterns

From the Strange Situation experiment, Ainsworth observed that infants explored the playroom and toys more freely in the presence of their caregivers than they did after a stranger entered or while the caregiver was absent (Ainsworth and Bell, 1970). On the basis of their reunion behaviour in the Strange Situation experiment, infants were categorised into different attachment types (Ainsworth et al, 1978; Parkes, 2006; Lohaus and Vierhaus, 2015), will be detailed.

Secure attachment (Attachment type Code B)

An infant securely attached to their parent (or other familiar caregiver) uses the caregiver as a secure base or a secure haven. They are able to explore the environment freely while the caregiver is present and frequently seeks contact with strangers. If the caregiver leaves, the child is often upset and a stranger is unable to completely comfort the child. On the return of the caregiver into the room, the infant is generally happy to see the caregiver return. Presuming the caregiver's response is helpful, the child experiences a sense of security, in which case a new learning can take place about how to cope with similar problems in the future. For this reason, secure attachment is perceived as the most adaptive attachment style. A child can become securely attached when the parent is available and able to meet the needs of the child in a sensitive and appropriate manner (Lohaus and Vierhaus, 2015). If parents are caring and sensitive towards their children in infancy and early childhood, those children will be more prone to secure attachment (Aronoff, 2012).

Anxious ambivalent attachment (Attachment type Code C)

In a strange situation, a child with an anxious–ambivalent pattern of attachment will generally explore little. At the same time, they are often wary of strangers, even in the presence of the caregiver. The child is frequently very distressed when the caregiver departs the room and reacts ambivalently when they return (Ainsworth et al, 1978). Often, the child cries after the return of the caregiver, even when the caregiver picks up the child in order to offer comfort. The researchers concluded that the anxious-ambivalent behaviour might be a response to caregiving that is characterised by unpredictable and unreliable parental behaviours (see Lohaus and Vierhaus, 2015). McCarthy and Taylor (1999) found in their empirical study that children with abusive childhood experiences were more likely to develop ambivalent attachments. The study also found that children with ambivalent attachments were more likely to experience difficulties in maintaining intimate relationships as adults.

Anxious avoidant or insecure avoidant attachment (Attachment type Code A)

An insecurely avoidant attached infant will generally ignore the caregiver and display very little emotion when the caregiver departs or returns. The infant is not very interested in the room and will not explore very much regardless of who is there. Ainsworth's interpretation showed that infants avoided the caregiver in the stressful Strange Situation experiment when they had a history of experiencing rejection of attachment behaviour. The infant had learned over time that their needs were often not met and had come to believe that signals of emotional needs had no or little influence on the caregiver (see Sroufe et al, 2005).

Mary Main, a student of Ainsworth, thought that insecure avoidant behaviour in the Strange Situation experiment should be regarded as a sort of paradoxical strategy that makes it impossible for the infant to seek proximity with the caregiver through not displaying attachment needs towards the caregiver. Unfortunately, this behaviour prohibits closeness to be possible with the primary caregiver. She suggested that this particular attachment behaviour has two functions for an infant:

- Avoidant behaviour allows the infant to maintain a close enough conditional proximity with the caregiver to maintain a certain amount of protection, but distant enough to avoid rejection.
- The cognitive processes that organise avoidant behaviour could direct attention away from the unfulfilled needs for proximity with the primary caregiver. In this way, the infant avoids the painful situation of being overwhelmed with emotion and as a result being unable to maintain control of themselves (Main, 1977).

Disorganised/disoriented attachment (Attachment type Code D)

A number of children showed contradictory behaviours in Ainsworth's Baltimore study and the Strange Situation Procedure. She and her colleagues (1978) observed strange behaviours in the infants, such as jerky or misdirected movements, freezing and apparent dissociation. Main and Solomon (1990) drew on records of behaviours that were discrepant with the prior three classifications. As a result of their analysis, they added a fourth classification, which they called disorganised/disoriented attachment. In 1990, Ainsworth (1990) introduced this new category, but urged that it should be used in a differentiated way in order to avoid subsuming the same forms of behaviour as if they were the same thing. This new category evoked much interest from researchers, policymakers and clinicians and some fear was expressed that this category was too encompassing. Crittenden (1999) points out that some behaviour in this category could be understood as more 'emergency' versions of behaviours of the avoidant and/or ambivalent/resistant behavioural strategies. He assumes that they might to some degree function to maintain the protective availability of the caregiver. Sroufe and his colleagues also stress that 'even disorganised attachment behaviour (simultaneous approach–avoidance; freezing, etc.) enables a degree of proximity in the face of a frightening or unfathomable parent' (Sroufe et al, 2005, p 245). However, often, children who are classified in this category have problematic interaction experiences with their caregivers, such as abuse (see Lohaus and Vierhaus, 2015).

Let us examine your understanding of these attachment types by considering Case Studies 7.1 and 7.2.

CASE STUDY 7.1

Oliver is aged 45. He is unemployed and lives with his wife, Susan, who is 42, his seven-year-old son Ben and 15-year-old daughter Amy. The family stay in a two-bedroom council flat in Manchester. Oliver is known to the police and social services for domestic violence towards his wife. Susan suffers from depression and frequently drinks too much alcohol. Their daughter Amy is withdrawn and has been caught shoplifting on several occasions. Ben is very aggressive towards other children in his school and wets his bed from time to time. The grandparents on both sides are living in London and have very little contact with the family.

Questions

1. Using the assessment types that we have considered, can you offer some explanations for both Ben's and Amy's current behaviour?
2. Do you think their current behaviours might be mitigated or altered by a change in their attachment experiences?
3. Who else might you be working with in this situation and how do you think knowledge of attachment theories may help you in this?

CASE STUDY 7.2

Joshua is ten years old and lives with his father, James. Joshua's mother, Anna, died when he was eight years old. He had a very close bond with her and suffered greatly following her death. He withdrew from his friends and his schoolwork suffered. James owns a travel agency and employed different nannies to look after Joshua. James travels a lot because of work commitments and he does not see his son very often. James did not know how to help his son through the loss of his mother and threw himself into his work. The death of his wife was very painful for James, who removed all the pictures of her from his house to help cope with the loss. Joshua does not understand why his father did this. The relationship between the two is distant. Joshua's grandmother, Mary, on his mother's side, is an important figure in Joshua's life and they are close. They see each other regularly because she lives in the same city quarter. The other grandparents are no longer alive.

Questions

1. How might you work with James to develop his attachment to Joshua and how might an understanding of attachment theory help you as a social worker to do this?
2. What contribution might the school make to your assessment of the situation?
3. Why might an understanding of attachment theory be helpful to Joshua's teachers?

Discussion

These two case studies illuminate some of the complexities that arise in the behaviours of children and young people when they have experienced problems with early attachments or have lost an immediate attachment figure. They show that, for social workers, these theories help to show what may have led to current behaviours, but also what might be needed to reinforce positive attachments from now on. Of course, early attachment is noted as central in one's development. However, later experiences can also be useful in adapting more helpful behaviours and providing the security a child or young person needs to explore the world in a healthy and positive way.

Of course, it is not only social workers who need a grounding in attachment theory. The teachers, health workers and police involved in these cases would all benefit from understanding the possible implications of poor attachment behaviours and seek to intervene to change this. Knowing the theories and research as a social worker will help give you credibility in working with other professionals – a lens through which you can begin to assess the situation you are working with and knowledge of what might assist in creating change.

Reactive attachment disorder

It is important to consider an atypical attachment pattern called 'reactive attachment disorder' (RAD), which is considered to be a psychological disorder within the two standard manuals of Mental Disorders. The *Diagnostic and Statistical Manual of Mental Disorders* (DSM 5) is published by the American Psychiatric Association. It is used by mental health professionals to diagnose mental conditions and by insurance companies to reimburse for treatment. The ICD-10 is the tenth revision of the International Statistical Classification of Diseases and Related Health Problems (ICD). It contains codes for diseases, signs and symptoms, abnormal findings, complaints, social circumstances, and external causes of injury or diseases. While there are questions raised by social workers and other professionals of the medicalisation of many of these conditions, RAD is listed in both manuals using the codes ICD-10 F94.1/2 and DSM 5, F 94.1 and it is suggested that it has to be distinguished from disorganised attachment. This code identifies any associated failure to thrive or growth delay, and the main characteristic of this disorder is a markedly disturbed and developmentally inappropriate social relatedness in most contexts (DSM 5, S. 362).

The DSM 5 gives the following criteria for RAD:

A. A consistent pattern of inhibited, emotionally withdrawn behaviour toward adult caregivers, manifested by both of the following:
- The child rarely or minimally seeks comfort when distressed.
- The child rarely or minimally responds to comfort when distressed.

B. A persistent social or emotional disturbance characterised by at least two of the following:
- Minimal social and emotional responsiveness to others
- Limited positive affect
- Episodes of unexplained irritability, sadness, or fearfulness that is evident even during nonthreatening interactions with adult caregivers.

C. The child has experienced a pattern of extremes of insufficient care as evidenced by at least one of the following:
- Social neglect or deprivation in the form of persistent lack of having basic emotional needs for comfort, stimulation, and affection met by caring adults
- Repeated changes of primary caregivers that limit opportunities to form stable attachments (e.g., frequent changes in foster care)
- Rearing in unusual settings that severely limit opportunities to form selective attachments (e.g., institutions with high child to caregiver ratios).

D. The care in Criterion C is presumed to be responsible for the disturbed behaviour in Criterion A (e.g., the disturbances in Criterion A began following the lack of adequate care in Criterion C).

E. The criteria are not met for autism spectrum disorder.

F. The disturbance is evident before age five years.

G. The child has a developmental age of at least nine months.

Specify if persistent: The disorder has been present for more than 12 months.

Specify current severity: Reactive Attachment Disorder is specified as severe when a child exhibits all symptoms of the disorder, with each symptom manifesting at relatively high levels.

REFLECTION POINT 7.2

Do you think that including reactive attachment disorder in these psychiatric manuals is useful for social workers?

According to Prior and Glaser (2006), RAD arises from a failure to form normal attachments to primary caregivers in early childhood. This kind of failure could result from very severe early experiences of abuse and neglect, as well as abrupt separation of children from caregivers while children are aged between six months and three years. A lack of caregiver responsiveness to the attempts of the child to communicate with the caregiver, or frequent change of caregivers, could also cause or contribute to this disorder. However, not all (or even a majority of) such experiences can cause the disorder. It is useful to know how other professionals might view certain forms of attachment experience and to be able to negotiate through these, even if you believe rather that the social experiences are interpreted differently by individuals according to a whole range of factors.

Temperament and attachment

In psychological theory, attachment and temperament are separate developmental concepts. However, aspects of these concepts contribute to a range of intrapersonal and interpersonal developmental results (Vaughn et al, 2008). Infant temperament refers to stable individual differences in the quality and intensity of emotional reactions in emotional self-regulation, as well as in the activity level of attention (Elsner and Pauen, 2012). Kagan (1997) conducted empirical research on a temperamental category termed 'reactivity'. This related to four-month-old children who became motorically aroused and distressed (showing signs of agitated physical movement) when exposed to presentations of novel stimuli (labelled as highly reactive), and children who remained motorically relaxed (showing no distressed movement) and did not cry or react in a distressed way to the same number of unfamiliar events (termed low reactive). In longitudinal studies (those taking place over time), he was able to confirm the relative stability of these two categories. Highly reactive infants were predominantly characterised by a profile of high fear to unfamiliar events, which Kagan termed 'inhibited'. Approximately one-third of highly reactive babies were still fearful when they reached two years of age and still showed introverted and negative behaviour when they were four-and-a-half years old. These children also experienced more adjustment problems as adolescents (such as school problems, delinquent behaviour and depression; Elsner and Pauen, 2012). In contrast to this pattern, low reactive children displayed minimal fearfulness to novel situations, and were characterised by an uninhibited profile (Kagan, 1997).

Not surprisingly, parents might react with more stress to 'difficult' children who show highly reactive responses to novel situations and are easily irritated. If children pick up from this that parents are more rejecting to their attachment needs, a cycle could develop that reinforces reactivity and rejection in the parent–child relationship. According to Marshall and Fox (2005), a particular type of child temperament can make some infants more susceptible to the stress of hostile or unpredictable relationships with caregivers in the early years. However, it seems that some children are particularly vulnerable to developing attachment disorders when there is an absence of responsive and available caregivers (Prior and Glaser, 2006). Spangler (2009) conducted a review of the literature on the role of child behavioural dispositions for their attachment development. He concluded that aspects of individual behavioural dispositions or aspects of temperament play – parallel to social processes – a role for individual differences in attachment quality.

We can conclude from the research that there are complex interconnections between temperament and attachment processes that are not yet fully understood, but certainly influence both the child's and their caregiver's attachment behaviour. These are important considerations to bear in mind as social workers when working with children and families.

Conclusion

Attachment is one of the most studied developmental processes of psychology. Secure attachment is an essential factor for the healthy physical, psychological and social development of a child. Therefore, it has central importance for you as a social worker in understanding and working with children and young people. The majority of children grow and develop within a complex network of attachment figures. Some of these attachment figures are enduring, while others change with time and circumstances (Howes and Spieker, 2016). Bowlby's and Ainsworth's studies on attachment have provided us with an understanding of how important early infant–caregiver relationships are. Attachment theory explains babies' behaviour towards their primary caregiver (usually the mother) during separation and reunion times. In summary, it is safe to say that attachment theory has inspired a huge body of empirical research and numerous practical applications in the field of psychology and many health professions. These applications will be discussed in respect of adults in Chapter 6 in Part II of the companion volume. Attachment theory offers a broad, far-reaching view of how humans develop affectional bonds with each other and which processes can interfere with this complex process. Being aware of these theories allows social workers to work with families to change attachment and affectional styles to foster enhanced relationships. What social workers need to know is summarised overleaf.

- Bowlby (1951) explains that infants and young children should experience warm, intimate and continuous relationships with their mothers, so that both can find satisfaction and enjoyment in their relationship. The lack of a nurturing infant–caregiver relationship may have significant and irreversible mental health consequences.
- Infants develop an internal working model, which is a set of expectations about parents' availability and responsiveness. Children try to make sense of their experience and in that process form models and ideas about who they are. They also conclude who their parents are based on the degree of their sensitivity and responsiveness towards them.
- Ainsworth's Strange Situation Procedure has revealed four attachment classifications: secure attachment, anxious ambivalent attachment, anxious avoidant or insecure avoidant attachment and disorganised/disoriented attachment.
- Reactive attachment disorder (RAD) arises from a failure to develop normal attachments to primary caregivers in early childhood. This kind of attachment disorder could result from very severe early experiences of neglect and abuse. Abrupt separation of children from caregivers while children are aged between six months and three years could also cause RAD.
- Both infant attachment behaviour and temperament may influence the quality of attachment, as they affect caregiver–infant interactions and relationships. There are complex correlations between attachment behaviour and temperament. It is certainly overstated that attachment is only a reflection of the child's temperament.

Reflective questions

1 What are the key points of attachment theory?

2 What do you think about the Strange Situation Procedure?

3 Describe a situation where your attachment needs were (a) met (that is, you were loved, accepted and included) and (b) not met (that is, you were rejected, excluded or ignored). How did the two situations make you feel? Compare your emotional and cognitive responses to the two situations.

4 How do you believe individual temperament and gender impacts on attachment behaviour?

Further reading

- Ainsworth, M.D.S. and Wittig, B.A. (1969) Attachment and the exploratory behavior of one-year-olds in a strange situation. In B.M. Foss (ed.), *Determinants of Infant Behavior* (Vol. 5). London: Methuen.

  Reading the original research that led to major developments in understanding attachment and bonding will help inform your professional literacy. This is important and often noticed, or otherwise, by other professionals, such as solicitors, judges and health professionals. So, reading this chapter will help embed your status as a social worker.

- Bowlby, J. (1969) *Attachment and Loss*, Vol. 1: *Attachment*. New York, NY: Basic Books.
- Bowlby, J. (1973) *Separation: Anxiety & Anger*, Vol. 2: *Attachment and Loss*. London: Hogarth Press.

  The two books by Bowlby provide the most comprehensive and original aspects of attachment theory. They are seminal texts – ones that have exerted a great deal of influence on the field – and as such should be read by you during your education to be a social worker.

References

Ainsworth, M.D.S. (1963) The development of infant–mother interaction among the Ganda. In B.M. Foss (ed.), *Determinants of Infant Behavior*. New York, NY: John Wiley & Sons.

Ainsworth, M.D.S. (1967) *Infancy in Uganda: Infant Care and the Growth of Love*. Baltimore, MD: Johns Hopkins University Press.

Ainsworth, M.D.S. (1990) Epilogue. In M.T. Greenberg, D. Ciccheti and E.M. Cummings (eds), *Attachment in the Preschool Years: Theory, Research, and Intervention*. Chicago, IL: Chicago University Press.

Ainsworth, M.D.S. and Bell, S.M. (1969) Some contemporary patterns in the feeding situation. In A. Ambrose (ed.), *Stimulation in Early Infancy*. London: Academic Press.

Ainsworth, M.D.S. and Bell, S.M. (1970) Attachment, exploration, and separation: Illustrated by the behaviour of one-year-olds in a strange situation, *Child Development*, 41(1): 49–67.

Ainsworth, M.D.S., Bell, S.M., Blehar, M.C. and Main, M. (1971) Physical contact: A study of infant responsiveness and its relation to maternal handling. Paper presented at the biennial meeting of the Society for Research in Child Development. April. Minneapolis, MN.

Ainsworth, M.D.S., Blehar, M., Waters, E. and Wall, S. (1978) *Patterns of Attachment*. Hillsdale, NJ: Erlbaum.

Ainsworth, M.D.S. and Wittig, B.A. (1969) Attachment and the exploratory behavior of one-year-olds in a strange situation. In B.M. Foss (ed.), *Determinants of Infant Behavior* (Vol. 5). London: Methuen.

Aronoff, J. (2012) Parental nurturance in the standard cross-cultural sample: Theory, coding, and scores, *Cross-Cultural Research*, 46(4): 315–347.

Bell, S.M. and Ainsworth, M.D.S. (1972) Infant crying and maternal responsiveness, *Child Development*, 43(4): 1171–1190.

Blehar, M.C., Lieberman, A.F. and Ainsworth, M.D.S. (1977) Early face-to-face interaction and its relation to later infant–mother attachment, *Child Development*, 48: 182–194.

Bowlby J. (1951) *Maternal Care and Mental Health*. Geneva: World Health Organization. Monograph Series, No. 2, 19–52 and 107–127.

Bowlby, J. (1958) The nature of the child's tie to his mother, *International Journal of Psycho-Analysis*, XXXIX: 1–23.

Bowlby, J. (1969) *Attachment and Loss*, Vol. 1: *Attachment*. New York, NY: Basic Books.

Bowlby, J. (1973) *Separation: Anxiety & Anger*, Vol. 2: *Attachment and Loss*. London: Hogarth Press.

Bowlby, J. (1977) The making and breaking of affectional bonds: I. Etiology and psychopathology in the light of attachment theory, *British Journal of Psychiatry*, 130: 201–210.

Bowlby, J. (1982) *Attachment* (2nd edn). New York, NY: Basic Books (original work published in 1969).

Bowlby, J. (1988) *A Secure Base: Parent–Child Attachment and Healthy Human Development*. London: Routledge.

Bowlby, J. (1991) Ethological light on a psychoanalytical problem. In P.P.G. Bateson (ed.), *The Development and Integration of Behavior: Essays in Honor of Robert Hide*. Cambridge: Cambridge University Press.

Bretherton, I. (1992) The origins of attachment theory: John Bowlby and Mary Ainsworth, *Developmental Psychology*, 28(5): 759–775.

Bretherton, I. (2009) Die Geschichte der Bindungstheorie. In G. Spangler and P. Zimmermann (eds), *Die Bindungstheorie: Grundlagen, Forschung und Anwendung* (5th edn). Stuttgart: Klett Cotta.

Bretherton, I. and Ainsworth, M.D.S. (1974) One-year-olds in the strange situation. In M. Lewis and L. Rosenblum (eds), *The Origins of Fear*. New York, NY: John Wiley & Sons.

Cox, M.J., Owen, M.T., Henderson, V.K. and Margand, N.A. (1992) Prediction of infant–father and infant–mother attachment, *Developmental Psychology*, 28(3): 474–483.

Crittenden, P. (1999) Danger and development: The organisation of self-protective strategies. In J.I. Vondra and B. Douglas (eds), *Atypical Attachment in Infancy and Early Childhood among Children at Developmental Risk*. Oxford: Blackwell.

Diagnostisches und Statistisches Manual Psychischer Störungen DSM-5 (*Diagnostic and Statistical Manual of Mental Disorders* (DSM V)) (2015) (German edn). Göttingen: Hogrefe.

Elsner, B. and Pauen, S. (2012) Vorgeburtliche Entwicklung und früheste Kindheit (0–2 Jahr). In W. Schneider and W. Lindenberger (eds), *Entwicklungspsychologie* (7th edn). Basel: Beltz.

Fremmer-Bombik, E. (1987) Beobachtungen zur Bindungsqualität im zweiten Lebensjahr und ihre Bedeutung im Lichte mütterlicher Kindheitserinnerungen. PhD thesis, University of Regensburg.

Fremmer-Bombik, E. (2009) Innere Arbeitsmodelle von Bindung. In G. Spangler and P. Zimmermann (eds), *Die Bindungstheorie: Grundlagen, Forschung und Anwendung*. Stuttgart: Clett Kotta.

Gerrig, R.J. (2015) *Psychologie*. Munich: Pearson.

Grossmann, K., Grossmann, K.E., Spangler, G., Suess, G. and Unzner, L. (1985) Maternal sensitivity and newborns' orientation responses as related to quality of attachment in Northern Germany. In I. Bretherton and E. Waters (eds), *Growing Points of Attachment Theory and Research, Monographs of the Society for Research in Child Development*, 50 (No. 1–2, Serial No. 209). Chicago, IL: University of Chicago Press.

Harlow, H. (1958) The nature of love, *American Psychologist*, 13: 573–685.

Howes, C. and Spieker, S. (2016) Attachment relationships in the context of multiple caregivers. In J. Cassidy and P.R. Shaver (eds), *Handbook of Attachment: Theory, Research, and Clinical Applications*. New York, NY: Guilford Press.

International Classification of Diseases, Tenth Revision (ICD-10). English Version.

Jacobson, T. and Hofmann, V. (1997) Children's attachment representatives: Longitudinal relations to school behavior and academic competency in middle childhood and adolescents, *Developmental Psychology*, 33(4): 703–710.

Kagan, J. (1997) Temperament and the reactions to unfamiliarity, *Child Development*, 68(1): 139–143.

Kail, R.V. and Cavanaugh, J.C. (2007) *Human Development: A Life-Span View*. Belmont, CA: Thompson.

Lamb, M.E. and Lewis, C. (2011) The role of parent–child relationships in child development. In M.E. Lamb and M.H. Bornstein (eds), *Social and Personality Development: An Advanced Textbook*. New York, NY: Psychology Press.

Lamb, M.E., Thomson, R.A., Gardner, W.P., Charnov, E.L. and Estes, D. (1984) Security of infantile attachment as assessed in the 'strange situation', *Behavioural and Brain Sciences*, 7: 121–171.

Lohaus, A. and Vierhaus, M. (2015) *Entwicklungspsychologie des Kinder und Jugendalters für Bachelor* (3rd edn). Berlin: Springer.

Main, M. (1977) Analysis of a peculiar form of reunion behavior seen in some day-care children. In R. Webb (ed.), *Social Development in Childhood*. Baltimore, MD: Johns Hopkins University Press.

Main, M., Kaplan, N. and Cassidy, J. (1985) Security in infancy, childhood, and adulthood: A move to the level of representation. In I. Bretherton and E. Waters (eds), *Growing Points of Attachment Theory and Research, Monographs of the Society for Research in Child Development*, 50 (No. 1–2, Serial No. 209). Chicago, IL: University of Chicago Press.

Main, M. and Solomon, J. (1990) Procedures for identifying infants as disorganized/disoriented during the Ainsworth Strange Situation. In M.T. Greenberg, D. Cicchetti and E.M. Cummings (eds), *Attachment in the Preschool Years: Theory, Research, and Intervention*. Chicago, IL: University of Chicago Press.

Marshall, P.J. and Fox, N.A. (2005) Relationship between behavioral reactivity at 4 months and attachment classification at 14 months in a selected sample, *Infant Behavior and Development*, 28(4): 492–502.

McCarthy, G., and Taylor, A. (1999) Avoidant/ambivalent attachment style as a mediator between abusive childhood experiences and adult relationship difficulties, *Journal of Child Psychology and Psychiatry*, 40(3): 465–477.

Miyake, K., Chen, S. and Campos, J.J. (1985) Infants' temperament, mothers' mode of interaction and attachment in Japan: An interim report. In I. Bretherton and F. Waters (eds), *Growing Points of Attachment Theory and Research, Monographs of the Society for Research in Child Development*, 50 (No. 1–2, Serial No. 209). Chicago, IL: University of Chicago Press.

Parkes, C.M. (2006) *Love and Loss: The Roots of Grief and Its Complications*. London: Routledge.

Prior, V. and Glaser, D. (2006) The nature of attachment disorder. In V. Prior and D. Glaser (eds), *Understanding Attachment and Attachment Disorders: Theory, Practice and Evidence*. London: Jessica Kingsley.

Reagan, P. (2011) *Close Relationships*. New York, NY: Routledge.

Rudolph, K.D., Hammen, C. and Burge, D. (1995) Cognitive representations of self, family, and peers in school children: Links with social competence and sociometric status, *Child Development*, 66(5): 1385–1402.

Sagi, A., Lamb, M.E., Lewkowics, K.S., Shoham, R., Dvir, R. and Estes, D. (1985) Security of infant–mother, –father, and metaplet attachment among kibbutz-reared children in Israeli children. In I. Bretherton and E. Waters (eds), *Growing Points of Attachment Theory and Research, Monographs of the Society of Research in Child Development*, 50 (No. 1–2, Serial No. 209). Chicago, IL: University of Chicago Press.

Spangler, G. (2009) Die Rolle kindlicher Verhaltensdispositionen für die Bindungsentwicklung. In G. Spangler and P. Zimmermann (eds), *Die Bindungstheorie: Grundlagen, Forschung und Anwendung*. Stuttgart: Clett Kotta.

Sroufe, A., Egeland, B., Carlson, E. and Collins, W.A. (2005) *The Development of the Person: The Minnesota Study of Risk and Adaptation from Birth to Adulthood*. New York, NY: Guilford Press.

Stayton, D. and Ainsworth, M.D.S. (1973) Development of separation behavior in the first year of life, *Developmental Psychology*, 9(2): 226–235.

Stayton, D., Hogan, R. and Ainsworth, M.D.S. (1973) Infant obedience and maternal behavior: The origins of socialization reconsidered, *Child Development*, 42: 1057–1070.

Tracy, R.L. and Ainsworth, M.D.S. (1981) Maternal affectionate behavior and infant–mother attachment patterns, *Child Development*, 52(4): 1341–1343.

Tracy, R.L., Lamb, M.E. and Ainsworth, M.D.S. (1976) Infant approach behavior as related to attachment, *Child Development*, 47: 511–578.

Vaughn, B.E., Bost, K.K. and Van Ijzendoorn, M.H. (2008) Attachment and temperament. In J. Cassidy and P.R. Shaver (eds), *Handbook of Attachment: Theory, Research and Clinical Applications*. New York, NY and London: Guilford Press.

8

Young people's transition to adulthood

Nick Frost and Melanie Watts

Introduction

The primary objective of this chapter is to explore the challenges facing young people in the modern world. Modern life is complex and demanding. The transitions that young people experienced previously have changed considerably and this chapter addresses some of the challenges that raises for young people and for social workers working with them. Making successful transitions into adulthood is important to establishing a secure and positive future. Much of what we say in this chapter can be used to underpin the other practice areas dealt with in this volume and to provide potential understanding for social workers. We draw on social theory, research and data to explore the issues around the transition from young person to adult.

Chapter objectives

- explore the transition from young person to adult in contemporary societies;
- analyse the role of families and alternative contexts;
- examine the significance of gender, sex and sexuality;
- explore the role of friends and relationships in this transition;
- understand the impact of living in a connected world;
- explore the challenges for the mental health and well-being of young people.

Background and context

This chapter explores the transition from 'young person' to 'adult' status in contemporary Western societies. We argue that being a modern young person is complex – the growth of individualism and neo-liberal forms of governance have placed a significant burden on young people. Neo-liberalism is an approach to understanding and acting in the world that prioritises the role of the market and places the emphasis on the individual person ensuring that they are self-sustaining and successful. This contrasts to socialist or social democratic ways of seeing the world, where there is more focus on the group and the collective.

As a result of the predominance of neo-liberalism, young people carry heavy expectations: they live in a highly achievement-orientated social context and face an array of choices – around sexuality, education, travel and lifestyle, to name just a few. All of this is underpinned, and to a degree, steered by, a rapid revolution in information technology, of which young people are among the earliest adopters and the most frequent users. For instance, the changes in mobile phone development often create 'in' and 'out' groups among young people and developments in social media reinforce this – those who are 'in' being adept users. This also creates class divides, with those who can afford the latest technology often assuming a predominant position.

We focus, in this chapter, on young people aged 13 to 18. The term 'young people' or 'young person' is used deliberately, reflecting a preference often expressed by young people themselves. 'Teenager' is in danger of suggesting some kind of age determinism, 'adolescence' implies that biology or psychology are the dominant factors and the term 'children', being applied until the age of 18, is often seen as patronising by young people. It is interesting to think back to how you felt about the terms applied to your age when you were growing up.

We will be reflecting upon significant elements of the transition to adulthood. This is a complex change in contemporary societies: in some ways, it is a more rapid transition than in the past, with easier access to information (about sex and sexuality, for example). But, in other ways, the transition is more extended, with the age at which people secure their first job, first house ownership, and of marriage and parenthood being later than in the past. We shall reflect upon and provide evidence about these factors in the discussion that follows. To build our argument, we will use social theory, data, research and case studies.

Our approach uses the concept of social construction (examined by Jo Finch in Chapter 4 in Part I of this volume) at its core – namely, that being a young person is not fixed by biology or neuro-science, but rather that youth varies according to time, place and social position, and thus is 'socially constructed' (Frost, 2011). This is an optimistic position in some ways, as social understandings can be changed over time in a way that biology and neurology cannot. So, we are not considering fixed transitions for being a young person to becoming an adult at certain clearly defined ages, but rather looking at people in their social world and environmental position, something that differs for everyone. Consider the young person who has just taken her A levels and is setting off to university. She has never been away from her parents for longer than a five-day school trip and has not yet had an intimate relationship. Think of some of the differences between a young person like this and one who worked from the age of 16 in a local shop to supplement her family income while she was studying for a BTEC. Now she has finished her studies, she is torn between going on to further study or setting up home with her boyfriend, whom she met when she was 15.

We will explore six keys issues for young people today and, in doing so, we hope to move towards a holistic approach to understanding young people today.

- being a young person – from child to adult;
- living contexts – families and alternative contexts;
- gender, sex and sexuality;
- friends and relationships;
- living in a connected world – the role of social media;
- mental health and well-being.

Key theories and thinkers

Being a young person: from 'child' to 'adult'

Being a young person in modern Western societies is highly complex and demanding. In England, higher education student finance provides perhaps the starkest example of this process. A student of the 1970s paid no fees, often received a means-tested grant and could also claim welfare benefits during holidays. Today, young people pay university fees, with no bursary or grant (with a few subject-related exceptions) and leave university with debts often exceeding £50,000. What is highly significant here is that the responsibility for higher education has passed from being funded as a collective social good towards being seen as an individual, personalised responsibility: a clear example of what was referred to earlier as 'neo-liberalism' (Pimlott-Wilson, 2011).

In the post-Second World War period, a 'connected transition', at least in traditional working-class communities, was perhaps the norm. By 'connected transition', we mean that leaving home, entering employment, getting married and achieving home ownership were closely temporally connected. Today, these events have been both deferred and separated – with a full transition to adulthood perhaps taking more than a decade, creating what we can conceptualise as a 'disconnected transition' (see Chapter 11 in this volume regarding cultural influence on transitional stages).

A similar challenge exists in terms of identity. In 1950s Britain, identity was relatively fixed to social positions and collectives. Being a working-class, coal miner, heterosexual, trade unionist would have been a dominant and relatively stable white, male identity (see Warwick and Littlejohn, 1992). The transition to adulthood in such communities was 'connected', with significant life transitions taking place in a relatively short period of time. In contrast, modern transitions are less connected; for example, the age of marriage has increased recently:

> For marriages of opposite-sex couples, the average (mean) age for men marrying in 2015 was 37.5 years, while for women it was 35.1 years.

This represents a slight increase compared with 2014 (37.0 years for men and 34.6 years for women) and continues the overall rise recorded since the 1970s. (ONS, 2016)

Today, many aspects of identity have become challenged and flexible. The working class, in terms of being involved in manual labour, has largely disappeared (for instance, most coal mines have closed), sexual identity is more fluid than previously and trade union membership has declined, thus making identity more flexible, complicated and demanding (Smith, 2017). The contemporary focus on young people's mental health, which we discuss in the following section, has perhaps come from these challenges, with identity being contested and negotiated, often under the incessant gaze of social media.

REFLECTION POINT 8.1

How do you think of yourself? What terms would you use to describe yourself? It may be that you use statuses and positions, but it may be that you consider qualities and attributes such as being outgoing or personable more than, say, being a social work student.

In an increasingly globalised world, developed economies are dependent on a highly educated, flexible, mobile workforce to face the challenge of being a 'value-added', knowledge-based economy (O'Reilly et al, 2015). This too places high expectations upon young people to achieve – a pressure which is seen at its most extreme in the Association of South-East Asian Nations 'tiger' economies: Taiwan, South Korea, Singapore and Hong Kong, the 'tiger cub' economies and China (Dayley, 2017). The young person today is the carrier, and to some extent the victim, of a modern competitive society with high expectations. This creates a double-jeopardy situation for young people. Imagine the young man who is striving to be the best footballer in his college, spending all his time training, keeping fit and eating healthily, but who becomes depressed because he has no time to spend with his friends or to socialise.

Once a young person enters employment – perhaps carrying and repaying a considerable student debt – the challenges continue. Working hours have often been extended, with 'presentee-ism' an expectation, pension contributions higher than in the past and the relentless pressures of targets and bonus-based pay. At the bottom end of the job market, the 'gig economy' predominates – being paid per journey or per delivery, without the benefits of contracted employment (Friedman, 2014). This is referred to as an 'hour glass' economy – with degree-level jobs at the top, low-paid 'gig economy' jobs at the bottom and few employment opportunities in the middle.

This complex and demanding world places new pressures and expectations on young people, which in turn has profound impacts on their relationships and mental health, as we will go on to explore in Case Study 8.1 and later in this chapter (see also Chapter 15 in Part III of this volume).

CASE STUDY 8.1

Joely is 17 years old, white British, and studying for her A levels at a local sixth-form college. She is predicted very high results in the exams and is being encouraged to try for Oxbridge. Joely has experienced low self-esteem throughout her life and does not believe she is good enough for university, thinks she must work harder and believes she is frumpy, overweight and not very likeable. She has started exercising to excess and stopping eating. She has lost weight rapidly, but still believes she must do more to be the person she thinks she ought to be.

Questions
1. What might be happening for Joely at the moment?
2. How might you as a social worker work with her?

Discussion
Joely seems to be struggling with her own self-concept, the pressures she feels she is under and how she ought to respond to these. It may be that she has tried to assume control over her life by slimming and stopping eating. This is a common reaction to contemporary pressures, alongside a patriarchal environment that focuses on looks and weight or size. Your role as a social worker is to help Joely explain how she is feeling and to ensure she is signposted to and receives specialist help, support and advice. You will be acting almost as a responsible team coordinator as described in the Norwegian system in Chapter 15 in Part III of this volume.

Living contexts: families and alternative contexts

As we have seen, new challenges have emerged in Western society for young people, who face a delay in achieving adult independence because of changes in an increasingly market-driven economy. Challenges such as high unemployment and rising costs of living mean that young people are staying at home much later than in previous generations, thus changing the process of family dynamics. Arnett (2004) coined the term 'emerging adulthood' to explain this contemporary phenomenon as a period of extended freedom to travel and try out lifestyles and jobs. Many young people, such as students, leave and then return to the family home over a number of years, before, finally, leaving home to set up their own homes at a much later stage in their lives.

However, this is not a pathway open to all, as socio–economic pressures, such as poverty and poor housing, mean that many families are living with increased stressors and the financial burden of younger adults remaining at home, which can contribute to family conflict. Prolonged transitions are more problematic for those young people who face disadvantages, who live in the care of the local authority or who are disconnected from their birth families (Stein, 2012). These young people may be forced to set up home earlier than their peers and will usually have limited family support and access to economic resources. This places young people who are vulnerable in very challenging circumstances and can cause feelings of isolation and stress (Wade, 2008; Stein, 2012). Coleman, referring to the research of Graber and Brooks-Gunn (1996), uses the term 'turning points' (2011, p 12) as a better way of describing the transitions young people face in an extended form, suggesting that seeing transition as a pathway with several turning points is a more helpful and focused model for adults to adopt, as it allows each life decision to be addressed one issue at a time. Tackling major decisions in this way is more applicable to the cognitive and psychological changes that are occurring for a young person and provides a framework to contain and cope with emotions, and to make rational consequential decisions in a safer and more considered manner.

For many young people, relationships with parents and birth family remain of key importance. While feeling connected and close to family is still a significant priority, increased feelings of personal agency and expressing personal choice take on greater emphasis. Coleman (2011) comments that there is less conflict with parents than commonly-held stereotypes would have us believe. Indeed, young people are likely to accept parental advice over moral and safety decisions about their care, but less likely to accept interference in the domestic personal sphere of life, such as what to wear and friendship groups. They are more likely to talk to fathers about career decisions, moral choices, politics and money, favouring mothers for emotional advice.

It is also the case that conflict can act as useful mechanisms for development and change in young people (Branje, 2018). Dowling et al (2006) refer to the importance of the environment and community on development, which can provide the young person with 'social capital' – a feeling from relationships with others of self-belief, trust and safety (2006, p 149). Social capital can be compromised by the effects of inequality and social disadvantage: poverty can affect family circumstances and parental functioning, which can result in poorer outcomes for young people, including for some exposure to abusive adult behaviours and child protection concerns. Social exclusion can also result from differences in ethnicity, race and religion, which can mean that some families will be exposed to greater external stressors in the environment around them. Good community resources and sensitive care-giving can act as protective factors to increase resilience levels to help deal with these stressors.

The concept of family has changed as social attitudes and values about marriage, sexuality, lone parenting, cohabitation and divorce have evolved. Many young people grow up with one parent or have 'blended' (or step-parent) families, as parents form new relationships. However, family breakdown and the effects of separation/divorce on children and young people remain a social concern. Young people cope best in such circumstances when parents manage disputes respectfully and come to early and consistent arrangements about where the young person wants to live and when they will see the non-resident parent.

School is an integral part of the community and can offer a positive resource for young people to support well-being in a shared setting which all attend. Therefore, there is an important emphasis for children 'looked after' by the state, in either foster care or residential care, to have personal educational plans and designated teachers to manage such plans within the school setting to raise the aspirations and attainment of these young people (Stein, 2012).

Becoming 'looked after' in childhood is a period when the state provides care on a temporary basis or for the duration of childhood. This happens when legal thresholds about the care and safety of the young person have been met and in order to protect from future abuse. Young people are placed in foster care and in residential settings, joining families made up of birth children, fostered children and/or residential social workers. They will face many challenges, including adjusting to feelings of loss and separation from their birth family. Carers work hard to promote the young person's identity and heritage so that emotional well-being is buffered in this context. In England, for example, arrangements such as Child Looked After Reviews offer a structured system which aims to be child-centred in ensuring that familial and educational links are promoted during this change in living arrangements (Cosis-Brown, 2014).

REFLECTION POINT 8.2

Think about your own upbringing, your experiences and how they helped or hindered your development towards becoming the adult you are today. Imagine how these experiences and emerging transitions feel to those young people you work with.

Gender, sex and sexuality

Powell writes that we are living in an age of 'sexualised consumer capitalism' (2010, p 13). There is a concern that commercial advertising presents an overt form of sexual behaviour and expectations, particularly in relation to young women, and thus it can be argued that this process is accelerating the normal rate of sexual maturation for young people. Again, this is a challenging time in which to grow up, as young people are exposed to external messages about idealised gender roles and conformity. Social media plays an important role in shaping youth culture around identity, gender and sexual relationships. For example, social media has changed dating rituals and expectations and has thus influenced behaviours between genders. The use of digital IT platforms provides opportunities for forming online connections with others; however, it comes with risks and the concept of 'sexting' – sending explicit messages/pictures – is a growing phenomenon. This has transformed the previously private sphere of sexual experimentation and curiosity into a potential arena for exploitation and abuse. Adults remain concerned about online safety and youth sexuality has become a modern-day 'moral panic' and a public health issue (Livingstone, 2016).

In the UK, concerns about teenage sexual health, contraception and reducing teenage pregnancy have been the source of numerous social policy initiatives (Department of Health, 2013). Powell (2010) suggests that, despite a growth in more liberal attitudes about sexual behaviours and an increase in sexual health programmes within schools, there remain unwritten rules between the sexes which have hardly changed and are commonly held views internationally. Inherently, males are seen as sexual instigators, with young men socialised within this context, which shapes their social interactions with young women. In general, there is an accepted 'script' about boys and male sex drives, which are seen as uncontrollable, as a result of high hormonal surges. Thus, males are forced to adopt competing roles of sexual instigator and chivalrous protector. For girls and females, the gender 'scripts' and accepted sexual identities are shaped by notions of romantic love and committed sexual behaviours taking part within relationships. Additionally, adults and professionals in caring and advisory roles need to be aware that these scripts tip over into the emotional aspects of the interaction between boys and girls when sexual behaviours can become violent, coercive and controlling. Sex and relationships programmes are better delivered holistically within a peer-based education setting that looks at scripts and the learned behaviours to which some young people who have had abusive home lives will have been exposed (Powell, 2010).

Temple-Smith et al (2015) comment that there is more recognition, and a greater acceptance of sexual diversity, with an increased visibility of the lesbian, gay, bisexual and transsexual (LGBT) community in wider society. There has also been a growing discussion about sexual violence, issues of consent and unacceptable behaviours, which has brought hidden areas of sexual behaviour into mainstream discourse. They describe the onset of the physical and hormonal stages of puberty as a 'critical period in the upsurge of sexual drives, the development of sexual values and the initiation of sexual behaviours' (Temple-Smith et al, 2015, p 3). Females are approximately two years ahead of males in their sexual maturation and the process of 'puberty' itself can last for around five to seven years. It is a period that can offer both positive and negative events to a sense of well-being, self-esteem and realisation that pleasure and desire is a normative human emotion. However, they stress that the 'context' in which sexual activity is experienced is fundamentally important for well-being. It should be within reciprocal healthy relationships; therefore, conversely, exploitative and unsafe relationships often happen in contexts which involve high-risk behaviours, such as the use of alcohol and drugs. These can reduce inhibitions and increase impulsive decision making. In such circumstances, Temple-Smith et al argue that 'wrong choices can lead to destructive outcomes' and feelings of 'unworthiness' (2015, p 4). Firmin et al (2016), researching the risks associated with child sexual exploitation, conclude that contexts of environment and peer pressure also play a role in factors pushing young people into risky situations. They argue for 'contextual safeguarding' (2016, p 2330), including assertive community outreach programmes which engage young people in discussions about consent and healthy relationships.

The discourse around accepted sexual behaviours for young people has changed. Research undertaken by Coleman (see Coleman, 2011, p 136) shows that, since the 1960s, the average age for sexual activity across Europe is steadily rising to age 16 for both genders; within the UK, 30 per cent of 16-year-olds reported being sexually active. Ethnicity and cultural differences are a factor, with young black males reporting higher percentages of activity and Asian young people the lowest.

Talking openly to young people about sex within their family context and contraception is likely to delay sexual activity and to encourage the use of safe-sex practices. However, to support this, sound educational programmes are essential and, in fact, young people report a preference for receiving information about sexual health within an educational setting rather than at home. Surveys about sexual health reveal a rise in the rate of sexually transmitted diseases among young people, with 63 per cent of UK chlamydia diagnoses in 2014 relating to those under the age of 25 (Young People's Health, 2015). Clearly, adults need to continue to hold open and honest conversations about sexual health to promote self-esteem and confidence in young people as they navigate tricky decisions about personal space and gender expression, and as they learn to forge intimate, loving relationships with each other.

Friends and relationships

The emotional and psychological changes that occur during the teenage years allow for a period of rapid self-discovery in relation to values, talents, hobbies and interests. For young people, this forging of a new autonomous self occurs through relationships with others. Importantly, peer relationships and friendships assume greater significance as the young person distances some aspects of self from parents and carers. The relationship between the young person and adults becomes one built more around negotiation and discussion. We have argued that all aspects of the developing young person are situational and socially constructed in relation to their environment (for example, when we consider identity development as the young person tries different personal narratives or 'ways of being' and seeing the world that may be different from the model they have received at home). They do this by aligning to peers to whom they are attracted, and from the 'ups and downs' of these friendships they receive feedback about how they integrate and are received into or excluded from social groups. In this respect, identity formation is fluid throughout the life course as we adapt and learn from our relationships and life experiences. During this phase of development, friendships and relationships with others are particularly powerful and emotive, as young people seek to find acceptance and support from others.

Primary attachment figures, usually parents, help to buffer the young person through this exciting, but often fraught, period of personal development, as friendship groups can change frequently, with rejection being a common experience. Friendship networks become more exclusive with increasing age. Younger children have more diverse group relationships and friendships and integrate better because they mix in a range of settings, such as sports or group activities. This provides a social identity and space to learn about rules and behaviour.

Friendships offer a person a sense of being accepted for shared interests and offer access to both social networks and validation by peers. Being popular is highly valued at this stage of development. Popularity for boys is often gained from having sporting talents or toughness; for girls, attributes which are valued include physical attractiveness and sociability, suggesting that selection of friends often follows gender stereotypes (Coleman, 2011). However, for some young people who have experienced challenges at home, such as looked-after young people, they may not have had a close attachment to an adult carer and may lack trust and self-esteem (Stein, 2012). Munford and Sanders (2015, p 1570) argue that this can lead to 'relational deprivation', which could cause them to form an over-reliance on the value of and emotional connection to peers. In turn, this could limit their narrative of self. These young people are more vulnerable to peer pressure, which could lead to high-risk-taking behaviours because of peer group norms and expectations about right and wrong. Reciprocal influence plays a feature as young people influence each other and are influenced by others; for instance, taking drugs, drinking and having sex is more likely to happen if you are with people who do these things. For these young people, this could lead to quite closed relationships with adult carers, who will need to work hard to overcome these barriers by building genuine, caring relationships to help young people see a possible version of self by offering alternatives and ways of being.

Maintaining friendships and keeping in touch in a digitally connected world has been transformed by social media. Young people are highly proficient in digital literacy and spend much of their time communicating digitally with friends and online acquaintances. A person's online identity can be changed and offers the possibility of showing the external world a different version of self; it provides an 'ideal forum for trying on different identities' (Coleman, 2011, p 188). For disadvantaged young people, the internet can provide a platform to broaden ideas and knowledge outside of the immediate environment that is otherwise inaccessible. However, the online world entails the risks of sexual grooming, availability of sexual material and online bullying from peers.

Because the young person is moving towards achieving more operational thinking, there is an increased capacity to reflect on self and on other people's perceptions of both them and the wider world. Daniel et al (2010) wrote that this can lead to a preoccupation and over-sensitivity in relationships with others, which can be felt as an 'imaginary audience' which magnifies the perceptions of self about which the young person is worried, such as body image and dress. This voice can often be quite self-critical and undermine the young person's self-esteem and ability to read ordinary social cues without this internal pressure. In this respect, the young person's preoccupation with self can appear to be quite egocentric and it can be challenging for their relationships with adults as they struggle to understand and to accept different points of view. The changes of biology, cognition and psychology during this part of development are huge and stressful for the young person, meaning they are prone to emotional reactivity and intense emotions which may be hard to regulate and to learn to control (Geldard and Geldard, 2009). However, this period of development is also intensely rich and rewarding, as young people grapple with moral thinking and ask 'big' questions about life and politics. This turbulent world can be all-encompassing, passionate and inspiring. It can challenge, remind and mobilise adults to acknowledge the energy and commitment required to strive for social change and personal responsibility.

REFLECTION POINT 8.3

Who do you keep in touch with from your childhood and youth? Why do you think these relationships have continued and what do they mean for your own development?

Living in a connected world: the role of social media

The world has changed dramatically since around the year 2000: life has been rapidly transformed through increasing globalisation and the impact of technology (Hynan et al, 2014). While these processes have impacted all of us, they have particularly transformed the lives of young people. Young people experience networked lives, where many hours per day are spent networked with others through forms of social media. These processes transcend time and space – we can network in real time with people many thousands of miles away.

As Geoffrey Pearson argued in his classic book *Hooligan* (1983), young people are often early adopters of new fashions, trends and developments. Pearson posits that even the early pedal cyclists were experienced as a threat to society! Equally recent developments in technology have become associated with social evils – sexual exploitation, grooming, pornography, suicidal ideation, eating disorders and bullying among them. However, young people grasp the positive opportunities to learn, network, campaign and support each other (Vromen et al, 2015).

Social media transforms their social and personal relationships, making relationships trans-global and immediate. It is easy to take for granted that we can take a photograph in, say, Australia and send it to someone in England in a just matter of seconds. One result of technology developments has been that young people become the experts and the early adopters; they have a world from which adults can be excluded and where they develop their own skill set and language. As Livingstone writes: 'Rather than concern for their welfare, I found myself encouraged at how well they managed the huge influx of digital devices and content that now fill their lives' (2016).

While having many advantages, of course, some of the dangers of social media are real. Young people have been groomed online and even eventually murdered, as illustrated by the death of Breck Bednar and the formation of the Breck Foundation (see http://www.breckfoundation.org).

How can these processes be negotiated between young people and their elders? Young people require their privacy and autonomy, but also require safeguarding from dangerous adults or peers who wish to exploit their power over others. There is a balance to be struck between privacy and protection, between autonomy and safeguarding. As adults and parents, we might spend less time worrying about what they get up to as teenagers and more time with them, discussing the challenges that lie ahead for them as adults in an increasingly connected world (Livingstone, 2016). An example is provided by the Childnet charity, which funds a competition to encourage safe use of the web:

> Over the past nine years, hundreds of young people have shown us how they can use their creativity, passion and skills to educate and inspire their peers to stay safe online. We are hugely excited to see the films that young people will be entering for this year's Childnet Film Competition and how they can help shape a respectful and better internet for all. (http://www.childnet.com/film-comp)

Initiatives like this demonstrate how adults and young people can work together to ensure that social media is a safe space.

Mental health and well-being

There is often a close connection made between the issue of social media, discussed in the previous section, and that of mental health and well-being. (This is explored in greater depth in Chapter 15 in Part III of this volume.) The mental health of young people has a high profile among the media, non-governmental organisations (NGOs) and governments (Lawrence et al, 2015): it often becomes a headline issue, for example, following a tragic school shooting in the US. Some of the measures and statistics demonstrate increased awareness, but nevertheless the official statistics are significant: 'Cases of self-poisoning among girls – ingesting pills, alcohol or other chemical substances – rose 50%, from 9,700 to 14,600 between 2005–06 and 2015–16. Similarly, the number of girls treated in hospital after cutting themselves quadrupled, from 600 to 2,400 over the same period' (Campbell, 2016).

There are a number of levels that we can use to understand the prevention of mental ill-health: primary prevention, secondary prevention and tertiary prevention (Greenberg et al, 2003). Each of these will be explored in turn.

Primary prevention explores the mental health of all young people: it takes a global approach and asks the 'big questions' about young people and their place in the world. As explored in our discussion of young people and transitions, the contemporary world is very complex and demanding for young people. Compared to industrial societies, which are largely organised around the collective identity of social class, post-industrial or neo-liberal societies are individualised and they place an expectation that the individual will negotiate their own pathway through life. To be a young person today is a pressurised, competitive and individualised experience: the 'selfie', and the implicit focus on 'self', perhaps carries a very significant social message. Modern youth are cut off from collective identities, such as being a 'worker' or being a 'local', which were taken for granted by previous generations. It is unsurprising that this places a heavy burden on the individual – and perhaps takes a toll on individual mental well-being. Primary prevention, then, is about young people having a valued and supported place in the post-industrial world.

Secondary prevention is about supporting those who are experiencing a degree of mental ill-health, which many of us do. Some young people may feel lonely, depressed, isolated, have a negative body image or be lacking in self-confidence. They require low-level support, including, for example, helplines, peer support, informative websites, mentors and counselling. This web of support is complex and difficult to map: it will differ significantly nationally, locally and from time to time. Such services need to be accessible and free from stigma. They need to be 'young-people-friendly' and responsive if young people with 'low-level' mental health challenges are to be supported so that their challenges do not become more severe.

Tertiary prevention applies to young people who may experience severe mental health challenges. They may be suicidal, self-harming and/or severely depressed. Support at this level needs to be delivered by highly qualified professionals, such as psychologists, psychiatrists and counsellors. Such services exist across the sectors – in the private sector and NGOs, and within the Health Service. In many parts of the world – including the UK – these services seem to be under considerable pressure, with extensive waiting lists. As with the previous levels, the services need to be accessible, young-people-friendly and free of stigma. At the top end of this service provision, there are specialist residential units for young people in severe need.

Making it real: applying knowledge to practice

This analysis matters in as much as it has implications for how young people, their parents and carers and relevant professionals act in the real world. Reading this book from the perspective of a student social worker, you will be aware of many of the issues explored and how challenging they are. We would argue for a young-person-centred practice, which works in partnership with young people and recognises the significance of their views and experiences. As well as having high expectations of young people, we need to make sure they are supported in negotiating many of the issues explored in this chapter (see Case Study 8.2).

CASE STUDY 8.2

Justin has been 'looked after' by the local authority since the age of 14. He is now 18 and on leaving college he is aiming to move on to his local university. Justin remembers his social workers. He has been lucky and there have not been many changes in the four years he has been in care.

Questions

1. What do you think Justin might say he valued most from his social workers?
2. What do you think the social worker should do when working with him?
3. How might you work with any gaps in provision?

Discussion

Justin may well say that it was the constancy of a known person and the relationship (see Chapter 4 in the companion volume) that he most valued. It is not unlikely that he would want this to continue and it is your role as a social worker to help Justin develop new bonds and friendships and to argue for the importance of consistency with your team, which is no doubt very busy and would want you to move on to other cases. However, just as with family and friends, a continuing bond with a trusted professional – in this case, a social worker – can be fundamental to his future success.

Having explored a number of issues confronting modern young people, we now go on to present two more brief, contrasting Case Studies (8.3 and 8.4) which help to explore some the issues previously discussed.

CASE STUDY 8.3

Sonia is a young woman of South Asian, Hindu heritage who attends a residential independent school. She is 17 and expects to obtain good A-level grades and hopefully attend a Russell Group University. She is captain of the school hockey team.

Sonia gets on well with her parents and her two younger siblings. Her dad is a chief executive of a large company and that means that she has private health insurance on her dad's policy. She hopes to have her own car next year. Her boyfriend is one year older and attends the same school. He is white British, and she is a little worried about telling her mum and dad about the relationship quite yet.

Questions

1. What do you think some of the key issues are for Sonia currently?
2. How do you think her lifestyle will affect her view of the world and transition within it?

CASE STUDY 8.4

Caroline is white British and is 15 years old. She lives with her mum in social housing in the centre of a large city. Her relationship with her mum is very difficult: she did spend a period of time in care when she was 13, after she had run away from home. Caroline hasn't seen her dad for about five years. She has asthma and has to regularly attend a clinic, which is a long bus journey away.

Caroline doesn't like school very much and is looking forward to leaving and perhaps attending college to study child care. She thinks she will leave home then and perhaps move in with Jim, who she has been going out with for a few months now.

Questions

1. What sort of transitions to you think Sonia and Caroline will experience?
2. What will these transitions have in common and how may they be different?
3. Why might there be different life trajectories for these two girls?

Discussion

Sonia and Caroline have very different social positions and we can see that this will, no doubt, have a major impact on their transition to adulthood. There is a complex interplay of gender, social class and ethnicity – what is sometimes referred to as 'intersectionality' (see Chapter 15 in Part III of the companion volume for more information on this).

They also have a differential relationship to the state: Caroline requires support from the state for housing, education, transport and health, and was also once looked after by the state. Sonia has housing, education, health care and, soon, transport which does not depend on the state at all. Their social position is very different and will have a considerable impact on their personal transitions and experiences.

REFLECTION POINT 8.4

Think of your own period as a young person. What were your strengths and talents? What did you find difficult and challenging? What helped you address these challenges? How would these experiences be different if you were a young person today?

Conclusion

This chapter has explored the experiences of young people in their transition from child to adult. We have argued that modern transitions are multidimensional and depend largely on the social position of the young person. These issues have been explored in a number of specific contexts – where complexity, choice, change and challenge are fundamentally common themes.

Our specific objectives in this chapter were to explore transitions, look at the role of families, friends and alternatives, gender and sexuality, and to consider the importance of the wider environment and society in which young people grow and make transitions into adulthood. These aspects of being a young person are all connected and have an impact on each other. How we understand these issues has implications for professional practice with young people.

Reflective questions

1 Think about your own transition to adulthood: how does it contrast with the experience of a young person you know?

2 If our argument that contemporary life is more complex for young people than for previous generations is correct, what can be done to support young people through this transition?

3 How has social media changed life for contemporary young people?

Further reading

- Coleman, J.C. (2011) *The Nature of Adolescence* (4th edn). Hove: Routledge.
  Perhaps the classic text book exploring the issues covered in this chapter using psycho-social perspectives.

- Frost, N. (2011) *Rethinking Children and Families: The Relationship between Childhood, Families and the State*. London: Continuum.
  Written by one of the authors of this chapter, this book explores many of the issues discussed here, while exploring younger children as well.

- Pearson, G. (1983) *Hooligan: A History of Respectable Fears*. London: Macmillan.
  Perhaps the classic study of adult attitudes to young people and how these change over time.

- Stein, M. (2012) *Young People Leaving Care: Supporting Pathways to Adulthood*. London: Jessica Kingsley.
  A very clear and research-informed study of the particular issues facing young people who have been in the care system.

References

Arnett, G. (2004) *Emerging Adulthood: The Winding Road from the Late Teens through the Twenties*. Oxford: Oxford University Press.

Branje, S. (2018) Development of parent–adolescent relationships: Conflict interactions as a mechanism of change, *Child Development Perspectives*, 12(3): 171–176.

Breck Foundation (no date) http://www.breckfoundation.org

Campbell, D. (2016) Stress and social media fuel mental health crisis among girls, *The Guardian*. 23 September. Available from: https://www.theguardian.com/society/2017/sep/23/stress-anxiety-fuel-mental-health-crisis-girls-young-women

Coleman, J.C. (2011) *The Nature of Adolescence* (4th edn). Hove: Routledge.

Cosis-Brown, H. (2014) *Social Work and Foster Care*. London: Sage/Learning Matters.

Daniel, B., Wassell, S. and Gilligan, R. (2010) *Child Development for Child Care and Protection Workers* (2nd edn). London: Jessica Kingsley.

Dayley, R. (2017) *Southeast Asia in the New International Era* (7th edn), New York: Routledge.

Department of Health (2013) A framework for sexual health improvement in England. March. Available from: https://www.gov.uk/government/uploads/system/uploads/attachment_data/file/142592/9287-2900714-TSO-SexualHealthPolicyNW_ACCESSIBLE.pdf

Dowling, M., Gupta, A. and Aldgate, J. (2006) The impact of community and environmental factors. In B. Daniel, S. Wassell and R. Gilligan (eds), *Child Development for Child Care and Protection Workers* (2nd edn). London: Jessica Kingsley.

Firmin, C., Warrington, C. and Pearce, J. (2016) Sexual exploitation and its impact on developing sexualities and sexual relationships: The need for contextual social work interventions, *British Journal of Social Work*, 46(8): 2318–2337.

Friedman, G. (2014) Workers without employers: Shadow corporations and the rise of the gig economy, *Review of Keynesian Economics*, 2(2): 171–188.

Frost, N. (2011) *Rethinking Children and Families: The Relationship between Childhood, Families and the State*. London: Continuum.

Geldard, K. and Geldard, D. (2009) *Relationship Counselling for Children, Young People and Families*. London: Sage.

Graber, J. and Brooks-Gunn, J. (1996) Transitions and turning points: Navigating the passage from childhood to adolescence, *Developmental Psychology*, 32(4): 768–776.

Greenberg, M.T., Weissberg, R.P., O'Brien, M.U., Zins, J.E., Fredericks, L., Resnik, H. et al (2003) Enhancing school-based prevention and youth development through coordinated social, emotional, and academic learning, *American Psychologist*, 58(6–7): 466–474.

Hynan, A., Murray, J. and Goldbart, J. (2014) 'Happy and excited': Perceptions of using digital technology and social media by young people who use augmentative and alternative communication, *Child Language Teaching and Therapy*, 30(2): 175–186.

Lawrence, D., Johnson, S., Hafekost, J., Boterhoven de Haan, K., Sawyer, M., Ainley, J. et al (2015) The mental health of children and adolescents: report on the second Australian child and adolescent survey of mental health and wellbeing. Canberra: ACER.

Livingstone, S. (2016) A day in the digital life of teenagers. Available from: http://theconversation.com/a-day-in-the-digital-life-of-teenagers-58553

Munford, R. and Sanders, J. (2015) Negotiating and constructing identity: Social work with young people who experience adversity, *British Journal of Social Work*, 45(5): 1564–1580.

ONS (2016) *Marriage in England and Wales 2015.* London: ONS.

O'Reilly, J., Eichhorst, W., Gábos, A., Hadjivassiliou, K., Lain, D., Leschke, J. et al (2015) Five characteristics of youth unemployment in Europe: Flexibility, education, migration, family legacies, and EU policy, *Sage Open*, 5(1): 1–19.

Pearson, G. (1983) *Hooligan: A History of Respectable Fears.* London: Macmillan.

Pimlott-Wilson, H. (2011) The role of familial habitus in shaping children's views of their future employment, *Children's Geographies*, 9(1): 111–118.

Powell, A. (2010) *Sex, Power and Consent: Youth Culture and the Unwritten Rules.* Cambridge: Cambridge University Press.

Smith, D. (2017) Exploring Bauman's liquid modernity, *Cultural Politics*, 13(3): 303–305.

Stein, M. (2012) *Young People Leaving Care: Supporting Pathways to Adulthood.* London: Jessica Kingsley.

Temple-Smith, M., Moore, S. and Rosenthall, D. (2015) Sexuality in adolescence the digital generation (3rd edn). Hove: Routledge. Available from: https://www-vlebooks-com.ezproxy.leedsbeckett.ac.uk/vleweb/Product/Index/633172?page=0

Vromen, A., Xenos, M.A. and Loader, B. (2015) Young people, social media and connective action: From organisational maintenance to everyday political talk, *Journal of Youth Studies*, 18(1): 80–100.

Wade, J. (2008) The ties that bind: Support from birth families and substitute families for young people leaving care, *British Journal of Social Work*, 38(1): 39–54.

Warwick, D. and Littlejohn, G. (1992) *Coal, Capital, and Culture: A Sociological Analysis of Mining Communities in West Yorkshire.* London: Taylor & Francis.

Young People's Health (2015) Available from: http://www.youngpeopleshealth.org.uk/wp-content/uploads/2015/09/KeyData2015_Chapter5.pdf

9

Developmental and life course criminology

Richard Heslop and Jonathan Parker

Introduction

Relationship development and social mores have a great impact on the ways in which norms are established and rules governing social behaviour are accepted by children and young people. Their social development and behaviour are influenced greatly by their relationships with peers, school teachers and professionals and within families. In turn, this affects the opportunities they get in society and their subsequent development through the life course, although, without doubt, this is subject to change. These issues, among others, will be explored within this chapter.

Separating children and young people from adults at the age of 18 years is arbitrary and if applied rigidly would not value the human and cultural differences that abound within society, communities and families. Thus, a fluid approach will be taken. Following an exploration of some of the key elements of the theories of life course criminology, we will explore some of the central theorists in the area before examining approaches developed to divert children and young people from crime.

Chapter objectives

- introduce life course criminology and key theorists and its importance for children and young people;

- consider the impact of family, friends, schooling and environment on the development of children and young people, focusing on the social constructs of crime and deviance;

- consider transitions in and out of crime and movement into adulthood.

Background and context

Although disputed, bio-genetic approaches to criminology and the development of criminal behaviour are important, although by no means exclusively so, of course, when considering life course criminology. However, it is important to point out the reductive and positivist nature of these theories at this juncture. By this, we mean that they pare down understanding to simple associations between biology and genetics and the development of crime, which in turn relies on an understanding of crime as being an entity that exists on its own and that we can identify as such, regardless of the context from which we are viewing it.

Clearly, such views are problematic, as we cannot identify specific biophysical or genetic traits that always lead to criminal behaviour. Neither can we specify exactly what is and what isn't a crime. There are no objective criteria to identify crime that are not contingent. Again, what we mean by this is that crime is defined by legislation and laws are made within societies according to social beliefs and customs that are ever-changing and developing. Of course, you may say that murder is always a crime and point to the brutal killing of a child to justify your position. However, even such crimes as murder and manslaughter are interpreted differently in different countries – for instance, even the US and the UK have different legislative understandings. Throughout this chapter, we will use a high-profile case from a number of years ago to illustrate some of the themes of life course development: the killing of two-year-old James Bulger by two ten-year-old boys, Jon Venables and Robert Thompson (see Case Study 9.1).

CASE STUDY 9.1

On 12 February 1993, a two-, nearly three-year-old boy, James Bulger, was abducted from his mother. They were out shopping in Bootle, a suburb of Liverpool in the UK. This toddler was taken by two ten-year-old boys, Jon Venables and Robert Thompson, and despite being seen as quite distressed by some passers-by, he was led to a train track a few miles away, where he was brutally killed by the two boys. It was not long before Thompson and Venables were arrested and admitted what they had done.

The two boys were tried, convicted and sentenced to be detained at Her Majesty's pleasure. The case raised many questions – not just because it was so shocking to think that two ten-year-olds were capable of brutally killing a toddler. Thompson and Venables were not allowed to remain anonymous despite being underage and, in fact, were tried in an adult court. The public outcry against them was vitriolic and called for the harshest of punishments and violence to be meted out to them. Once sentenced, the populist newspaper *The Sun* took a moralistic position in calling for the Home Secretary to increase the minimum number of years they were to serve. He subsequently stated that they should serve at least 15 years. The House of Lords in the UK, followed by the European Court of Human Rights, claimed that the Home Secretary had acted illegally and the boys had not had a fair trial. The Lord Chief Justice restored the original eight-year minimum term and Thompson and Venables were released after having served this sentence.

On their release, the boys were granted lifetime anonymity and a change of identity. This has been challenged, but maintained. Concerning Thompson, it seems that he has integrated back into society and has not reoffended, despite being labelled the ringleader of the attack. (Little evidence for this was produced, except for his impassive response during questioning and the trial.) Venables, on the other hand, was rearrested for fighting and possessing cocaine in 2008, was sent to prison in 2010 for possessing child abuse images and was again sent to prison in 2018 after being found in possession of further child abuse images.

Questions
1. Thinking of this case study, how does it make you feel?
2. Do you think trial, in an adult court, of the two boys who killed James Bulger led to a fair hearing and sentence?
3. Why do you think Thompson and Venables acted in this way?

Discussion
The case led to highly-charged emotional outbursts and, because of its nature, still evokes such. When we have used the case as a reflection point in our classes, it is sometimes hard at first for students to move beyond the horror of the crime to consider aspects of fairness and the effects on young people's development.

After reviewing some key elements of theory relating to life course criminology and applying this in particular to children and young people, we will explore further elements of these two boys and their backgrounds, alongside using other cases, to illustrate how this model may provide useful ways of understanding how crime and behaviour may develop.

The importance of life course criminology as a model is that it also considers the centrality of environmental factors – who one lives with, where one lives and what relationships one has with others. It recognises that environmental factors such as these interact with bio–genetic make–up and offers possible ways of understanding how a child or young person may be affected by crime and criminality. Some of this has already been alluded to in Chapters 1 and 5 in Part I of this volume. Thus, the concept of criminogenic families, relationships and environments represents an important area to consider regarding the development of children and young people. This suggests that certain relationships and environments are more likely to lead to criminal behaviour than others. What it does not explain, of course, is why some children and young people behave differently in similar settings; individual experiential, interpretive and personality factors are needed. For instance, thinking of Case Study 9.1, we may ask why boys in similar positions to Thompson and Venables do not kill other children: what is it that is different? If we could answer this with precision, of course, it would make a fundamental difference to the criminal justice and social work systems across the world. However, as we have seen in Chapter 5 in Part I of this volume, the complex environments in which children and young people live and the different interactions and experiences they have led to a range of varied responses which we can only hint at through the application of theory. This does not make it any less useful, but represents an important caveat when we are assessing theory.

Life course criminology relies on a range of explanatory approaches in particular life course developmental psychology, alongside the multiple interacting influences we have begun to set out (some of which have been explored in respect of social learning theories in Chapter 1 in Part I of this volume). It represents a growing area of academic research and even has its own journal dedicated to its explication and research: the *Journal of Development and Life Course Criminology*.

Key theories and thinkers

In this section, we examine key theorists and theories within life course criminology and seek to apply this to children and young people. However, we must remember that the theories and models have been developed across the life course and are therefore difficult to separate entirely; to do so between young people and adults remains somewhat artificial. In Chapter 9 in Part II of the companion volume, we seek to do the same in respect of adults. There will be some overlap and repetition here, as social and emotional growth do not always follow the same pattern as chronological growth. Life course criminology represents a long-standing and well-rehearsed approach to crime that links age and criminal behaviour. These models and underpinning theories are critiqued, recognising that children and young people live in a complex human context in which differences, diversity and multiple perspectives abound. We will draw upon international as well as local theoretical perspectives.

Despite the notions of crime and criminality being highly contested concepts, we can say that criminology is concerned with both the systematic study of crime and the causes of crime (Newburn, 2017). Using this definition as our starting point, we can suggest that there are two central challenges in youth criminology: (1) why certain young people or groups of young people commit crimes; and (2) why others do not. Throughout history and into the present day, most academics, professionals (social workers and criminal justice workers) and policymakers who are concerned with crime and criminal behaviour expend a great amount of energy thinking about and developing ways of how to deal with them. This subject taxes the general public and is portrayed in the media often with great sensation and moral opprobrium, especially where young people are concerned (Cohen, 1972).

Ever since Cain murdered his brother Abel, a well-known story in the three Abrahamic religions (Judaism, Christianity and Islam), people have been asking why crime happens. However, it is only in relatively recent times that the systematic study of crime and offending (which is the academic discipline of criminology) has gained acceptability and, now, popularity. Many contemporary criminology textbooks date the emergence of criminological thinking to an era between the late 17th and early 18th centuries (see, for example, Chamberlain, 2015; Newburn, 2017).

The 18th-century philosophers

The focus in criminological thinking did not discriminate between young people and adults in its stages, since the notion of childhood is also relatively recent (as already discussed in Chapter 4 in Part I of this volume). The traditional or 'classical' criminology of earlier times emerged through the writings of 18th-century philosophers promoting social reform, most notably, Jeremy Bentham and Cesare Beccaria. These arose in response to many of the inhumane and cruel forms of punishment that operated at that time. As part of the broader Enlightenment movement, classical criminologists not only advocated humanising responses to crime, but also rejected traditional religious interpretations of individual behaviour and concepts associated with individual 'sin' (Chamberlain, 2015). These ideas about the 'rational subject' and a social contract led to new legal and criminal justice systems, under which the punishment should be proportionate to the crime (Bowling, 2006).

Positivism

It is interesting to note that, by the middle of the 19th century, this 'enlightened' approach to the problem of crime was overturned by 'positivist' criminologists. Positivism represents a philosophical notion that knowledge about a thing can only come from observation in the real world and can be verifiable. Positivist criminology states that criminals are born and not made; in other words, it is the biophysical nature of the person rather than their environment, upbringing and socio-political conditions around them which results in their criminal behaviour. Most notably and notoriously, the Italian physician and psychiatrist Cesare Lombroso (1835–1909), who counted himself as a criminal anthropologist, dissected and studied the cadavers of soldiers and executed criminals to determine 'scientifically' the physiological reasons for 'criminal' and 'non-criminal' behaviour. Believing that criminality was an inherited trait, Lombroso's research claimed that the inherited facial features of criminals, for example, large jaws and bloodshot eyes, showed their criminality. His work also influenced racist stereotyping of physiological features to determine superiority and inferiority across different ethnic groups. Quite rightly, his ideas were subsequently discredited. However, despite this, Lombroso was one of the first people in history to use scientific methods – systematic experimentation – to study crime. He is regarded by some as the 'father' of modern criminology.

More recent theories

Since the times of Bentham, Beccaria and Lombroso, modern criminology has evolved into a vast and ever-expanding multidisciplinary field of study and practice, and study in criminology degree programmes in the UK and internationally (Loader and Sparks, 2012). This has led to significant growth of criminological research and theories which claim to explain criminal propensities and behaviour. These include:

- strain theory
- labelling theory
- control theory
- social bonds theory
- rational choice theory
- broken windows theories
- life course and development criminology

Alongside these theories, there has been considerable development in sociologically-grounded 'critical' approaches, such as Marxism, feminism and cultural criminology (see Chapter 5 in Part I of this volume for further details on these). Criminology is, of course, like social work, an interdisciplinary field of study which borrows theories about criminality that are drawn from economics, politics, sociology, psychology, psychiatry, biology and, perhaps most controversially, genetics. The original crude forms of positivism, such as that of Lombroso, have long since been discredited. However, many scholars and commentators insist that criminality can and must be studied using the same methods and ideas drawn from the natural sciences. Of course, not everyone shares this view, but what most academic criminologists usually agree upon is that criminology is both a theoretical and an empirical subject (one that can be observed in the natural world). In other words, criminology emphasises the importance of both theoretical work and a firm evidence base for its theories. Keeping this overview of criminology in mind, we turn now to an examination of life course and developmental criminology.

Life course and developmental criminology

The broad term 'life course perspective' is a wide-ranging approach which may be used in a variety of fields of enquiry, including, history, biology, human geography and, as covered by this chapter, criminology as it relates to children and young people. The idea of life course indicates a range from birth to death. However, as we have seen in Part I of this volume, it is possible to a lesser or greater extent to identify different stages within that course. From a criminological perspective, then, it is distinguished from other subject matters by its conceptual focus on crime and offending behaviour across the lifespan of an individual and how this may change over time (McAra and McVie, 2012). Before we go on to examine the background and theory to the life course as it relates to children and young people, it will be helpful to make two further initial points.

Firstly, the focus of life course criminology is crime, and therefore on one of the most problematic and contested concepts in the social sciences, which involves 'endless disputes' about its meaning (Reiner, 2016). We do not have space within this chapter to engage in a deep philosophical discussion of the (ever-changing) meaning of crime and criminal acts. However, even at a superficial and everyday practical level, it is clear how the concept of crime changes over time and across different locations. For example, in October 2018, the Canadian government introduced legislation to legalise the possession and use of marijuana – a substance which, at that time, remained a controlled drug and was therefore illegal even to possess, let alone 'smoke', in the UK. In this example, if we smoked 'pot' outside our university offices in Bournemouth, England, we would be criminals, but if we boarded a plane and smoked a 'joint' in Toronto, Canada, we would be within the law. In a similar vein, we can readily think of examples of how laws in England have changed over time. In what now seems to him like a 'previous life', one of the authors (Heslop), when a serving police officer in Yorkshire, was required in the late 1980s and early 1990s to arrest adult gay men for homosexual conduct and acts in 'public'. In 1967, the Sexual Offences Act was passed. This decriminalised private homosexual acts between adult males aged over 21 (in England and Wales), while at the same time imposing heavier penalties on street offences (although the law was not changed for Scotland until 1980, or for Northern Ireland until 1982). In 1994, the Criminal Justice and Public Order Act lowered the age of consent for gay men from 21 to 18, and in 2001 it was further lowered to 16. Thus, in the UK, some acts have been decriminalised, making the conception of crime complex and fluid. However, even today, in countries such as Sudan, Saudi Arabia and Iran, homosexuality can still be punished by death. We can see, then, that there is nothing 'objective' about the concept of crime, or to put this more academically: crime is a 'socially constructed concept' which has 'no ontological reality' (Dorling et al, 2008, p 7), which means arguments about its meaning will always be open to debate. While the changing nature of crime and criminal acts is problematic for most if not all established theories of criminal behaviour, this argument can be deployed as a devastating critique of life course criminology, which both theoretically and methodologically is predicated on establishing patterns of offending over time.

Secondly, a range of different terms are employed when referring to the life course approach. Some understanding of these will be useful when reading in this area. This chapter is entitled 'Developmental and life course criminology' following the work of David Farrington (see overleaf). The range of the terms employed tend to be used interchangeably. While this can be confusing for those new to criminology, the terms can be differentiated somewhat. For instance, the life course perspective is a longitudinal approach which is used in a range of subject matters, all of which share the common idea of exploring individual change over time (the life course). Strictly speaking, developmental criminology (or developmental psychology) is a narrower term/approach which relates to exploring children's development from birth to young adulthood. Henceforth, in this chapter, we will predominantly use the term 'developmental and life course criminology' (DLC). At times, however, we may use other terms as employed by specific authors.

As noted, the defining feature of DLC is its specific focus on children and young people's developments in offending over time and relating this to their life circumstances. In other words, as Chamberlain (2015, p 155) more theoretically puts it: 'the life course perspective can best be conceptualised as viewing life events in the context of life changes, turning points and pathways, all of which are embedded in social institutions; specifically the family, the school, the work place and so on'. Development and life course criminologists, therefore, are concerned with issues of both continuity and change in behaviour, especially as these relate to offending in children and young people. A great deal of current research in this area focuses in practice on childhood and youth (Homel and France, 2005), which is our primary focus in this chapter. Indeed, this key focus on trying to explain why some young people commit crime and others abstain or discontinue makes sense from both theoretical and practical policy (including policing and broader criminal justice) perspectives, as the majority of officially recorded crime in Western nations is committed by young people (Chamberlain, 2015).

A foundational theoretical assumption of the DLC approach is that childhood criminality often represents a precursor to an adult life of crime. However, it is, of course, recognised that not all antisocial children and young people or those who have committed offences become adult offenders. This axiom is itself based on the arguably common-knowledge recognition that 'baggage' we may all carry from the past, such as the continuing effects of a happy and carefree childhood or, at the other extreme, experiences of neglect and other forms of early abuse, affects our attitudes and behaviour in the present. Even for readers new to theoretical criminology, this idea may seem quite obvious, but, of course, for DLC to become an established, coherent theory of criminal behaviour in children and young people, this required sustained methodological, empirical and intellectual academic endeavour.

As with many ideas in criminology, identifying the precise origins of DLC is not a straightforward task (Blokland and Nieuwbeerta, 2010); however, in broad terms, it 'has its roots in mainstream criminology and positivist social science' (Homel and France, 2005, p 1). Methodologically, the development of DLC theory has been heavily informed by quantitative (particularly statistical) methods, with the aim of measuring and establishing the relationship between life events and changes and patterns of offending behaviour. As such, DLC research fits closely methodologically to longitudinal study – a research design in which data is repeatedly gathered for the same subjects over time, with the aim of establishing correlations between risk factors, such as neglect or poverty and offending.

Many texts mention Sheldon and Eleanor Glueck (1930) as being among the first early proponents of the developmental approach (Blokland and Nieuwbeerta, 2010; McAra and McVie, 2012). The Gluecks were among the first criminologists to perform studies of persistent juvenile offenders and they made attempts to predict criminality using statistics. During the 1930s, they began a ten-year longitudinal research project following a cohort of 500 boys who had been remanded to Massachusetts reform schools (Glueck and Glueck, 1930). This led to the publication in 1950 of their controversial work *Unravelling Juvenile Delinquency*, which contained 'social prediction tables' and claimed to show that potential deviants could be identified by as young as six years of age.

The developmental perspective snowballed over the course of the 20th century, particularly from the 1970s onwards within US Criminal Justice Studies (McAra and McVie, 2012). Of particular note during this period, the American sociologist and criminologist Marvin Wolfgang and his collaborators successfully completed one of the most well-known studies of the longitudinal progression of crime. This research, usually referred to as the 'Philadelphia Birth Cohort Study' (Wolfgang et al, 1972), was a retrospective study of criminal activity among nearly 1,000 males up to the age of 17 born in Philadelphia during 1945. Importantly, this study was among the first to highlight that a small group of offenders were responsible for committing a disproportionately high number of offences (behaviour which in these days would probably result in them being labelled as 'repeat' or 'persistent' offenders (Whitehead, 2011)). This generated the interest of both academics and politicians (particularly in the US) in attempts to identify this active delinquent subgroup and subject the individuals to policies aimed at redirecting their criminal development (Blokland and Nieuwbeerta, 2010).

Blokland and Nieuwbeerta (2010) indicate that the key element of DLC here is that criminal involvement results from a lack of social control and that this itself changes and develops at various turning points as children and young people grow. Prior to these changes, the child or young person may still receive greater reward for engaging in criminal behaviour than they would if they refrained; whereas as they grow, other responsibilities and a desire for stability and life structure assumes greater importance.

Similar ideas about patterns of offending over time being influenced by stability or change can be found in Terrie Moffitt's (1993) much-cited 'dual taxonomy' of offending behaviour theory. However, in contrast to the aforementioned work of Laub and Sampson (2003), at the heart of Moffitt's theory '[l]ies a biologically grounded model of criminal behaviour which holds that the life course of a small proportion of adult offenders demonstrates that the roots of their offending behaviour lead back not only to their childhood but the fact that they possess neuropsychological defects' (Chamberlain, 2015, p 160).

Moffitt's theory was based on a longitudinal research of a cohort of just over 1,000 New Zealand children born in the early 1970s. Moffitt proposed that there are two main types of antisocial offenders in society: (1) the adolescence-limited offenders, who exhibit antisocial behaviour only during adolescence; and (2) the life course persistent offenders, who begin to behave antisocially early in childhood and continue this behaviour into adulthood. As indicted, this theory tends be used with respect to the notion of antisocial behaviour rather than the concept of crime due to the culturally specific and problematic nature of the latter (although we could just as easily argue that the term 'antisocial behaviour' is equally socially constructed and problematical).

Finally, then, we cannot conclude our brief summary of key DLC theorists without mentioning the British criminologist and forensic psychologist David P. Farrington. Farrington is well known for his research on the development of criminal behaviour throughout the life course and was largely responsible for the term 'developmental and life course criminology' entering the criminological lexicon (Farrington, 2003). Perhaps most notably, Farrington collaborated on the *Cambridge Study in Delinquent Development*, which followed 411 London boys born just before and after 1953, and was conducted over 24 years (Farrington et al, 1998). The study found that the persistent criminal is typically male, and is brought up within economically-deprived large families, in which parents are likely to be divorced or separated. It also found that poor parenting, including the use of harsh punishment, was an important factor predicting future criminality. At school, typical offenders had low educational attainment and associated with friends who also exhibited antisocial behaviour. Importantly, the study also found that the typical offender provided the same kind of disrupted and deprived family life for his own children, and thus the social conditions and experiences that produce delinquency are transmitted from one generation to the next.

In summary, then, DLC has made a significant contribution to our understanding of the relationship between offending and antisocial behaviour and age and a wide range of factors that vary over the life course. After *gender* (males in all countries for all periods of history have been shown to commit more offences than females – Leonard, 1982) comes the relationship between *age* and offending as the most established feature of recorded crime. Furthermore, as McAra and McVie (2012, p 556) helpfully point out, 'the findings from the development and life course perspective remind us that young people who offend most seriously and those who come into conflict with the law, are amongst the most vulnerable and victimised groups in our society'. That said, the DLC approach has a number of limitations, some of which we have already alluded to or mentioned. First and foremost is the well-rehearsed critique that developmental criminologists tend to see the relationship between offending and non-offending as unproblematic, having little to say about the socially constructed nature of the concept of crime and the role of states in defining what is and is not 'criminal', and how this itself changes over time. Secondly, and returning to the point made immediately above, for the most part, DLC theories are relatively quiet on how other key sociological categories of gender (and race) may matter in relation to patterns of offending and how they intersect with other variables, such as age, poverty and family adversity. Finally, while there is no doubt that DLC approaches may help us understand patterns of criminal and antisocial behaviour, it can be argued that the theory is too broad and, as such, in essence is only an expansion of other more established and focused criminological theories, such as strain, rational choice, labelling and control.

The importance of family, attachments and bonds

REFLECTION POINT 9.1

Think of a serious crime that has been reported in the media and pick up any newspaper or search the stories online. What do you notice?

It is a fair assumption that something will be said about the family background and upbringing of the child or young person responsible or alleged to be so. Whether this is a stable and loving family, of whatever composition, or a family that is 'dysfunctional' in some way, news media will impose or imply that a moral position should be taken to both the family and the environment of the child or young person involved.

Of course, there are some sound reasons for applying particular understandings to the ways we 'perform' family. For instance, we know from research that secure attachments are more likely to lead to positive outcomes than insecure, avoidant or dysfunctional attachments in one's family (see Chapter 7 in this volume for a comprehensive introduction to attachment theory). However, these stories also tend to demonise, through their explanations, certain groups or individuals who challenge the social mores of the time. This happened with single-parent families, and children and young people from 'broken homes' in the 1960s, 1970s and 1980s. Such thinking avoids a critical approach to the structural and environmental factors; therefore, it can be politically useful in deflecting attention from governmental or organisational responsibilities.

Hirschi's (1969) social bond theory reverses the frequently accepted idea that good children and young people are drawn into or learn criminal behaviour. He poses the question why most people behave reasonably or within the law most of the time. He draws on concepts aligned with attachment theory that indicate it is the strength of our ties to others, especially those close to us, that socialises us into behaving pro-socially.

To underpin his theory, Hirschi (1969) articulated a number of assumptions that are set within a particular social and historical context which have led to some degree of criticism. He suggested, according to Walsh (2012), that the 'typical' criminal was a young man, brought up in a fatherless, single-parent family in an urban slum and with school problems. This young person's difficulties stemmed from attachment problems, which in turn led to a lack of commitment to lawful behaviour, lack of involvement in social life and lack of belief in conventional morality. Gottfredson and Hirschi (1990) developed this thinking further in their social control theory. Low self-control develops in childhood as a result of inadequate boundaries and socialisation, and incompetent rather than loving and guiding parents.

Walsh (2012) recognises that there are many criticisms of these approaches to crime, including a focus on disrupted and non-conventional parents, which does not explain why most people do not enter crime. The parts played by genetics and child personality are also ignored. However, while more sophisticated understandings are required, a focus on childhood bonds and attachments is useful when seeking to understand criminal behaviour and its development in children and young people.

If we return to our Case Study 9.1 of Jon Venables and Robert Thompson, we can see that early socialisation, attachment and bonds played a significant part in their early lives and development. The public, the media and the judge blamed the parents and their dysfunctional lifestyles for the boys' subsequent behaviour. It is interesting that the mothers – Ann Thompson and Susan Venables – attracted most criticism. Mrs Thompson's alcoholism and Mrs Venables's 'loose morality' attracted comment, as though this explained the boys' crime. There is something in this understanding that stems from normative thinking about gender roles and responsibilities. It may also unwittingly indicate that the boys had no clear male role model to follow, which again fits into a normative model of heterosexual parenting, no doubt with asymmetric gender roles, being 'best'.

What this interpretation fails to take into account is the many children and young people who experience adverse family environments and negative attachment experiences who do not commit crime, especially such violent crime as evidenced in the Bulger case. While early attachment experiences and the support, guidance and authority or otherwise of a parent or guardian is important, there needs to be a wider approach. The environment in which children and young people grow is wider than the family: the structural aspects – quality of accommodation, neighbourhood, poverty, playgrounds and so on – interact with family relations and other factors.

School

After one's family, the strongest relationship to have an impact on children and young people is the one made with school. This includes relationships with teachers and other professionals, as well as peers. One of us remembers clearly an incident in primary school that shows the power of schooling. When 'lining up' to move to a different classroom, there was a 'disturbance' – some talking in the line – which was immediately blamed on one boy who was often picked out as a troublemaker. He became very upset and stormed out of school shouting and cursing, which confirmed the label to the teachers, who pointed out his 'bad behaviour' to us and inculcated in us a sense of how we should respond to our colleague. Throughout this boy's adolescence, he became increasingly disenchanted with school, truanting often and becoming involved in criminal behaviour because of the opportunities presented outside of school. The causes of his criminal behaviour are, of course, open to much debate, but lack of schooling and his negative experiences with those in authority, the teachers, certainly facilitated his move into crime. This young man grew up in a two-parent family, both of whom were in employment, and had a brother and sister who did not become involved in criminal behaviour.

Jon Venables and Robert Thompson are reported to have had an uneasy relationship with their primary school and were, in fact, truanting on the day they killed James Bulger (Morrison, 2011). There are many reasons for truanting, and this changes as the legislation and social and political meanings associated with education change. However, the fractured relationship with school indicated that these two were in a position to commit crime, as they were unsupervised and away from the authority provided by school. This is similar to Hirschi's (1969) social bond theory.

School, at its best, not only provides an educative environment in which children and young people can grow and develop into fulfilled human beings, but also provides an environment for safe experimentation, and social and emotional growth. However, it also represents an environment which, as the young man described, can label children and channel them into certain expectations that become embedded in their behaviour repertoire, as seen in Case Study 9.2.

CASE STUDY 9.2

Wesley was a 16-year-old African Caribbean young person who had recently been caught stealing cash from the school office. He had not been in trouble previously and his teachers, alongside his parents, talked to him in a firm but understanding way about what he had done, why he had done it and why it was wrong.

Peter, a white British 16-year-old, attended a different school. He had recently been caught demanding money from younger boys, who had become very frightened of him and of coming to school. The incidents came to light following a complaint by one of the parents of the boys from whom he had extorted money. The head teacher said she was not surprised by Peter's behaviour as he had always been a 'bad lot' and came from 'that estate' – a local housing estate that had experienced increased deprivation over the last ten years.

Questions
1. How might you explain the different reactions to the boys at each school?
2. Using your understanding of life course development and crime, can you think of explanations for the boys' behaviour?
3. How might you as a social worker work alongside the schools to support the boys in steering them away from crime?

Discussion

No model ever fits real-life practice in a perfect way. However, it does seem that some degree of labelling may have been used in each case – good boy Wesley/bad boy Peter. Both boys had done something wrong and, in Peter's case, of course, the consequences for other people may have been greater and this may also have led to the response. If Wesley could be considered through 'radical non-intervention' (see the transitions section overleaf), which seems appropriate, something had to be done to divert Peter from bullying and stealing from younger boys. This is perhaps where the social worker could be most useful in planning self-esteem building with Peter, who, if the head teacher's reaction about him and his environment were found to be commonplace, could have a profound effect on his behaviour. There may be housing and accommodation issues, there may be financial needs and there is most likely a need for positive leisure time activities to steer him away from future crime.

Friends, peers and forming relationships

Friendships at schools and in our neighbourhoods are highly influential, but as the child matures into a young person, relationships change. With puberty, especially, thoughts turn to more intimate relationships, which in turn raises questions of sexuality. However, before that, it is one's peers who help us to grow and find our place within the world. The importance of friendships is highlighted when we remember our own experiences of growing up and parents telling us not to play with certain peers at school or in the neighbourhood because they were 'a bad influence'. The assumption was that certain children or young people were predisposed to crime and antisocial behaviour because of their background, environment or experiences, and that this might be picked up through association (as already mentioned in Chapter 5 in Part I of this volume). Thompson and Venables had a relationship that guarded against some of their negative experiences of the world, family and school, although their friendship with each another was so powerful that it exerted a huge influence on their behaviour that led to the brutal killing of a toddler.

The development of one's sexuality and sexual experimentation associated with this has an interesting and, again, complex relationship with crime in young people. For instance, one of us (Parker) worked with a young man, aged 16, who was convicted of incest with his younger sister – a very serious crime. He was kept in local authority secure accommodation following his conviction, which also led to him becoming a Schedule 1 offender. This meant that he was recorded as an offender under Schedule 1 of the Children and Young Person's Act 1933, and his offence would never be considered a 'spent' crime under the Rehabilitation of Offenders Act 1974. Sexual development represents a powerful influence in most young people's lives and the need to contain, hold and master it is important (see Chapter 2 in Part I of this volume for an introduction to this idea).

The labels associated with sexual expression and development may also lead to crime, antisocial behaviours and repression of feelings. A young person who is gay may attract responses that are, at the very least, hate incidents, if not hate crimes, in a society that still oscillates around patriarchy and heterosexual hegemony.

Of course, friendships can be very positive as well as negative, and they can increase a sense of positive inhibition that prevents young people from engaging in behaviours that would be frowned upon by peers. Thus, encouraging and developing pro-social relationships can be a positive influence on moving people away from crime. Some earlier criminologists identified a shift away from crime in heterosexual young men once they began to engage in serious intimate relationships and assume a sense of responsibility. This change was rooted in a particular social and political landscape and it is likely that the situation is more complex. However, it shows that life course development can exert a profound influence on one's propensity to crime.

The social environment

The 'broken windows' hypothesis reflects a politically right-wing approach to the influence of socio-structural environments on people and their propensity to crime. The metaphor of broken windows is used to suggest that lack of attention to environmental breakdown, social incivility and minor misdemeanours is liable to create an atmosphere of disrespect towards the law and therefore to increase the likelihood of more increased crime or more 'windows being broken' (see Peter in Case Study 9.2).

Proposed by Wilson and Kelling in 1982, the theory had a profound effect on US policing. It has led to zero tolerance campaigns in the belief that immediately clamping down on criminal behaviour will deter its future occurrence. Labelling theory and the concept of radical non-intervention, introduced in the following pages, offer a different interpretation.

Transitions to young adulthood

When one of us (Parker) was undertaking qualifying education as a social worker, great store was being put on the concept of 'radical non-intervention' in probation work (Bottoms and McWilliams, 1979; McNeill, 2006). This suggested that young people tended to 'grow out' of criminal behaviour as they became more responsible for holding a job, for beginning families and changing their relationship with the world around them. The idea was that it was better not to intervene with young people who had committed a crime in a way that either labelled them as 'criminals' or exposed them to others who had committed perhaps more serious offences. In the former case, it was hoped that these young people would not see themselves as without hope and belonging to a group shunned by society. In the latter, it was hoped they would not 'learn' criminality for the future. This approach had considerable merit and, indeed, 'worked' to borrow a phrase for the neoliberal 'what works' school. This led to other scholars adopting this approach (Raynor and Vanstone, 1994, 2016; McNeill, 2006). However, doing nothing was not something that a popularly minded government could accept and the call for 'short, sharp shocks' grew in political attractiveness.

What lay in these changes was an association between political and structural approaches to youth offending and the experience of young people themselves, who desisted or otherwise according to the political life course as much as their own.

Making it real: applying knowledge to practice

Asking yourself some key questions when working with children and young people who have offended is important. The need to maintain a critically reflective stance should be uppermost in your mind. So, asking how you perceive certain environmental situations, what you think of parents, siblings and friends in a very honest way can help you identify some of the prejudices you might have that may suggest simplistic cause-and-effect understandings of these young people's lives. Identifying your own biases and prejudices (and we all have them, however unconscious these are!) will allow you to move beyond them to see the young people and the ecological systems they inhabit. In social work and other human service professions, it is crucial to develop your reflexivity.

In general terms, we can see children and young people develop across the life course depending on different experiences, and environmental and personal factors. Understanding the impact of these influences and experiences is important in understanding people in their context and offers ways of comprehending how they might best be helped. So, a young person who is exposed to criminal behaviour and experiences rejection may be in need of positive role models, nurture and respect. Much of this could have come from youth and community work in the past. However, with continuing austerity measures exerting great pressure on public services, many of these have been cut. This means that those professionals working with young people in these settings will need to find creative ways of working and to use themselves as role models for emulation. This is not, perhaps, something that comes naturally to many of us, but is an important part of working within a life course perspective with young people who have offended.

Conclusion

We return to the chapter objectives here regarding what the theories of life course criminology offer to our understanding of growth and development. Life course theories applied rigidly are normative and reductive, and as such require challenge. However, examined in context, they offer useful explanatory frameworks.

We have examined how relationship development and social mores have a great impact on the ways in which norms are established and rules governing social behaviour are accepted by children and young people. Relationships with a range of people – distant and proximal – exert a significant impact on the social development and behaviour of children and young people. In turn, this affects the opportunities they get in society and their subsequent development through the life course.

Reflective questions

1 Name some of the key theories of life course criminology and describe their underlying premises.

2 What do you think some of the criticisms of life course criminology are when considering children and young people?

3 As someone working with children, young people and families, consider how useful these life course theories are for understanding or explaining how a child or young person can be diverted from criminal behaviour.

Further reading

- Farrington, D.P. (2017) *Integrated Developmental and Life-Course Theories of Offending*. London and New York, NY: Routledge.
  This book provides a most comprehensive and rigorous approach to life course criminology. For anyone wishing to explore this area more deeply, this would be the text to consider.

- France, A. and Homel, R. (eds) (2007) *Pathways and Crime Prevention: Theory, Policy and Practice*. Cullompton: Willan Publishing.
  Theories and models are designed to be practical in terms of their explanatory power and their potential to determine ways of helping people move out of crime and criminal environments. This book provides a range of ideas to assist here, which focus on the criminal justice systems, but equally apply to social workers.

- McAra, L. and McVie, S. (2012) Critical debates in developmental and life-course criminology. In M. Maguire, R. Morgan and R. Reiner (eds), *The Oxford Handbook of Criminology*. Oxford: Oxford University Press.
  For a less thorough but nonetheless important introduction to life course criminology, this chapter provides a useful overview of the key concepts.

- Sampson, R.J. and Laub, J. (2005) A life-course view of the development of crime, *Annals of the American Academy of Political and Social Science*, 602(1): 12–45.
  Sampson and Laub's original research and the development of the Gluecks' work underpins much of what we know about how the life course potentially moulds and changes one's involvement with crime. To keep abreast of current research, this provides a good read.

References

Blokland, A.A.J. and Nieuwbeerta, P. (2010) Life course criminology. In P. Knepper and S.G. Shoham (eds), *International Handbook of Criminology*. London: CRC Press.

Bottoms, A.E. and McWilliams, W. (1979) A non-treatment paradigm for probation practice, *British Journal of Social Work*, 9(2): 159–202.

Bowling, B. (2006) A brief history of criminology, *Criminal Justice Matters*, 65(1): 12–13.

Chamberlain, J.M. (2015) *Criminological Theory in Context*. London: Sage.

Cohen, S. (1972) *Folk Devils and Moral Panics: The Creation of the Mods and the Rockers*. London: MacGibbon & Kee.

Dorling, D., Gordon, D., Hillyard, P., Pantazis, P., Pemberton, S. and Tombes, S. (2008) *Criminal Obsessions: Why Harm Matters More than Crime*. London: Centre for Criminal Justice Studies.

Farrington, D.P. (2003) Developmental and life-course criminology: Key theoretical and empirical issues. The 2002 Sutherland Award address, *Criminology*, 41(2): 221–256.

Farrington, D.P., Lambert, S. and West, D.J. (1998) Criminal careers of two generations of family members in the Cambridge study in delinquent development, *Studies on Crime and Crime Prevention*, 7: 85–106.

Glueck, S. and Glueck, E. (1930) *500 Criminal Careers*. New York, NY: Knopf.

Gottfredson, M. and Hirschi, T. (1990) *A General Theory of Crime*. Stanford, CA: Stanford University Press.

Hirschi, T. (1969) *The Causes of Delinquency*. Berkeley, CA: University of California Press.

Homel, R. and France, A. (2005) *Youth Justice Dictionary*. Cullompton: Willan.

Laub, J.H. and Sampson, R.J. (2003) *Shared Beginnings, Divergent Lives: Delinquent Boys to Age 70*. Cambridge, MA: Harvard University Press.

Leonard, E.B. (1982) *Women, Crime and Society: A Critique of Theoretical Criminology*. London: Longman.

Loader, I. and Sparks, R. (2012) Situating criminology: On the production and consumption of knowledge about crime and justice. In R. Maguire Morgan and R. Reiner (eds), *The Oxford Handbook of Criminology*. Oxford: Oxford University Press.

McAra, L. and McVie, S. (2012) Critical debates in developmental and life-course criminology. In M. Maguire, R. Morgan and R. Reiner (eds), *The Oxford Handbook of Criminology*. Oxford: Oxford University Press.

McAra, L. and McVie, S. (2012) Negotiated order: towards a theory of pathways into and out of offending. *Criminology and Criminal Justice*, 12(4): 347-376.

McNeill, F. (2006) A desistance paradigm for offender management, *Criminology and Criminal Justice*, 6(1): 39–62.

Moffitt, T. (1993) Adolescence – limited and life course persistent antisocial behaviour: A developmental taxonomy, *Psychological Review*, 100(4): 674–700.

Morrison, B. (2011) *As If*. London: Granta.

Newburn, T. (2017) *Criminology* (3rd edn). London: Routledge.

Raynor, P. and Vanstone, M. (1994) Probation practice, effectiveness and the non-treatment paradigm, *British Journal of Social Work*, 24(4): 387–404.

Raynor, P. and Vanstone, M. (2016) Moving away from social work and half way back again: New research skills in probation, *British Journal of Social Work*, 46(4): 1131–1147.

Reiner, R. (2016) *Crime: The Mystery of the Common Concept*. Oxford: Oxford University Press.

Walsh, A. (2012) *Criminology: The Essentials*. Los Angeles, CA: Sage.

Whitehead, T. (2011) Repeat offenders responsible for half a million crimes, *The Telegraph*, 27 October. Available from: https://www.telegraph.co.uk/news/uknews/law-and-order/8852705/Repeat-offenders-responsible-for-half-a-million-crimes.html

Wilson, G.L. and Kelling, J.Q. (1982) Broken Windows: Police and Neighborhood Safety. *The Atlantic*. March 1982 issue, Available from https://www.theatlantic.com/magazine/archive/1982/03/broken-windows/304465/

Wolfgang, M.E., Figlio, R.M. and Sellin, T. (1972) *Delinquency in a Birth Cohort*. Chicago, IL: University of Chicago Press.

10

Loss and bereavement in childhood

Sue Taplin

The father came back from the funeral rites.

His boy of 7 stood at the window, with eyes wide open and a golden amulet hanging from his neck, full of thoughts too difficult for his age.

His father took him in his arms and the boy asked him 'Where is mother?'

'In heaven,' answered his father, pointing to the sky.

The boy raised his eyes to the sky and long gazed in silence. His bewildered mind sent abroad into the night the question 'Where is heaven?'

No answer came: and the stars seemed like the burning tears of that ignorant darkness.

Tagore (1970), cited in Devlin (1996, p 63)

Introduction

Children and young people's experiences of loss and bereavement may include both the external losses of significant others, including siblings, parents, relatives and friends, and 'internal' losses of their own which, for some, may include the knowledge of their own impending death (this consideration is continued in Chapter 11 in Part II of the companion volume). The journey of loss and bereavement takes place alongside the child's development and transition to adulthood, in which many interrelating risk and protective factors mediate or moderate the child's experiences (Aynsley-Green et al, 2012; Aynsley-Green, 2017; Brewer and Sparkes, 2011; Ribbens McCarthy, 2006; Rolls, 2011; Rolls and Payne, 2007).

In this chapter, the profound and often lasting influence of loss and bereavement will be explored in the context of the growth and development of children and young people as they learn to negotiate their social worlds.

Chapter objectives

- explore children and young people's experiences of loss and bereavement;

- examine the concept of resilience and how it may relate to better outcomes for young people following a bereavement;

- outline theories of understanding and models of intervention which can inform human service practice in supporting children and young people following a bereavement.

Background and context

Bereavement is one of a range of difficult life events that children and young people may face. Fauth et al (2009) reported that, among a nationally representative sample of children aged five to 16, 3.5 per cent had experienced the death of a parent or sibling. Since many of these children were still young, the likelihood of losing a parent or sibling throughout the whole range of childhood into young adulthood is likely to be higher. A more recent analysis of data from the 1970 British cohort study (a longitudinal study of over 11,000 children born in 1970) reported that 5 per cent of these children when interviewed at age 30 had experienced the death of a parent or sibling by the time they were 16 years old (Parsons, 2011). Children may also experience the death of a friend and/ or other close relatives apart from their immediate family. One in 16 five- to 16-year-olds had experienced the death of a friend, according to the Office for National Statistics survey data (Fauth et al, 2009). In a further study of 11- to 16-year-olds, over three-quarters (78 per cent) reported that at least one of their close relatives or friends had died (Harrison and Harrington, 2001). This indicates the significance of loss and bereavement as an area of knowledge that social workers require.

REFLECTION POINT 10.1*

Think of a time where you experienced loss as a child or young person. That might be the loss of a toy, or a friend moving away from school or to another area. It may be the separation or divorce of your parents, the loss of a pet or the death of someone close. Consider how the experience made you feel and act and what helped to mitigate some of your upset and distress.

We all experience loss in different ways and the loss of different things is felt differently depending on who we are. However, what this reflection point helps to identify is that the experience of loss in childhood or as a young person is felt very deeply indeed. As a social worker, it is important to keep this in mind.

* Note: This reflection can be quite emotional, and it might be useful to undertake it when you have friends, family or other support close by and you do not need to complete it if it is too difficult at the moment (that is learning in itself).

Reviews of numerous studies on bereavement in childhood or adolescence following parental death report that young people in this situation do experience a wide range of emotional and behavioural responses to grief (Dowdney, 2000; Haine et al, 2008). These studies suggest that parents tend to report fewer symptoms and disorder in their children than children do themselves. The child often experiences an increase in anxiety, with a focus on concerns about further loss, the safety of other family members and fears around separation.

Haine et al (2008) reported that many children who are bereaved of a parent adapt well and do not experience serious problems. However, Fauth et al (2009) suggest that bereaved children are approximately one-and-a half times more likely than other children to be diagnosed with 'any' mental disorder. However, the analysis did not indicate whether these conditions were present before the bereavement and so was not able to comment on whether or not the bereavement could be said to have contributed to the child's diagnosis of mental ill health. However, the study found that children whose parent or sibling had died were more likely than other children to have problems with anxiety or alcohol use, whereas children who had experienced the death of a friend were more likely to display behavioural problems – for example, substance misuse, staying out late and truanting. This study did not find higher rates of 'clinical levels' of depression among bereaved children, although this is a high threshold and so milder forms are likely to have remained hidden.

Significantly, Christ (2000) found that difficulties may be experienced by bereaved children later in their lives, when subsequent life changes occur – for example, the remaining parent remarrying or the bereaved person having a child of their own. Haine et al (2008) suggest that a bereaved child's resilience or ability to cope with future adverse circumstances may be compromised by the earlier loss, although it may be that difficulties are being wrongly attributed to the bereavement – it is impossible to know the course the child's life would have taken if the bereavement had not occurred.

Children's perceptions of death

Following the death of a close family member, a child may not only experience the loss of the person who has died, but also, through identification, a loss of part of their own self (Fell, 1994). According to Randall (1993, cited in Devlin, 1996, p 64): 'Much of the behaviour of a child's grief represents their search for a new identity.' He illustrates this point when discussing the reaction of a five-year-old boy following the death of his mother, suggesting that the phrase 'Mummy's little boy' may be interpreted by a child as meaning: 'I was my mother's property, but she is dead, so who do I belong to now? Who *am I* now?'

Young children often have a limited understanding of the concept of death: they may have difficulty in accepting that it is irreversible and may wonder why the dead person has abandoned them (Furman, 1974). Wass (1984) suggests that children's understanding of death may be characterised by both 'magical thinking' and 'psychological causality', the former being a belief that 'wishes can come true' and that 'willing' something could in fact cause it to happen, and the latter being a belief that they had somehow caused the death because they had done something wrong.

Children's perceptions of death can also be influenced by their past experiences of loss and how these were 'managed' – for example, when a much-loved pet 'survives' serious illness because it is secretly replaced with a healthy but otherwise very similar creature. It can also be confusing for children to see a famous actor die in one film or programme, only to return alive in another the next day. This can lead to a belief that death is reversible.

There is a clear role for children and families practitioners in helping a dying parent to prepare even very young children for the time when they are no longer present to parent 'in person', as can be seen from the Case Study 10.1.

CASE STUDY 10.1

Adele was four when her mother Maria was diagnosed with advanced-stage breast cancer.

She died 18 months later, the week after Adele's sixth birthday. During the time of her illness, and aware of her prognosis, Maria met with a Bereavement Support Worker to prepare a 'memory box' containing a variety of objects, each one reflecting a memory of her daughter's early childhood, which she knew she would not be able to share with Adele when she grew up. The box also contained a bottle of Maria's favourite perfume and some letters which Maria wrote specifically to be read by Adele as she entered her teenage years, and others as she approached adulthood.

Adele took great pride in her memory box, and for the first few months after her mother's death, she looked through it with her father every night before she went to bed. As time moved on, Adele looked through the memory box less frequently, and only showed it to people she really trusted.

Adapted from Stokes, 2007, pp 60–61

Questions
1. As a social worker, how would your knowledge of human growth and development inform your practice with Maria and Adele?
2. How would you use social work theories to help you to understand their situation and which theories would help you to intervene?

Discussion
The memory box can be seen as a 'transitional object' which took the place of the physical bond between mother and child. As Adele grew up, she was able to

develop her own mechanisms for remembering her mother and 'holding on' to her memory, while also 'letting go'. Memories helped Adele reaffirm her sense of self as she encountered future changes, such as changing school, and gaining a step-mother and step-siblings.

Adolescents have also been identified as a vulnerable group, as they try to cope with the physical, psychological and emotional developments that accompany the transition from childhood to adulthood. Morgan (1991) suggests that adolescents 'need' to grieve in order to find the meaning of loss and its place within their world and individual value system. He observes that it is unlikely that a child will reach adolescence without experiencing the pain of loss. This may be associated with illness or death, or it may be the loss of a peer group when moving house or changing school, or the divorce or separation of parents or carers. Grief can therefore be seen as an essential component of the developmental process (Machin, 2009). Morgan (1991) contends that adolescents require support in order to deal effectively with loss and that, in the absence of effective support, the pain of grief may manifest itself in violence towards self or others. Adolescence can be a difficult time in terms of bio-psycho-social development and change, and a significant loss experienced at this time may magnify these difficulties, as can be seen in Case Study 10.2.

CASE STUDY 10.2

Matthew's father died suddenly when Matthew was 16. He was referred to the local Child Bereavement Service as his behaviour was becoming increasingly challenging: he was unable to manage his feelings of anger, not communicating with his mother and siblings, refusing to attend school and regularly using cannabis.

Matthew received one-to-one support sessions with a qualified Bereavement Worker. Following these, his drug use reduced significantly, his communication with his family improved and he returned to school just in time to take his GCSEs.

Matthew is still in touch with the Bereavement Support Service on an occasional basis, and is looking forward to pursuing a career in construction.

Questions

1. As a social worker, how would your knowledge of Human Growth and Development help you to understand Matthew's behaviour following his father's death?

2. Which theories would inform your intervention with Matthew and how would you work with him to complement the work of the Bereavement Support Service?

3. Which other services and professionals might you be working with to support Matthew?

Discussion

Matthew's father's death was unexpected, which further compounds the experience for Matthew. He is at a difficult stage in his development. Often, teenagers are struggling with bodily and hormonal changes that, in adolescent boys, can lead to aggression and, at times, violence. Your knowledge of this can assist in developing a plan with him. It is important for Matthew to recognise that it is not just the bereavement and subsequent grief that is affecting him, but his stage of development makes this potentially more difficult to deal with. He is also at that stage in life when peers and the wider environment begin to offer more opportunities, some of which may not be very positive for him. In Matthew's case, he began to use drugs, which again had a 'knock-on' effect on his schoolwork. The conditions for a serious situation developing were all present.

As a social worker, you would want to bring together those significant people involved in Matthew's life at that time. Working with the Bereavement Support Service would be likely to provide him with the space to talk and vent his emotions, to offer him some counselling support. Alongside this, you would want to work with the school in developing a supportive plan to ensure that his educational as well as pastoral needs were met.

It is unclear whether his drug use requires specialist intervention or indeed if he has wider family support and what his living environment was like. You would, of course, as a social worker undertake a comprehensive assessment that looked at the whole picture in order to form a plan of intervention with him. However, probably the most important aspect of your work is to develop a supportive, strengths-focused relationship with Matthew from which he can move forward at his own pace.

It is important to emphasise that children and adolescents may have different perceptions of loss and death depending on their age, intellectual development and life experience. For example, where children are more commonly exposed to death, as in times of war or civil disturbance, they are likely to have a more advanced understanding of its consequences. An example of this was reported by McWhirter et al (1983) in relation to children living in Northern Ireland at the height of the 'Troubles' (the name given to the period of sectarian conflict prior to the 'Good Friday Agreement', which began a peace process in 1998).

It is likewise important to be aware of the needs of children and young people whose vulnerability after bereavement may be increased because of adverse life experiences – for example, those who are 'looked after' (in the care of the local authority) or those within the youth justice system. Liddle and Solanki (2000) found that 22 per cent of young offenders from an outer London borough had experienced the death of a close relative. However, significant life events, such as a death in the family, appear often to have been omitted from an individual's case history. According to the Youth Justice Trust (UK), this is to the detriment not only of the young people involved, but ultimately of society as a whole, as it would seem that 'crime prevention would follow when grief, loss and rejection issues were acknowledged and attended to' (cited in Stokes, 2007, p 47). (See Chapter 9 in this volume for further discussion of the life course and criminal behaviour.)

Post-traumatic growth and resilience in children

Stokes (2007, p 40) provides the following case study:

> A five-year-old watches helplessly as his younger brother drowns. In the same year glaucoma begins to seriously impair his vision. His family are unable to fund the medical care that may save him from becoming blind. Both parents later die during his teenage years. Eventually he is taken into care and not permitted access to leisure activities, including music …

Stokes goes on to reveal that the individual in question is Ray Charles, who went on to become a world-renowned singer and musician. His life story is similar to that of other individuals who have faced great emotional, physical and social adversity, yet have somehow not only survived, but indeed can be said to have thrived. However, there are others who face ongoing struggles, underachieving educationally, with a series of failed relationships and impaired mental and emotional health. Clearly, what is of interest to social work practitioners is to ascertain what it is that determines whether or not a young person thrives, and what interventions may be helpful in facilitating a bereaved child's capacity to rebuild their life.

Developing resilience: the provision of specialist support

> A resilient child is not a child in a certain set of circumstances, but rather a child with a certain set of attitudes. (Stokes, 2007, p 40)

Machin (2009, p 15) contends that 'an apparent absence of distress is most likely where the process of change is a shared transition': a child's response to grief can be seen to be influenced by the reaction of those around them to the loss. Children and young people usually grieve within a family context, and this may work either to promote or to inhibit the expression of grief (Machin, 1993).

Stokes (2007, p 42) suggests that children and young people who have been bereaved of a parent are more likely to thrive if they:

- have a secure attachment and positive relationship with at least one 'competent' adult (see Chapters 7 and 13 in this volume);
- maintain a healthy 'connection' to the person who has died;

- engage successfully with their peers (see Chapter 4 in this volume); and
- are able to value themselves and feel valued by and valuable to others (see Chapter 4 in this volume).

REFLECTION POINT 10.2

How can a child or young person who has been bereaved maintain a 'relationship' with the person who has died? Might attachment theory help us to understand this? The idea that people can have a continuing relationship with people who die is clearly seen in research, where memory and evaluation of the dead person continues (Klass et al, 1996; Walter, 2018). This can be used very positively, especially if there has been a stable and secure attachment with the dead person. However, having the opportunity to talk through the experience and the feelings surrounding bereavement can also help where attachment has been more problematic – feelings can be revised.

The death of someone significant in the life of a child or young person is a key challenge for any child to cope with. However, an understanding of the features of a resilient 'mindset' can facilitate the ability of both formal and informal carers to nurture optimism and increase the potential of the young person to thrive. As previously mentioned, opportunities to talk about the person who has died in a way that brings comfort is a key aspect of this, particularly in cases where the relationship may have been broken or where the circumstances around the death were complex or violent. Above all, the child or young person will need to find a way to make sense of the loss that is appropriate to their age and cognitive ability (Stroebe and Schut, 1999).

REFLECTION POINT 10.3

Return to your own experiences of loss and identify your own ways of coping: what helped, what hindered and what you wanted. What is resilience to you? Consider what this might mean for your own social work practice.

Resilience implies energy, creativity and the flexibility to 'move on' with life, to encounter new situations and to dare to trust others and form appropriate secure attachments. While it may be possible to promote a resilient 'mindset' through existing services, it is important to be aware of what specialist child bereavement support is available in your local area, in order that referrals are made that are both appropriate and timely. The list below, adapted from Stokes (2007, p 55), provides suggestions as to what such services may provide:

- Encourage the child to construct a *coherent narrative* about their life, including their experience of loss and bereavement, which they can tell with emotional integrity throughout their lives.
- Develop cognitive and behavioural strategies to help a child rewrite negative scripts and challenge negative beliefs.
- Help the child to develop effective communication skills and strategies to use with their family and friends to talk about their loss, and the confidence to 'own' their story and communicate it to those they trust.
- Provide opportunities for bereaved children to develop empathy and have positive connections with others of a similar age who have been bereaved.
- Help children who have been bereaved to feel understood and confident with their peers and with teachers at their school or college.
- Create services that foster family cohesion and adaptability to future changes (for example, new partners, step-siblings).
- Provide a range of age-appropriate activities that encourage children to maintain continuing attachments to the person who has died, recognising that these will need to change and be re-offered as the child matures and develops.

If children are supported throughout the grieving process, they are less likely to develop problems in adulthood as a result of unresolved grief (Devlin, 1996). Child bereavement services that are timely and targeted, recognising those who may be particularly vulnerable or 'at risk', may prevent a significant number of children and young people being referred to mental health or youth justice services later in life.

Examples of what child bereavement services look like, and how and to whom they could be targeted, are provided in Figures 10.1 and 10.2.

Supporting children and young people in bereavement

Clearly, the needs of bereaved children should not be seen as the sole province of specialist bereavement support agencies; all human service practitioners can play a role in building resilience and in recognising the particular needs of children who are bereaved (Jewett, 1982). There would seem to be a particular role for schools here, as the place where most children spend a large proportion of their daily lives. According to Akerman and Statham (2014), 'whole-school' policies on promoting emotional well-being could act as a protective factor for bereaved children, alongside training staff about how to respond 'in-house' when a child has experienced the death of someone close, and being prepared to refer children to more specialist support where appropriate. Case Study 10.3 provides an example of how services can work together to ensure that a child or young person has consistent support following the death of a parent.

Figure 10.1: Irish Childhood Bereavement Network

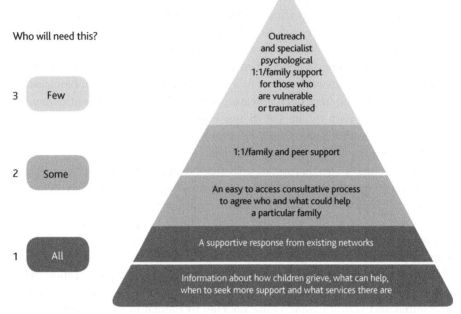

What good provision for bereaved children and young people
and their parents and carers looks like

Who will need this?

3   Few

2   Some

1   All

Outreach
and specialist
psychological
1:1/family support
for those who
are vulnerable
or traumatised

1:1/family and peer support

An easy to access consultative process
to agree who and what could help
a particular family

A supportive response from existing networks

Information about how children grieve, what can help,
when to seek more support and what services there are

Source: With kind permission from the Irish Childhood Bereavement Network, https://www.childhood
bereavement.ie

CASE STUDY 10.3

Chloe was 17 when her father died of lung cancer. During the last phase of his illness and following his death, Chloe's relationship with her mother had become increasingly difficult – Chloe was reluctant for anyone outside the family to know that her father had died, and she had stopped caring about her appearance or personal hygiene. Her college work was also affected as she was experiencing intrusive thoughts about death and she found it difficult to concentrate on academic work.

Chloe's Bereavement Support Worker gained Chloe's permission to involve the college in supporting her to build her self-esteem, to make sense of what had happened and to begin to rebuild her relationship with her mother. Through attending a Therapeutic Weekend run by the local Child Bereavement Support Service, Chloe was also introduced to a supportive peer group, with whom she has continued to meet.

As a result of this, Chloe gradually started to take better care of herself and is now planning to take up the offer of a place at university.

Figure 10.2: The Irish Childhood Bereavement Care Pyramid

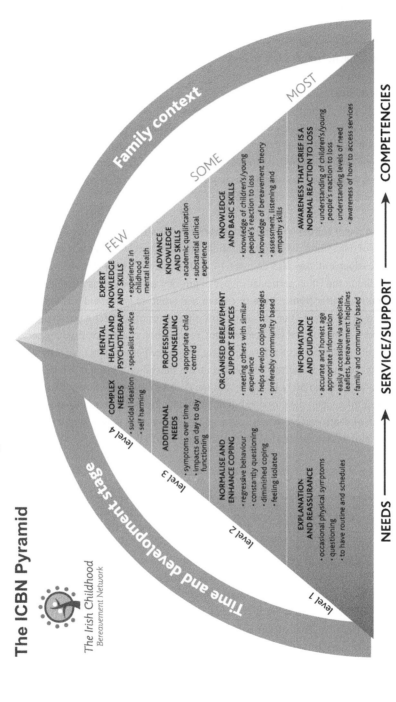

Source: With kind permission from the Irish Childhood Bereavement Network, https://www.childhoodbereavement.ie

Questions

1. How might your knowledge of Human Growth and Development inform your understanding of Chloe's behaviour following her father's death?
2. Which theories would inform your intervention with Chloe and how could you, as a social worker, promote a multi-disciplinary approach to her care?
3. How might culture exert an impact on this case?

Discussion

You may have gone back to some of the ideas discussed in Case Study 10.2. Again, there is a constellation of things happening for Chloe that add up and create great difficulties for her. She tries to master these by ignoring her appearance and personal hygiene, which remain things under her control. As a social worker, your main task here is to find ways in which she can regain mastery of other aspects of her life that she can influence and promote.

Questions of culture are central to sensitive social work practice. (See Chapter 5 in Part I of this volume, which covers taking culture into account in critical approaches to development. See also Chapter 11 in this volume, which focuses on Muslim families in the UK in particular.) Ways of grieving and the rituals associated with them may differ from culture to culture and group to group and it is important that you are aware of or ask about how differences may affect a young person's outward display of grief and bereavement. For instance, a white British young person may be considered to be acting strangely, or labelled pathological in grief by some, if they screamed, shouted and wailed at the funeral of a loved one rather than sobbing more demurely. However, this may not be the case with another culture. In countries where heat makes burial, or bodily disposal, necessarily speedy, the shock of death can be so immediate as to provoke such strong reactions, and it may also be an expected element of showing your loss.

Conclusion

This chapter has explored children and young people's experiences of loss and bereavement and considered some of the factors which can influence their ability to thrive. In particular, we have explored the concept of resilience and how it relates to improving outcomes for children and young people following a bereavement. Lastly, we have considered relevant theories of understanding and models of intervention which can inform our practice in supporting children and young people. As human service practitioners, we have a responsibility to offer support which can help a bereaved child grow into adulthood, empowered with personal resources that can enable them to live a satisfying and successful life in which, despite adverse circumstances, they can realise their full potential (Stokes, 2007).

Reflective questions

1 What do you understand by the concept of resilience?

2 Do you consider some children and young people to be less likely than others to thrive after a bereavement and, if so, who and why?

3 If a child or young person with whom you are working experiences an unexpected bereavement, would you know what support might be available to them in your local area?

4 Are you aware of what support might be available to you in working with children and young people who have been bereaved?

Further reading

- Akerman, R. and Statham, J. (2014) *Bereavement in Childhood: The Impact on Psychological and Educational Outcomes and the Effectiveness of Support Services*. London: Childhood Wellbeing Research Centre.
  This research shows the importance of offering support and intervention to children and young people when they are bereaved. It also shows the potential effects of bereavement if it is not dealt with constructively.

- Aynsley-Green, A., Penny, A. and Richardson, S. (2012) Bereavement in childhood: Risks, consequences and responses, Editorial, *BMJ Supportive and Palliative Care*, 2(1): 2–4.
  This research paper provides empirical evidence for some of the impacts and long-lasting effects that bereavement of a significant person can have on children and young people. This provides important knowledge for social work practice, as social workers need to be up-to-date in their knowledge of research to work alongside other professionals.

- Childhood Bereavement Network (2009) *Grief Matters for Children: A Call to Action*. London: National Children's Bureau.

- Dyregrov, A. (2008) *Grief and Young Children*. London: Jessica Kingsley.
  This practice volume examines the grief of young children in particular. It does not consider adolescence, however. Describing different effects of bereavement and the grieving process, it offers social workers a good knowledge base from which to practise.

References

Akerman, R. and Statham, J. (2014) *Bereavement in Childhood: The Impact on Psychological and Educational Outcomes and the Effectiveness of Support Services*. London: Childhood Wellbeing Research Centre.

Aynsley-Green, A. (2017) Think adult – think child! Why should staff caring for dying adults ask what the death means for children in the family? Invited Review, *British Medical Bulletin*, 123(1): 5–17.

Aynsley-Green, A., Penny, A. and Richardson, S. (2012) Bereavement in childhood: Risks, consequences and responses, Editorial, *BMJ Supportive and Palliative Care*, 2(1): 2–4.

Brewer, J. and Sparkes, A. (2011) Parentally bereaved children and post-traumatic growth: Insights from an ethnographic study of a UK childhood bereavement service, *Mortality*, 16(3): 204–222.

Christ, G. (2000) *Healing Children's Grief: Surviving a Parent's Death from Cancer*. New York, NY: Oxford University Press.

Devlin, B. (1996) Helping children to grieve, *International Journal of Palliative Nursing*, 2(2) https://doi.org/10.12968/ijpn.1996.2.2.63

Dowdney, L. (2000) Annotation: Childhood bereavement following parental death, *Journal of Child Psychology and Psychiatry*, 41(7): 819–830.

Fauth, B., Thompson, N. and Penny, A. (2009) *Associations between Childhood Bereavement and Children's Background, Experiences and Outcomes: Secondary Analysis of the 2004 Mental Health of Children and Young People in Great Britain Data*. London: National Children's Bureau.

Fell, M. (1994) Helping older children grieve: A group therapy approach, *Health Visitor*, 67(3): 92–94.

Furman, F. (1974) *A Child's Parent Dies*. London: Yale University Press.

Haine, R.A., Ayers, T.S., Sandler, I.N. and Wolchik, S.A. (2008) Evidence-based practices for parentally bereaved children and their families, *Professional Psychology: Research and Practice*, 39(2): 113–121.

Harrison, L. and Harrington, R. (2001) Adolescents' bereavement experiences: Prevalence, association with depressive symptoms, and use of services, *Journal of Adolescence*, 24(2): 159–169.

Jewett, C. (1982) *Helping Children Cope with Separation and Loss*. Boston, MA: Batsford.

Klass, D., Silverman, P.R. and Nickman, S.L. (1996) *Continuing Bonds: New Understandings of Grief*. London: Routledge.

Liddle, M. and Solanki, A.R. (2000) *Missed Opportunities: Key Findings and Implications from Analysis of the Backgrounds and Life Experiences of a sample of Persistent Youth Offenders in Redbridge*. London: NACRO.

Machin, L. (1993) *Working with Young People in Loss Situations*. Harlow: Longman.

Machin, L. (2009) *Working with Loss and Grief: A New Model for Practitioners*. London: Sage.

McWhirter I., Young, V. and Majury, J. (1983) Belfast children's awareness of violent death, *British Journal of Social Psychology*, 22(2): 81–92.

Morgan, J.D. (ed.) (1991) *The Dying and the Bereaved Teenager*. Philadelphia, PA: Charles Press.

Parsons, S. (2011) Long-term impact of childhood bereavement. CWRC Working Paper. Childhood Wellbeing Research Centre.

Randall, P. (1993) Aspects of bereavement 4: Young children grieve differently from adults, *Professional Care of Mother and Child*, 3(2): 36–37.

Ribbens McCarthy, J. (2006) *Young People's Experiences of Loss and Bereavement: Towards an Interdisciplinary Approach*. Maidenhead: Open University Press.

Rolls, L. (2011) Challenges in evaluating childhood bereavement services: The theoretical and practical issues, *Bereavement Care*, 30(1): 10–15.

Rolls, L. and Payne, S. (2007) Children and young people's experiences of UK child bereavement services, *Mortality*, 12(3): 281–303.

Stokes, J. (2007) Resilience and bereaved children: Helping a child to develop a resilient mind-set following the death of a parent. In B. Monroe and D. Oliviere (eds), *Resilience in Palliative Care: Achievement in Adversity*. Oxford: Oxford University Press.

Stroebe, M. and Schut, H. (1999) The dual process model of coping with bereavement: Rationale and description, *Death Studies*, 23(3): 197–224.

Tagore, R. (1970) *Lectures and Addresses*, A. Soares (ed.), Madras: Macmillan.

Walter, J. (2018) How continuing bonds have been framed across millennia. In D. Klass and E.M. Steffan (eds), *Continuing Bonds in Bereavement: New Directions for Research and Practice*. London: Routledge.

Wass, H. (1984) Concepts of death – a development perspective. In H. Wass and C.A. Corr (eds), *Childhood and Death*. Washington, DC: Hemisphere.

11

Culture and coming of age:
the example of Muslims in Britain

Sara Ashencaen Crabtree

Introduction

There are few minority ethnic groups in the UK that have come under the levels of political and media scrutiny experienced by the wider Muslim community in the past decades, particularly in relation to the family, and especially in terms of the transitional years leading from adolescence towards young adulthood. This carries implications for social work practice in relation to working with Muslim families in a culturally sensitive way.

This chapter covers a number of interlinked areas in exploring the implications of this topic from a social work perspective. These include a focus on understanding the context of the family in Islam, using a combined religious, social and cultural lens. Through this focus, social workers are urged to adopt a wider social science view, prevalent in anthropological and sociological ethnography, to seeing the family as functioning within psychosocial and ecological frameworks (Parker and Ashencaen Crabtree, 2018).

The chapter also considers the position of Muslims in the UK using current demographic data, which is important for professionals to be aware of in terms of connecting this information to practice priorities. Here, we will consider the concept of transition, exploiting a social work understanding, as relating to the changes affecting the growing child, returning to an ecological framework that considers the implications of living within a multicultural contemporary society.

Islamophobia is critically discussed within an analysis of how social work concepts and theorisation, so relevant to a professional understanding of human growth and development, have sought to challenge oppression – a range of social or political acts that limit the ability of certain groups to act independently and leave them open to exploitation and abuses of power. Islamophobia is contextualised as operating within social attitudes of pejorative discrimination, as well as the wider and prevailing political discourse concerning terrorism and Islam. The impact on families of counter-terrorist strategies targeting Muslim youth and their families will also be discussed.

Gender norms play an important role in Islam and require some explanation for social work practice. The overlapping contentious issues of culture and religion are explored in relation to expectations of modesty and propriety, particularly regarding girls and young women, together with guardianship of such by their families and communities. This follows a discussion of the evidence base regarding the abuse of young Muslim girls.

Moving on, a review of research data examines examples of Muslim youth's successful negotiation of transitions to adulthood in the European/British context using, once again, social work concepts.

The chapter concludes with a critical discussion of social work reflectivity (Fook, 2007) and ethnographic self-reflexivity in terms of applying the ideas covered in this chapter to other domains and contexts in a multicultural setting. Anti-oppressive practice is reliant on the basic principle that good practice operates within an appreciation of and adaptation to the issues and implications of diversity. To reside and practice in a multicultural society requires a particular attitude – namely, that there is much to learn from unfamiliar cultures and much to offer in return, within interactive power relations of equality and respect.

Chapter objectives

- introduce the context of Islam and Muslim families;

- explore the rise of Islamophobia in its impact on families;

- critique notions of gender in Muslim families;

- examine the importance of critical reflection and reflexivity when working in multicultural settings.

Background and context

Difference and diversity are arguably the focus of the social work profession, and equally characterise what constitutes a multicultural and therefore multi-faith modern European society, like the UK. Yet few groups have been subject to so much misunderstanding as British Muslims (with the recent exception, perhaps, of American Muslims); and there has been such an accentuated general public attitude towards the idea of Muslims as different to an unbridgeable degree compared to other groups in society. Muslims are now viewed by some as holding extreme views, lifestyles and behaviours – a relatively recent phenomenon. This is in contrast to the historic past, where Muslim societies were seen as either opulent, luxurious and decadent, epitomised by the Turkish Ottoman Empire, or as austere and insular desert cultures of the impoverished Middle East (long before the discovery of oil fields). Or, to delve further into history, Muslim societies of the Middle Ages were associated with great scholarship, artistry and religious plurality, typical of the Moorish civilisation of Andalusia. Even further back than this, they were seen as the Saracen rival for the holy prize of Jerusalem.

Occidental (Westernised European) views of Islam have not, with few exceptions, regarded the faith and the faithful as familiar aspects of the known landscape. Instead, as Edward Said (1978) famously argued, the Muslim world has been the colonised canvas upon which many fantasies and misconceptions have been projected. The notion of the languorously inviting, sexually wanton harem is one such Western, masculinised fantasy. The Moroccan feminist and writer, Fatima Mernissi (1975), has shown this to be false: drawing on her own family experiences, she described the Muslim world as a location of active, gendered resistance. This is in stark contrast to the projections of the contemporary period. Since the Al-Qaeda terrorist attacks on the Trade Center Building in New York (more commonly known as 9/11), Muslims and Islam have been more likely to be associated, in the public imagination, with erratic extremism than with sensuality, medicine and mathematics.

The Muslim family

The family is the central unit of social organisation in Islam, from which nurture and care, welfare, education, community allegiances and, in particular, religious piety spring. The role and value of parenting, in particular that of motherhood, are celebrated highly in Islam through references in the Holy Qur'an and the hadiths (sayings) associated with Prophet Mohammed (peace be upon Him) – an aspect explored in more detail in Chapter 7 in Part II of the companion volume. Mothers are duty-bound to provide a solid foundation for their children on the path to adult responsibility. Their teaching and example is expected to provide essential guidance to the growing child within the Muslim community of believers – the *Ummah* (Stang Dahl, 1997). If the responsibilities of mothers are primarily located directly within the bosom of the family, those of fathers are more external, in terms of being expected to provide financial support and protection for the family. Gendered roles for parents are therefore considered to be more distinctly delineated in Islam than in Westernised feminism and/or metrosexual ideals of overlapping and blurred parenting roles for mothers and fathers.

A more traditional family structure where mothers carry the responsibility for day-to-day care within the home and fathers are external providers may be expected to be common among many, but not all, Muslim families in the UK (Ashencaen Crabtree et al, 2016). It is within these structures that girls and boys will be raised, with a general expectation that these values will be passed on to the younger generation. Access to tertiary (university) education is also a feature of Muslim participation in civic society across Europe and, indeed, is encouraged in Islam, which sets high store by education (Haw et al, 1998). Nor does faith prevent women from taking up paid work if they so wish, although it is not their responsibility to earn the family income.

Demographic data gathered by the Muslim Council of Britain (MCB) provides very useful statistics on young Muslim women's rate of employment (about half of the national average), with a higher unemployment rate across genders, which may result from Islamophobic prejudice (MCB, 2015). Statistics are also available on Muslim youth's access to tertiary education, which is slightly lower than the national average, although there is a low proportion of black and minority ethnic student uptake by Russell Group universities (MCB, 2015). Overall, the statistics presented in the MCB report show a decidedly upwards trend compared to the previous decade, when weaker educational levels, lower employment rates, low income rates, poorer housing and generally much higher levels of under-privilege characterised the socially marginalised position of British Muslims compared to the general population (Ashencaen Crabtree et al, 2008). Nevertheless, poor health status – both physical and mental – remains a concern for British Muslim minority ethnic (ME) groups (Ashencaen Crabtree et al, 2016).

The vulnerability of particular ME groups – in terms of social oppressions, the associated marginalisation of communities, and individual and family stress – is a concern for social work. For example, the much-condemned Islamophobic, facetious remarks by the then Foreign Secretary, Boris Johnson, about burqa-wearing Muslim women resembling 'bank robbers' and 'letter boxes' were followed by a 375 per cent spike in hate crimes the following week (Parveen, 2019). Case Study 11.1 is illustrative of the impact of Islamophobic attacks on individual family members and how such reactions may play out in the immediate ecological and socially interactive environment of such families.

CASE STUDY 11.1

Nazir is a 14-year-old British Bangladeshi boy with four siblings, living with his family in council accommodation in London. The family are close-knit, have extended family living close by and have good relationships with most of their neighbours, some of whom share their cultural beliefs. Nazir's parents, however, have struggled to support their family. His father, the sole family breadwinner, has found it difficult to obtain regular work outside of zero-contract, low-skilled, temporary labour.

The family used to regard life in the UK as hard, but not threatening. Recently, however, Nazir's elder sister was subject to a racist attack when a man in the street called her a terrorist and tried to pull off her traditional headscarf. Nazir's mother has become very anxious since this event, and while she has always spoken only very basic English, she was previously not worried about leaving the house. She is now afraid to go shopping without her husband and Nazir in case she attracts the same abuse as her daughter.

The anxiety felt by the family weighs heavily upon Nazir. Although he has good friends at school and likes most of his teachers, he has also experienced episodes of name-calling, bullying and harassment. He has chosen not to tell his family about one of these incidents, when a small group of strangers taunted him at the bus stop, saying his family would soon be rounded up and sent back to where they came from. Nazir is increasingly beginning to wonder where he fits into British society and what the future holds for them all. He has begun to find it a relief to speak in private to other Muslim teenagers he knows in the neighbourhood about his pent-up feelings of fear, resentment and anger.

Questions

1. How would you describe the different pressures experienced by each member of this family?
2. What concerns might you have for any of the family members?
3. Is there a role for social work in relation to any of the issues you have identified? If so, what would that be?

Discussion

The impact of negative stereotyping is never easy for a person to deal with. However, in respect of Islamophobia, it can be exacerbated by pressures from media, and political statements can make its experience very frightening indeed. While Nazir appears to be on the receiving end of this discrimination, he is likely to be mindful of the effects it can have on his wider family. As a social worker, you should take into account this wider, social and environmental aspect. You are working with communities and other groups – not only families and individuals – and you may have a role within the community to dispel myths and to listen to fears and concerns, as well as to provide individual and family support where requested.

REFLECTION POINT 11.1

Think of your own positions you hold in society. For example, do you consider yourself to be a young person or an older adult, a Muslim or non-Muslim, a person with a disability or no disability? Think of as many positions as you can. How do you think being targeted for occupying one of those positions may impact on your development from a young person to an adult?

Think what this might mean for working as a social worker with people who have experienced a hate crime. (Important: if you have experienced such an event and need help or support, please talk to your university tutors in the first instance and to the police.)

Transitions

The concept of transition, commonly used in both psychology and social work, relates to moving through the stages of human life – in this case, from childhood to adulthood (Walker, 2017). Such phases are replete with individual events and experiences which can be either very positive, life-enhancing and ego-boosting, or, at the other extreme, highly traumatic and destructive. The idea of formally becoming an adult may be liberating for some teenagers and dreaded by others, but, in general, mixed feelings and stress are to be expected by most people in relation to change. Families may also struggle with adolescent transitions – formerly-close parent–child relations may become tense and uncertain; yet strong bonds of intimacy can also be forged during this time as identities and roles begin to change. Beckett and Taylor (2016) refer to transition as reaching a 'turning point' in human life, where some turbulence may be expected; although this, they posit, may be exaggerated given the following factors:

- atypical timing – puberty arrives out of synchronisation with other teenage peers;
- too many turning points – rapid and multiple changes create individual coping problems;
- unsupportive context – the young person does not find the level of intimate support and acceptance needed to cope with transitional changes.

Unequal social positions combined with discriminatory attitudes are the context in which many Muslim children will grow up in the West. The transition from young childhood to adolescence and onwards towards adulthood will be marked by such inequalities to a lesser or greater degree. Other factors, such as migration (forced or voluntary), the parental country of origin and/or cultural variations, as well as conversion to Islam, will shape individual attitudes and experiences, which may have an impact on the material outcomes for such youngsters and their families.

Furthermore, transitions and other human growth changes do not only take place within the inclusive context of the family: they will be directly influenced by the mores and values of surrounding communities and wider society. How these vectors of influence may in turn be accommodated, adapted, challenged or resisted may vary widely across groups, but where there is an obvious gulf between dominant social values and those of particular ME families and communities, then these gulfs are likely to represent significant terrains of contested values, through which young people will need to tread a cautious path.

Stigma

Following 9/11, uniquely among other European nations, the UK rushed towards developing a raft of anti-terrorist legislation (Ashencaen Crabtree et al, 2008). Since then, there have been a number of other terrorist attacks in Europe (and globally), including the 2017 Manchester bomb attack targeting young fans leaving an Ariana Grande concert (Dodd et al, 2017). A few days later, eight people were killed in London when a van was used as a terrorist weapon to deliberately plough into pedestrians on London Bridge and other bystanders were stabbed (BBC, 2017). These events preceded and followed in the wake of a number of attacks in Europe and beyond, drawing widespread condemnation of Islamist violence, which added to a turbulent wave of anxiety and insecurity through stigma by proxy (the stigmatising labelling of individuals by association) among law-abiding Muslim communities.

Such stigmatisation carries serious implications for Muslim families; where the exclusive authority of parenting has been undermined in Western societies at many levels, including by the media. However, the control of state intervention can be particularly felt through social work, education, health care and youth services, where no other parenting group has come under as much state suspicion as Muslim parents in the UK. In 2008, Ashencaen Crabtree and colleagues described the Muslim family as being the first buffer for security offensives: these Muslim families were often viewed as inculcating, nurturing or failing to extinguish seeds of religious extremism in young relatives. The family home itself has been seen as the toxic nest where extremism thrives – and it was here that the focus of social policy strategies and professional surveillance would be exercised as a risk-prevention strategy (Ashencaen Crabtree, 2017a, 2017b).

The UK's counter-terrorist strategy 'Prevent', designed to detect and deal with so-called 'radicalisation' in Muslim youth, illustrates this heavy-handedness in seeking to draw a contested comprehensive surveillance net across UK services serving families and children (Ashencaen Crabtree, 2017b). For example, non-voluntary referrals have been made to Prevent counter-terrorist teams by a variety of professional staff in relation to: an old, disabled man planning his pilgrimage to Mecca; spotting a child on a domiciliary health visit watching an Arab television programme beside various Arab language literature (Taylor, 2018); and seeing a student reading literature about terrorism at his university library for the purpose of his course work. Parents have been charged with the responsibility of policing their children for radicalism and are expected to confiscate the passports of any child considered at risk of absconding to Islamist causes; those failing to carry out these precautions face the jeopardy of suspect citizenship allegiance (Ashencaen Crabtree, 2017a).

Understanding and using relevant concepts, principles and theorisation

The concept of 'culture' is too often applied from a strongly ethnocentric position, where culture invariably appears to be associated with other groups, rather than with ourselves; and where an unthinking assumption is often made regarding our normality versus other groups' differences that pose as 'culture'. In social work, 'cultural competence' has been an idea framing the education of social workers to be able to negotiate different cultures in their work by understanding the broad parameters of beliefs and lifestyles relating to them. The danger has lain in potential homogenisation or 'essentialisation' of stereotypic ideas about different groups (Parker et al, 2018), such as 'Asian families look after their own', 'all Muslim families accept men's authority over women' and so on.

To practise with cultural 'sensitivity' means knowing some general norms, behaviours and etiquette, but equally remaining aware that all groups and families hold differences even within highly homogenous settings (which is not a general feature of a diverse Europe, including the UK). Thus, in respect of Muslim families, these constitute a very heterogeneous grouping in the UK in terms of ethnicity, migration, generational differences, conversion, secularisation and religious interpretation, into which we can add the influential strands of cultural and intercultural notions, politics, education, employment and health, to name but some variations. However, this is not to say that identifying as a Muslim is a completely fluid category. We need to bear in mind that some Muslims, like Jews and Christians (all being Abrahamic religions), embrace secularity and might regard themselves as conforming more to a cultural heritage or ethnic mould rather than being a fully signed-up member to a faith.

> ## REFLECTION POINT 11.2
> Consider how much you know about Islam and what you need to know to work as a social worker with Muslim young people.
>
> Much may depend on whether you are a Muslim or non-Muslim, but this is also important in determining how your knowledge may influence your practice as a social worker. Being reflective and questioning your knowledge, understanding and the influence of your own position is important in developing social work practice wisdom. Think about these issues as you read the following section.

Piety in Islam

To be a practising, pious Muslim, certain conditions apply where the five duties must be observed:

1. *Shahadah* – bearing witness to the monotheistic nature of Islam and the prophecy of Mohammed.
2. *Salat* (prayer) – five times a day, facing Mecca and fixed according to the movement of the sun.
3. *Zakat* – an alms-giving tax aimed at benefiting the needy in society.
4. S*aum* (fasting) – Ramadan, the ninth month in the Muslim calendar, is the month of fasting, when practising Muslims refrain from eating, drinking and smoking from sunrise to sunset. Children often commence initiation into adult religious practice by beginning to observe Ramadan.
5. *Hajj* – pilgrimage to the sacred monument, the *Ka'aba* in Mecca, Saudi Arabia, which all pious Muslims are encouraged to take in their lifetime.

These duties are complemented by the six pillars of faith, which are summarised as: a belief in Allah as the One Creator and Sustainer of all beings, followed by a belief in angels, the revealed scriptures of Allah, belief in and reverence for all of Allah's prophets, including Moses and Jesus Christ, belief in the hereafter and belief that Allah ordains (for a fuller explanation, see Ashencaen Crabtree et al, 2016). Thus, while diversity is a feature of Muslims universally, the precepts of faith remain unchanged across the Muslim community of believers, the *Ummah*. It is into this community that many children of Muslim background will be born and raised. While this may seem somewhat abstract knowledge, it is important for social workers to hold a basic understanding of the holistic framework that orders the daily lives of Muslims across the globe and which acts as a universal identifier of what it is to be seen to be a Muslim. This relates to cultural sensitivity, without which a social worker practises at a severe disadvantage to their credibility in the eyes of service-users and their families, thus jeopardising the helping, working relationship, without which little constructive work can be undertaken.

Social inequality and oppression

In considering issues of social inequality, many years have lapsed since Lena Dominelli (1994) first drew social workers' attention to the impact of institutionalised racism on black families in Britain and how this influenced social work services and professional attitudes to 'client' groups, as they were then predominantly and not incorrectly called. The conceptualisation of 'black' in relation to 'race'/ethnicity overarched many different peoples at the time. Asian groups were also subsumed under this category at a polemic, politicised level. Thus, many groups that might be identified by contemporary social workers as Muslim were not viewed as such for the purposes of addressing racism.

Messages such as Dominelli's did not fall on deaf ears in the social work profession, but formed part of an anti-racist *zeitgeist* (dominant spirit of the age) of the time – this being a new social consciousness that had given rise to the earlier 1976 Race Relations Act. Anti-racism played a strong role in social work education and in turn gave way to the new model of anti-discriminatory practice as qualifying social work education changed. Later still, anti-oppressive practice was introduced – a familiar model to most social work graduates of the past decade or more (Keating, 2000). However, these changes were not always accepted as a natural evolution; instead, critiques were levelled against anti-oppressive doctrine by such writers as Graham (2009) and Bhatti-Sinclair (2011), writing regretfully of the eclipsing of anti-racism by newer models, now viewed as levelling hierarchies of discrimination and where anti-racism no longer occupied the summits.

As anti-oppressive practice took into account 'wider structural issues and inequalities' (Parker, 2007, p 151), a wider overview permitted bigger panoramas of inequality and discrimination to be explored, much of which is relevant to the milestones and experiences of human development. Here, sociological thinking, which has always permeated and influenced social work theorisation, for example, deepens our understanding still further. Today, the more traditional concept of diversity as pertaining to, for example, gender, ethnicity, class and sexuality, has been greatly expanded by the concept of 'super-diversity' as referring to multiple variations of difference interacting within individuals, groups and communities (Vertovec, 2007).

Understanding Islamophobia

One significant advantage of an anti-oppressive approach is that it allows Islamophobia to be understood as a pernicious form of discrimination, which otherwise was not easily accommodated conceptually by the old framework of anti-racism. Islamophobia cuts across two different forms of prejudice – biological racism and cultural racism (Lorente, 2010; Hussain and Bagguley, 2012) – to create a hybrid 'new racism' (Grosfoguel and Mielants, 2006; Ashencaen Crabtree, 2014). In fact, Islamophobia is not a new discovery, being first flagged up in the far-sighted UK Runnymede Report of 1977, 'Islamophobia: A challenge for us all', where the characteristics are summarised as:

1. Monolithic & static
2. Separate and 'other' – not sharing other values
3. Inferior to the West
4. An aggressive enemy
5. Muslims as manipulative
6. Critical of the West
7. Patriarchy and sexism are implicit to Islam. (Ashencaen Crabtree, 2014; Runnymede Trust, 1997)

Critics like Taras (2013) have added additional variants to Islamophobia, such as viewing Muslims as inherently aggressive and hostile, where Islamic ideology is used for political and military agendas. Benighted intolerance has also been associated with the faith; and a general Islamophobic attitude that Muslims are deemed by non-Muslims to be deserving of marginalisation and that hostility and suspicion towards them is normal and natural (Taras, 2013).

Taras's list is obviously open to qualification in terms of such beliefs being generally held towards all Muslims. Notoriously dangerous Islamist groups such as the Islamic State (of Syria and Levant), also known as Daesh/ISIS, have obviously been intent on imposing extreme forms of Islam on non-Muslims and Muslims alike through acts of extreme violence. We should view such groups as indisputably criminal aberrations of an otherwise peace-loving and tolerant religion (Ashencaen Crabtree et al, 2016).

This apart, instead of beginning to decline in everyday language and behaviour through more enlightened social attitudes, as has generally taken place in the UK towards most ME groups, Islamophobia has instead, unfortunately, been given a tremendous boost through current political discourse. Notorious examples of this are connected through Alt-right populist political rhetoric. The first example relates to the anti-migrant sentiment, largely focusing on Muslim migrants as potential terrorists, as espoused by UKIP and their political allies; the second is the presidential election of Donald Trump, who, supported by his Republican allies, has permitted (indeed, many would argue, has actively encouraged) a wave of deeply racist views in the US, together with draconian anti-immigration policies, which again are predominantly directed against Muslims (and Latin Americans) for the same spurious reasons as given by UKIP. Trump's continued and ill-informed Twitter attacks on the reputation of London Mayor, Sadiq Khan, have been viewed as being directly connected to Khan being a Muslim. Finally, the charge of the Conservative Party's institutional Islamophobia by Baroness Warsi, a Muslim peer, together with human rights groups' accusations of 'structural Islamophobia' relating to the routine stopping and harassments of Muslims by British immigration authorities (CAGE, 2019), works to legitimise Islamophobic public insults. These are likely to increase the sense of insecurity and alienation among British Muslims, with due ramifications on both social and civic participation and physical and mental health.

Gender normativity and Islam

Most communities observe gendered norms to some degree, even if these are contested or resisted. Among Muslim families, gendered norms may form an important social construction of how women and men are expected to conduct themselves; and these may be viewed as part of the social, cultural and religious worldview guiding them. Gendered normativity in the West exists from the very moment a child is born, when the family is anxious to know whether the newborn is a boy or a girl. In the UK, the gendering of children's toys is probably more prevalent now than at any other time in history; and the contemporary 'pinkification' of a little girl's world, irrespective of cultural background, carries worrying implications in any quest to achieve gendered equality in the adult world (Valenti, 2014).

In Islam, clearly-demarcated gendered roles, where such exist, may not be viewed as detrimental to the dignity and status of women (Stang Dahl, 1997). This is particularly the case where gendered roles are viewed as symmetrical in worth, if different in definition and enactment. The onset of puberty will usually herald the transition from young childhood to emerging adulthood for young Muslims, if a traditional, culturally socialised route is followed. Girls in this case may be expected to alter their dress to more adult, female attire, adapting school uniform to suit; although in some cases even pre-pubescent children may be expected to cover their hair. Virtues of propriety and modesty may well be reinforced and both sexes made aware of their responsibilities regarding upholding the family name and honour (*izzat*).

Yet, as in most patriarchal structures, these burdens will be laid more heavily upon the shoulders of girls and women than boys or men, and perceived impropriety of the former may receive greater punishment. Impropriety in the multicultural context of the UK, for example, may be regarded by dominant society as perfectly normal conduct, such as the wearing of fashionable dress or mixing socially with unrelated males (although Muslims must consider the boundaries concerned with mixing with related males as well). The oft-quoted analogy used in many Muslim cultures describes this attitude of reinforced propriety well, where women are equated to silk, and men to gold. If the former is dropped into the mud just once, then it will be permanently soiled, whereas gold – no matter how often dirtied – can always be washed clean again. Such concepts lie at the core of the belief that male relatives are the guardians of females and that the latter have a particular power to dishonour the family, as exemplified in Case Study 11.2. Such attitudes can lead to domestic violence and so-called 'honour-based violence' (see Chapter 7 of the companion volume for a more in-depth discussion of this). Case Study 11.2 is adapted from that of Ashencaen Crabtree et al (2016).

CASE STUDY 11.2

17-year old Asma has been locked in her bedroom by her brother and has been violently beaten with a belt by him for two days. Allowed out of her room to eat, she manages to phone a Muslim helpline and tells the listener that, driving by in his car, her brother her saw her talking to a male classmate on her way home. He stopped the car, dragged her inside and drove her home. Her parents are aware of the violence, but have permitted it to continue without intervening. Her brother has now forbidden her to return to sixth-form college, threatening her with death if she disobeys. She tells the helpline how frightened and desperate she is and asks if her brother's conduct is acceptable in Islam and what help she can get.

Questions

1. What kind of statutory and additional community help might be available to Asma in a situation like this?
2. How far do you think social workers should be involved in such cases?
3. Are there any other professionals with whom social workers may work in this case?

Discussion

While all social workers, whatever their ethnic and/or religious background, need to develop culturally sensitive ways of working, there is never an excuse for violence, of any form, and this situation constitutes violence. The family may argue that this is a question of honour and that such matters go beyond the individual to the family and group as a whole. However, Asma's brother is holding her against her will and is threatening her. It is likely that there will be community groups who can assist in such cases and you should, as a social worker, have a good in-depth knowledge of community resources to draw upon – never be afraid to ask if you don't know!

Given the situation, it may be that it is not just the community group who might be involved, but also the college and the police if a crime is suspected.

Domestic violence implicating Muslim families, again like other forms of violence, can take many forms – but all are classified as abusive. Forced marriage (typically where an unwitting girl is taken out of the country by her family, usually under the excuse of a holiday) is a crime that is finally receiving the state's concerted attention. Thousands of British schoolgirls over the years have disappeared from public view only to be found to have been married off to strangers in their parents' country of origin (Ashencaen Crabtree et al, 2016). Until relatively recently, there was little concerted action taken to prevent or prosecute this crime, where victims were also inhibited to press a charge. However, in May 2018, a Birmingham woman was sentenced to jail for duping her teenage daughter into marrying an older relative in Pakistan (Summers, 2018). Legal activists seeking more robust sentencing argue that such abuses constitute a form of modern slavery, where victims are treated as possessions (chattels).

The notorious Huddersfield and Rotherham, Yorkshire, and Rochdale, Greater Manchester, sexual abuse cases pivoted on the deeply violent exploitation of young girls, mostly white, working-class children, used as modern slaves. Two gangs of men were later arrested for these atrocities, which had spanned several years and dozens of victims (Ashencaen Crabtree et al, 2016) (for more details, see the Jay Report, listed in the 'Further reading' section at the end of this chapter). At first, this was viewed as a form of religio-ethnic violence: Muslim adult perpetrators, white minors as victims. However, research by the UK Muslim Women's Network revealed the extent of abuse, very similar in brutality, of young Muslim girls within their own communities (see the report 'Unheard Voices' for more information [Gohir, 2013]). The conclusion to be drawn is that gross, deep-rooted misogyny lies at the root of all such crimes preying on vulnerable females. Yet while the relevant authorities seemed uninterested in what was happening to the Rotherham and Rochdale victims for years, Muslim girls may also be trapped by issues of family honour and shame should they reveal what is happening to them at the hands of their own relatives and neighbours.

Negotiating transition successfully

The concept of a dominant culture suggests a homogeneity of values and beliefs among prevalent communities, which runs counter-intuitive to the notion and factual existence of multicultural societies. Even within certain ethnic categories and class factors (for example, white middle-class), numerous differences in outlook and lifestyle will be found. Nevertheless, it would also be disingenuous to argue that, consequently, this must mean that the social and civic space is composed of nothing but relativity and a complete democratisation of cultural and ethnic difference. We know that this is not true: some beliefs and behaviours are regarded as conventional and normal in society, being more expected and legitimised, while others will occupy more marginal spaces and may be regarded as, at best, unusual, at worst, deviant and suspicious.

For young ME people experiencing the transition from childhood to adulthood, the difficulties of this journey can be compounded by the need to negotiate differing cultural norms that may be viewed as a collision course. The accepted values and conduct in the home environment may be quite dissimilar from those espoused in mainstream education, for instance. Friendship groups across ethnic groups and cultures are a healthy and positive development that should be encouraged, yet these can also magnify a range of alternative perspectives and lifestyles that are viewed as incongruent or incompatible among individual group members or their families. Tiptoeing a path through these human complexities is an additional task for transitional youth, which, as we saw in Asma's case (Case Study 11.2), can become explosively difficult. Yet successful negotiation of pathways that honours different perspectives and values will be found among many young ME people. An example of this is a study by Afshar and colleagues (2005), commenting on how young Muslim girls may combine the hijab with fashionable jeans, jackets and heels. The greater parental trust shown to religiously and culturally respectful teenagers can reward young people with greater latitude in forging pathways to a fulfilling adult life.

So-called 'radicalisation' is a dangerous term that labels dissenting views as deviant. Youth is a time of experimental enquiry and occasionally extreme positions, so there needs to be a clear distinction between holding views with which the majority population may disagree and causing actual physical harm. Oppressive state tactics to suppress opposing views create far greater dangers to all who live in a democratic liberal society than radical ideas unaccompanied by violence. It is worth noting the research findings of Fleischman et al (2011), who find that Muslim youth are more likely to construct a religiously based identity that may also be associated with political action, based on their perceptions of Islamophobia, compared to the previous Muslim migrant generation.

For professionals working in multicultural and multi-faith contexts, we return to the earlier caveat of avoiding essentialist assumptions that ME communities are similar to each other or carry great similarities within them. Islam, being a global religion, like Christianity, has attracted a huge diversity of peoples who bear little in common with each other apart from a shared religion. Cultural variations are much more likely to influence idiosyncrasies than religion, although here it is well worth acquainting oneself with the denominational differences found within Islam – which are as profound and important as those found in Christianity, with equally serious sectarian tensions (see Ashencaen Crabtree et al, 2016 for more information on this topic).

Conclusion

While a good awareness of general Islamic precepts is very important for social workers to avoid undue offence, taking time to learn more about cultural variations is equally important to understand how these are interpreted and enacted within families and communities, with an expectation that, while similarities will be discerned, the uniqueness of human autonomy and experience will be continually demonstrated. Developing authentic professional practice demands a critical understanding developed through self-reflectivity of not only how we relate to the 'other', but also where we stand in relation to the norms and conventions we have grown up with. We are also the 'other' in this sense, both to those we interact with and through apperception – namely, recognising the boundaries of the social constructs that have shaped our understanding of the world. By attempting to step outside of these normative lenses (an exercise of imagination and objectivity that is never fully achieved), we begin to shed so many of the assumptions and preconceptions that hinder our ability to work more meaningfully with unfamiliar people and cultures. Through this process, we may find a new humility, greater psychological agility and reinvigorated professional strengths that, taken together, create a professional expertise and wisdom sought, but not always found, by service-users in professionals.

Reflective questions

1 How much do you think social workers should learn about ethno-cultural and religious diversity as part of their social work education? Give reasons for your answers.

2 How far do you feel that differences in diversity should be accommodated in social work practice? Describe and explain.

Further reading

• Ashencaen Crabtree, S., Husain, F. and Spalek, B. (2016) *Islam and Social Work: Culturally Sensitive Practice in a Diverse World* (2nd edn). Bristol: Policy Press.
In this book, we offer a comprehensive introduction to theory, models and practice implications for social workers working with Muslim families and communities where they may not be Muslim themselves.

• Jay, A. (2014) Independent inquiry into child sexual exploitation in Rotherham 1997–2013. Rotherham Metropolitan Borough Council. Available from: http://www.rotherham. gov.uk/downloads/file/1407/independent_inquiry_cse_in_rotherham
This shocking report illustrates how complex it is to tread a culturally sensitive path, but how important it is to name abuse as abuse. It makes difficult reading, but it is important for all social workers to be aware of this matter.

• MCB (Muslim Council of Britain) (2015) *British Muslims in Numbers: A Demographic, Socio-Economic and Health Profile of Muslims in Britain Drawing on the 2011 Census.* London: Muslim Council of Britain.

The Muslim Council of Great Britain is a rich source of information and data relating to British Muslim communities. This report uses the last census to create a profile of Muslims in Britain and shows some of the differences from non-Muslim communities, which is important for social workers to take into account in their work.

• Mlcek, S. (2014) Are we doing enough to develop cross-cultural competencies for social work?, *British Journal of Social Work*, 44(7): 1984–2003.
This article draws on an Australian study into ways in which social work students might be introduced to and challenged in respect of cross-cultural competencies or being able to practise in culturally appropriate and sensitive ways. While written within the Australian education system, it has equal relevance to social work students wherever they are completing their qualification.

References

Afshar, H., Aitken, R. and Franks, M. (2005) 'Feminisms, Islamophobia and Identities', *Political Studies*, 53: 262–283.

Ashencaen Crabtree, S. (2014) Islamophobia and the Manichean constructions of the 'Other': a contemporary European problem. In: S. Ashencaen Crabtree, (ed.), *Diversity and the Processes of Marginalisation and Otherness: a European Perspective*. London: Whiting & Birch, pp. 33–48.

Ashencaen Crabtree, S. (2017a) Social work with Muslim communities: Treading a critical path over the crescent moon. In B. Crisp (ed.), *Routledge Handbook of Religion, Spirituality and Social Work*. London: Routledge.

Ashencaen Crabtree, S. (2017b) Problematizing the context and construction of vulnerability and risk in relation to British Muslim ME groups, *Journal of Religion & Spirituality in Social Work*, 36(1–2): 247–265.

Ashencaen Crabtree, S., Husain, F. and Spalek, B. (2008) *Islam and Social Work: Debating Values and Transforming Practice*. Bristol: Policy Press.

Ashencaen Crabtree, S., Husain, F. and Spalek, B. (2016) *Islam and Social Work: Culturally Sensitive Practice in a Diverse World* (2nd edn). Bristol: Policy Press.

BBC (2017) London Bridge attack: The victims. 9 June. Available from: https://www.bbc.co.uk/news/uk-40153090

Beckett, C. and Taylor, H. (2016) *Human Growth and Development*. London: Sage.

Bhatti-Sinclair, K. (2011) *Anti-Racist Practice in Social Work*. Houndmills: Palgrave Macmillan.

CAGE (2019) Schedule7: Harassment at Borders, the impact on the Muslim community. London: CAGE Advocacy Ltd.

Dodd, V., Pidd, H., Rawlinson, K. Siddisque, H. and MacAskill, E. (2017) At least 22 killed, 59 injured in suicide attack at Manchester Arena, *The Guardian*, 23 May. Available from: https://www.theguardian.com/uk-news/2017/may/22/manchester-arena-police-explosion-ariana-grande-concert-england

Dominelli, L. (1994) *Anti-Racist Social Work*. Houndmills: Macmillan Press.

Fleischman, F., Phalet, K. and Klein, O. (2011) Religious identification and politicization for political Islam and political action among the Turkish and Moroccan second generation in Europe, *British Journal of Social Psychology*, 50(4): 628–648.

Fook, J. (2007) Reflective practice and critical reflection. In J. Lishman (ed.), *Handbook for Practice Learning in Social Work and Social Care* (2nd edn). London: Jessica Kingsley.

Gohir, S. (2013) *Unheard Voices: The sexual exploitation of Asian girls and young women*, Birmingham: Muslim Women's Network.

Graham, M. (2009) Reframing black perspectives in social work: New directions?, *Social Work Education*, 28(3): 268–280.

Grosfoguel, R. and Mielants, E. (2006) The long-durée entanglement between Islamophobia and racism in the modern/colonial capitalist/patriarchal world-system, *Human Architecture: Journal of the Sociology of Self-Knowledge*, V(I), 1–12.

Haw, K.F. with Shah, S. and Hanifa, M. (1998) *Educating Muslim Girls: Shifting Discourses*. Buckingham: Open University Press.

Hussain, Y. and Bagguley, P. (2012) Securitized citizens: Islamophobia, racism and the 7/7 London bombings, *Sociological Review*, 60(4): 715–734.

Keating, F. (2000) Anti-racist perspectives: what are the gains for social work?, *Social Work Education*, 9(1): pp 77-87.

Lorente, J.R. (2010) Discrepancies around the use of the term 'Islamophobia', *Human Architecture: Journal of the Sociology of Self-Knowledge*, VIII(2): 115–128.

MCB (Muslim Council of Britain) (2015) *British Muslims in Numbers: A Demographic, Socio-Economic and Health Profile of Muslims in Britain Drawing on the 2011 Census*. London: Muslim Council of Britain.

Mernissi, F. (1975) *Beyond the Veil*. Cambridge, MA: Schenkman.

Parker, J. (2007) Social work, disadvantage by association and anti-oppressive practice. In P. Burke and J. Parker (eds), *Social Work and Disadvantage: Addressing the Roots of Stigma through Association*. London: Jessica Kingsley.

Parker, J. and Ashencaen Crabtree, S. (2018) Wisdom and skills in social work education: Promoting critical relational social work through ethnographic practice, *Relational Social Work*, 2(1): 13–29.

Parker, J., Ashencaen Crabtree, S., Reeks, E., Marsh, D. and Vasif, C. (2018) 'River! that in silence windest': The place of religion and spirituality in social work assessment: Sociological reflections and practical implications. In C. Spatscheck, S. Ashencaen Crabtree and J. Parker (eds), *Methods and Methodologies of Social Work: Reflecting Professional Intervention*. Erasmus SocNet (Vol. III). London: Whiting & Birch.

Parveen, N. (2019) Boris Johnson's burqa comments led to surge in anti-Muslim hate crimes, *The Guardian*, 2 September. Available from: https://www.theguardian.com/politics/2019/sep/02/boris-johnsons-burqa-comments-led-to-surge-in-anti-muslim-attacks

Runnymede Trust (1997) *Islamophobia, A Challenge for Us All*. London: Runnymede Trust.

Said, E. (1978) *Orientalism*. London: Penguin Books.

Stang Dahl, T. (1997) *The Muslim Family: A Study of Women's Rights in Islam*. Oxford and Oslo: Scandinavian University Press.

Summers, H. (2018) Woman jailed for duping daughter into forced marriage, *The Guardian*, 23 May. Available from: https://www.theguardian.com/uk-news/2018/may/23/birmingham-woman-jailed-duping-daughter-forced-marriage

Taras, R. (2013) 'Islamophobia never stands still': Race, religion and culture, *Ethnic & Racial Studies*, 36(3): 417–433.

Taylor, D. (2018) Report finds some NHS Trusts screen all patients for radicalization, *The Guardian*, 19 March. Available from: https://www.theguardian.com/uk-news/2018/mar/19/report-finds-some-nhs-mental-health-trusts-screening-all-patients-for-radicalisation-prevent

Valenti, J. (2014) Let's end pink-ification: Must the 'girls' aisle be full of sexist toys and clothes?, *The Guardian*, 5 August. Available from: https://www.theguardian.com/commentisfree/2014/aug/05/girls-aisle-sexist-toys-clothes

Vertovec, S. (2007) Super-diversity and its implications, *Ethnic and Racial Studies*, 30(6): 1024-1054

Walker, J. (2017) *Social Work and Human Development* (5th edn). London: Learning Matters/Sage.

PART III

Professional practice

In Part III, authors will take a social work practice perspective and utilise the theoretical models and factors explored in Parts I and II. Service-user accounts will be included wherever possible. The advantages and disadvantages of the model and theories will be identified and an approach that focuses on the person will be emphasised. The examples and case studies are designed to embed and generate learning and application specific to social work practice, but also to other forms of human service professions. This is important because it allows you to enter the world of social work, which necessarily involves working with other professionals and dealing with their sometimes different interpretations of theories and models and different ways of practising. This helps you to identify what is unique about your practice as a social worker, while respecting the particular contribution made by others.

Chapter authors are all social work academics, but from Britain, Norway and Northern Ireland, and bring together their perspectives. This is useful for your learning as you begin to make connections between theories and models that are common across social work practice and to consider the similarities and differences in social work practice.

Part III objectives

- understand how theories and models are used to help children and young people facing particular problems in life;
- identify some of those elements that make social work unique as both a local and a global profession.

This part of the book includes chapters that cover disabled children and young people, mental health and ill-health, maltreatment or abuse and its effects, being an unaccompanied minor and negotiating complex and often hostile policies and agencies, and moving to and living in substitute families. Chapter authors use many of the theories and models that have been introduced in Parts I and II and demonstrate how they can be applied to achieve best outcomes for those children and young people under discussion.

12

Impacts of child maltreatment: critical considerations

Lisa Bunting

Introduction

Child maltreatment is a global problem affecting millions of children across the world. Experience of abuse and neglect has well-evidenced links with poorer physical, emotional and mental health across the life course, making it a key concern for professionals working in clinical, education and community settings with both children and adults. It is important that social workers have a sound knowledge of research and this chapter provides theories and models that will underpin your understanding and knowledge base of how such experiences might influence the life course.

Chapter objectives

Drawing on recent systematic reviews, this chapter provides an overview of:

- the research evidence identifying the long-term impacts of maltreatment on children's physical, cognitive, social and emotional development;

- current understanding of the mechanisms by which the developmental trajectory is thought to be affected;

- the limitations of the literature, critiques of contemporary neuroscience and neurobiology, and the implications for professional practice.

Background and context

Although definitions may vary, it is estimated that nearly a quarter of adults (22.6 per cent) worldwide have suffered physical abuse as a child, 36.3 per cent emotional abuse, 16.3 per cent physical neglect and 11.8 per cent sexual abuse (Stoltenborgh et al, 2015). The World Health Organization (2016) defines maltreatment as including 'all forms of physical and emotional ill-treatment, sexual abuse, neglect, and exploitation that results in actual or potential harm to the child's health, development or dignity'. This, in itself, provides a clear case for ensuring your knowledge is developed and based in up-to-date research evidence.

A child is considered to be sexually abused when they are forced or persuaded to take part in sexual activities; physically abused when they are deliberately caused injury; neglected when there is an ongoing failure to meet basic developmental needs such as food, clothing, medical and educational needs; and emotionally abused when they are psychologically mistreated or their basic emotional needs, such as needs for affection, emotional warmth and comfort, are not met. Although these forms of maltreatment are commonly identified as the focus of intervention within Western child welfare systems, legal definitions vary and there are substantial differences in child abuse reporting rates between countries (Bunting et al, 2010; Gilbert et al, 2011). While all forms of maltreatment are, to varying extents, culturally constructed (see Chapter 5 in Part I of this volume), neglect and emotional abuse, in particular, grounded as they are in judgements about acceptable parenting practices and appropriate levels of care, are subject to particular variation over time and between cultures (Green, 2017). A little bit of history will help to illustrate this.

Since the discovery of 'battered child syndrome' (Kempe et al, 1962), there has been exponential growth in research attempting to elucidate both the causes and consequences of child maltreatment, what works in terms of prevention and how best to address the long-term needs of those affected by abuse. We now know that multiple child, parent, family and neighbourhood factors interact in complex ways to increase the risk of child maltreatment (Petersen et al, 2014). We also know that, although the long-term consequences of maltreatment vary significantly, depending on the severity, chronicity and timing of the abuse, as well as the protective factors present, abused and neglected children are more prone to experience poor mental and physical health, behavioural and relationship problems and diminished economic well-being (Dube et al, 2003; Felitti and Anda, 2010). As we have already seen in Chapter 4 in Part I of this volume, in recent decades, developments in brain-imaging techniques and integration of evidence from neuroscience, psychology and the social sciences have also enabled greater understanding of the factors which influence brain development and functioning over the life course. This has fuelled international recognition of the need for early intervention involving a coordinated response from diverse professional groups, such as social workers, nurses, teachers and criminal justice professionals.

In the following section, we will relate some of the impacts that abuse and maltreatment have on children and young people. Some of the descriptions make for harrowing reading, but it is important for you as a social worker to grapple with this since it forms a large part of the work in which social workers are engaged.

Impact of maltreatment on development

Physical and cognitive development

One of the most serious consequences of maltreatment is the risk of serious injury or, in the most extreme cases, death. In 2003, UNICEF stated that 3,500 children under the age of 15 die each year from abuse or neglect in the 27 richest countries worldwide, while the World Health Organization estimates that 57,000 children die annually from maltreatment. While the majority of these deaths are attributable to physical abuse, notably injuries caused by head trauma, child maltreatment deaths caused by child neglect, including starvation, failure to provide potentially life-saving medical care and inappropriate supervision of dangerous activities or substances can also occur (Jenny and Isaac, 2006). Owing to their physical vulnerability and dependence on adult caregivers, very young children, particularly those under the age of one, are at most risk. Common non-fatal injuries, especially in cases involving infants, include fractures, traumatic brain injury, bruises, burns and subdural haematoma (Leeb et al, 2011). Some physical injuries can result in permanent disability or impairment, while neglect leading to nutritional deficits can produce long-term physical effects, including limited physical stature, smaller size, learning difficulties and developmental delays (Boddy et al, 2000). Sexual abuse may involve genital and anal injury and can result in sexually transmitted infections and, in adolescent girls, unwanted pregnancy (Leeb et al, 2011).

Child abuse and neglect have much broader and longer-lasting effects than accidental injuries and children who experience maltreatment are also at increased risk of adverse health effects and certain chronic diseases as adults. Irish et al's (2010) systematic review and meta-analyses demonstrated that child sexual abuse was systematically related to higher rates of physical health symptoms, including gastrointestinal health, gynaecologic pain, cardiopulmonary symptoms and obesity. Focusing on neglect, physical and emotional abuse, Norman et al's (2012) systematic review also found some evidence for an association between child physical abuse and arthritis, ulcers and headache/migraine in adulthood, but noted that associations for other health outcomes were mostly weak and inconsistent. They did, however, find that physical abuse significantly increased the risk of problem drinking and drug use and that both physical abuse and emotional abuse increased the risk of adult obesity and smoking. Those who were physically abused, emotionally abused or neglected were at a significantly higher risk of sexually-transmitted infections and engaging in risky sexual behaviour, while those who experienced physical abuse or neglect were at increased risk of suicidal behaviour.

Developments in neuroscience have also highlighted how maltreatment can affect brain development, altering the physical structures and functioning of the brain. A recent systematic review of more than 200 neuroimaging studies (Teicher et al, 2016) found consistent evidence that maltreatment can lead to structural deficits in the adult hippocampus, corpus callosum, anterior cingulate cortex, orbitofrontal cortex and dorsolateral prefrontal cortex. It also highlighted marked differences between the sexes, with several studies reporting a twofold greater reduction in the corpus callosum area in maltreated males than in maltreated females. In males, the corpus callosum area, which joins the right- and left-hand sides of the brain together, was most affected by exposure to neglect, whereas, in females, it was most affected by exposure to sexual abuse. These alterations in brain maturation are considered to have long-term consequences across a range of domains, including cognitive function, linguistic development and academic ability.

Research provides evidence of an association between maltreatment and lower levels of educational attainment in children ranging from infancy to older adolescents (Meadows et al, 2011; Pacheco et al, 2014). Perez and Widom's (1994) study compared 413 individuals with substantiated child maltreatment reports before age 11 with a matched sample of 286 individuals who had not been maltreated. Twenty years later, when participants were re-interviewed and their educational outcomes measured, the maltreatment group averaged a sixth-grade reading ability compared to an eighth-grade reading ability for the control group. Pacheco et al's (2014) systemic review also found that maltreated children tended to exhibit greater disciplinary problems and higher rates of school absence and grade repetitions than those who had not experienced abuse. Neglect was more strongly associated with negative academic performance, while physical abuse was associated with problems related to discipline and aggressiveness. Irigaray et al's (2013) systematic review also points to deficits in cognitive function with both children/teenagers and adults exposed to abuse during childhood performing more poorly on cognitive tasks to assess verbal episodic memory, attention and executive functions, such as problem solving, planning, working memory, inhibition, mental flexibility, information processing speed and abstract reasoning.

Social and emotional development

As we saw in Chapters 4 and 6 of Part I of this volume, social and emotional development is just as important as physical and cognitive development and involves the acquisition of a wide range of abilities and skills, including the ability to experience and control emotions, understand the feelings of others, build relationships with peers and adults and develop a positive sense of self. There is an extensive literature highlighting the negative effects of child maltreatment on an array of psychosocial outcomes, including poor mental and emotional health, low self-esteem, poor social skills, behavioural difficulties, juvenile delinquency and adult criminality. Sexual abuse, in particular, has a well-established association with increased risk of mental and behavioural problems in childhood and adulthood (Hillberg et al, 2011; Cashmore and Shackel, 2013). These include post-traumatic symptoms, substance abuse, feelings of helplessness, negative attributions, aggressive behaviours, conduct problems, eating disorders, anxiety and, more recently, psychotic disorders, including schizophrenia and delusional disorder. A prospective study comparing almost 3,000 children who experienced sexual abuse with general population peers found that 12.4 per cent in the maltreatment group had received psychiatric treatment during childhood compared to 3.6 per cent of controls (Spataro et al, 2004). Rates were higher for childhood mental disorders, personality disorders, anxiety disorders and major affective disorders, but not for schizophrenia, and male victims were significantly more likely to have had treatment than females (22.8 versus 10.2 per cent).

Physical abuse, emotional abuse and neglect have been shown to significantly increase the risk of depressive and anxiety disorders in adulthood and an almost three-fold increased risk of eating disorders (Norman et al, 2012). Physical abuse and neglect doubled the odds of childhood behavioural and conduct disorders, while, for physical abuse, significant increases were observed in relation to post-traumatic stress disorder (PTSD) and panic disorder diagnoses. Norman et al (2012) also found consistent evidence that increasing levels of exposure, both in terms of frequency and severity, to physical abuse, emotional abuse and neglect produced higher rates of mental disorders. Neuroimaging studies involving patients diagnosed with psychiatric disorders point to specific differences in the brain structures and functioning of maltreated individuals compared to non-maltreated individuals. It has been argued that those with maltreatment histories should be recognised as a specific subgroup, with distinct clinical, neurobiological and genetic features (Teicher et al, 2016).

Studies have demonstrated that maltreatment has a negative impact on self-esteem as well as the development of emotional and social skills. Pacheco et al (2014) found that maltreated adults showed significantly lower levels of self-esteem than non-maltreated adults, with those exposed to multiple maltreatment types tending to have poorer self-esteem than those who had not experienced abuse or had experienced a single type of abuse. They also highlighted poorer social competence and peer relationships among those with maltreatment histories.

Similarly, Luke and Banerjee (2013) found consistent evidence of an association between child maltreatment and deficits in emotional skills, such as emotion understanding, knowledge and recognition, with more pronounced effects evident for those in early and middle childhood than for adolescents and adults.

A longitudinal study of 215 maltreated and 206 non-maltreated children aged six to 12 years (Kim and Cicchetti, 2010) elucidates the possible pathways by which poor emotional skills contribute to social and psychological difficulties. At baseline, children who experienced neglect, physical and/or sexual abuse exhibited lower levels of emotion regulation, as measured by socially appropriate emotional displays, empathy, and emotional self-awareness. This was associated with higher levels of aggressive and delinquent behaviours, which were, in turn, associated with later rejection by peers and subsequent increases in the levels of these behaviours.

REFLECTION POINT 12.1

Thinking of what you have just read concerning the impacts and outcomes of experiencing abuse as a child or young person, note down some of the reasons why you believe a social worker should keep up-to-date with research.

You may have noted down reasons of professional competence, ensuring your knowledge is as good as that of other professionals working in this area, and especially that a good knowledge base will prepare you for working in these complex and challenging areas and providing the best possible service for children and young people.

Critically evaluating the literature

The various reviews discussed all highlight wide variability in the ascertainment of maltreatment and in the contexts samples were drawn from (such as residential settings, home environments and clinical settings). Many studies focused on generic constructs of 'child maltreatment', making it difficult to disentangle the effects of different forms of abuse on outcomes. In studies investigating exposure to specific maltreatment types, the types of behaviours covered within abuse definitions varied considerably and a predominant focus on sexual and physical abuse was noted in several reviews. Maltreatment definition is crucial to understanding how findings may vary across studies and over time and what conclusions may be drawn. A particular issue for professionals in evaluating and interpreting maltreatment research is the extent to how far these definitions reflect the legal and practice context they operate within. For example, several reviews included studies of children who experienced global neglect in institutional settings – a severe form of sensory deprivation across multiple domains, including minimal exposure to language, touch and social interaction (see Teicher et al, 2016). While such research provides valuable insight into the enduring impact of prolonged and extreme deprivation in the first few years of life, this form of neglect arguably bears limited resemblance to the cases of neglect which are common to most Western child welfare systems.

Many of the reviews highlighted the preponderance of cross–sectional research designs in the maltreatment literature, noting the difficulty this poses for establishing maltreatment as the cause of negative outcomes. One of the most difficult things to do in social science research is to prove a causal relationship between two variables. A key component of this is establishing temporal order, whereby the research design clearly demonstrates that the cause preceded the effect, that the maltreatment happened before the outcome. Randomised controlled trials are considered the 'gold standard' in terms of establishing a causal link. However, the obvious legal and ethical problems involved in randomly allocating children to a 'maltreatment' group and a 'control' group to study subsequent outcomes means that other research designs have to be used.

Cross-sectional studies measure both maltreatment exposure and outcomes at one point in time and although temporal order can be established through retrospective reports of abuse in childhood, there are concerns that errors in memory recall and the willingness of participants to disclose maltreatment can bias results. There is also concern that, because participants will have already developed the outcome of interest, those experiencing difficulties may be more inclined to interpret parental behaviours as abusive (Teicher et al, 2016). Longitudinal studies, on the other hand, measure the cause before the outcome and are widely considered quite robust means for making causal attributions. While many of the reviews drew on findings from longitudinal studies (Petersen et al, 2014), this still represented only a minority of studies and was notably rare within the neuroscientific literature.

Although prospective measures are generally considered more reliable than retrospective measures, they have particular limitations in maltreatment research. Prospective maltreatment measures which collect data on current or past-year exposure at various points during childhood are relatively rare, mainly because of reporting requirements to notify statutory authorities once abuse has been identified (Kendall-Tackett and Becker-Blease, 2004). As such, prospective maltreatment measures identified within the reviews were primarily based on official records of substantiated maltreatment collected when the child first came to the attention of child welfare professionals.

However, it is recognised that child welfare records only capture a portion of child maltreatment cases which occur within a given population. Additionally, they may, themselves, reflect biases in professional decision making and may contain missing or incomplete data that do not allow for disaggregation by abuse type (Kendall-Tackett and Becker-Blease, 2004). They are also likely to represent the most serious cases and the findings may, potentially, be biased by any subsequent professional intervention. In assessing their applicability, professionals also need to consider the legal and practice context in which these cases became known to statutory authorities, how this compares to their own and how this may have changed over time.

Child maltreatment rarely occurs in isolation and there are a wide range of individual, family and neighbourhood factors that not only increase the likelihood of child abuse and neglect, but are, in turn, associated with negative adult outcomes (Petersen et al, 2014). In order to disentangle the specific effects of child maltreatment from the effects of other childhood and family factors, consideration needs to be given to how studies have taken account of these potentially confounding factors. Depending on the study design, this can be achieved by matching maltreated participants with non-maltreated peers across relevant factors at the design phase, or by using statistical techniques which 'control' for the presence of these factors at the analysis phase. For example, in Irigaray et al (2013), several studies found that controlling for IQ and socio-economic status tended to reduce or remove the association between abuse and some measures of cognitive function.

The aforementioned is not just an issue for researchers and statisticians, but has important implications for professionals and policy makers. If, in the presence of child or family risk factors, maltreatment is no longer associated with poor outcomes, or the relationship is significantly weakened, this suggests that maltreatment is not the key driver in producing these outcomes. This is not to say that maltreatment should be ignored or children left in situations that are clearly unsafe, but it does suggest that efforts to address a broader range of risk factors, including those related to poverty, may have greater positive benefits for children in the long term. The impact of wider structural factors is important for social workers to keep in mind to offset the personalised blame that is often attached to individuals. This blame deflects attention away from social and political factors that affect the growth and development of children and young people: a more holistic approach is needed. Although multivariate analytic models are used, lack of adequate controlling for co-morbid risk factors remains a frequent criticism of much of the maltreatment literature (Petersen et al, 2014).

It is important to understand a little about neuroscience. For instance, functional brain imaging techniques such as fMRI do not measure brain activity as such, but rather changes in blood oxygenation and flow which are thought to be related to neural activity. Moreover, the fact that the relevant signal must be detected from a sea of other activity means that fMRI neuroimaging studies can only be said to study neural activity in a gross sense (Munro and Musholt, 2014). Images of brains which frequently appear in the neuroscientific literature are not 'photographs' of individual brains, but are best understood as graphs representing the average levels and location of brain activity across the research sample and which use differing colours for differing degrees of statistical significance. As with the social science literature, much of the data on which these images are based are correlational in nature and collected primarily from retrospective self-reports.

Equally, many studies of children and adults have tended to recruit individuals with PTSD or other mental health diagnoses (McCrory et al, 2012; Teicher et al, 2016), making it difficult to determine whether the changes in brain volume observed in the literature are a result of the abuse, the psychiatric conditions or an interaction between the two. It is only when integrated with knowledge derived from social science that neuroscience can contribute to a better understanding of the effects of maltreatment at different stages in the life course. Integration of the findings from neuroscience and neurobiology within the psychological perspective of attachment theory now provide the dominant framework for understanding how maltreatment and trauma produce negative outcomes. Read Case Study 12.1 and consider how neuroscience and social environmental factors may combine to influence growth and development.

CASE STUDY 12.1

Darren is a six-year-old boy who has been referred by his teacher for behavioural problems. Although small for his age, he is frequently aggressive in class, both towards his peers and staff, often has difficulties concentrating and listening to instructions and is considerably behind the rest of his class in terms of his literacy and numeracy. Darren's mother, Chloe, aged 25 years, is a single parent who has been previously known to social services. Darren had a low birth weight when born, which resulted in a three-week stay in an intensive baby unit. Chloe experienced severe post-natal depression and was referred to social services by her health visitor when Darren was four months old because of his continued low weight and concerns over Chloe's mental well-being and ability to care for Darren.

During the course of social services involvement, it emerged that Chloe was in an abusive relationship with Darren's father, Mike, and had limited social support or contact with family and friends. The relationship subsequently ended and Mike moved out when Darren was six months old; since then, he has only had sporadic contact with Darren.

On initial contact, Chloe presents as tired and under pressure, struggling to manage the demands of full-time work and childcare. She pays little attention to Darren, who, more often than not, is left watching TV, and appears irritated when he interrupts her or seeks her attention. When asked to describe what Darren is like, there is little positive assessment, and she describes him as 'exhausting', 'hard to control/manage' and 'draining'.

Questions

Consider the following questions and write down some ideas, giving reasons for your answers:

1. To what extent do you think the issues/difficulties experienced by Darren are potentially attributable to maltreatment?
2. What other explanations are possible and what role might structural/cultural factors also play?
3. If we knew for sure that Darren's brain was not developing along a 'normal' trajectory, what would be the best course of action: removal from the care of Chloe in an effort to stimulate better developmental outcomes or the provision of family support services to keep parent and child together? Are there other options?

Discussion

We have seen that any attribution of issues such as those shown by Darren are not easily explained. As a social worker, you will need to consider scientific and environmental evidence and to test this as a hypothesis against what is happening. You must recognise that other factors may also be at play, although Darren's experiences of early ill-health and current lack of stimulation represent good starting points to explore. As a social worker, you will want to consider a range of options to help Darren remain at home, while ensuring that Chloe is supported in looking after him.

Mechanisms underpinning the impact of maltreatment

The neurobiology of attachment

Theorists like Allan Schore (1994), Dan Siegel (1999) and Peter Fonagy (2001) have integrated findings from neuroscience and neurobiology to support the idea of the attachment relationship as critical to the development of structural neurobiological systems involved in processing emotion, stress modulation and self-regulation. In Bowlby's (1969, 1973) attachment theory, attachment refers to a long-lasting emotional and psychological bond between an infant and caregiver. (For an introduction to attachment theory, see Chapters 7 in Part II of this volume. Chapter 13 in this volume expands on the concept and examines how it might apply to looked-after children.)

To recap a little, a central function of the attachment relationship is emotional regulation in the first few years of life. Infants have limited ability to manage their own levels of arousal and rely on caregivers to co-regulate their emotions to decrease emotional distress. Through repeated emotionally positive interactions with caregivers, over time children become increasingly autonomous in regulating their own emotional arousal. Where a caregiver is emotionally unavailable, or where parent–child interactions are characterised by fear, hostility and unpredictability, children are at risk of failing to develop effective strategies for regulating emotions in interactions with others. This can produce disorganised patterns of attachment which have been shown to predict very poor outcomes, including low levels of social and emotional well-being, and later psychopathology in adolescence and adulthood.

In integrating neurobiological perspectives, Schore (1994) and Siegel (1999) have drawn on neuroscientific insights into how the brain develops during childhood. Children are born with billions of neurons – nerve cells which form the basic building blocks of the nervous system, but which have few connections between them. The brain develops sequentially over time, starting with the most primitive functions of the body (such as heart rate and breathing) to the most sophisticated functions (such as complex thought), and is not fully developed until the age of 20 to 25 years (Giedd et al, 1999). Over the first two years of life, the number of neural connections grows exponentially, after which those connections that are used are strengthened and those that are not are gradually discarded up to adolescence (synaptic pruning) (Brown and Ward, 2013). Although many aspects of brain development are genetically controlled, many, particularly after birth, are thought to be experience-dependent (Greenough and Black, 1992). This leads many developmental psychologists and neuroscientists to consider the first few years of a child's life to be a sensitive or critical period during which lack of a specific experience or exposure to the wrong type of experience can change the developmental trajectory of the brain by altering its structure and functionality.

They have also incorporated the growing literature which investigates how stress-induced changes in a child's neurobiological systems affect development and functioning (McCrory et al, 2012). The body's stress response is highly adaptive and learning how to cope with stress and adversity is an important part of healthy development. While moderate or short-lived stress can promote growth, severe or prolonged adversity can potentially alter the architecture of the brain, establishing neurobiological responses associated with a higher biological cost and increased risk of mental and physical health problems. For example, in longitudinal research with children who experienced global neglect in Romanian orphanages (Gunnar et al, 2001), those who were institutionalised for eight or more months before adoption had higher levels of the stress hormone cortisol levels at age six than those institutionalised for shorter time periods. Persistent threat is considered to be a form of toxic stress which sensitises the fear response, putting the child in a persistent fear state and causing exaggerated reactivity. As a consequence, the child may become hyperactive, over-sensitive and hyper-vigilant, moving quickly from anxiety to terror. Children exposed to severe trauma and maltreatment may also exhibit dissociative tendencies, whereby they withdraw attention from the outside world and focus instead on their own inner world in an attempt to manage the stress response (Perry, 2001). While either of these stress responses can be adaptive within the context of abuse, they may become problematic in normal environments, limiting the child's ability to learn, manage emotions and develop social relationships.

Schore (1994) draws on findings from infant MRI studies which show that the early maturing right brain undergoes a growth spurt in the first two years, before the verbal left, and is dominant in the first years after birth. Non-verbal communication between mother and baby is thought to form the basis of attachment, overlapping this growth spurt and shaping the early organisation of the right brain. Schore (2000) also notes that implicit memory is the primary form of memory in the first two years of life. This differs from explicit memory in that recollection does not require focused attention and there isn't a sense of remembering – rather, just experiencing in the form of automatic behaviours, emotions and thought processes. Within the neurobiology of attachment, early attachment patterns are viewed as implicit memories formed by repeated interactions with caregivers which provide the cognitive foundation for the child's understanding of the world, the self and others and which encodes future coping strategies for managing stress and emotion.

Critical considerations

REFLECTION POINT 12.2

Before reading this section on critical approaches to scientific and psychological theories, think about some of the reasons why social workers need to know these theories and why it is important to approach them sceptically – to critique them. Write down some of your ideas and check these against the subsequent discussion.

It should also be noted that, while attachment theory and neuroscience are widely drawn upon in professional practice with children and families, they are also subject to various critiques. Neuroscience has come under criticism, particularly, in relation to how it has been used to inform early intervention and child welfare policy within the US and the UK. For the most part, this has centred on the claim of the first three years of life as a critical time period during which sub-optimal parenting can cause significant and potentially irreversible damage to child development. Wastell and White (2017) contend that over-simplification and misrepresentation of the scientific literature has fuelled a 'now or never' policy and early intervention imperative. Evidence showing how parenting behaviours predetermine the rest of an infant's life has been overstated, while evidence of brain plasticity and individual differences in resilience to adversity have been understated.

Likewise, Bruer (1999) argues that birth to three years of age is not the clear-cut critical period for brain development it is often professed to be, and that different neural systems have their own sensitive periods – some stretching into the teenage years. He also contends that the assumption that socio-emotional development is subject to critical period constraints has little empirical support. Over-reliance on findings from animal and human studies focusing on clinical or institutional populations are also highlighted as weaknesses within the current evidence base, a criticism to which the various systematic reviews discussed in this chapter also draw attention. Of particular concern is the shift from relatively well-defined conceptualisations of physical and sexual abuse towards less well-defined concepts of emotional abuse and neglect which encompass an ever-widening range of parenting behaviours. Despite engendering the greatest definitional ambiguity at an international level, these forms of maltreatment now account for the majority of identified child protections cases in countries such as the US, England and Australia (Munro and Manful, 2012).

Dawson et al (2000) point to an array of literature demonstrating the relationship between maternal depression, a fairly common risk factor, and longer-term social and emotional difficulties, highlighting emerging evidence that the behaviour of depressed mothers can influence patterns of infant frontal brain activity. They also note that there is little disagreement that the early years of life represent a peak period of synaptic formation which coincides with the emergence of important cognitive and social skills (Dawson et al, 2000). Equally, there is consensus that the process of brain development and associated learning continues throughout childhood and that different brain regions develop at different rates (McCrory et al, 2012). Indeed, there is emerging evidence that stress-sensitive brain regions have their own developmental time windows which can vary as a function of genetic factors and which may be differentially affected depending on the age at which maltreatment occurs (Andersen et al, 2008; Choi et al, 2012). While Belsky and de Haan's (2011) review of the impact of parenting on children's brain development reiterates the limits of the research literature noted previously, it concludes that there is evidence to suggest that parenting conditions of extreme adversity, including maltreatment and institutionalisation, affect the structure and functionality of the developing brain. However, the extent to which less extreme parenting behaviours affect brain development remains less clear. Read Case Study 12.2 and reflect on the extent to which neuroscience might contribute to contemporary social work practice and child safeguarding.

CASE STUDY 12.2

Figure 12.1 shows a controversial picture of 'neglected' versus 'non-neglected' brains which has been widely used within the UK government's early intervention policy agenda, most prominently on the cover of Graham Allen's various early intervention reports as shown (Allen, 2011). Taking a critical look at the study from which this emotive image was originally derived (Perry, 2002), Wastell and White (2012) raise important questions about the scientific methods employed,

Figure 12.1: 'Neglected' versus 'non-neglected' brains

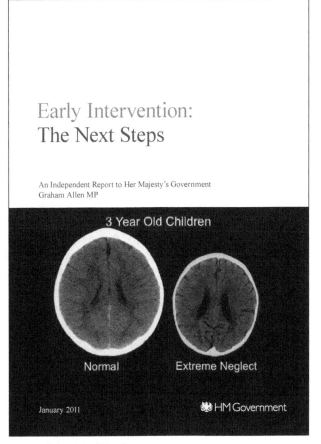

Source: HM Government of the United Kingdom

the conclusions reached and their applicability to practice. In summary, Perry's study involved the following:

Study focus and participants

Measures of growth for 122 children who had experienced neglect were compared to standard norms developed and used in major paediatric settings.

Definitions

A history of maltreatment was obtained from multiple sources (for example, investigating Crown Prosecution Service (CPS) workers, family and police). Neglect was further subdivided into four categories: global neglect; chaotic neglect; global neglect with pre-natal drug exposure; chaotic neglect with pre-natal drug exposure. Neglect types were defined as follows:

- Global neglect – a history of relative sensory deprivation in more than one domain was obtained (for example, minimal exposure to language, touch and social interactions).
- Chaotic neglect – a history was obtained that was consistent with physical, emotional, social or cognitive neglect.

Method

Measurement of the frontal-occipital circumference (FOC), a measure of head size used to estimate brain size; interpretation of MRI and CT brains scan in cases where available (n = 43, 35 per cent of sample).

Findings

Dramatic differences from the norm were observed in FOC. For the globally neglected children, the group mean was below the fifth percentile and suggested abnormal brain growth, while the chaotically neglected children did not markedly differ from standard norms. In cases where MRI or CT scans were available, neuro-radiologists interpreted 11 of 17 scans as abnormal from the children with global neglect (64.7 per cent) and only three of 26 scans abnormal from the children with chaotic neglect (11.5 per cent). The authors also note that one-year follow-up of children with experience of sensory deprivation neglect showed increases in FOC measurement following removal into foster care. Improvements were less marked for those who had spent most time in the neglectful environment.

Questions

Thinking of the critical examination of Perry's research study and your critical notes made at the outset to this section (in Reflection Point 12.2):

1. Reflect on the assumptions made that often remain unquestioned in professional practice with children and young people.

2. How important is it for you as a social worker to have knowledge of these natural science and bio-medical perspectives, but to ensure that you take a critical, reflective and analytic approach to them at all times?

Discussion

This natural science approach is controversial in social work because it is contested and, on the surface, excludes the social and environmental factors that buffer against or exacerbate human problems. It is very important for you to know about these approaches, however, as they have found traction in medical circles. To ensure that a balanced approach is taken, you will need, as a social worker, to be able to argue with and use models outside your everyday field.

The picture shown at the beginning of the case study is controversial because it presents the idea that a child's brain is fixed within the first three years of life. We have seen in Chapter 1 in Part I of this volume that this is not the case and that brain plasticity (the ability to grow and adapt) continues into early adulthood at least. So, having knowledge of these important steps forward and their weaknesses is important to ensure the best interests of the child are served.

The assumptions underpinning attachment theory have also come in for criticism (see Chapter 7 in Part II and Chapter 13, both in this volume, for more on attachment theory). In reviewing the empirical literature, Bolen (2000) found consistent empirical support for the idea that attachment is relatively stable over time, is predictive of negative outcomes and is intergenerationally transmitted. However, they noted inconsistent and contradictory evidence for the claims that attachment is universal to all cultures, has a physiological basis and is transmitted from caregiver to infant in a linear fashion. In a more recent systematic review, McCrory et al (2012) also point to mixed findings from neurobiological studies comparing levels of the stress hormone cortisol among maltreated and non-maltreated children. Nevertheless, they conclude there is general agreement that dysregulation of the hypothalamus–pituitary–adrenal axis, one of the body's core stress response systems, likely mediates the link between early stress and later psychopathology. Similarly, neuroimaging research also highlights emerging evidence that maltreatment alters brain development to affect sensory systems, network architecture and circuits involved in threat detection, emotional regulation and reward anticipation (Teicher et al, 2016). However, as yet, we do not have a reliable understanding of the 'dose' of stress or trauma needed to produce such changes.

While attachment theory is understood as important in social work with children, the privileging of attachment theory may lead to an overemphasis on the parent–child relationship to the exclusion of broader structural issues such as poverty, which also have a well-documented relationship with negative psychosocial and health outcomes (see Bolen, 2000). The complex interplay between family factors and the wider social and physical environment in both increasing maltreatment risk and affecting outcomes needs to be recognised. Five decades of research suggest that 'resilience rests, fundamentally, on relationships' (Luthar, 2006, p 780), and while positive relationships with parents or carers will always be a significant element of this, positive relationships with peers and other supportive adults can act as protective factors, encouraging the development of functional coping behaviours.

Implications for social workers

Child maltreatment is a complex and multi-faceted issue linked to a variety of negative physical, cognitive, social and emotional outcomes. Experiencing it may alter the structure and functioning of the developing brain. Integration of neuroscience, neurobiology and attachment theory frame current understanding of the mechanisms by which the developmental trajectory is thought to be affected. It is posited that exposure to chronic stress impacts both the growing brain and the emerging attachment relationship with a parent/caregiver to produce high levels of stress and physical arousal, without the accompanying ability to regulate these powerful emotional states. This limits the child's ability to learn, manage emotions and develop social relationships, affecting both child and adult functioning across a variety of domains. However, critical consideration of the literature and current debates reveals a more nuanced picture than many media and policy representations would suggest. Thus, it is essential that social workers are able to evaluate the evidence base and its applicability to their own practice setting.

Key research considerations include how maltreatment had been defined, how the study design enables causal links to be established and how other risk factors have been accounted for within analyses. There is no doubt that integration of neurobiology with attachment theory has contributed significantly to recent theoretical developments, providing a cohesive framework for understanding how parent–child relationships may affect social and emotional development through the regulation of the stress response. Nevertheless, the neuroscience which supports this is still in its infancy. There is a danger of simplistic interpretation fostering an overly deterministic view of parenting behaviours which does not adequately take into account the broad range of circumstances which contribute to both child maltreatment and associated outcomes. Even if the science was to achieve a level of certitude about the impact of abuse on the brain, what follows from this in terms of policy and practice implications is by no means clear – should we intervene and remove children from the care of their parents earlier or should we invest in earlier and more intensive family support? Such consequential decisions should be informed by a more fine-grained understanding of the available evidence and wider debate about the moral and practical implications they have for both professionals and families.

Conclusion

This chapter has examined the ways in which child maltreatment can influence child development across a range of domains, significantly affecting physical, cognitive, social and emotional development across the life course. We have an increasingly sophisticated understanding not only of the ways, but also the whys, of how abuse can alter the developmental trajectory. The emergence of disciplines like neuroscience and neurobiology and their integration with older theoretical approaches, such as attachment theory, continue to enhance our understanding, although it is also apparent there is still much to be explained. While it is essential that child care professionals have a sound understanding of child development and the factors which can disrupt and damage developmental processes, it is equally important that they approach and evaluate evidence from a critical perspective. Research provides invaluable insight into potential risk factors and outcomes at a group level, guiding who we intervene with and how. Nevertheless, it remains the role of the professional to exercise professional judgement, assessing and evaluating how such findings can meaningfully inform their work at an individual level and in ways which take account of the wider moral implications for children and their families.

Reflective questions

1 What are the long-term impacts of maltreatment on children's physical, cognitive, social and emotional development and do they vary by maltreatment type?

2 Through what developmental processes are maltreatment experiences thought to affect outcomes in adolescence and adulthood?

3 What are the implications and possible limitations of applying research findings to professional practice?

Further reading

- Belsky, J. and de Haan, M. (2011) Annual research review: Parenting and children's brain development: The end of the beginning, *Journal of Child Psychology and Psychiatry*, 52(4): 409–428.
  This article explores ways in which a child's brain development is physically affected by parenting experiences.

- Brown, R. and Ward, H. (2012) Decision-making within a child's timeframe. Working Paper 16. London: Thomas Coram Research Unit, Childhood Wellbeing Research Centre.

This paper argues for the inclusion of all approaches to child development, including neuroscience, and suggests that this has implications for the time scales on which decisions are made in the lives of children who experience abuse and maltreatment.

• Teicher, M.H., Samson, J.A., Anderson, C.M. and Ohashi, K. (2016) The effects of childhood maltreatment on brain structure, function and connectivity, *Nature Reviews Neuroscience*, 17(10): 652–666.
This article links the experiences of maltreatment in early childhood to later psychiatric ill-health and calls for earlier recognition and intervention to prevent this from happening.

• Wastell, D. and White, S. (2012) Blinded by neuroscience: Social policy, the family and the infant brain, *Families, Relationships and Societies*, 1(3): 397–414.
Wastell and White provide an important social work critique to the neuroscientific evidence presented. They bring back to centre stage the adaptability and mutability of children and young people and the socio-environmental factors, the structural parts of life, that affect people's development and experience.

References

Allen, G. (2011) *Early Intervention: The Next Steps. An Independent Report to Her Majesty's Government*. January. HM Government.

Andersen, S.L., Akemi T., Evelyn S. Vincow, E. Valente, A.P. and Teicher, M.H. (2008) Preliminary evidence for sensitive periods in the effect of childhood sexual abuse on regional brain development. *Journal of Neuropsychiatry and Clinical Neurosciences*, 20(3): 292–301.

Belsky, J. and de Haan, M. (2011) Annual research review: Parenting and children's brain development: the end of the beginning, *Journal of Child Psychology and Psychiatry*, 52(4): 409–428.

Boddy, J., Skuse, D. and Andrews, B. (2000) The developmental sequelae of nonorganic failure to thrive, *Journal of Child Psychology and Psychiatry*, 41(8): 1003–1014.

Bolen, R. (2000) Validity of attachment theory, *Trauma, Violence and Abuse*, 1(2): 128–153.

Bowlby, J. (1969) *Attachment and Loss*, Vol. 1: *Attachment*. New York, NY: Basic Books.

Bowlby, J. (1973) *Attachment and Loss*, Vol. 2: *Separation*. New York, NY: Basic Books.

Brown, R. and Ward, H. (2013) Decision-making within a child's timeframe. Working Paper 16. London: Thomas Coram Research Unit, Childhood Wellbeing Research Centre.

Bruer, J.T. (1999) *The Myth of the First Three Years: A New Understanding of Early Brain Development and Lifelong Learning*. New York, NY: Free Press.

Bunting, L., Lazenbatt, A. and Wallace, I. (2010) Information sharing and reporting systems in the UK and Ireland: Professional barriers to reporting child maltreatment concerns, *Child Abuse Review*, 19(3): 187–202.

Cashmore, J. and Shackel, R. (2013) The long-term effects of child sexual abuse. CFCA Paper No. 11. Canberra, Australia: Commonwealth of Australia.

Choi, J., Jeong, B., Polcari, A., Rohan, M.L. and Teicher, M.H. (2012) Reduced fractional anisotropy in the visual limbic pathway of young adults witnessing domestic violence in childhood, *Neuroimage*, 59(2): 1071–1079.

Dawson G., Ashman S.B. and Carver, L.J. (2000) The role of early experience in shaping behavioral and brain development and its implications for social policy, *Development and Psychopathology*, 12(4): 695–712.

Dube, S., Felitti, V., Dong, M., Giles, W. and Anda, R. (2003) The impact of adverse childhood experiences on health problems: Evidence from four birth cohorts dating back to 1900, *Preventive Medicine*, 37: 268–277.

Felitti, V.J. and Anda, R.F. (2010) The relationship of adverse childhood experiences to adult health, wellbeing social function and healthcare. In R. Lanius, E. Vermetten and C. Pain (eds), *The Hidden Epidemic: The Impact of Early Life Trauma on Health and Disease*. Cambridge: Cambridge University Press.

Fonagy, P. (2001) *Attachment Theory and Psychoanalysis*. New York, NY: Other Press.

Giedd J., Blumenthal J., Jeffries N.O., Castellanos, F.X., Liu, H., Zijdenbos, A. et al (1999) Brain development during childhood and adolescence: A longitudinal MRI study, *Nature Neuroscience*, 2(10): 861–863.

Gilbert, N., Parton, N. and Skivenes, M. (2011) *Child Protection Systems: International Trends and Orientations*. New York, NY: Oxford University Press.

Green, L. (2017) *Understanding the Life Course: Sociological and Psychological Perspectives* (2nd edn). Cambridge: Polity Press.

Greenough, W. and Black, J. (1992) Induction of brain structure by experience: Substrate for cognitive development. In M.R. Gunnar and C.A. Nelson (eds), *Minnesota Symposia on Child Psychology 24: Developmental and Behavioural Neuroscience*. Hillsdale, NJ: Lawrence Erlbaum.

Gunnar, M., Morison, S., Chisholm, K. and Schuder, M. (2001) Salivary cortisol levels in children adopted from Romanian orphanages, *Developmental Psychopathology*, 13(3): 611–628.

Hillberg, T., Hamilton-Giachritsis, C. and Dixon, L. (2011) Review of meta-analyses on the association between child sexual abuse and adult mental health difficulties: A systematic approach, *Trauma Violence & Abuse*, 12(1): 38–49.

Irigaray, T.Q., Pacheco, J.B., Grassi-Oliveira, R., Fonseca, R., Leite, P. and Kristensen, C.H. (2013) Child maltreatment and later cognitive functioning: A systematic review, *Piscologia: Reflexao e Critica*, 26(2): 376–387.

Irish, L., Kobayashi, I. and Delahanty, D.L. (2010) Long-term physical health consequences of childhood sexual abuse: A meta-analytic review, *Journal of Pediatric Psychology*, 35(5): 450–461.

Jenny, C. and Isaac, R. (2006) The relation between child death and child maltreatment, *Archives of Disease in Childhood*, 91(3): 265–269.

Kempe, C.H., Silverman, F.N., Steele, B., Droegemueller, W. and Silver, H.K. (1962) The battered child syndrome, *Journal of the American Medical Association*, 181(1): 17–24.

Kendall-Tackett, K. and Becker-Blease K. (2004) The importance of retrospective findings in child maltreatment research, *Child Abuse Neglect*, 28(7): 723–727.

Kim, J. and Cicchetti, D. (2010) Longitudinal pathways linking child maltreatment, emotion regulation, peer relations, and psychopathology, *Journal of Child Psychology and Psychiatry*, 51(6): 706–716.

Leeb, R.T., Lewis, T. and Zolotor, A.J. (2011) A review of physical and mental health consequences of child abuse and neglect and implications for practice, *American Journal of Lifestyle Medicine*, 5(5): 454–461.

Luke, N. and Banerjee, R. (2013) Differentiated associations between childhood maltreatment experiences and social understanding: A meta-analysis and systematic review, *Developmental Review*, 33(1): 1–28.

Luthar, S. S. (2006) Resilience in development: A synthesis of research across five decades. In D. Cicchetti and D.J. Cohen (eds), *Developmental Psychopathology: Risk, Disorder, and Adaptation*, New York: John Wiley & Sons, pp 739–95.

McCrory, E., De Brito, S. and Viding, E. (2012) The link between child abuse and psychopathology: A review of neurobiological and genetic research, *Journal of the Royal Society of Medicine*, 105(4): 151–156.

Meadows, P., Tunstill, J., George, A., Dhudwar, A. and Kurtz, Z. (2011) *The Costs and Consequences of Child Maltreatment – A Literature Review for the NSPCC*. London: NSPCC.

Munro, E. and Manful, E. (2012) *Safeguarding Children: A Comparison of England's Data with that of Australia, Norway and the United States*. London: Department for Education.

Munro, E. and Musholt, K. (2014) Neuroscience and the risks of maltreatment, *Children and Youth Services Review*, 47(1): 18–26.

Norman, R.E., Byambaa, M., De, R., Butchart, A. and Scott, J. (2012) The long-term health consequences of child physical abuse, emotional abuse, and neglect: A systematic review and meta-analysis, *PLOS Medicine*, 9(11): 1–31.

Pacheco, J., Irigaray, T., Werlang, B., Nunes, M. and de Lima Argimon, I. (2014) Childhood maltreatment and psychological adjustment: A systematic review, *Psicologia Refl exão e Crítica*, 27(4): 815–824.

Perez, C.M. and Widom, C.S. (1994) Childhood victimization and long-term intellectual and academic outcomes, *Child Abuse and Neglect*, 18(8): 617–633.

Perry, B. (2001) The neurodevelopmental impact of violence in childhood. In D. Schetky and E.P. Benedek (eds), *Textbook of Child and Adolescent Forensic Psychiatry*. Washington, DC: American Psychiatric Press.

Perry, B.D. (2002) Childhood experience and the expression of genetic potential: What childhood neglect tells us about nature and nurture, *Brain and Mind*, 3(1): 79–100.

Petersen, A.C., Joseph, J. and Feit, M. (2014) *New Directions in Child Abuse and Neglect Research*. Washington, DC: Institute of Medicine and National Research Council.

Schore, A. (1994) *Affect Regulation and the Origin of the Self: The Neurobiology of Emotional Development*. Hillsdale, NJ: Lawrence Erlbaum.

Schore, A. (2000) Attachment and the regulation of the right brain, *Attachment & Human Development*, 2(1): 23–47.

Siegel, D. (1999) *The Developing Mind*. New York, NY: Guilford Press.

Spataro, J., Mullen, P., Burgess, P., Wells, D. and Moss, S. (2004) Impact of child sexual abuse on mental health – a prospective study in males and females, *British Journal of Psychiatry*, 184(5): 416–421.

Stoltenborgh, M., Bakermans-Kranenburg, M.J., Alink, L.R. and IJzendoorn, M.H. (2015) The prevalence of child maltreatment across the globe: Review of a series of meta-analyses, *Child Abuse Review*, 24(1): 37–50.

Teicher, M.H., Samson, J.A., Anderson, C.M. and Ohashi, K. (2016) The effects of childhood maltreatment on brain structure, function and connectivity, *Nature Reviews Neuroscience*, 17(10): 652–666.

UNICEF (2003) *A League Table of Child Maltreatment Deaths in Rich Nations. Innocenti Report Card*. Florence: Innocenti Research Centre.

Wastell, D. and White, S. (2012) Blinded by neuroscience: Social policy, the family and the infant brain, *Families, Relationships and Societies*, 1(3): 397–414.

Wastell, D. and White, S. (2017) *Blinded by Science: The Social Implications of Epigenetics and Neuroscience* (Kindle edn). Bristol: Policy Press.

World Health Organization (2016) Child maltreatment – fact sheet. Available from: http://www.who.int/mediacentre/factsheets/fs150/en/

13

Substitute care: moving into a new family

Christine Cocker

Introduction

For those children and young people in local authority care, substitute state care arrangements can take many forms. This may include family/friends or 'connected persons' placements, 'stranger' foster care placements, residential placements and, for a few younger children, adoption. Many of the children coming into care each year will return home to their families of origin. However, a considerable number of children will require ongoing substitute care, with local authority social work involvement.

Many children enter care following a specific incident or event where concerns are raised about the welfare, safety and/or quality of care the child has been receiving. At the point when children enter care, there are often many worries about their health and well-being. Children may have physical or mental health difficulties, behavioural problems and educational difficulties, and may in addition be angry, upset, confused, bewildered, anxious, afraid, worried, withdrawn and/or unhappy. This list is by no means exhaustive. Some children may be relieved to be in a safe space. Providing good quality and nurturing care for children facing these types of difficulties is challenging, but foster carers and residential carers undertake this sterling work with looked-after children every day. As a result of experiences of abuse and neglect prior to care, children often face developmental delays in their overall progress. It is therefore imperative that care offers children and young people an opportunity to do as much 'catching up' on their development as possible. We know a little about what makes a difference to developmental outcomes for children, and this is explored in the following pages.

Chapter objectives

- consider the impact of separation and loss for children entering care;
- enable the reader to develop a critical understanding of the concepts of attachment and resilience and how they might apply to looked-after children;

- reflect how different types of placements and caring arrangements can meet the needs of looked-after children;

- consider ways in which social workers can help children and young people make sense of these life-changing events;

- help social workers think about some of the challenges for children's development.

Separation and loss

The looked-after children population is not homogeneous. Every one of the 72,670+ children in care in England on 31 March 2017 is unique (Department for Education, 2017), and individual circumstances need to be taken into consideration when formulating an appropriate care plan for each child. The only two features that all looked-after children have in common are their experiences of separation and loss. Individual experiences will, of course, differ, but at the point at which they enter care, each looked-after child experiences separation from immediate family and attachment figures, with the devastating sense of loss of connection with external loci such as people and places. There are always reasons why such moves are deemed necessary; however, the psychological effect upon the child's inner world should not be underestimated. One of the most important roles of social workers and carers is to support children through those first few days/weeks/months where grief may surface for the child in a number of different ways, depending on their age, most often through their behaviour. This is a completely appropriate response to an experience of loss, and should be understood as such.

As we have seen in Chapter 7 in Part II of this volume, John Bowlby has written extensively about attachment, separation and loss (Bowlby, 1969, 1973, 1980) and his ideas are highly influential in social work practice. His work has helped us think about the psychological effects of separation and loss on children. Although his early work concentrated on mothers and maternal behaviours, it is now accepted that his ideas apply to all parental behaviours and it is the child's attachment figure rather than the sex of the parent that is most important (Green, 2017).

Michael Rutter refers to separation as the physical loss of a 'mother figure' (now more accurately described as 'attachment figure'), but this does not mean the loss of 'mothering' (now described as 'parenting'), which he thought could be provided by another person (1981). For those children entering foster care, they will have a different experiences of family life with other people providing good quality, nurturing and appropriate care and parenting.

According to Vera Fahlberg, loss is something that is experienced after separation, whether or not that separation is temporary or permanent: 'It is an affectual state that an individual experiences when something of significance is unexpectedly withdrawn' (2012, p 133). Jane Aldgate reminds us that for looked-after children, 'separation involves fear, which needs to be mastered, and that loss involves grief which needs to be expressed' (cited in Fahlberg, 2012, p 133). For those of us working with looked-after children, acknowledging and supporting them through these experiences of grief is important, because, as Fahlberg contends, unresolved grief can introduce a range of difficulties for children, including forming new attachments and moving forward positively.

Children's behaviours can indicate their reaction to separation from parents and there is a continuum of identifiable responses. At one end, some children who are not particularly attached to their parents may not demonstrate any reaction, while at the other end children may find the separation from parents traumatic. Fahlberg identified a number of factors that influence a child's reaction to parental separation (2012, p 134):

- the child's age and stage of development;
- the child's attachment to the parent;
- the parent's bonding to the child;
- past experiences of separation;
- the child's perceptions of the reasons for separation;
- the child's preparation for the move;
- the 'parting message' the child receives;
- the post-separation environment;
- the child's temperament;
- the environment from which they are being moved.

Each of these factors is important on its own, but it is the interplay of these factors that social workers must also consider when they are working with children. There are many ways that social workers can approach dealing with children's feelings of sadness and being upset. Age-appropriate books may help. An example of one is *Michael Rosen's Sad Book* (Rosen, 2011), which recounts how Michael felt after his son died suddenly. Some social workers may think that raising topics like this with children is unhelpful, as children's parents won't have died and it may make children even more upset, but this negates the opportunity it provides for children to express their feelings. Coram BAAF and Jessica Kingsley Publishers both publish books for children that are specifically about children moving to a new home, and also about children's feelings, including grief. Social workers should have the skills to deal with children expressing their feelings by crying, screaming or acting out their feelings through their behaviours, assist foster carers in understanding the reasons for the behaviours, and also deal with their own feelings. Fahlberg comments:

> When children use unacceptable behaviours to show strong feelings, adults can accept the emotions at the same time as they confront the behaviours. They can teach the child new and more acceptable ways to express emotions. For example, if a child is angry and hits a sibling,

the adult might say, 'I know that you are really mad and that is ok, but it is not right to hurt others when you are angry. When you are mad and feel like hitting, you can punch a pillow.' (2012, p 148)

Fahlberg talks about the difference between responding to 'naughty behaviours' by isolating children (sending them to their room), which she argues may reinforce a message of 'this time you have been sent away only as far as your room, but if you continue to misbehave you may be sent away from this home' (2012, p 148). Instead, she suggests:

> ... having a child sit on a chair in the same room as the adult until the child has calmed down. This action gives the message ... when you have strong feelings, you need to be close to people, not separated from them ... it gives the message that the adult is not afraid of the child's anger. (2012, p 149)

There are a number of ways in which children can be helped to adjust to their new placements. Supporting children to manage new routines, to have regular contact with their parents and other significant people, such as extended family members or siblings, is important. New experiences of family life and the opportunities that may present themselves are also important, but they may also be frightening. Social workers should talk with children about their feelings and their behaviours arising from being upset and distressed, and offer support to the foster carers who are doing the everyday caring tasks, including responding to these behaviours. Case Study 13.1 explores this further.

CASE STUDY 13.1

Jamil (age eight) and Jaya (age three) are black British children. They were placed together with foster carers in your local authority a year ago, following an incident occurring in their family home where Jamil's arm was broken by an adult staying at the home. Both children were known to social services since Jaya's birth. Prior to coming into care, they lived with their mother. She was diagnosed with bi-polar disorder and has a history of drug misuse. There have been many reports received from the school about Jamil's chaotic attendance and concerns expressed about his behaviour in class when he lived with his mother. Prior to coming into care, both children were the subjects of child protection plans. There were concerns about whether the children's mother could put the children's needs ahead of her own, given her drug addiction and mental health issues. The children are transracially placed with experienced foster carers (male and female) who are white British, who also have two teenage birth children (both boys) living at home.

Jamil and Jaya have settled well into the placement. Jamil's behaviour at school has recently improved, but the foster carer provides considerable support to the school to manage this. Additional school resources have been slow to materialise to support Jamil in the classroom. Jaya has very little speech and is quiet and reserved, especially after contact with her mother, and the foster carers are becoming more concerned about her. Jamil also sees his mother regularly for contact (once a fortnight), but has recently said he does not want to go to contact.

Questions
1. How have these children's experiences of separation and loss affected them?
2. What does this case say to you about social work practice in this area?
3. As their social worker, what do you need to consider?

Discussion
Separation from their mother will have affected each child in different ways. Refer back to Chapter 2 concerning psychoanalytic explanations that might be useful to consider here and Chapter 7's extended discussion about attachment, some of which we rehearse next in this chapter. As a social worker, you will need to consider the short, medium and long term plans for each child, including maintaining some sort of contact with their birth mother, whilst recognising that this may be creating some difficulties currently and will therefore need to be closely monitored. You would also need to consider how Jamil and Jaya's black British heritage can be nurtured in a white British family.

Attachment and resilience

Attachment theory has become one of the most enduring psychological theories for describing the development of social and emotional relationships of children with their principal caregivers (see Chapter 7 in Part II of this volume for a detailed account of attachment theories). In this chapter, we will consider Fahlberg's approach. She uses the definition of attachment offered by Klaus and Kennel (1976, cited in Fahlberg, 2012, p 14): 'an affectionate bond between two individuals that endures through space and time and serves to join them emotionally'. Fahlberg (2012) talks about an arousal/relaxation cycle – attachment-seeking behaviour as initiated by the child – and the positive interaction cycle – interaction between a caregiver and child as initiated by the adult – as examples of bonding and attachment behaviours in action. The adults' responses to these cycles will have implications for how reliable and available babies and children view their caregivers.

Attachment theory holds that, within close relationships, young children acquire mental representations, or internal working models, of their own worthiness based on other people's availability and their willingness to provide care and protection (Ainsworth et al, 1978, cited in Howe et al, 1999, p 21). It is through the world of relationships that children begin to understand themselves and their relationship with others (Howe, 1996). As already discussed in Chapter 7 in Part I of this volume, Mary Ainsworth documented three types of attachment behaviours for children aged between one and three years (Ainsworth et al, 1978; Daniel et al, 2010).

- Type A: Anxious, avoidant, insecure attachment, where toddlers experience their caregivers as consistently rejecting, and themselves as insecure but compulsively self-reliant. They show little distress when the caregiver leaves, and avoid contact with the caregiver on their return – some will avoid the caregiver completely. Toddlers with an avoidant attachment will react to a stranger in the same way that they do with their caregiver (Daniel et al, 2010).
- Type B: Secure attachment, where toddlers experience their caregiver as available and they see themselves positively. They explore when their caregiver is present, show upset at the caregiver's departure and stop exploring. They show interest in reuniting with the caregiver upon return but then want to explore. They will cling to their caregiver in the presence of a stranger (Daniel et al, 2010).
- Type C: Anxious resistant or ambivalent insecure attachment, where toddlers experience their caregiver as inconsistently responsive and themselves as dependent and poorly valued. They are anxious before their caregiver leaves, distressed while their caregiver leaves and will demonstrate a mix of resisting and seeking contact with their caregiver on return (Daniel et al, 2010).

Main and Hesse (1990, cited in Schofield and Beek, 2006, p 38) identified a further group of children who were insecurely attached and yet did not fall into either Type A or C. This further type of insecure attachment is Type D:

- Type D: Disorganised, disoriented insecure attachment, where toddlers experience their caregivers as either frightening or frightened, and themselves as helpless, angry and unworthy. Toddlers' behaviours are contradictory and high levels of negative emotions are expressed (Daniel et al, 2010).

Many looked-after children will have some sort of attachment difficulty. Bearing in mind that a difficulty is not the same thing as a disorder, Meltzer et al (2003) suggested the rate of looked-after children who had attachment disorders was significantly higher than in the general population.

> Looked after children are thought to be at much greater risk than other children of having an attachment disorder. Inhibited attachment disorders are characterised by marked difficulties with social interactions that are usually attributed to early and severe abuse from 'attachment figures' such as parents. Disinhibited attachment disorders are characterised by diffuse attachments, as shown by indiscriminate sociability without the usual selectivity in choice of attachment figures – often attributed to frequent changes of caregiver in the early

years ... Using a standard definition, around 2.5% of looked after children had an attachment disorder, but this rate rose to around 20% using a broader definition ... the overwhelming majority of children with attachment disorders also meet the diagnostic criteria for other psychiatric disorders. (2003, p. xvii)

In terms of thinking about what might make a difference to children's experiences within fostering or adoption placements, Schofield and Beek's work on the secure base model (2014), builds on what is known about attachment theory and resilience and translates it into an environment where it can be applied to foster care with looked-after children and also adoption placements. We know that the need for continued support for carers is important in supporting placements because of the continued difficulties that children face as a result of experiences of early adversity. It sets out the dimensions of caregiving that can support children to thrive.

The five points of the model are the five dimensions of caregiving, and are represented in Figure 13.1.

The model is predicated on the caregiving relationship. It focuses on the interaction between the caregiver and the child, but also considers how that relationship can enable the child to develop competence in the outside world and manage often complex relationships with birth family members (Schofield

Figure 13.1: Five dimensions of caregiving

The Secure Base model

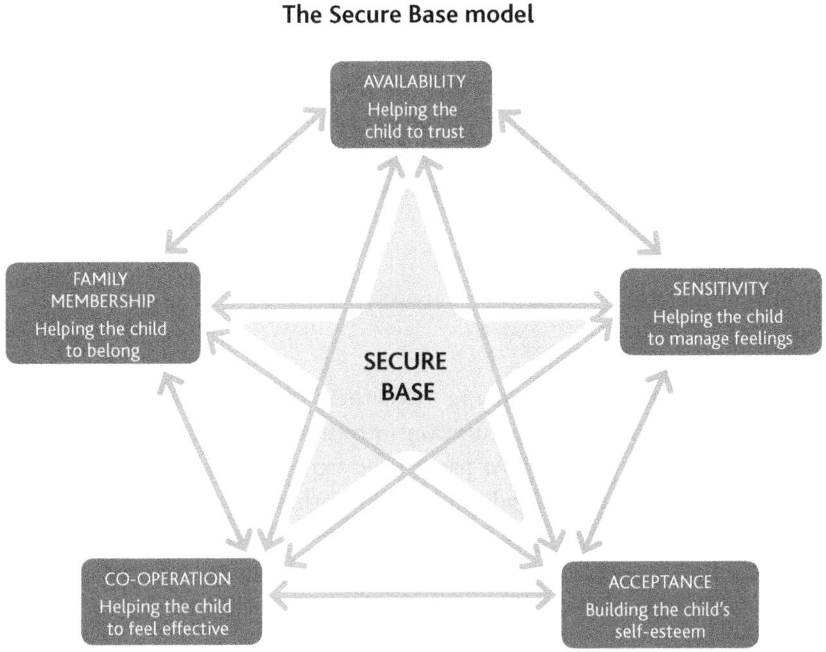

Source: Schofield and Beek (no date)

and Beek, 2014). Each of the five caregiving dimensions (availability, sensitivity, acceptance, cooperation and family membership) has an associated developmental benefit for the child, with some overlap also occurring between the five dimensions. While this model has been developed for use with foster carers and adopters, it is important that social workers also understand the principles underpinning the model so that they can support the use of this model in practice. Case Study 13.2 encourages you to apply this model.

CASE STUDY 13.2

Use the secure base model to think about the caregiving relationships that Jamil and Jaya (Case Study 13.1) have in their lives. Use the five different dimensions to expand and deepen your ideas.

Questions

1. What are the differences between the children in terms of the support that they each require?
2. Think about the differences between the foster carers and parent relationships with each of the children.
3. What support do the carers need?
4. How might this be provided?

Discussion

It is important that each child's needs are considered individually. The provision of a stable, loving environment in which they are both accepted, included and in which sensitive care-giving is available will help each child to develop trust in care-giving relationships and to develop from there. The foster carers are providing a great deal of support to the children, to the school, and will require help and support themselves to deal with their feelings and concerns, to ensure their family can work together to help Jamal and Jaya, and to ensure that questions concerning their birth family and cultural and ethnic heritage are dealt with appropriately and sensitively.

Placements

When a child cannot remain living with their birth family, where they are looked after is significant. The transition into that place and space is important as everything will be different. As part of the experience of separation and the feelings of loss, the sights, sounds and smells within the new foster/residential home will all be different, as will the food, the household rules, the people within the home, and the opportunities for play and for exploration – all require some adjustment for the child. It will also take some time for the carers to get to know the child.

Placements include fostering placements (emergency, respite care, short-term and long-term fostering, family and friends fostering), residential placements and adoption. There are many laws and regulations that govern a local authority's responsibilities towards looked-after children. For an overview, see sections 22 and 23 of the Children Act 1989; Children Act 1989 guidance on placements (Department for Education, 2015a); national minimum standards for fostering (Department for Education, 2011) and adoption (Department for Education, 2014); and children's homes regulations and standards (Department for Education, 2015b). It is important that the quality of the substitute care provided to children is very good; that is the reason for the government setting 'minimum' standards when caring for someone else's child. The use of the term 'minimum' is unfortunate, however, as why would the lowest common denominator be the aim when thinking about the quality of alternative care provision for children, especially given the poor parenting experiences many of the children requiring care and protection have received? In order to identify what is known about what brings about success in placements and good outcomes for children, two broad areas are identified in the literature: children's characteristics and placement characteristics.

REFLECTION POINT 13.1

What do you think you need to know about children's and placement characteristics in order to make an appropriate match? Think how, as a social worker, you might take these considerations into account when working with children and young people needing substitute care.

Systematic literature reviews of outcomes in foster care have identified a number of characteristics known about children at the point they enter care that can positively or negatively affect psychosocial or placement outcomes. These include the numbers of placements that children have while in care; the age children come into care, with younger children having better permanency arrangements than older children (Pritchett et al, 2013); children's externalising behaviours; and older age of children and children's experience of multiple social workers having a negative effect on outcomes (Rock et al, 2015).

Forrester et al (2009) investigated the impact of public care on the outcomes for looked-after children and identified 12 studies in the British literature that either compared children in care with children from similar backgrounds that had not entered care (three studies), or tracked children in care over time (nine studies). These studies consistently reported the serious emotional problems that looked-after children have when they enter care, likely because of their abusive and neglectful experiences, living with parents who have drug or alcohol problems or mental illness, and showed that these problems improved for children in care over time (Forrester et al, 2009). This finding is consistent with the international literature.

Placements, particularly foster placements, are viewed as the cornerstone to the outcomes that children are able to achieve in public care. The warmth of the carer's parenting relationship with the child or young person, including their persistence or 'stickability' and ability to set boundaries, is critical, as is the interplay between the two (Pritchett et al, 2013). Rock et al's (2015) review also acknowledged a number of protective factors, including more experienced foster carers with strong parenting skills, older foster carers and placements where foster carers enable children's academic development. Common to both these systematic reviews is the 'concept of "fit" between the child and the foster family' (Rock et al, 2015, p 197), linked to the child and carers liking each other and the child being treated equally alongside other children living with the foster carers, with no rivalry within these relationships. The importance of models like the secure base model then come into their own, as the focus is on developing the relationship between the carer and the child. This becomes the primary focus, as it is through this relationship that change has the potential to occur (Howe, 2005). While many different kinds of people become foster carers, in terms of considering whether there is a preferred 'type' of family that looked-after or adopted children would do best in, Golombok (2000) believes that the opportunities to form positive attachments is central.

Two of the more controversial placement topics in fostering and adoption over recent years have been lesbian and gay fostering and adoption, and transracial placements. There is now a growing body of research to show that children growing up in lesbian and gay households are just as well adjusted as children growing up in heterosexual households (Golombok et al, 1983; Golombok and Tasker, 1996; Barrett and Tasker, 2001, 2002; Golombok et al, 2003; Patterson, 2005; Tasker and Golombok, 2005; Goldberg, 2010). More recently, research into outcomes for children adopted by lesbians and gay men found these parents were highly motivated and more actively involved in the lives of their adopted children than heterosexual parents (Mellish et al, 2013). Outcomes for adopted children placed with gay fathers have been found to be particularly positive (Golombok et al, 2014). While mostly comparative and based on small samples, these studies have contributed to an increasing body of positive research evidence on outcomes for children adopted by lesbians and gay men in terms of children's functioning, family relationships and quality of parenting (Erich, 2005; Kindle and Erich, 2005; Leung et al, 2005; Erich et al, 2009; Farr et al, 2010). They challenge earlier concerns about the impact of lesbian and gay fostering and adoption on children facing adversity in their early lives and their potential for adjustment later on (Cocker, 2015).

Ethnicity, culture and transracial placements became a topic of interest for the coalition government in 2010, when Michael Gove was the Secretary of State for Education. The government's view at that time was that a child's ethnicity, although important, should not be an over-riding concern when placing that child for adoption, as it led to unnecessary delays for children from ethnic minorities in securing permanency, because of a shortage of adopters from ethnic minority backgrounds. Local authorities were encouraged to consider permanency for children where their needs could be met, and this included within transracial placements. The same approach to placement choice was also encouraged within fostering placements, although because of shortages in foster placement nationally, transracial placements were more commonplace, as foster care was considered to be a short-term arrangement for the majority of children, and a child's need for care and protection was seen as paramount, over-riding the need for an ethnic placement match.

There are strong opinions about the so-called 'correctness' of transracial placements in the UK. Selwyn and Wijedasa provide an overview of the key debates:

> … the placement of minority ethnic children has been dominated for the last forty years by competing arguments about the benefits and disadvantages of 'trans-racial' placements. The debate is often polarised with one camp (Gilroy, 1990; Macey, 1995; Hayes, 2003) arguing that placing children according to 'race' is a form of apartheid, not supported by the research evidence and deeply divisive. The opposite camp (Maxime, 1993; Small, 2000) argues that research has been Eurocentric and children's mental health needs are best met in an ethnically matched placement to allow the development of a 'Black' identity. Both camps accuse each other of racism and this has limited the willingness of others to become involved and engage with the issues. (2009, p 363)

Most of the transracial placements commented about in the literature involve black and ethnic minority children or children of dual/mixed heritage being placed with white carers. However, there have been a number of high-profile cases that have hit the media over the last few years, where white children have been placed with non-white carers. The London Borough of Tower Hamlets found itself on the front page of *The Times* newspaper on 28 August 2017 under the headline, 'Christian child forced into Muslim foster care – concern for girl who "had cross removed and was encouraged to learn Arabic"' (Norfolk, 2017). In April 2018, *The Times* was forced to issue an apology stating that it had misrepresented the facts of the case in how it had reported the story (Grierson, 2018). Although a number of political drivers appeared to affect how and why this story was picked up and then dominated national media for a number of days in August 2017, there were also a number of more considered accounts of Muslim foster carers looking after a number of children who were not Muslim, which identified the strengths in the care that was offered by the carers and the enjoyment that the carers had experienced in fostering (Manzoor, 2017).

REFLECTION POINT 13.2

What do you think are the key elements of matching for placement? Do you believe that transracial placements should be discouraged where possible or supported as providing a stable home? Reflect on why you might be thinking in these ways and how your thoughts might influence your practice.

Matching children to placements is a complex process, and there are a number of different factors that guide decision making, including practical issues like availability of placements. Professional bias and opinion can also influence decision making on what is viewed as in the 'best interests' of individual children. Social workers are also likely to have prejudices that impact on their decision making (Brown and Cocker, 2011), particularly in the area of lesbian and gay fostering and adoption, but some positive change is reported (Brown, 2011). The important point is whether carers can adequately meet the developmental needs of the looked-after children in their care, and that applies to all carers, regardless of ethnicity or sexuality.

A minority of looked-after children are cared for in residential settings. In 2018, this number was 11 per cent. For many years, residential care has been viewed as a last resort for children entering care because of the high-profile inquiries and investigations into abuse and neglect within children's homes throughout the UK. These included: the Waterhouse inquiry, which investigated abuse in Welsh children's homes in the 1970s and 1980s; and the Pindown inquiry, investigating conditions in a number of Staffordshire children's homes in the 1980s. However, foster care is not appropriate for all children, as some children cannot live in a family setting because of their own experience of dysfunctional family life. Clough et al (2006) believe that effective residential child care can be achieved, but it is important to correctly assess the needs of young people and match these to placements.

In England, there are a number of well-established therapeutic communities, such as Childhood First and the Caldecott Foundation, which have psychosocial or psychotherapeutic approaches to caring for vulnerable children in residential settings. Residential care often deals with young people who are in crisis, have a variety of complex needs and have often experienced several placement moves. While suggesting that the outcomes for these children are often perceived as negative, these 'challenges' to good quality residential care – high levels of behavioural problems, further placement instability, and the poor education and health outcomes that have been the focus of recent concern, and the continuing personal and social difficulties faced by those young people who become care-leavers (Scottish Institute for Residential Child Care, 2006) are challenges to quality care for all looked-after children. Residential care remains an important and valuable placement option for some looked-after children. We consider transracial placement further in Case Study 13.3.

CASE STUDY 13.3

Jamal and Jaya's placement is transracial, as we have seen in Case Study 13.1. Consider the following questions.

Questions

1. How might this affect the care planning and support you offer the children and the foster carers?
2. What are the markers you look for to indicate that this placement is meeting the needs of the two children?
3. How would you assess the warmth of the foster parenting relationship?
4. How would you describe the attachment between the foster parents and each of the children?

Discussion

In the next section, we will consider the role of the social worker in supporting children who are looked after. As a social worker for looked after children, your primary focus is on Jamil and Jaya; you will work with the foster carers to ensure that they meet the specific needs of each child. The warmth in the relationship between the foster carers and each child will be important to assess. As a fostering social worker, your role is different; you will support the foster carers in their caregiving work with all children placed within their home. As this is a transracial placement, care will need to be taken by both social workers to ensure that the foster carers can meet the specific needs of the children, for example, ensuring they have appropriate skin and hair products available, and that other aspects of their identity and heritage are prioritised in the care they receive.

The role of the social worker

The role of social work is key in the life of a looked-after child. Social workers are responsible for assessing many aspects of a child's well-being: planning for where they will live; ensuring that they have a care plan, a plan for permanency, an education plan that addresses any support needs they might have; and that any health and mental health needs a child may have will be addressed via the placement or through additional specialist services. Social workers need to spend time with the child in order that they know the child well enough to be able to represent their needs in decision-making fora. This is a huge undertaking, bearing in mind that a social worker will have a number of children for whom they are responsible at any one time. Arranging regular visits and ensuring that children are well cared for, that their relationships with parents and siblings are nurtured where possible and enabling them to have a voice in their own futures, are all part of the social work role. There is a presumption of contact between children and their families of origin for all children who are in care. Research evidence shows that there are better outcomes for children if this occurs (Thoburn, 1994). The frequency of contact will be determined by the age of the child and the child's wishes and feelings, among other factors, covered in an assessment relating to the relationship between the parent and child.

In terms of children's development, there are a number of key tasks that social workers can undertake or promote to ensure that children have the best chance at developing resilience and overcoming the adversity they have experienced. There is evidence to suggest that those children who enter care do better than those children who are from similar backgrounds, but remain living in the community (Forrester et al, 2009). Research in Practice (2014) suggest that social workers should ensure that a looked-after child is able to develop a close and secure relationship with at least one key person while in care (this might be the social worker or foster carer). The child needs nurturing routines and clear boundaries so that they begin to learn that the world is predictable and safe. While the foster carer is most likely to be the person implementing boundaries and nurturing routines, it is the social worker's role to ensure this is taking place.

It is also important that children have opportunities for talking about their experiences. This helps them learn to name and manage feelings and to develop a narrative for understanding their experiences. For young children, messy and sensory play can be helpful as an opportunity to experience different textures and sensations (such as play involving sandpits, water, bubbles and paint), and provides a vehicle for creativity, as well as the expression of unconscious worries, thoughts and feelings. Allowing children to experiment with food is also important, as many children who are maltreated have food issues. Often, looked-after children present and need to be cared for like a much younger child. This includes allowing children to revisit earlier stages of play to catch up on what they may have missed (Research in Practice, 2014). Social workers need to have awareness about the overarching issues and plans for children, as well as the specific day-to-day worries and concerns that children may have. Their relationship with the child is critical in ensuring their work is effective.

For social workers working with adolescent young people, knowledge about child development is critical, as young people go through a great deal of developmental change during this period of their lives. It is important that social workers have a good understanding about some of the physical, social and emotional changes and challenges young people will be experiencing. As with any other looked-after child, experiences of abuse and neglect may have affected any young person's developmental progress and so young people may also need the opportunity to 'catch up' on their development in a foster placement or residential setting. Adolescents will continue to need support and help in many aspects of their lives, as they move towards independence (see Case Study 13.4 to consider this in relation to Jamil and Jaya). This might consist of helping with organising day-to-day tasks, helping them with skills in setting priorities and providing opportunities for them to practise making decisions. A number of social and environmental influences will also be present in terms of peer influence, other risk-taking behaviour, such as using drugs, drinking and becoming sexually active. Being aware of and attuned to situations that some of the potentially more vulnerable young people may be at risk of involvement in is also important; for example, the risks of young people becoming involved in sexual exploitation or in 'county lines' activities should not be underestimated.

CASE STUDY 13.4

Imagine you are a social worker newly allocated to Jamil and Jaya (Case Study 13.1). Jamil has expressed his sadness and anger at his mother, but also at being in foster care. He worries about his sister and about what is going to happen to them both. These children have no other birth family living locally.

Questions

1. How would you go about building effective relationships with Jamil and Jaya, both individually and together?
2. How would you address Jamil's and Jaya's needs to maintain their cultural and ethnic roots?

Discussion

The following section considers what we know about child development and how this might help you in your work with Jamil and Jaya. Being reflective and enquiring is central to using this knowledge. You will also need to be confident in who you are, and how you understand your upbringing as a child and the attachments you had, in order that your experiences do not overly influence your responses to children's situations, including their distress. Understanding how your own position can influence how you approach that of your work with others is important.

Child development for looked-after children

Having a robust awareness of child development theories and the different ages and stages of cognitive, language, physical, social and emotional development that such theories espouse is essential for a social worker. Most social workers will cover this on their qualifying training and will be familiar with the work of Freud and psychosexual development (see Chapter 2 in Part I of this volume for further details), Piaget and cognitive development, and Erikson and psychosocial development (both discussed in Chapter 3 in Part I of this volume) as a minimum. Some students will have also completed a child observation while on their course and applied child development theory to their observations. There are many other theories and theorists (such as Bandura and social learning theory, Vygotsky and sociocultural theory, Bronfenbrenner and ecological theory) whose work is influential. Altogether, these theories help social workers understand the impact of adversity, abuse, poor parenting, poor attachments and experiences of separation and loss on children and their development.

Wilson et al (2011) suggest that it is not helpful to think of development as either 'normal' or 'abnormal'. Instead, it is the behaviour and the context in which it is observed that is important. It is this that helps social workers determine whether what they have observed is concerning. There will be times where children's behaviours are well outside of what could be considered to be 'normal' in the circumstances and it is important to note that there can be wide variations in what is considered 'normal'. There can also be medical or organic reasons for children experiencing some delays in development. However, children who have experienced abuse and neglect in their early years often show developmental delay in some areas, such as language acquisition. If, once in foster care, a child's development suddenly improves so that the child is playing 'catch up' and reaching appropriate developmental milestones, then it is highly likely that the developmental delay experienced by a child was due to the environment in which they were living and their experiences within that environment. Theories of human development provide a means for assessing children, including evaluating the quality of relationships they have with their parents. They can also help social workers understand the impact of trauma by observing children's behaviour and thinking about this within the context of their overall development. It can help social workers think about interventions that might be necessary, including from specialist services, and it can also help social workers think about permanence options for children, including placement choices (Wilson et al, 2011).

Parental problems such as domestic violence, substance misuse and mental ill-health can have an impact on all aspects of children's development. Any assessment undertaken by a social worker should consider these factors. After 20 years of use, the Assessment Framework (Department of Health, 2000) still helpfully sets out the key areas for social workers to consider when assessing children's circumstances (the child's developmental needs; parenting capacity; and social and environmental context). In terms of developmental issues specifically affecting children in care, the American Academy of Pediatrics Committee on Early Childhood Adoption and Dependent Care (2000) identified the following priorities:

1. the implications and consequences of abuse, neglect, and placement in foster care on early brain development;
2. the importance and challenges of establishing a child's attachment to caregivers;
3. the importance of considering a child's changing sense of time in all aspects of the foster care experience; and
4. the child's response to stress. (p 1145)

The age of the child will have an impact on how any developmental issues manifest. Within social work, there is some contention regarding the literature that describes the effect of abuse and neglect on early brain development. Researchers such as Woolgar (2013) and Brown and Ward (2013) have examined the scientific evidence that discusses the effect of abuse on children's brain development, commenting on the importance of the early years for the developing brain. White and Wastell (2013) are more circumspect in their positioning, and have expressed misgivings with the weighting given by Brown and Ward, in particular, to their findings after reviewing the literature.

These differences in opinion are useful in ensuring that, as a profession, we are critically considering the research data of other professions, especially where positivist methodologies are used. Research investigating neuroscience is still developing, as is research that investigates the use of cortisol as a biological stress indicator. While some of these findings are considered 'facts' and cannot be disputed (for example, when under stress, humans produce cortisol), these fields are complex areas of study. Translating the results of the research to general policy in work with looked-after children, or children who have experienced abuse and neglect and are 'in need', is not straightforward. The blanket application of scientific findings to individual children is another source of controversy, as the impact of this for individual children will differ.

Conclusion

This chapter explored five areas: the impact of separation and loss for children entering care; the concepts of attachment and resilience and how they might apply to looked-after children; placements; the role of social workers; and the importance of child development theory and knowledge. Most children are in care because of abuse and neglect and enter care with some aspect of 'delayed development'. Some of the important ways in which children can be nurtured while in care are through developing a warm, caring and reciprocal relationship with their carer. Research tells us that it is not the make-up of families that is important, but what happens within them that matters, in terms of the effect on children (Golombok, 2000).

Attachment theory, concepts of separation, loss and resilience help social workers make sense of their observations and understand the effect that a child's experiences are having on their development. Social workers need to have a comprehensive knowledge of child development and to be able to apply it to individual children to understand how children's experiences of abuse and neglect can affect their development and consequently how best to support them in their new environments.

Reflective questions

1 Think about one looked-after child you have worked with. How has separation and loss manifested for this child? How has it affected their behaviour and understanding about their life at this point? What role can you have in the looked-after child's life to assist them in coming to terms with being looked after?

2 There are a number of different models that provide information about how to support a child's attachment and resilience while in care. Using the Secure Base Model, think about the child you identified in question 1 and apply the model to their care. Where are the strengths and where are the gaps? What is your role in supporting this child within their current placement?

3 In terms of child development, can you identify any areas that are unique to looked-after or adopted children? An example of this might be children aged between seven and eight years becoming very interested and curious about their birth families. How might you respond?

Further reading

- Cocker, C. and Allain, L. (2019) *Social Work with Looked After Children* (3rd edn). London: Sage/Learning Matters.
  In this book, we offer a more detailed consideration of what social workers need to know and how they might practise with children who are 'looked after'.

- National Institute of Clinical Excellence (2015) Children's attachment: Attachment in children and young people who are adopted from care, in care or at high risk of going into care – NG26. Available from: https://www.nice.org.uk/guidance/ng26
  This guide provides a useful overview of attachment in children and expands what we have discussed here and in Chapter 7 in Part II of this volume. It is important knowledge that covers a range of disciplines – not only social work, and so is useful for you, as a social worker, to know what other people you may be working with will know.

- Schofield, G. and Beek, M. (2018) *Attachment Handbook for Foster Care and Adoption* (2nd edn). London: Coram BAAF.
  This book offers a comprehensive introduction to the importance of attachment theories in fostering and adoption, something that is key to successful working in these areas.

- Smith, M., Fulcher, L. and Doran, P. (2013) *Residential Child Care in Practice: Making a Difference*. Social Work in Practice Series. Bristol: Policy Press.
  Residential child care in many countries in the UK is not discussed or is relegated as a less preferred option to foster care or adoption. However, it can provide a useful place of safety and nurture for children and it is important that, as a social worker, you are cognisant of what it can offer.

References

Ainsworth, M., Blehar, M., Waters, E. and Wall, S. (1978) *Patterns of Attachment: A Psychological Study of the Strange Situation*. Hillside, NJ: Erlbaum.

American Academy of Pediatrics Committee on Early Child Adoption and Dependent Care (2000) Developmental issues for young children in foster care, *Pediatrics*, 106(5): 1145–1150.

Barrett, H. and Tasker, F. (2001) Growing up with a gay parent: Views of 101 gay fathers on their sons' and daughters' experiences, *Educational and Child Psychology*, 18(1): 62–77.

Barrett, H. and Tasker, F. (2002) Gay fathers and their children: What we know and what we need to know, *Lesbian and Gay Psychology Review*, 3(1): 3–10.

Bowlby, J. (1969) *Attachment*. London: Pimlico.

Bowlby, J. (1973) *Separation*. London: Pimlico.

Bowlby, J. (1980) *Loss*. London: Pimlico.

Brown, H.C. (2011) The assessment of lesbian and gay prospective foster carers: Twenty years of practice and what has changed? In P. Dunk-West and P. Hafford-Letchfield (eds), *Sexual Identities and Sexuality in Social Work: Research and Reflections from Women in the Field*. Farnham: Ashgate.

Brown, H.C. and Cocker, C. (2011) *Social Work with Lesbians and Gay Men*. London: Sage.

Brown, R. and Ward, H. (2013) *Decision-Making within a Child's Timeframe*. London: Childhood Wellbeing Research Centre, Institute of Education.

Clough, R., Bullock, R. and Ward, A. (2006) *What Works in Residential Child Care: A review of Research Evidence and the Practical Considerations*. London: National Centre for Excellence in Residential Child Care/National Children's Bureau.

Cocker, C. (2015) Social work and adoption: The impact of civil partnerships and same sex marriage. In N. Barker and D. Monk (eds), *From Civil Partnership to Same Sex Marriage: Interdisciplinary Reflections*. Abingdon: Routledge.

Daniel, B., Wassell, D. and Gilligan R. (2010) *Child Development for Child Care and Protection Workers*. 2nd edn. London: Jessica Kingsley Publishers.

Department for Education (2011) *Fostering Services: National Minimum Standards*. London: Crown Copyright.

Department for Education (2014) *Adoption: National Minimum Standards*. London: Crown Copyright.

Department for Education (2015a) *The Children Act 1989 Guidance and Regulations*, Vol. 2: *Care Planning, Placement and Case Review*. London: Crown Copyright.

Department for Education (2015b) *Guide to the Children's Homes Regulations Including the Quality Standards*. London: Crown Copyright.

Department for Education (2017) Children looked after in England including adoption: 2016 to 2017. Available from: https://www.gov.uk/government/statistics/children-looked-after-in-england-including-adoption-2016-to-2017

Department of Health (2000) *Framework for Assessment of Children in Need and Their Families*. London: HMSO.

Erich, S. (2005) Gay and lesbian adoptive families: An exploratory study of family functioning, adoptive child's behaviour and familial support networks, *Journal of Family Social Work*, 9: 17–32.

Erich, S., Hall, S.K., Kanenberg, H. and Case, K. (2009) Early and late stage adolescence: Adopted adolescents' attachment to their heterosexual and lesbian/gay parents, *Adoption Quarterly*, 12(3–4): 152–170.

Fahlberg, V.I. (2012) *A Child's Journey through Placement*. London: Jessica Kingsley.

Farr, R.H., Forsell, S.L. and Patterson, C.J. (2010) Parenting and child development in adoptive families: Does parental sexual orientation matter?, *Applied Developmental Science*, 14(3): 164–178.

Forrester, D., Goodman, K., Cocker, C., Binnie, C. and Jensch, G. (2009) What is the impact of public care on children's welfare? A review of research findings from England and Wales and their policy implications, *Journal of Social Policy*, 38(3): 439–456.

Goldberg, A.E. (2010) *Lesbian and Gay Parents and Their Children: Research on the Family Life Cycle*. Washington, DC: American Psychological Association.

Golombok, S. (2000) *Parenting: What Really Counts?* London: Routledge.

Golombok, S., Mellish, L., Jennings, S., Casey, P., Tasker, F. and Lamb, M. (2014) Adoptive gay father families: Parent–child relationships and children's psychological adjustment, *Child Development*, 85(2): 456–468.

Golombok, S., Perry, B., Burston, A., Murray, C., Mooney-Somers, J., Stevens, M. et al (2003) Children with lesbian parents: A community study, *Developmental Psychology*, 39(1): 20–33.

Golombok, S., Spencer, A. and Rutter, M. (1983) Children in lesbian and single parent households: Psychosexual and psychiatric appraisal, *Journal of Child Psychology and Psychiatry*, 24(4): 551–572.

Golombok, S. and Tasker, F. (1996) Do parents influence the sexual orientation of their children? Findings from a longitudinal study of lesbian families, *Developmental Psychology*, 32(1): 3–11.

Green, L. (2017) *Understanding the Life Course: Sociological and Psychological Perspectives* (2nd edn). Cambridge: Polity Press.

Grierson, J. (2018) Complaint upheld over Times story about girl fostered by Muslims, *The Guardian*, 25 April. Available from: https://www.theguardian.com/media/2018/apr/24/complaint-upheld-over-times-story-about-london-girl-fostered-with-muslim-family

Howe, D. (1996) *Attachment and Loss in Child and Family Social Work*. Aldershot: Avebury.

Howe, D. (2005) *Child Abuse and Neglect: Attachment, Development and Intervention*. Basingstoke: Palgrave.

Howe, D., Brandon, M., Hinings, D. and Schofield, G. (1999) *Attachment Theory, Child Maltreatment and Family Support*. Basingstoke: Palgrave.

Kindle, P.A. and Erich, S. (2005) Perceptions of social support among heterosexual and homosexual adopters, *Families in Society*, 86(4): 541–546.

Leung, P., Erich, S. and Kanenberg, H. (2005) A comparison of family functioning in gay/lesbian, heterosexual and special needs adoptions, *Children and Youth Services Review*, 27(9): 1031–1044.

Main, M. and Hesse, E. (1990) Parents' unresolved traumatic experiences are related to infant disorganized attachment status: Is frightened and/or frightening parental behavior the linking mechanism?, In M. Greenberg, D. Cicchetti and M. Cummings (eds) *Attachment in the Pre-School Years*. Chicago: Chicago University Press, pp 161–182.

Manzoor, S. (2017) Muslim foster parents: 'We'd never had a Christmas tree – it made them so happy', *The Observer*, 3 December. Available from: https://www.theguardian.com/society/2017/dec/03/muslim-foster-parents-it-has-been-such-a-blessing

Mellish, L., Jennings, S., Tasker, F., Lamb, M. and Golombok, S. (2013) *Gay, Lesbian and Heterosexual Adoptive Families: Family Relationships, Child Adjustment and Adopters' Experiences*. London: British Association for Adoption and Fostering.

Meltzer, H., Gohuard, R., Corbin, T., Goodman, R. and Ford, T. (2003) *The Mental Health of Young People Looked after by Local Authorities in England: The Report of a Survey Carried Out in 2002 by Social Survey Division of the Office for National Statistics on behalf of the Department of Health, Great Britain*. London: Office for National Statistics/HMSO.

Norfolk, A. (2017) Christian child forced into Muslim foster care – concern for girl who 'had cross removed and was encouraged to learn Arabic, *The Times*, 28 August. Available from: https://www.thetimes.co.uk/article/christian-child-forced-into-muslim-foster-care-by-tower-hamlets-council-3gcp6l8cs

Patterson, C.J. (2005) *Lesbian and Gay Parenting*. Washington, DC: American Psychological Association.

Pritchett, R., Gillberg, C. and Minnis, H. (2013) What do child characteristics contribute to outcomes from care: A PRISMA review, *Children and Youth Services Review*, 35(9): 1333–1341.

Research in Practice (2014) Early brain development and maltreatment. Available from: https://fosteringandadoption.rip.org.uk/topics/early-brain-development/

Rock, S., Michelson, D., Thomson, S. and Day, C. (2015) Understanding foster placement instability for looked after children: A systematic review and narrative synthesis of quantitative and qualitative evidence, *British Journal of Social Work*, 45(1): 177–203.

Rosen, M. (2011) *Michael Rosen's Sad Book*. London: Walker Books.

Rutter, M. (1981) *Maternal Deprivation Reassessed*. Harmondsworth: Penguin.

Schofield, G. and Beek, M. (no date) The Secure Base model. University of East Anglia, Norwich. Available from: https://www.uea.ac.uk/providingasecurebase/home

Schofield, G. and Beek, M. (2006) *Attachment Handbook for Foster Care and Adoption*. London: British Agency for Adoption and Fostering.

Schofield, G. and Beek, M. (2014) *Promoting Attachment and Resilience: A Guide for Foster Carers and Adopters on Using the Secure Base Model*. London: Coram BAAF.

Scottish Institute for Residential Child Care (2006) *The Contemporary Role and Future Direction of Residential Care for Children and Young People in Scotland*. Glasgow: SIRCC.

Selwyn, J. and Wijedasa, D. (2009) The placement of looked after minority ethnic children. In G. Schofield and J. Simmons (eds), *The Child Placement Handbook: Research Policy and Practice*. London: British Agency for Adoption and Fostering.

Tasker, F. and Golombok, S. (2005) Adults raised as children in lesbian families, *American Journal of Orthopsychiatry* [online]: 65(2): 203–215.

Thoburn, J. (1994) *Child Placement: Principles and Practice*. Aldershot: Ashgate.

White, S. and Wastell D. (2013) A response to Brown and Ward, 'Decision-making within the child's timeframe', *Social Science Research Network*. http://dx.doi.org/10.2139/ssrn.2325357

Wilson, K., Ruch, G., Lymbery, M. and Cooper, A. (2011) *Social Work: An Introduction to Contemporary Practice*. Harlow: Pearson Longman.

Woolgar, M. (2013) The practical implications of the emerging findings in the neurobiology of maltreatment for looked after and adopted children: Recognising the diversity of outcomes, *Adoption and Fostering*, 37(3): 237–252.

14

Working with disabled children and young people

Louise Oliver and Sally Lee

… we have a moral duty to remove the barriers to participation, and to invest sufficient funding and expertise to unlock the vast potential of people with disabilities. Governments throughout the world can no longer overlook the hundreds of millions of people with disabilities who are denied access to health, rehabilitation, support, education and employment, and never get the chance to shine. (Hawking, 2011, p 3)

Introduction

In this chapter, the social and historical contexts of social work with physically and learning-disabled children and young people will be described and critiqued as socially constructed leading to value-based assumptions about how disabled children and young people and their families should behave and interact with wider society. These constructed ideas will be dismantled to understand the social, cultural and economic contexts in which children and families live. Concepts of social role valorisation, discrimination and oppression will be introduced, and the meanings and applications of how social constructs can influence beliefs and behaviours will be explored to aid professional practice in these areas.

Chapter objectives

- critically review some of the paradigms of disability in relation to children and young people;

- examine approaches that take account of the social, structural and personal contexts of disabled children and young people;

- offer ways in which social workers can negotiate the complexities of working with disabled children and young people and their families.

The chapter is written from the UK perspective; however, the issues discussed in relation to human development and disability are readily applicable to the international context, as the social construction of both childhood and disability require examination in all cultural contexts.

Background and context

The World Health Organization (WHO, 2011) define disabilities as an umbrella term used to include impairments as well as activity limitations and participation restrictions; therefore, including both the individual and the socio-structural aspect of disability in terms of the individual's specific impairment and how the individual interacts with the world. The UK defines disability for statutory purposes in section 6 of the Equality Act 2010, which states that a person has a disability if they have 'a physical or mental impairment which has a long term and substantial adverse effect on their ability to carry out normal day to day activities'. This definition includes physical, sensory and mental impairments or severe disfigurement and includes individuals born with impairments and those who become disabled at any stage in life (Lee, 2020). This definition of disability is used within human services and locates disability with the individual, not their social or physical environment. Many people in the UK live with disability: the office of National Statistics Family Resources Survey 2016/17 showed there were 13.9 million people with a disability, 8 per cent of whom are children. The statistics include the diverse range and experience of disability, including physical, learning and behavioural impairments.

In the UK, disability is a protected characteristic under section 6 of the Equality Act 2010, which means that it is illegal to discriminate (treat unfairly) on the grounds of that characteristic. Disabled children and young people are also safeguarded and their welfare promoted by legislation, including the Children Act 1989 and the Children and Families Act 2014. In addition, the UK government statutory guidance, entitled Working together to safeguard children: A guide to inter-agency working to safeguard and promote the welfare of children (2018), informs social workers' and other professionals' practice with disabled children and young people. Section 17 of the Children Act 1989 includes disability in the indicators of a child in need, and requires statutory agencies to inform children, young people and their parents what they need to know about their disability and what support is available, with a cooperative approach to meeting the individual's education, health and social care needs (Lee, 2020). Despite these safeguards, disabled children remain the most marginalised citizens globally and are more likely to experience some form of abuse (Carpenter and McConkey, 2012; WHO, 2019). This means that it is essential for human service professionals to understand key theories of human development in relation to disability to be able to use this knowledge to promote the rights and welfare of children who have a disability.

History and development of theories and models

In this section, we will explore a range of perspectives to explain and help negotiate working with disabled children and young people and their families. This will include an examination of medical perspectives, challenges to the predominance of this model by social models and theories, and a critical consideration of the importance of social context to the relevance of all models and theories.

Bio-physical and medical models of disability

The medicalisation of disability developed from the link with the medical profession using the dominant biomedical perspective of health (Oliver and Barnes, 2012), which presupposes that disability results from impairment; it is an individual experience. This model values medical diagnosis and treatment to 'cure' the disability or illness in order to improve quality of life. The medical intervention aims to correct or reduce the impact the disability has upon the person, focusing on clinical outcomes and solutions. The medical approach is valuable in that, for some, medical treatment can save lives and improve quality of life. However, it does not holistically consider the needs and wants of the person; rather, it tries to locate 'faults' and fix what is 'wrong' so people can be 'normal'.

The emphasis on normalcy has led to the pathologising of atypical bodies, leading to their being viewed as though the impairment was a symptom of disease rather than embodied diversity (Simcock and Castle, 2016, cited in Lee, 2020). Therefore, it could be argued that the medical model sustains the societal belief and attitude towards impairment, that there is something wrong with disabled people, which, Oliver and Barnes (2012) argue, distracts us from the very important discussion of marginalisation and the impact this has upon the lived experiences of disabled people.

Social model of disability

The social model was generated through the work of activists and academics trying to alter perceptions of disability, leading to the reformation of policies (Oliver et al, 2012; Simcock and Castle, 2016). The model describes how society's perception of impairment, and the physical environment designed by non–disabled people, creates disability. The social model locates disabling factors in how society is organised in terms of access to participation and the status given to people who have a disability. It also considers ways in which barriers to equality and inclusivity can be removed. It is a dynamic concept and reflects how disablism influences society's experience of disability, but also how the individual personally experiences their environment and social world (Swain et al, 2003, cited in Lee, 2020). Oliver (2013) explains that the social model is not meant to be an all-encompassing framework, but was generated as a tool for understanding disability.

Affirmative model

Disability studies and debates informed by the social model have led to alternative understandings of disability, including the 'affirmative model', which arose from the disability arts movements and offers an alternative view of disability to the powerfully negative perception dominant within our society (Swain et al, 2014). It incorporates the positive social identities of disability and the benefits disability brings to life. This model offers a different perspective such as the relief from some social expectations, leading to a sense of freedom disability (Swain and French, 2000).

The affirmative model challenges the notion of disability as a tragedy, calling into question the notion that disabled people want to be 'normal' and/or 'independent'. It questions the assumption that the only response to impairment is one of negativity and sorrow (Swain and French, 2000). However, Swain and French (2000) do not deny that some people do experience their disability as tragic and it would be very difficult not to do so, with today's dominant negative discourses surrounding disability (Quarmby, 2011; Briant et al, 2013).

REFLECTION POINT 14.1

Consider the different models of disability that we have reviewed. Thinking of disabled children and young people, identify the possible impacts of each model on those young people. Examine each for their relevance to social work practice.

In Case Study 14.1, we consider the models of disability more closely. The case study illustrates how professional perspectives, informed by different models of disability, can impact on individuals' experiences and life chances. We return to Mary's story to illustrate further points as the chapter progresses.

CASE STUDY 14.1

Mary has limited mobility due to cerebral palsy. She uses a wheelchair when she goes out, but is reliant on carers (usually her parents) to propel her chair, so has to make arrangements according to their availability. Mary could operate the mechanism for a powered chair. She has just turned 16 and wants to increase her personal independence, including going out without the assistance of a carer.

Assessment informed by the medical model might focus on her medical and physical need and, therefore, a powered wheelchair may not be considered necessary to meet Mary's basic needs. An approach informed by the social model would consider how her disability is created by barriers within her social and physical environment, and consider her wish and right to become more independent and opportunities for social engagement and inclusion. Thinking about Mary's situation from an affirmative model approach, Mary's strengths, skills and unique perspectives would be promoted within the assessment – privileging her voice.

Questions

1. If you were working with Mary, what questions might you ask her to find out what you want to know?
2. Taking each model in turn, how can each support Mary to achieve her needs and rights?
3. What are the deficits of each model when considering Mary's needs and rights?

Discussion

In your thinking about this case study, you will probably recognise the need to establish rapport, to take things slowly and to ensure you are asking 'open questions' – those that explore more than simply asking for 'yes' or 'no' answers. You will want to identify with her the things she enjoys, and the skills and strengths she has in everyday life, always being led by Mary. You will also note that each model has strengths, benefits and some potential disadvantages, so taking a mixed approach is important – again, being led by Mary's wishes and needs. It is important in social work to ensure that the model fits the need rather than the need or person fitting the model.

Latent influences

The theory of social construction is based on the idea that society, through social interchange, generates and sustains a very powerful but hidden force which normalises values and beliefs, affecting our thinking, decision making and, in turn, our actions (or in-actions), thereby creating and sustaining dominant discourses (Korobov, 2010). Discourses are systems of representation that produce our reality, constructed through the use of language and social symbols to create our sense of identity (Burr, 1995). Social constructionist theory offers an explanation as to why inequality and difference has developed, and is often sustained by our society, through the meaning-making processes, generating discrimination and oppression (Foucault, 1967, 1977; Burr, 1995).

Sexism, racism, classism, ageism and disablism are examples of often passive social constructions which sustain this discrimination and oppression, filtered throughout our society, and which have a significant impact on people's well-being and outcomes. The following is an example of this:

> … disabled pupils in England, Wales and Scotland have much lower attainment rates at school than non-disabled pupils, and are significantly more likely to be permanently or temporarily excluded … in Britain in 2015/16, less than half of disabled adults were in employment (47.6%), compared with almost 80% of the non-disabled adult population, and

the gap between these groups has widened since 2010/11. (Equality and Human Rights Commission, 2017, p 8)

These statistics suggest that some invisible force could be acting within our society to lead to these inequalities, which discriminates against some and privileges others.

Oliver and Barnes explain that 'despite environmental and attitudinal barriers many disabled people compete successfully in the labour market and acquire a wide range of jobs' (2012, p 13). So why, then, is there such a gap between disabled people and their peers who do not have disabilities? They explain that this must be a structural issue and not individualistic. It could be argued that this situation is generated and sustained through hegemonic discourse privileging people who do not have disabilities. This is when theory becomes important, because it explains why such inequalities are still occurring and, with that, ways of promoting equality.

Contemporary society is only starting to understand how these invisible forces of privilege (the unconscious advantages for specific dominant groups – for example, white people, men, heterosexuals and people without disabilities, in other words, the hegemonic 'norm' (McIntosh, 1988)) impact on all citizens. These powerful social constructs go unnoticed or unchallenged and become ingrained in thinking through socialisation, and therefore affect social work and cognate disciplines unless *we* challenge our own ontological and epistemological processes and those which underpin legislation and policy. (Ontology 'refers to claims regarding the nature and structure of being' (Rawnsley, 1998, p 2). It concerns how *we* understand and theorise about the world we live in. 'Epistemology is the theory of knowledge. It is concerned with what knowledge is, and what counts as good knowledge ... Epistemology examines what counts as truth (if, indeed, anything at all falls into that category), what we can say we know and how we know what we know' (Greener, 2011, p 4).

The more dominant paradigms surrounding disability include the notion that a disability should be fixed in some way – for example, through the use of medication or surgery, or the view that someone with a disability should be pitied, infantilised and overprotected, as discussed earlier. Such views could lead to disablism which constructs disability in wholly negative ways (Oliver and Barnes, 2012).

What is disablism?

Disablism is oppression stemming from the subordination of people who have disabilities. Barnes and Mercer (2007) argue that disablism is ingrained within our culture, thinking and belief systems and is socially constructed, so has no evidential, factual or natural foundation. Disablism infringes human rights, and generates powerlessness within individuals and communities at every level of life (Thompson, 2006). The UN Convention on the Rights of Persons with

Disabilities advocacy toolkit 2008 comments on this, when it states: 'though all of the international human rights treaties extend to persons with disabilities, this large group of persons continues to suffer from discrimination and often does not enjoy respect for their human rights on an equal basis with others' (2008, p 15).

Disabled children and young people are the most marginalised people in society today (Carpenter and McConkey, 2012). Marginalisation occurs when people are pushed to the edges of society, with little engagement in social processes or activities (Thompson, 2006; Parker and Ashencaen Crabtree, 2018). It can be experienced differently – for example, some disabilities are visible, and therefore it is easier for people to empathise, although this sometimes goes too far and becomes pity, marginalising people through condescension.

When people are marginalised, their 'voice' is not heard and their opinions are not meaningfully gathered to influence social policy, which directly impacts upon their lives. A slogan which started to address this issue became the title of the book by James Charlton (1998): *Nothing about Us without Us*. He explained that he first heard this slogan in 1993 from two leaders of the organisation Disabled People South Africa, who said they encountered this expression at an international disability rights conference. Charlton noted: 'The slogan's power derives from its location of the source of many types of (disability) oppression and its simultaneous opposition to such oppression in the context of control and voice' (1998, p 3). This idea is one which remains relevant today in terms of marginalisation and people being silenced.

Hodges et al consider the lived experience from the perspective of disabled young people and question attitudes and behaviours towards disability, arguing 'the lived experiences of many disabled young people are linked to negative attitudes, beliefs and prejudices that constitute barriers to education, employment, and social participation (WHO, 2011). Those who face specific communication challenges may be further marginalised' (2014, p 2). Marginalisation exposes people to risk as discussed earlier in this chapter and supported by evidence that disabled children and young people are more likely to experience abuse than their non–disabled peers (Jones et al, 2012). In addition, if a disclosure is made, it is more likely to be under-reported, and there have been cases when the disabled child was not considered a reliable witness, even when a direct disclosure had been made by the child (Taylor et al, 2014).

REFLECTION POINT 14.2

As a social worker, how do you think your role can and should give voice to young people and children with disabilities?

Note down the possible ways in which voice could be given and critique the idea that you (in a position of authority and privilege) are able to 'give' that voice. What does that say about power relations between young people with disabilities and those in a societally legitimised position of helping?

Disablism is a global issue (UN Convention, 2008; WHO, 2011), with disabled children being silenced and hidden. The prejudicial social construct of disability, if not challenged, can affect practice in terms of risk assessments, decision making and safeguarding. Because of the ingrained nature of the hegemonic discourses which *silence* disabled children, practice which occurs within the social context is affected, demonstrating the importance of reflectivity that examines the human service professionals' own understanding of disability. Case Study 14.2 provides an example in which some of the more 'hidden' and the unquestioned aspects of disability can be seen. We will take Mary's case study further to show how addressing some aspects of disability may illuminate other points that are not always seen on the surface – in this case, different treatment as a result of disability.

CASE STUDY 14.2

Mary was successful in applying for funding for a powered wheelchair. She is now about to leave her home without her carer for the first time. She is going to the cinema with her friends. She needs to use public transport to get there (during the afternoon on a Saturday when it is really busy), and will meet her friends outside the cinema. Mary has had to pre-book her cinema ticket, as this is the cinema's policy for all wheelchair users.

Questions

1. Think about when you go out and the different stages of your journey. Now think about Mary's journey (starting with leaving the house and making her way to the bus/train stop). What practical barriers do you think Mary might encounter getting to the cinema?
2. Are these barriers the same ones that someone without a disability might encounter?

Discussion

It seems very positive that Mary now has a powered wheelchair and this is something that should help her become more mobile and independent. However, we note in the case study that she, unlike non-disabled young people, has to pre-book her cinema tickets – thus marking her out as different. This may seem like quite a small matter. However, we have seen in Chapter 5 in Part I of this volume the potential effects of labelling and stereotyping. Also, we have not considered the road and pavement surfaces, whether or not there are accessible places for wheelchairs to get across each road or how long pelican crossings stay in red to let people cross. We do not know if there are accessible buses or staff to assist if she goes by train, or indeed whether she must arrange travel beforehand – unlike non-disabled young people.

Critical perspectives and thinking

A core aspect of human service work with disabled children and young people is involvement in making life-affecting or -altering decisions within complex situations, which can hold high levels of risk. Knowledge about human development is key to understanding the complexities faced by children who have disabilities and their families. In addition, the wider social context of disability has to be acknowledged to enable a holistic understanding of an individual situation.

To guide practise, all human service professionals use evidence-based practice, theory, legislation, policy and procedures related to their discipline and the objectives of the intervention. Theories including the nature and significance of secure attachments (Ainsworth and Bell, 1970; Aldgate and Jones, 2006) are essential in how impairment can impact on human development. For example, where the impairment interferes with the opportunity for babies and young children to receive the physical contact which often communicates security and love, alternative methods of establishing these attachments need to be explored. Parents who have disabled children and young people are more likely to focus on how to communicate with their child. If this involves difficulties and/or the child is not perceived to be able to respond to the parent's caregiving, this can lead to parental stress, which in turn can negatively impact on the child–parent relationship (Simcock and Castle, 2016).

Professional decision making is also underpinned by values and ethics which, in the UK, are laid out by the Health and Care Professions Council (2018) and the British Association of Social Workers *Professional Capabilities Framework* (2018). Personal values may also influence decision making and these are shaped through culture, history and personal and professional experiences, affecting conceptualisation of risk and subsequent decisions (Helm and Roesch-Marsh, 2017). However, decisions are not made in a vacuum, and a partnership working with the child or young person, their family and other agencies is an essential part of human service work (see HM Government, 2018).

Macdonald et al (2014) state that poor-quality decision making and assessments are due to:

> … an inability or failure critically to appraise information collected, random errors, and our susceptibility to sources of bias such as 'observation bias' (a tendency to see things and people in a particular way, based either on what we are told about them beforehand, or on the basis of certain features), 'cultural relativism' (the tendency to exercise different standards across different cultures) and the dominance of first impressions. (2014, p 4531)

However, strengths in practice were identified in terms of information gathering, especially in complex cases (Barlow et al, 2012; Macdonald et al, 2014). This suggests that multi-disciplinary approaches can strengthen intervention, especially in high-risk and complex situations, with different professions bringing a range of skills to decision-making processes.

Decision making can become additionally complex when a child or young person's ability to communicate their views is limited by impairment, which includes their capacity to understand any 'future talk' or make significant decisions about their lives. Communication tools such as visual aids and sign language can become essential, in combination with observation, talking with the family/ carers and multi-agency working to understand the worldview of the child, their wishes and feelings, so decision making does not lead to you, the social worker, imposing your own views on the child or their family.

Complexity is created for people living with impairments because the world is designed by non-disabled people and this impacts on how the individual interacts with the world (accessibility and opportunities) and how the world interacts with them (attitudes towards disability). Therefore, it is essential that human service professionals use reflection (Schön, 1991) to consider the unconscious (latent) influences constructed and sustained by society which may inform their practice. Without considering these latent influences, practice with disabled children and young people may fail to recognise how the socio-political and economic context in which they develop will influence the experiences of those who have a disability (Oliver and Barnes, 2012).

All children and young people face challenges as they grow up. However, disabled children and young people often face additional barriers in accessing the opportunities that facilitate personal growth and development. Nevertheless, it should not be up to those directly affected by disablism and other such social constructs to counter the negative impact of such hegemonic ideologies; this is a societal responsibility alone. Therefore, human service professionals need to do two things. Firstly, they should appropriately challenge the dominant discourse to make long-lasting change. This requires putting the individual at the centre of their thinking, planning and decision making, by working with them and, when needed, advocating for disabled children and young people, who are the most marginalised people in our society (Carpenter and McConkey, 2012). Secondly, human service professionals need to work towards understanding the lived experiences of disabled children and young people and their families and to use this understanding to empower them (Hodges et al, 2014).

To show what these two core elements of progressive practice look like in action, three key areas of work with disabled children and young people will now be discussed.

Economic well-being

An individual's or family's economic context is key to how they engage with the world and the opportunities they may be able to take up. Professionals working with disabled children and young people, and their families, need to be aware of the potential impact disability has on economic well-being due to related expenses, and the impact on poverty and employment prospects. Families are more likely to experience financial pressures and/or be living in poverty and living in social housing, and to have little or no social support (Oliver et al, 2012).

When considering economic well-being, it is of value to link this back to the social construction of disability. It is important to remain reflective when working with the child and/or family and to work in an anti-oppressive way. We need to ensure that, in a world where such marginalisation exists, we appropriately promote and support the child/young person and family, enabling them to meaningfully express their views and wishes, with the understanding that they are the experts of their lived experiences.

In terms of practical support and advice, it is useful to be aware of which agencies/services can offer guidance on benefits or funding applications. It is imperative to know about and be able to signpost to the different services and charities that could help with an aspect of the child's life – for example, sensory equipment, communication aids or sports equipment. Therefore, interactions with professionals are significant to the child's and family's lives, because they relate to whether they are offered correct and appropriate advice and support that meet the child's needs, as well as having the balance of support to help meet the rest of the family's needs.

It is also essential that the human service professional has the skills/awareness and abilities to recognise and appropriately respond to discrimination, abuse and neglect, due to the increased vulnerability to these issues among young people who have a disability. This work is underpinned by legislation, policy and procedures to safeguard vulnerable citizens.

Relationships (balancing autonomy and risk)

The child/young person and their family are very likely to experience individual pressures from within the family, as well as external pressures (for example, social and economic). When looking at the first point, there is an expectation for family members to meet the care needs of their child who has a disability, for which they may be eligible for a carers allowance (Oliver et al, 2012). (For eligibility criteria and further information about the carers allowance in the UK, please see the GOV.UK website.) The carer–child relationship can place a strain on the carer, both physical and emotional, and may impact adversely on their ability to care for a child with additional needs. From the perspective of the child who depends on their parent to meet their needs, it is vital to explore with the person how they feel about their parent having to bath or toilet them. Making sure the child's wishes, thoughts and feelings are sought and applied to any assessment is crucial, as well as hearing the carer's opinions.

Looking at the latter point, Oliver et al (2012) note that having family members as carers has generated a debate – that by promoting familial carers, the government are saving money. Taking a feminist stance, the duty of care often sits more with the mother than any other family members. This is another example of socially constructed ideology, which sits within the notions of hegemonic discourses sustaining the belief that women should be carers. However, could it also be argued that, if the carer is a family member, this is a way of supporting the person with the disability, by being cared for by someone who knows and loves them? This is when garnering the individual child/young person's views and wishes and the parent/carer's is essential to any assessment.

Regarding friendships and romantic relationships, many disabled young people engage in positive and fulfilling relationships. Yet, it should be noted that Mencap (2016) found 'almost 1 in 3 young people with a learning disability spend less than 1 hour outside their home on a typical Saturday'. This issue could be because there are often difficulties with transport to and from social activities, coupled with a lack of resources and funding to, if required, support an active social life, leading to social isolation (Mencap, 2016). There may also be barriers to socialising influenced by societal structures being arranged so as not to meet people's needs and wants when they have a disability (Oliver et al, 2012; Oliver and Barnes, 2012). For example, these barriers may include inaccessible toilets or café menus written in small print and without pictures.

To challenge such discourses, the use of language needs to remain anti-oppressive. Furthermore, there is a need to challenge personal judgements or the judgments of others to promote the understanding that friendships and/or romantic and/or sexual relationships are important and should be supported, not hindered. Once the practical aspects have been addressed, such as how a young person would manage to get to and from an activity or out with friends, a further layer of difficulty needs to be considered in terms of their safety. For example, young people with learning disabilities are more at risk of abuse than non-disabled children (NSPCC, 2016). In addition, if a sexual relationship is desired by the young people, then for some, capacity to consent needs to be assessed, possibly with the need to conduct a mental capacity assessment (Mental Capacity Act 2005). Therefore, it is essential to maintain the young person's dignity and right to privacy, balanced against any potential risks of harm they may encounter.

Transitions to adulthood

Disabled children and young people who have a disability, aged 14 to 18, and are moving from children to adult services may be supported through this period of transition. Young disabled people face the same issues as any other young person, but may have additional barriers in attaining the markers of adulthood, such as 'employment, independent housing and the establishment of one's own family' (Simcock and Castle, 2016, p 43, cited in Lee, 2020).

A core part of human service professional work with disabled children and young people is working with them to support the development of social networks, life goals and personal identity (Lee, 2020). This involves, whenever possible, the professionals working together, especially between children's services and adult services, to create a strong 'handover' between the children's professionals and the adult's professionals. It could also mean, if possible, offering training opportunities to businesses so that they can employ young people who have disabilities. This, in turn, would start to positively influence society's perceptions of disability. Case Study 14.3 provides examples where such training may be needed, such as in the cinema Mary goes to.

CASE STUDY 14.3

Mary tells you (as her social worker) about her trip to the cinema and explains there were not enough places on the first bus for her wheelchair, so she had to wait for another bus, making her late to meet her friends. Also, the allocated seating for wheelchair users at the cinema meant that she and all her friends could not sit together. This made her feel excluded from the group.

Questions

1. How could you support Mary to participate in enjoyable and inclusive social experiences?
2. Mary also wants more independence at home and wishes that someone other than her mother could assist with her personal care needs. Think about how you wash, dress and use the toilet. Who would you want to assist with those tasks?
3. What reasons can you think of why Mary wishes for more independence at home?
4. What do you think Mary's mother would be thinking when considering Mary no longer wanting her to meet these needs?

Discussion

Thinking about how you could support Mary, you may have thought about the social aspects of the work here which may be seen as outside the remit of many social workers. However, working with community groups and local businesses represents a core part of the social element of the social work role. So perhaps helping Mary to articulate her concerns to the cinema is one way of addressing these issues. As Mary grows and desires more independence, you could also negotiate how a personal assistant may help. When considering such things, you need a sensitivity to the feelings of all involved, especially Mary's mother, who may feel very protective towards her and struggle to see her becoming more independent, while Mary is growing and developing as a young woman. You will need, as her social worker, skills in negotiating sensitive interpersonal issues and excellent communication skills at both organisational and political levels – a tall order!

Conclusion

This chapter has critically reviewed some of the accepted paradigms of disability in children and young people by examining approaches to working with disabled children and young people that emphasise the importance of social, structural and personal contexts. The influence of disablist attitudes on human service professional work have been highlighted, and alternative ways in which human service professionals can negotiate the complexities of working with disabled children and young people and their families which challenge disablist attitudes have been discussed.

It is essential that the influence of hegemonic discourses is acknowledged. Human service professionals, like other individuals, are socialised into dominant social constructs. However, they need to take conscious steps to challenge accepted norms and reveal the underlying assumptions. Professionals also need to be consciously aware of the societal privilege they as individuals may have, but also the power associated with the role of a human service professional, which can reinforce oppressive social constructs. This illuminates the necessity to challenge such constructs to alter the lived realities of disabled children and their families. Finally, let us return to Mary's situation in Case Study 14.4.

CASE STUDY 14.4

In a couple of years, Mary will turn 18. Many of the professionals and services she is currently involved with will change. Mary has established long-term relationships with her professional support network. Professionals are working with her to support her unique transition to adulthood when she will need to access support from adult services.

Questions

1. For most children, growing up is both exciting and scary. How do you think Mary is feeling as she physically, emotionally and socially matures?
2. What opportunities and barriers do you think she may face as she reaches adulthood?

Discussion

In answering these questions, it would be useful to re-read the earlier chapters in Part I of this volume to gain an insight into what Mary may be experiencing in terms of her growth and development and how these are shaped and influenced by her experiences in the world and with others. As she moves into adulthood, she will experience a number of transitions and she may be excluded from life experiences open to others because of society's reaction to her disability (see Chapter 12 in Part II the companion volume for guidance on working with adults with disabilities).

Reflective questions

1 How might traditional theories of human growth and development be a barrier to working with disabled children and young people?

2 In what ways might human service professionals use critical reflexivity in their work with disabled children and young people and their families?

3 What theoretical perspectives might help human service professionals in their practice with disabled children and young people?

Further reading

- Adams, J. and Leshone, D. (2016) *Active Social Work with Children with Disabilities*. St. Albans: Critical Publishing.
  This book covers a range of aspects of working with children with disabilities as a social worker. It is written by two people well versed in experience and practice providing academic, practice and experiential insights.

- HM Government (2018) Working together to safeguard children: A guide to inter-agency working to safeguard and promote the welfare of children. Available from: http://www.gov.uk
  As a social work student, you should ensure familiarity with government guidance. The 'working together' guidance is updated continually and offers a wide range of information necessary to working with children and young people – not just in the arena of disability.

- Oliver, M., Sapey, B. and Thomas, P. (2012) *Social Work with Disabled People* (4th edn). Basingstoke: Palgrave Macmillan.
  This is the fourth edition of this seminal work from the 1980s. It provides a critical and important introduction to social work and disabled people across the life course. The book challenges mainstream thinking.

- Simmock, P. and Castle, R. (2016) *Social Work and Disability*. Cambridge and Malden, MA: Polity Press.
  This volume provides another introduction to working with people with a disability and brings in the important perspective of sensory impairments.

References

Ainsworth, M.D.S. and Bell, S.M. (1970) Attachment, exploration, and separation: Illustrated by the behaviour of one-year-olds in a strange situation, *Child Development*, 41(1): 49–67.

Aldgate, J. and Jones, D. (2006) The place of attachment in children's development. In J. Aldgate, D. Jones, W. Rose and C. Jeffery (eds), *The Developing World of the Child*. London and Philadelphia, PA: Jessica Kingsley.

Barlow, J., Fisher, J.D. and Jones, D. (2012) *Systemic Review of Models of Analysing Significant Harm*. Oxford: Oxford University Press.

Barnes, C. and Mercer, G. (2007) *Disability: Key Concepts*. Malden, MA: Polity Press.

Briant, E., Watson, N. and Philo, G. (2013) Reporting disability in the age of austerity: the changing face of media representation of disability and disabled people in the United Kingdom and the creation of new 'folk devils', *Disability and Society*, 28(6): 874–889.

British Association of Social Workers (2018) *The Professional Capabilities Framework (PCF)*. Available from https://www.basw.co.uk/professional-development/professional-capabilities-framework-pcf

Burr, V. (1995) *An Introduction to Social Constructionism*. London and New York, NY: Routledge.

Carpenter, J. and McConkey, R. (2012) Disabled children's voices: The nature and role of future empirical enquiry, *Children and Society*, 26(2): 251–261.

Charlton, J.I. (1998) *Nothing about Us without Us: Disability Oppression and Empowerment*. Berkley, CA and London: University of California Press.

Equality and Human Rights Commission (2017) Being disabled in Britain: A journey less equal. Available from: http://www.equalityhumanrights.com

Foucault, M. (1967) *Madness and Civilization*. Translated by R. Howard (ed.). London and New York, NY: Routledge.

Foucault, M. (1977) *Discipline and Punish*. Translated by A. Sheridan (ed.). London: Penguin Books.

Greener, I. (2011) *Designing Social Research: A Guide for the Bewildered*. London and Thousand Oaks, CA: Sage.

Hawking, S. (2011) (WHO) *World Report on Disability*. 3(0). Geneva: WHO and World Bank.

Health and Care Professions Council (HCPC) (2018) Standards of Performance, Conduct and Ethics, available at https://www.hcpc-uk.org/standards/standards-of-conduct-performance-and-ethics/

Helm, D. and Roesch-Marsh, A. (2017) The ecology of judgement: A model for understanding and improving social work judgements, *British Journal of Social Work*, 47(5): 1361–1376.

HM Government (2018) Working together to safeguard children: A guide to inter-agency working to safeguard and promote the welfare of children. Available from: http://www.gov.uk

Hodges, C.E.M., Fenge, L. and Cutts, W. (2014) Challenging perceptions of disability through performance poetry methods: The 'Seen But Seldom Heard' project, *Journal of Disability and Society*, 29(7): 1090–1103.

Jones, L., Bellis, M.A., Wood, S., Hughes, K., McCoy, E., Eckley, L. et al (2012) Prevalence and risk of violence against children with disabilities: A systematic review and meta-analysis of observational studies, *Lancet*, July 380(9845): 899–907.

Korobov, N. (2010) A discursive psychological approach to positioning, *Qualitative Research in Psychology*, 7(3): 263–277.

Lee, S. (2020) Social work with disabled children, young people and adults. In J. Parker (ed.) *Introducing Social Work*. London: Sage.

Macdonald, G., Lewis, J., Macdonald, K., Gardner, E., Murphy, L., Adams, C. et al (2014) The SAAF Study: Evaluation of the Safeguarding Children Assessment and Analysis Framework (SAAF), compared with management as usual, for improving outcomes for children and young people who have experienced, or are at risk of, maltreatment: Study protocol for a randomised controlled trial, *BioMed Central*, 15(453). doi:10.1186/1745-6215-15-453

McIntosh, P. (1988) White privilege: Unpacking the invisible knapsack. In M. McGoldrick (ed.), *Re-visioning Family Therapy: Race, Culture, and Gender in Clinical Practice*. New York, NY: Guilford Press.

Mencap (2016) Sexuality and relationships advice and support. Available from: https://www.mencap.org.uk/learning-disability-explained/research-and-statistics/friendships

NSPCC (2016) Deaf and disabled children: Learning from case reviews. Available from: https://learning.nspcc.org.uk/media/1333/learning-from-case-reviews_deaf-and-disabled-children.pdf

Oliver, M. (2013) The social model of disability: thirty years on, *Disability and Society,* 28(7): 1024-1026.

Oliver, M. and Barnes, C. (2012) *The New Politics of Disablement*. Houndmills and New York, NY: Palgrave Macmillan.

Oliver, M., Sapey, B. and Thomas, P. (2012) *Social Work with Disabled People*. Houndmills and New York, NY: Palgrave Macmillan.

Parker, J. and Ashencaen Crabtree, S. (2018) *Social Work with Marginalised People*. London: Sage.

Quarmby, K. (2011) *Scapegoat: Why We are Failing Disabled People*, London: Portobello Books.

Rawnsley, M.M. (1998) Ontology, epistemology, and methodology: A clarification, *Nursing Science Quarterly*, 11(1): 2–4.

Schön, D. (1991) *The Reflective Practitioner: How Professionals Think in Action*. London and New York, NY: Routledge.

Simcock, P. and Castle, R. (2016) *Social Work and Disability*. Cambridge and Malden, MA: Polity Press.

Swain, J., French, S., Barnes, C. and Thomas, C. (2014) *Disabling Barriers – Enabling Environments* (3rd edn). London: Sage.

Swain, J., French, S. and Cameron, C. (2003) *Controversial Issues in a Disabling Society*. Buckingham: Open University Press.

Swain, J. and French, S. (2000) Towards an affirmation model of disability, *Disability and Society*, 15(4):569-582.

Taylor, J., Stalker, K., Fry, D. and Stewart, A.B.R. (2014) Disabled children and child protection in Scotland: Investigation into the relationship between professional practice, child protection and disability, *Social Research*, 127: 1–4.

Thompson, N. (2006) *Anti-Discriminatory Practice* (4th edn). London: Palgrave Macmillan.

UN Convention on the Rights of Persons with Disabilities (2008) Advocacy toolkit: Professional training series No. 15. Office of the High Commissioner for Human Rights. Available from: https://www.ohchr.org/Documents/Publications/AdvocacyTool_en.pdf

WHO (World Health Organization) (2011) *World Report on Disability*. Geneva: WHO and World Bank.

WHO (World Health Organization) (2019) Health topics: Disabilities. Available from: https://www.who.int/topics/disabilities/en/

15

Mental health and children

Elisabeth Willumsen, Siv E.N. Sæbjørnsen
and Atle Ødegård

Introduction

Children and young people with mental health problems and the question of how to treat them has become a great concern across many different services in most welfare states (WHO, 2005a; Sixty-sixth World Health Assembly, 2013; Nordic Welfare Research, 2017). According to Patel and colleagues (2007), the mental health of young people is a global public health challenge, related to health, social problems, lower educational achievement, substance abuse, violence, and poor reproductive and sexual health. These psychosocial problems are complex to interpret and assess, and often require coordinated efforts across disciplines (Willumsen, 2006). The public health perspective may serve as a unifying concept, including health, social and educational issues, with which different professions and agencies can associate. Social workers need to know their core competence and professional identity to be able to take part in collaborative work. It is likely that social workers' education and practice particularly help to coordinate services for citizens with complex problems (Willumsen, 2015). The case study of 12-year-old Emily will be presented and developed throughout the chapter. Students are encouraged to connect Emily's situation to theory and practice, and reflect on the questions posed alongside the case.

This chapter begins with an examination of the models, approaches and ideas surrounding mental health, and presents the prevalence and some characteristics of mental health problems. This is followed by Case Study 15.1 concerning 12-year-old Emily, and we use this as a starting-point to examine collaborative work and how children and young people can participate in such processes. Next, we introduce a model of problem perception and role expectations that illustrates four collaborative relationships and discuss how collaboration and participation can contribute to human growth and development.

Chapter objectives

- apply a 'multidisciplinary public health' perspective, as an overarching and unifying inter-professional framework, including all areas that impact on the health, development and well-being of individuals and communities (Green and Tones, 2010; Reeves et al, 2010);

- discuss mental health problems in children and young people and connect to social work practice;

- describe children's participation in inter-professional collaborative work processes and the role of social workers.

Professional contexts

Collaboration between health, education and social services, as well as families and volunteers, is essential for improving the mental health of children and young people (WHO, 2001). The World Health Organization (WHO) has for many years highlighted the need for inter-professional collaboration, both in the education system (inter-professional education/learning (IPE/IPL)) and in practice (inter-professional collaboration (IPC)). The main idea of IPL is to improve collaborative practice in order to enhance the quality and safety of care (CAIPE, 2002). Hence, IPE/IPL and IPC are closely connected.

According to article 12 of the UN Convention on the Rights of the Child (CRC) (United Nations, 1989) and section 6-3 of the Norwegian Child Welfare Act 1992 (NCWA), children and young people have the right to express their views in cases concerning themselves. Similarly, in section 3 of the Children Act (1989) in the UK, children have the right to have their views taken into account. This also relates to child and adolescent mental health services and collaborative work (WHO, 2005b). However, how or to what extent children can participate is not described in detail in either the convention or the legislation. This means that different services must find ways to encourage and safeguard the right of children and young people to participate. The extent and form of children's participation varies in different organisations, as well as geographically. It is evident that children benefit from participation in professional meetings, even when they have psychosocial difficulties and complex service needs (Vis et al, 2011; Sæbjørnsen and Willumsen, 2015).

On a national level, countries organise their services differently. There are reasons to believe that the varying perspectives are social configurations rooted in each country's traditions and visions of family life, children, communities and societies. The perceptions are affected by public debates following the tragic deaths of abused and neglected children, resulting from cultures of blame and responsibility (Freymond and Cameron, 2006; Samsonsen and Willumsen, 2014).

Hence, although the mental health problems of children and young people are global issues, they have to be approached in diverse local contexts, thus affecting priorities and professional practices, the opportunities for young people to participate and ultimately the help provided to them. As illustrated in this chapter, social workers can play an important role in collaborative work and supporting children's participation, but let us first examine the characteristics and prevalence of mental health problems.

Models, approaches and ideas

Prevalence and causes of mental health problems

According to the World Health Organization (2001), mental health is broadly defined as a state of well-being in which an individual realises their own abilities, can cope with the normal stresses of life, can work productively and is able to make a contribution to their community. It is difficult to determine the prevalence rate of mental health disorders in young people. In a systematic review, Patel et al (2007, p 1303) found a large variation in prevalence: rates of mental disorders ranged from 8 per cent (in the Netherlands) to 57 per cent (for young people receiving services in five sectors of care in San Diego, California, USA).

Patel et al summarised findings from earlier studies, concluding that: 'at least one out of every four to five young people in the general population will suffer from at least one mental disorder in any given year' (2007, p 1303).

The difficulties may surface in a mild form, after which most children grow out of them. However, if the difficulties become serious, the young person may be unable to behave appropriately in school or at work. Children with more serious problems, such as a behavioural disorder, may ignore social norms and rules, possibly resulting in physical and psychological abuse of other persons. Conduct disorder affects between 1.5 and 3.4 per cent of children and young people and is more common among males than females (ratio 5:1) (Barton and Parry-Jones, 2004, p 1632).

With such a high prevalence of mental health problems, it is impossible to identify a single cause. Based on the evidence, Patel and colleagues (2007) report multifactorial risk factors – physical, psychological and social. However, these factors seldom occur in isolation. Instead, the development of mental health problems is usually complex, where several factors interact over time. Based on the evidence, Patel et al provide the following example: 'growing up in a poor household increases the risk of exposure to adversities such as scarcity of food, poor nutrition, violence, inadequate education, and living in a neighbourhood characterised by absence of social networks, all of which are risk factors for mental disorder' (2007, p 1304).

However, some children and young people who experience very difficult life situations do not develop mental health disorders. According to Patel et al (2007), our understanding of 'protective factors' is very important for reducing, modifying and eliminating risk factors. For example, how do we involve more children in sports to increase their physical health, which is a strong protective factor for mental health? How can schools (teachers and peers) help a child develop higher self-esteem? Or, if a child cannot live with their parents, how do we recruit resourceful and appropriate foster parents?

Mental health problems appear to change over time; therefore, it is helpful to understand such issues from a lifespan perspective. According to the WHO: 'Early intervention with children and adolescents, as well as with their parents/families, can reduce or eliminate the manifestations of some mental disorders and foster the integration into mainstream educational and health services of children and adolescents who would otherwise require specialized, intensive services' (2005a, p 13). Hence, mental health conditions need to be addressed by applying a broad perspective ranging from emotional well-being to mental illness and disorder (WHO, 2005b). Children and young people with mental health problems are a diverse group that pose a considerable risk to their own health and development, as well as to their families and society.

REFLECTION POINT 15.1

Early intervention is often highlighted in social work education. What do you as a social worker understand by early intervention and what can you contribute to it in respect of children and young people with mental health problems?

This may constitute (some of) your contribution to collaborative work with other professionals. However, when starting work with children and young people with a mental health problem, due to the complexities surrounding such problems, you probably lack a great deal of information about the specific case in question. Identify some questions about what you need to know and to whom (professions/ others) you will present the questions.

As we have seen, the causes of mental health problems among children and young people are multifaceted and complex. Several evidence gaps have been identified, including the effects of: feedback on outcome measures in relation to treatment effectiveness; group interventions for children who experience family disruption; internet-based interventions for children, young people and young adults with anxiety and/or depression; and school-based interventions for preventing self-harm and suicide attempts.

However, we know a great deal about the effect of different treatment approaches to child and adolescent mental health problems. Weisz et al conducted a meta-analysis of 447 randomised controlled trials (RCTs) including 30,431 young people carried out over the past 50 years. The main findings were that 'psychological therapy points to beneficial effects that are moderate in magnitude and relatively durable' (Weisz et al, 2017, p 93). However, the researchers also found that some problems were easier to treat than others – for example, the outcome of treatment for anxiety was far better than that for depression.

Collaborative work in child mental health care

The health and social care system has become increasingly specialised, decentralised and professionalised (Willumsen et al, 2012). In Norway, as in the UK, it is common for several professionals to be involved when a child has a mental health issue. The child may display poor behaviour at school and be referred to a school nurse. The nurse might consider it best for the child to talk to a psychologist and therefore sends a referral (in collaboration with the parents) to the youth mental health services. This calls for collaboration between professionals – an activity that is often taken for granted.

According to the WHO: 'Collaborative practice happens when multiple health workers from different professional backgrounds work together with patients, families, carers and communities to deliver the highest quality of care' (2010, p 7). In addition, it is suggested that professionals achieve a double identity, both as a professional carrying out particular (uni-professional) tasks and as a welfare worker who understands and is able to grasp the wholeness of the welfare system, with the ability to interact with other professionals and participants (collaborative work) in order to meet the child or young person's needs (Norwegian White Paper, no. 13, 2011–12, p 45; Welsh Government, 2016). The latter includes the ability to engage in inter-professional collaboration, possessing knowledge of the welfare system and a comprehensive understanding of the framework of professional performance, as well as the competence to work with individuals who have complex problems.

It is useful to have many resources available when a child experiences mental health problems. Several professionals may support the needs of the child and together deliver high-quality treatment and care in collaboration with parents and the school system. However, this does not always happen (Ødegård, 2006; Ødegård and Bjørkly, 2012). Researchers have found it difficult to identify a strong connection between inter-professional collaboration and patient or service-user outcomes (Reeves et al, 2010). One plausible reason for this could be that inter-professional collaboration per se is multifaceted and contextual in nature. It is difficult to design research projects (such as RCTs) that make it possible to investigate the relationship between independent variables (for example, different collaboration arrangements) and dependent variables (for example, outcomes for service-users and/or their family network). One solution to achieving higher quality and developing more rigorous research designs is to focus on different aspects of collaboration, such as communication, social support and group leadership (Ødegård, 2006) and their outcomes.

Children and young people's participation

Children have the legal right to participate in their own cases (United Nations, 1989; NCWA, 1992), which suggests that they can benefit from involvement. Although it does not always happen, when children's effective participation in social work decision making is achieved, it is associated with improved service outcomes (Gallagher et al, 2012).

The three strands of effective participation identified by Gallagher and colleagues (2012) were: the importance of good relationships; the provision of information; and, in some cases, ensuring support to enable participation. These findings are supported by Cossar et al (2013), but several studies conclude that children's effective participation in terms of influencing decision making is rare (Vis and Thomas, 2009; Warming, 2011; Vis et al, 2012; van Bijleveld et al, 2015).

Adolescent service-users' subjective views about participation were explored by Sæbjørnsen and Willumsen (2015) and Sæbjørnsen and Ødegård (2016). The adolescents involved in these studies had experience of participating in inter-professional teams called 'responsible teams', which will be described later in this chapter. The findings emphasise that children and young people appreciate and benefit from participation when they feel welcomed and recognised by their professional helpers.

An important 'indicator' of feeling welcomed and recognised seemed to be that the young people were allowed to influence decisions – not only being present at meetings, but also being permitted to speak and be listened to. Simply being present but having no influence is not consistent with children's right to 'have their views taken into account' (United Nations, 1989; NCWA, 1992) or effective participation (Vis et al, 2011). Let us now turn to the example of Emily in Case Study 15.1.

CASE STUDY 15.1

Emily, aged 12, was moved to a foster home two years ago. Her parents could no longer take care of her, mainly due to their own drug problems and unemployment. During those two years, Emily became increasingly anxious and now suffers from severe depression. She began cutting her underarms in recent months. She has a few friends at school, but is not really close to anyone. Her teachers report that Emily scores below average in most subjects.

Questions
1. What would be the best way to help Emily?
2. Does she need medication, hospitalisation, to change schools, psychological treatment or something else?
3. How might Emily be included in discussions about her situation?

Discussion

In the following sections, we will look into some issues that may enable Emily to move forward and increase her chance of achieving a better quality of life. We examine in more detail how service-users can be included in their own treatment plans. We introduce a model for problem perception and role expectations, which may strengthen collaborative processes. As you read through the following sections, keep Emily's case in mind.

Service-user involvement and empowerment

Service-user involvement has been a priority in health and welfare policies in Norway for decades. Participation is considered particularly relevant for tackling health inequalities (Green and Tones, 2010). The concept of service-user involvement is difficult to describe and has been referred to as a concept of honour that has a low level of precision (Humerfelt, 2005). Service-user involvement is partly derived from the concept of empowerment, which stems from the civil rights movement and the struggle for black people's rights in America in the 1960s (Croft and Beresford, 1996). Empowerment is related to the promotion of people's control over their own lives and increased participation in the community (Rappaport, 1981). However, some authors have questioned whether empowerment really provides more power to vulnerable groups of people, or if it is merely a subtle form of (ab)use of power by the authorities. Illusions of autonomous choice are created, but increased self-regulation may be oppressive instead of empowering (Powers, 2003; Dean, 2010; Juritzen et al, 2012).

Although service-user involvement does not have similar political roots, it is nevertheless a necessity for achieving empowerment for individuals and social groups, as well as at community level. Service-user involvement is a prerequisite for empowerment, but does not necessarily lead to it. Its aim is for the citizens to become active and better members of society, as well as users, by participating and developing their competencies and capabilities (Humerfelt, 2005). In the case of Emily (Case Study 15.1), her participation is highly important and service providers need to reflect on how she can be involved in the best possible way.

Children's participation

Research indicates that children and young people's participation is rare, despite their legal right and the knowledge that such participation is beneficial (Vis and Thomas, 2009; Warming, 2011; Vis et al, 2012; Cossar et al, 2013; van Bijleveld et al, 2015). One frequently used argument against involving children in professional meetings is the need to protect them from risk of harm. However, children and young people benefit more from being involved as participants than from being protected (Vis and Thomas, 2009; Vis et al, 2011). This is also reflected in the shift of professionals' perspective from 'children are vulnerable and need protection' to 'children need protection *and* are competent participants' (NESH, 2006; Strandbu and Thørnblad, 2010). Nevertheless, as Vis et al (2012) demonstrate, if caseworkers, such as social workers, are of the opinion that it is better for the child not to participate, they will often prevent them from doing so, despite the child's legal right. This highlights the power that many caseworkers possess. Professional caseworkers intend to help and support the child, but their efforts are not necessarily consistent with the child's best interests. We will look at two approaches that may empower Emily: the use of responsible teams and the basic need for recognition.

Responsible teams

Due to the range of bio-psycho-social factors involved, there are many approaches to working with children with mental health problems. This calls for inter-professional collaboration, as one approach is rarely sufficient for solving the problem. When inter-professional teams are functioning well, they have the potential to improve patient or service-user outcomes (Reeves et al, 2010). Therefore, identifying well-functioning ways to collaborate in relation to and together with children and young people who have complex needs may be one way to improve the professional help for children suffering from psychosocial problems.

The Norwegian inter-professional team organisation, called responsible teams (RTs) or *ansvarsgruppe* in Norwegian, has the potential to be a well-functioning method for collaboration in relation to and together with the target group (Sæbjørnsen and Willumsen, 2015; Sæbjørnsen and Ødegård, 2016; Sæbjørnsen, 2017). RTs have been used in Norway since the 1980s to coordinate and organise collaboration for a child with complex needs. Different RT guidelines exist and there are variations in practice due to the procedures of the municipality and initiating agency involved, but they share some key characteristics. We will now apply RTs to Emily's situation in Case Study 15.2.

CASE STUDY 15.2

In the case of Emily, it is reasonable to assume that an RT would be established and chaired by Emily's caseworker. In RTs, professionals involved in the treatment and care of the child collaborate across professions, services and agencies. As in most RTs for young people, Emily is included as an RT-member, as are her foster parents. The aim of the RT is to ensure coordination and to create an environment where Emily and her foster parents can take part in the collaboration among her inter-professional helpers.

The professionals involved in Emily's RT include her caseworker (social worker), a therapist from the children's mental health services, a school teacher and a community nurse alongside her foster carers and herself. Her RT comprises seven persons in total, which is common in many RTs for young people in similar situations to Emily. The RT makes plans for and follows up on the help and support that Emily needs. Status updates, evaluations and round-table discussions take place at the meetings. Although RT members may change as a result of staff turnover and the child's evolving needs, an RT can be established when the child is young and remain in place for several years (Sæbjørnsen, 2017).

In Emily's case, the subjects discussed in her RT were very important in her life. Therefore, she disregarded the unpleasant feeling of being the object of attention and attended every RT meeting. Fortunately, she found most of the people in the RT really nice and welcoming, especially her caseworker. Emily trusted her caseworker and believed that the feeling was mutual. During the meetings, the caseworker invariably focused on Emily in a positive way. Emily always knew the meeting agenda well because she was involved in planning it with her caseworker. However, she did not always feel comfortable talking at the meetings, thus it was reassuring to know that her caseworker could speak on her behalf.

Questions
1. Do you think RTs might offer a valuable way of working with Emily?
2. How do you think you can best serve Emily as a social worker and as part of her RT?

Discussion
You will gain more information about Emily's situation as this case study develops throughout the rest of the chapter. However, being part of an RT might allow you to help coordinate and address a range of different needs expressed by Emily. It may also be the case that the RT can work with her to develop confidence and ways of speaking up for herself, rather than leaving this to members of the RT – although we must accept that sometimes young people need the social worker to be active on their behalf. We must think interdependence rather than dependence and independence.

Sæbjørnsen and Willumsen (2015) and Sæbjørnsen and Ødegård (2016) found that some adolescents perceived RTs as very useful and felt that they had a positive impact on their outcomes. However, the same studies also show that others perceived RTs as useless and even as making their life situation more complicated. As a collaboration model, RTs will not necessarily ensure improved outcomes and there is a need for more research to explore their impact on, for example, quality of life. It has been suggested that a central feature of RTs and other approaches to the participation of young people is how the clients are recognised, as explored in more detail overleaf.

Recognition

Service-user involvement and children and young people's participation are strongly connected to recognition. According to Honneth (2008), recognition is necessary to be a human being and is crucial for the development of a sound self. Central to his theory are the three modes and spheres of recognition: love – private sphere; rights – rights sphere; and solidarity – sphere for social valuation. The recognition modes should not be mistaken for rungs on a developmental ladder, but rather as constant movements where the rungs build on one another and work simultaneously. People grow and change throughout life. Experiences of being recognised are of great importance for human growth and development from a life-course perspective.

Recognition by love in the private sphere, such as feelings of being unconditionally loved by a parent or other close relative, is necessary in order to develop self-confidence. Although recognition in childhood is important in this sphere, it is not limited to childhood. For example, experiences of recognition by love from a fiancé also have the potential to strengthen an individual's self-confidence. However, love is the most important and basic recognition mode, thus experiences in this sphere will impact on all other spheres. Recognition by rights, such as the legal right to participate, contributes to the development of self-respect. The recognition mode termed 'solidarity' concerns being recognised for valuable contributions to society. One example of such recognition is feedback from the whole team to a team member that their knowledge is valuable for achieving the goals of the team. Experiences of recognition by solidarity contribute to the development of self-esteem and potentially self-realisation. On the other hand, lack of recognition, as well as violation, may limit and impair the development of the self in a number of serious ways. Violation in the private sphere is the most harmful factor for the development of the self. However, experiences of violation may also stimulate a struggle for recognition (Honneth, 2008).

We will now examine a model of problem perception and role expectations that illustrates four collaborative relationships. This next section will build on the discussion thus far by examining how, as well as being beneficial for children and young people with mental health problems, collaboration and participation can also contribute to human growth and development.

A model for problem perception and role expectations

Ødegård and Bjørkly (2012) constructed an analytical model based on a literature review that can be used as a tool to grasp different perspectives about collaboration between parents and professional partners. The model facilitates discussion about problem perception and role expectations, which are both closely linked to service-user participation and offer alternatives on how a 'problem' can be understood. This multifaceted collaboration model suggests that first- and second-order therapy positions may have a different impact on collaborative relationships. Hence, the model has the potential to be of high relevance for practice and collaborative work.

When a child needs help from the mental health services, in most cases this will also involve the parents and/or caregivers, at least up to a certain age. Parents are, in one sense, collaborative partners with the professionals. For the partnership to develop in a positive direction, it is recommended in this model that professionals and parents clarify their respective expectations and perceptions.

Ødegård and Bjørkly (2012) suggest that parents, as well as professionals, hold either a first- or a second-order position in therapeutic processes and that this may lead to different collaborative relationships. A first-order position means that 'the problem' is understood/interpreted in a way that assumes there is something wrong with the child or their family system. Therapists working within this framework are most likely to think that an expert who intervenes in one way or another, preferably based on existing evidence, can 'fix' the problem. For example, the causal factors that maintain the problem should be changed or medication used to 'remove' the problem.

A second-order position suggests that the problem creates the 'meaning system': 'The problem is the meaning system created by the distress, and the treatment unit is everyone who is contributing to the meaning system. This includes the treating professional as soon as the client walks in the door' (Hoffman, 1985).

The implications of professionals (or parents or child) holding a first- or a second-order position may have a major impact on the delivery of treatment and care. As suggested in the model described previously, differences between professionals holding either first- or second-order positions in therapeutic processes may give rise to different collaborative relationships. Here are two examples:

> Shared first-order perspective: In this position, we would expect that the family system (for example parents/caregivers) acknowledges the expertise of the professionals and acts in accordance with this. The professional takes the role of an expert (position 1) – conducting the assessment and presenting results and relevant solutions to the problem. (Ødegård and Bjørkly, 2012, p 102)

> Different perspectives (professionals take 2nd and parents/caregivers take 1st): In this position, the family system may expect expert solutions from experts (position 1) who do not want to, or cannot, meet their demands (position 2). Professionals may find it more relevant to reflect on the situation – for example by trying to engage parents to explore new meaning through dialogues. (Ødegård and Bjørkly, 2012, p 103).

This means that the very 'starting point' for understanding a 'problem' may lead to positive or negative collaborative processes, which will influence how the child is involved. Professionals are advised to explore the current understanding of the situation – by the child/adolescent, the family system and even the community. Unless this is done properly, issues that could lead to misunderstanding and difficult communication among the collaborative partners may not be revealed.

One example that we think many clinicians encounter is when a child seems restless at school. Is this an indication of ADHD, or is it something else, or both? An assessment of the child within the youth mental health services may show indications for ADHD and therefore medication is chosen as the appropriate solution. But the symptoms might be signs of something else, such as child sexual abuse or exposure to violence.

REFLECTION POINT 15.2

In relation to Emily's case, how will you proceed after listening to the different partners' presentations and possible solutions? Can you identify a first-order and/ or a second-order perspective? Who holds a first-order versus a second-order position? Reflect on how different perspectives affect the interaction between professionals and between professionals and users (Emily and/or parents). What are the consequences for Emily's participation?

Practice moving forward

As illustrated in the previous section, children and young people's mental health problems are characterised by complexity and unpredictability in terms of prevalence, severity, types of treatment and recovery, as well as whether or not participation is effective. If applying a public health perspective, including biological, psychological and social causes, we need to acknowledge the variety of perceptions and experiences among the professionals and children/families in collaborative work. It is essential to explore and nuance participants' views and hopes for recovery.

Given that there is no single understanding of a mental health problem, we assume that many risk and protective factors are involved and, in addition, the complexity surrounding the child is often vast. Sometimes, a single factor may explain why a child has developed a mental health problem (for example, abuse), whereas in other cases we have to look for multifactorial explanations. In the latter situation, it is possible that a second–order perspective will make it possible to find new solutions through the creation of new meaning developed in dialogue between all participants surrounding the child.

Our presentation of the complex field of children and young people with mental health problems suggests that solutions are needed on several levels (individual, group and community) and from policy to practice. Across these levels, there are many obstacles and opportunities, but these are far beyond the scope of this chapter. A central issue should be to focus on how the systems are organised and how leadership can increase positive outcomes.

When several professionals have different roles in the treatment of a child and their family network, some kind of role clarification is necessary. It is important not to expose the family to uncoordinated interventions. Experiences from professional practice demonstrate that parents often have to elaborate on their family history several times to various services, which some have described as exhausting. In Norway, the introduction of an 'individual plan' was meant to address coordination problems, as a discussion of the plan, including its aims, should also clarify the responsibilities of the professionals and services involved.

Ødegård and Bjørkly suggest that inter-professional collaboration in mental health services for children and adolescents may benefit from routinely discussing meta-positions, for example: 'a) as an introductory theme in the opening stages of the collaboration between professionals; b) as an introductory theme in the first meeting with the child and the family system; and, c) as a theme throughout the course of treatment for both professionals and the family network' (2012, pp 107–108).

'How the problem is understood' (first- or second-order perspective) may well be an introductory theme in the opening stages of the collaboration between professionals, discussion of which could take place prior to their meeting with the parents and child. However, it can be difficult for parents when the professionals all have very different perspectives. Alternatively, the perception of the problem could also be an introductory theme in the first meeting with the child and family. The professionals could explore the expectations on the service system at a later stage. If the parents appear to have unrealistic expectations, this issue must be addressed. Other parts of the child's network may also have unrealistic expectations – for example, the school.

CASE STUDY 15.3

So, we may ask: Where does this leave the child while undergoing treatment for mental health problems? For example, if Emily's (foster) parents believe that her behaviour is abnormal, they will possibly make an appointment to see a GP as a first step in contacting the mental health services. They may also feel a certain amount of pressure to do so (for instance, from the school) if her teacher has indicated that Emily's behaviour is problematic and should be dealt with. To provide the GP with the information needed to write a referral to the mental health services, 'the problem' must be described. The description itself may support and maintain a first-order perspective and contribute to both the parents' and Emily's expectations that the experts can 'fix' the problem.

Questions
1. What information might be collected regarding Emily and who do you think should be able to have access to it?
2. What else might be needed?

Discussion

Emily would probably be present at meetings with the GP, but not necessarily involved in decision making. She would possibly perceive herself as the subject of the dialogue between the GP and her (foster) parents. In order to understand the problem, would it not be helpful to know about her views, interests, school, family, thoughts and dreams? Do we know whether or not her views and perspective are included in the information given to the GP? What if the problem is considered a symptom by the family or her school? Would that necessarily have been brought to the surface based on the information provided by the parents and the teacher? Hence, Emily's own views would be useful, irrespective of the causes of the problem, and could help to highlight her strengths. The question should therefore instead be *how* she should be involved.

According to Vis et al (2011), children and young people have more to gain than to lose from participation at meetings. However, they should be seen as both vulnerable and competent participants (Strandbu and Thørnblad, 2010). The GP needs to be skilled in communicating with children and young people in order to make them feel supported by someone they can trust (Sæbjørnsen and Willumsen, 2015; Sæbjørnsen and Ødegård, 2016). If Emily feels recognised and taken seriously by professionals regarding her problem as discussed in Case Study 15.3, instead of *her being* the problem, the meeting could be a positive and self-strengthening experience for her (Honneth, 2008). It is important to note that inviting Emily to be present without allowing her effective participation in the sense of taking her views into account (United Nations, 1989) is unlikely to imply anything positive for her, instead leaving her with a negative experience (Sæbjørnsen, 2017). In other words, it is recommended that a second-order perspective be applied to explore her views and how she perceives various solutions presented to her.

Conclusion

As described earlier in this chapter, experiences of recognition contribute to the development of a sound self and may even promote healing the self of an individual who has been exposed to violation (Honneth, 2008). Considering that medication constitutes an essential part of the treatment offered to children who suffer from psychosocial problems, it can be questioned whether the potential of recognition by love, rights and solidarity is sufficiently used. Conceivably, involving the child in the treatment from the very beginning, that is, moving from a first-order towards a second-order perspective, could improve the outcome of the mental health intervention. It is possible that other professionals, such as teachers, could be helpful for meeting the needs of a specific child.

Such a shift would require knowledge and communication skills among professionals, as well as a willingness to recognise service-users' points of view and share their 'expert power' with them. As indicated by Sæbjørnsen and Ødegård (2016), it would be useless to try to impose such a shift on the mental health service system without the professionals genuinely wishing to do so. This also requires recognition of the importance of taking into account the range of factors that are necessary for the healthy growth and development of the child or young person.

A child in need of help will most often go through a process including assessment (for example, different kinds of tests) and interventions (individual or family therapy and/or prescriptions of medication). This means that collaboration issues should be a theme throughout the course of treatment for both professionals and the family network. The situation may be unstable and the expectations of the participants may change. The child may decide that they no longer want to see the therapist. Will this lead to the professionals ending their contact with the entire family system, or could there be other treatment approaches – for example, closer collaboration with the parents and/or the school? Depending on the magnitude and changing nature of these problems over time, it is quite possible that there will be a need for more dialogue about expectations and other issues associated with collaboration. If these matters are not discussed regularly, misunderstandings may arise.

In this chapter, we have presented and discussed global issues concerning mental health problems related to children and young people, focusing on inter-professional work. Global issues may appear differently in a local context due to national legislation and regulations. However, based on policy documents from the EU and the WHO, some overarching global standards and rights exist that we are all obliged to implement. This gives us an opportunity to learn from one another's practice, as well as to try out and develop high-quality services. With reference to the presentation of mental health issues, we are all aware that this is a complex and demanding area with no quick fixes. We hope this chapter will contribute relevant knowledge and inspire professionals to try out alternative solutions.

Reflective questions

1 Focus on one child or young person that you know/are working with. Consider how you might characterise their problems. Please reflect on different biological, psychological and social perspectives when trying to interpret the situation. What aspects do you focus on and how do you think these influence your interpretation and practice?

2 How can you as a social worker contribute support and prevention when such problems occur?

3 How can you organise inter-professional collaboration to address problems like this?

4 Based on your professional context, how would you describe the service you are part of and how it functions for children and young people with mental health problems? Please include inter-professional collaboration and identify possible changes you want to propose.

5 Reflect on how you involve children in your work. In what ways do you think they experience participation? Please reflect on your role as social worker and possible coordinator of the collaborative work. Any suggestions for improvement?

Further reading

- Sæbjørnsen, S.E.N. and Willumsen, E. (2015) Service user participation in inter-professional teams in child welfare in Norway: Vulnerable adolescents' perceptions, *Child & Family Social Work*, 22(S2): 43–53. doi: 10.1111/cfs.12242
  In this article, we explore the centrality of involvement and inclusion of children and young people to working successfully as a social worker.

- Sæbjørnsen, S.E.N. and Ødegård, A. (2016) Adolescents' subjective views about interprofessional team participation: A Q-methodological study, *Journal of Comparative Social Work*, 11(2): 1–26.
  The views of children and young people assisted by RTs – members of wider responsible teams – were considered in this research, recognising the value of a wider disciplinary base to work with difficult problems.

- Weisz, J.R., Ng, M.Y., Ugueto, A.M., Jensen-Doss, A., Marchette, L.S.K., Weersing, V.R. et al (2017) What five decades of research tells us about the effects of youth psychological therapy: A multilevel meta-analysis and implications for science and practice, *American Psychologist*, 72(2): 79–117.
  This article is helpful in comparing numerous research studies testing the effects of psychological treatment for young people experiencing anxiety disorders.

- Ødegård, A. and Bjørkly, S. (2012) The family as partner in child mental health care: Problem perceptions and challenges to collaboration, *Journal of the Canadian Academy of Child and Adolescent Psychiatry*, 21(2): 98–104.
  In this article, we deal with the complexities of recognising and dealing with emotional and psychiatric problems in children and young people.

References

Barton, J. and Parry-Jones, W. (2004) Adolescence. In R. Detels, R. Beaglehole, M.A. Lansang and M. Gulliford (eds), *Oxford Textbook of Public Health*. Oxford: Oxford University Press.

CAIPE (Centre for the Advancement of Interprofessional Practice) (2002) Interprofessional education: today, yesterday and tomorrow, available from https://www.caipe.org/resources/publications/caipe-publications/caipe-2002-interprofessional-education-today-yesterday-tomorrow-barr-h

Cossar, J., Brandon, M., Bailey, S., Belderson, P., Biggart, L. and Sharpe, D. (2013) *'It Takes a Lot to Build Trust': Recognition and Telling: Developing Earlier Routes to Help for Children and Young People*. London: Office for Children's Commissioner.

Croft, S. and Beresford, P. (1996) The politics of participation. In D. Taylor (ed.), *Critical Social Policy — A Reader: Social Policy and Social Relations*. London: Sage.

Dean, M. (2010) *Governmentality: Power and Rule in Modern Society*. London: Sage.

Freymond, N. and Cameron, G. (2006) *Towards Positive Systems of Child and Family Welfare: International Comparisons of Child Protection, Family Service and Community Caring Systems*. London, Toronto and Buffalo, NY: University of Toronto Press.

Gallagher, M., Smith, M., Hardy, M. and Wilkinson, H. (2012) Children and families' involvement in social work decision making, *Children and Society*, 26(1): 74–85.

Green, J. and Tones, K. (2010) *Health Promotion: Planning and Strategies*. London: Sage.

Hoffman, L. (1985) Beyond power and control: Toward a 'second order' family systems therapy, *Family Systems Medicine*, 3(4): 381–396.

Honneth, A. (2008) *Kamp Om Anerkjennelse: Om De Sosiale Konfliktenes Moralske Grammatikk* [*The Struggle for Recognition: The Moral Grammar of Social Conflicts*]. Oslo: Pax.

Humerfelt, K. (2005) Begrepene brukermedvirkning og brukerperspektiv — honnørord med lavt presisjonsnivå [The concepts service user involvement and service user perspective — words of honour with low level of precision]. In E. Willumsen (ed.), *Brukernes medvirkning!* [*The Service Users' Participation!*]. Oslo: Universitetsforlaget.

Juritzen, T., Engebretsen, E. and Heggen, K. (2012) Myndiggjøringens forførende makt [The seductive power of empowerment]. In E. Engebretsen and K. Heggen (eds), *Makt på nye måter* [*New Ways of Power*]. Olso: Universitetsforlaget.

NESH, De nasjonale forskningsetiske komiteer (2006) Forskningsetiske retningslinjer forsamfunnsvitenskap, humaniora, juss og teologi. Available from: http://www.etikkom.no/

Nordic Welfare Research (2017) *Unge i Norden — tilhørighet og sammenhenger*, 2. Available from https://www.idunn.no/nordisk_valfardsforskning/2017/01/unge_i_norden_tilhoerighet_og_sammenhenger

Norwegian White Paper, no. 13 (2011–12) Utdanning for velferd [Education for welfare]. Norwegian Ministry of Education and Research.

Ødegård, A. (2006) Exploring perceptions of interprofessional collaboration in child mental health care, *International Journal of Integrated Care*, 6(4):1–13.

Ødegård, A. and Bjørkly, S. (2012) The family as partner in child mental health care: Problem perceptions and challenges to collaboration, *Journal of the Canadian Academy of Child and Adolescent Psychiatry*, 21(2): 98–104.

Patel, V., Flisher, A.J., Hetrick S. and McGorry, P. (2007) Mental health of young people: A global public-health challenge, *Lancet*, 369(9569): 1302–1313.

Powers, P. (2003) Empowerment as treatment and the role of health professionals, *Advances in Nursing Science*, 26(3): 227–237.

Rappaport, J. (1981) In praise of paradox: A social policy of empowerment over prevention, *American Journal of Community Psychology*, 9(1): 1–25.

Reeves, S., Lewin, S., Espin, S. and Zwarenstein, M. (2010) *Interprofessional Teamwork for Health and Social Care*. Oxford: Blackwell and CAIPE.

Samsonsen, V. and Willumsen, E. (2014) Assessment in child protection: Social workers' voices in England and Norway, *Journal of Comparative Social Work*, 10(1): 1–25.

Strandbu, A. and Thørnblad, R. (2010) 'Sårbare' barn som deltakere i kvalitativ forskning ['Vulnerable' children as participants in qualitative research], *Forskningsetikk og etisk forskning*, 1: 27–41.

Sæbjørnsen, S.E.N. (2017) Exploring adolescent service users' subjective views about participation in responsible teams. PhD thesis, Molde University College.

Sæbjørnsen, S.E.N. and Ødegård, A. (2016) Adolescents' subjective views about interprofessional team participation: A Q-methodological study, *Journal of Comparative Social Work*, 11(2): 1–26.

Sæbjørnsen, S.E.N. and Willumsen, E. (2015) Service user participation in interprofessional teams in child welfare in Norway: Vulnerable adolescents' perceptions, *Child & Family Social Work*. 22(S2): 43–53.

Sixty-sixth World Health Assembly (2013) Comprehensive mental health action plan 2013–2020. Available from: http://apps.who.int/gb/ebwha/pdf_files/WHA66/A66_R8-en.pdf

United Nations (1989) Convention on the Rights of the Child. Available from: http://www.ohchr.org/Documents/ProfessionalInterest/crc.pdf

van Bijleveld, G.G., Dedding, C.W. and Bunders-Aelen, J.F. (2015) Children and young people's participation within child welfare and child protection services: A state-of-the-art review, *Child & Family Social Work*, 20(2): 129–138.

Vis, S.A., Holtan, A. and Thomas, N. (2012) Obstacles for child participation in care and protection cases – why Norwegian social workers find it difficult, *Child Abuse Review*, 21(1): 7–23.

Vis, S.A., Strandbu, A., Holtan, A. and Thomas, N. (2011) Participation and health – a research review of child participation in planning and decision-making, *Child & Family Social Work*, 16(3): 325–335.

Vis, S.A. and Thomas, N. (2009) Ikke bare snakk–barns deltakelse i Norske barnevernssaker [Beyond talking – children's participation in Norwegian care and protection cases], *European Journal of Social Work*, 12(2): 155–168.

Warming, H. (2011) Children's participation and citizenship in a global age: Empowerment, tokenism or discriminatory disciplining?, *Social Work & Society*, 9(1): 119–134.

Weisz, J.R., Ng, M.Y., Ugueto, A.M., Jensen-Doss, A., Marchette, L.S.K., Weersing, V.R. et al (2017) What five decades of research tells us about the effects of youth psychological therapy: A multilevel meta-analysis and implications for science and practice, *American Psychologist*, 72(2): 79–117.

Welsh Government (2016) Collaborative working between CAMHS and the Counselling Service. Available from: https://gov.wales/sites/default/files/publications/2018-03/collaborative-working-between-child-and-adolescent-mental-health-services-and-the-counselling-service.pdf

WHO (World Health Organization) (2001) *The World Health Report 2001: Mental Health: New Understanding, New Hope*. Geneva: WHO. Available from: https://www.who.int/whr/2001/en/

WHO (World Health Organization) (2005a) Child and adolescent mental health policies and plans. Mental health policy and service guidance package. Available from: http://www.who.int/mental_health/policy/services/9_child%20ado_WEB_07.pdf?ua=1

WHO (World Health Organization) (2005b) Atlas: Child and adolescent mental health resources. Global concerns: implications for the future. Geneva: WHO. Available from: https://apps.who.int/iris/handle/10665/43307

WHO (World Health Organization) (2010) Framework for Action on Interprofessional Education & Collaborative Practice. Available from: http://apps.who.int/iris/bitstream/handle/10665/70185/WHO_HRH_HPN_10.3_eng.pdf;jsessionid=A9E1BCD3FD66FB197078D7EBFE2F0505?sequence=1

Willumsen, E. (2006) Interprofessional collaboration in residential child care. PhD thesis, Nordic School of Public Health, Gothenburg, Sweden.

Willumsen, E. (2015) Tverrprofesjonelt samarbeid i sosialt arbeid [Interprofessional collaboration in social work]. In I.T. Ellingsen, I. Levin, B. Berg and L.C. Kleppe (eds), *Sosialt arbeid – en grunnbok* [*Social Work – Basic Introduction*]. Oslo: Universitetsforlaget.

Willumsen, E., Ahgren, B. and Ødegård, A. (2012) A conceptual framework for assessing interorganizational integration and interprofessional collaboration, *Journal of Interprofessional Care*, 26(3): 198–204.

16

Working with unaccompanied migrant children and young people seeking asylum

Deborah Hadwin, Gurnam Singh and Stephen Cowden

Introduction

Over the last few years, there has been an increase in the number of children and young people entering Europe alone, without a parent or other carer accompanying them. Usually from countries experiencing war or severe political instability, these young people are in need of care and protection from further vulnerability to abuse and exploitation. Since many of these children and young people are 'looked after' by local authorities, it is vital that social workers – and any other professionals involved in their care and support – understand the issues they face and can support them during this period in their lives. This stage is often marked by issues and challenges with which other young people whose futures in the UK are determined do not have to contend.

Chapter objectives

This chapter seeks to support social workers and professionals working with unaccompanied migrant children and young people to:

- understand how the legislative and social policy contexts affect their lived experiences;

- consider the complexities in assessing the individual needs of these children and young people, being mindful of safeguarding risks, such as the vulnerability to modern–day slavery (including trafficking) and how their experiences prior to coming to the UK (including the impact of trauma) can influence this;

- understand the resettlement process and how claiming asylum and subsequently a young person's immigration status can be a challenge;

- consider how the quality of and access to services can promote the well-being of unaccompanied migrant children and young people, including how best to prepare them for the particular challenges they face as they approach adulthood and/or when the young person's eligibility to gain access to some services may come to an end.

Background and context

In January 2016, the then British Prime Minister David Cameron stated that he was standing firm in the face of the call to allow an additional 3,000 unaccompanied asylum-seeking children to enter the UK. Taking a resolute stance against the calls for humanitarian intervention that were gaining traction with the public, he argued that increasing numbers would only make Britain a 'magnet' for even more people to attempt this journey (Perraudin and Mason, 2016). This type of reasoning, as reflected here, is one of the key issues framing contemporary populist understandings of unaccompanied minors. Accordingly, this demonstrates how a real crisis born out of the displacement of children has come to be viewed through the lens of ongoing moral panics about immigration. What lies behind these headlines are a range of push-and-pull factors linked to the devastating impact of ongoing political conflicts, increasing levels of poverty and inequality between and within countries, and an increasing body of evidence which demonstrates the abuse, exploitation and harm these children suffer, all of which have an impact on the young people's health and development.

Although collecting reliable data on flows of child migrants is difficult, the scale of the current situation globally is shown by a UNICEF report entitled 'Uprooted', which estimates that around 50 million children are currently displaced, with 28 million of them driven from their homes by conflicts (UNICEF, 2016). In 2015, over 100,000 unaccompanied minors applied for asylum in 78 countries – triple the number in 2014. The UK currently hosts approximately 3 per cent of these young people (UNHCR, cited in Refugee Council, 2017b).

A small number of media reports and charities, such as Save the Children, focused on the inhumane conditions in the migrant camps in Calais and Dunkirk, in which many of these young people found themselves. They argued that, under the Dublin III Regulations (Refugee Council, 2015) to promote 'family reunion' and the initiative known as the 'Dubs Amendment', which constitutes part of the 2016 Immigration Act, the UK should provide sanctuary to its fair share of unaccompanied migrant children and young people. However, the majority of media coverage has emphasised the 'danger' of the UK becoming a 'magnet' for still more asylum seekers, and claimed that the UK is already 'doing enough'. Alongside this has been a highly destructive set of claims presenting these young people as seeking to deceive British authorities by understating their age, and gaining the support of welfare services in the UK through devious means.

A Conservative Blog UK Rants (2016) is typical of much of the sort of material that circulates on the internet on this issue:

> Show me these 3,000 'children', let me see they ARE indeed children. Let UK public see where they are, where they are coming from and WHO they actually are. Then we'll accept all the kids you want, as any human would.

It was against this background that the UK government decided to end the transfer of children and young people in February 2017 after just 350 young people had been brought to the UK under the 'Dubs' initiative. Any serious analysis of UK policy and practice needs to be set against the fact that, compared to counties bordering major conflict zones, where refugees can make up over 10 per cent of the population, in the UK there is one refugee for every 530 people.

This chapter begins with a discussion of the way a 'common-sense' discourse has been constructed around unaccompanied migrant children and young people which sets the context not just for how they are perceived by the public at large, but also by the way they interact with state and non-state agencies, including social work. Our argument is that this discourse must be explicitly countered and challenged if we are to understand and help with the situation of young people who have arrived in the UK alone, have sought asylum, and some of whom may be the victims of modern-day slavery, including human trafficking. The chapter then goes to discuss the support social workers and other professionals need to work with unaccompanied migrant children and young people seeking asylum. We argue that it is crucial to understand how the legislative and social policy contexts in the UK at the moment impact on the lived experiences and growth and development of unaccompanied migrant children and young people. We also consider the complexities associated with assessing the needs of unaccompanied migrant children and young people, specifically in relation to how their experiences prior to coming to the UK, including the impact of trauma, and of the need to be mindful of safeguarding issues such as vulnerability to modern-day slavery, including trafficking. We conclude by discussing how best to prepare young people for the challenges they face as they approach adulthood and/or when the young person's eligibility access to some services may come to an end.

What do we mean by 'unaccompanied migrant'?

The definition of who is an unaccompanied migrant child or young person can be complex. According to the Committee on the Rights of the Child (CRC), unaccompanied children are those persons 'who have been separated from both parents and other relatives and are not being cared for by an adult who, by law or custom, is responsible for doing so' (CRC, cited in Matthews, 2014, p 16).

Matthews explains that children who have been separated from their parent or other legal caregiver, but not necessarily from other family members, are often referred to as 'separated children', and these children in some literature and statistics may also be defined as unaccompanied minors, or unaccompanied migrant children and young people. Unaccompanied migrant children and young people within official government discourse and often within local authorities are regularly referred to as 'unaccompanied asylum-seeking children' (UASC), the language of which locates the child very much in terms of the 'immigration status' first, and location as a child, second.

Even within official government publications, there has been development of the definition used and the preferred terminology that perhaps reflects changing, and generally harsher, rhetoric towards people seeking asylum more generally, to which young people are also subjected. For example, the 2014 Statutory Guidance for local authorities, defined a UASC as 'a child who is applying for asylum in their own right and is separated from both parents and is not cared for by an adult who in law or by custom has the responsibility to do so' (Department for Education, 2014, p 5).

By the time the government redrafted this guidance in March 2017, the title referred to 'Unaccompanied Migrant Children and Child Victims of Modern Slavery' (Department for Education, 2017). Within it, the guidance identified several categories of unaccompanied child:

- unaccompanied children who had made a claim for asylum;
- unaccompanied migrant children who are in the UK, not seeking asylum;
- asylum-seeking child, in the UK with family members, or transferred to the UK to be with family members;
- unaccompanied European Economic Area (EEA) national child, who may have entered the UK with a family member or entered independently;
- EEA family member, defined as a child who may be a family member of an EEA state without being a national of that country themselves;
- a child victim of modern-day slavery, which includes human trafficking, slavery, servitude and forced or compulsory labour for the purpose of exploitation.

Interestingly, the National Statistics on unaccompanied migrant children and young people detailing the period October to March 2016 referred to:

> UASC as a person under 18, or who, in the absence of documentary evidence establishing age, appears to be under that age, is applying for asylum in his or her own right and has no relative or guardian in the United Kingdom. (Home Office, 2007)

This represents a change of definition to include a question mark over the age of unaccompanied migrant children and young people, and therefore by implication, a negative discourse suggesting that these young people are untrustworthy and dishonest.

Common-sense discourse around asylum seekers

A key question surrounds how this sense of asylum seekers as untrustworthy became part of a 'common-sense' discourse. Such discourse plays an important role when the complexity of world events is such that many would not have the time or interest to engage with the issues on a deeper level (Hall and O'Shea, 2015).

Contemporary attitudes towards asylum-seeking young people do not take place in a socio-political vacuum, and it is important to situate negative attitudes to asylum as not simply an expression of callousness or xenophobia. Rather, they are part of discourses of competitive individualism, where people who require state support are often described as people 'wanting something for nothing'. The dichotomy of 'strivers or skivers' expressed by the former UK Chancellor of the Exchequer George Osborne epitomises this. As we have argued elsewhere, 'as welfare states and social protection systems are dismantled, neoliberal structures have called forth a new social imagery of "functional" and "dysfunctional" people' (Singh and Cowden, 2015, p 376). Viewed through this lens, asylum seekers are rarely seen as people with whom we should identify or sympathise, let alone to whom we owe an obligation.

It is not coincidental that the change in definition of an unaccompanied young person discussed previously took place following the media coverage on unaccompanied migrant children and young people in October 2016, when the age of young people entering the UK was the lead headline news. Conservative MP David Davis had said that mandatory dental checks including X-rays would reassure the public that the young people being brought to the UK were children and had commented that one of the young people looked older than he did (Travis, 2016). However, the British Dental Association has disputed the accuracy of dental radiographs and 'vigorously opposed' their use where there were no health benefits (Electronic Immigration Network, 2015). Judith Dennis, Policy Advisor at the Refugee Council, commented that she was highly concerned by the way the media was representing these young people and asserted that it was not possible to tell the age of young people by physical appearance alone (BBC, 2016). However, only a month later, a judge accepted that undertaking a forensic orthodontist examination may add value to a holistic age assessment, and that a young person subject to an age dispute could not fail to cooperate with this examination (*ZM and SK, R (on the application of) v. The London Borough of Croydon (Dental Age Assessment)* [2016] UKUT 559 (IAC)). Yet there was still much caution to be applied to an examination of this nature (Yeo, 2016).

This form of common-sense is directly contradicted by research into the reasons why people migrate, which identifies the drivers for this as diverse and complex. Research identifies that refugees have little 'information about migration policies in particular countries and decisions about where to go are usually made ad hoc, along the route' (Crawley, 2016, p 1), where people migrate across Europe because they cannot see a future for themselves either in their country of origin or in transit (Crawley, 2016). Masocha and Simpson, in considering the role of social workers, state that professionals need to be aware of 'the ever-shifting parameters of exclusionary discourses' and understand how knowledge of these can help to combat 'complicity in oppressive and racist-practices' (2011, p 5). The shaping of social policy through anti-asylum discourses in parliamentary debates and the media can be very subtle where moral duties are offset against economic priorities (see Betts and Collier, 2017).

Masocha and Simpson (2011) argue that the rhetoric of Britain's long and proud history of providing sanctuary serves to disarm criticism for restrictive measures with politicians who oppose policy constituted as weak. The tougher asylum system is legitimated on the grounds of protecting the genuine refugee, as well as restoring public confidence in the political system, where asylum seekers are often constructed as 'bogus', again providing justification for a strict immigration policy. Goodman et al (2017) reiterate how the media adopts emotive terminology such as 'floods, delude, massive flows and swamps' to construct a refugee threat to British society.

REFLECTION POINT 16.1

As social workers and other professionals working with unaccompanied migrant children and young people seeking asylum, it is essential that you understand how your own views could impact on your practice. It is crucial to continually be reflective and responsive to adapting these. Consider the following:

1. What do you think about unaccompanied migrant children and young people coming to the UK and seeking asylum?
2. Who should be responsible for the care and support of these young people and why?
3. From reading 'The truth about asylum', how does this information impact on your views? Has anything changed?

Discussion:

There are likely to be a range of responses to these questions and these will have been informed by a number of factors, including your political views, your own lived experiences, your professional values and information from various media platforms. The Refugee Council each year produces a document entitled 'The truth about asylum', which attempts to convey accurate information about people seeking asylum. This is available from: https://www.refugeecouncil.org.uk/information/refugee-asylum-facts/the-truth-about-asylum/

The impact of the legislative and social policy framework

Working with unaccompanied migrant children and young people arriving in the UK seeking asylum presents particular practical, as well as ethical, challenges for professionals, as immigration status directly impacts on their qualification for support and care, regardless of the impact the experiences have on their development. Even if these young people's asylum claims are not upheld, the Home Office generally grants some form of leave to remain on grounds that they are unable to guarantee safe return to their countries of origin. However, far from resolving their problems, this limbo existence can have very negative material and psychological consequences (Chase, 2017). As these young people approach adulthood, their precarious immigration status can begin to significantly impact on their access to services more widely. Critically, once they become adult and have exhausted all appeal rights, they may not be entitled to any local authority support at all. Current government policy, based on the Immigration Act 2016, is likely to exacerbate the situation over the next few years, with some highly vulnerable young people being left without appropriate support at a range of levels.

While each unaccompanied migrant child or young person will have their own particular set of circumstances, there is a growing body of evidence that highlights some common features of their experience. Research by Wade et al (2012) identifies that seeking asylum alone is a mixed blessing. The young person is chosen to travel, leaving behind family members who may continue to be exposed to danger. Hope may be placed on the young person's shoulders that they will be able to establish a new life for themselves, which might include a return on the family's investment. Young people are initially often at a loss and formal encounters can be scary. While claiming asylum is essential, maintaining silence or telling only an official version of the past may or may not help to achieve it. The impact for unaccompanied minors can mean their emotions are in turmoil (Wade et al, 2012).

Crawley (2017) argues for a holistic and joined-up policy model to address the issue of refugee and asylum seekers, noting that 'what is needed is the political will to address the drivers of refugee flows across policy areas: conflict, development, foreign policy and trade' (Crawley, 2017, p 27). Unaccompanied migrant children and young people, by definition, are excluded from participation in anything but minimal legal economic activity and are therefore a group who depend almost entirely on state provision for support, which may have a bearing on how policy is shaped. Thus, keeping the humanity of asylum seekers as a foremost consideration, professionals must combine a critical understanding of dehumanising rhetoric and its influence on social policy to help unaccompanied minors access services to which they are entitled. It may help them to challenge when resources or access to services appears to be contrary to the promotion of the well-being of the child (Children Act 1989) and not in their best interests (section 55 of the Borders, Citizenship and Immigration Act 2009).

Assessing individual needs

So far, we have focused on the broader policy context, but ultimately the job of a social worker working with unaccompanied migrant children and young people is to is to conduct a fair and comprehensive assessment of need and then to develop strategies for addressing identified needs. The assessment task requires a sound knowledge of developmental and life course needs. A unique and critical feature in assessing the needs of these young people is to understand their experiences prior to coming to the UK, including the impact of trauma, and being mindful of safeguarding risks, such as the vulnerability to modern-day slavery, including trafficking.

Unaccompanied migrant children and young people do not constitute a homogenous group. Indeed, they are made up of individuals with their unique identity, histories and perspectives. While it is true that currently 93 per cent of unaccompanied migrant children and young people entering the UK are male, in 2016, 65 per cent of those arriving were 16–17 years old, 24 per cent 14–15 years old, 8 per cent under 14 and 3 per cent age unknown (Refugee Council, 2017a), many different nationalities, ethnicities, languages and religious beliefs are represented, as well as other factors, such as individual mental health needs, possible physical or learning disability, and sexual orientation.

Assessing an individual child's or young person's needs means creating an environment whereby they feel safe enough to begin to share details of their life. Social workers and other professionals who are conducting assessments are generally assessing a young person from a different culture and possibly religion, whose first language is not shared, and whose view and experience of the world could be entirely different. Effective communication is vital, including ensuring access to appropriate interpreters and understanding why unaccompanied migrant children and young people share the information in unexpected ways. At times, children and young people may appear to present an official version of events, possibly a version an influential person in their lives has told them to say. This may be a family member or friend, an agent who has facilitated their entry into the UK, or a trafficker, whom they probably fear, while maintaining silence may preserve their own sense of agency (Chase, 2010a).

Unaccompanied migrant children and young people may have had to survive difficult and traumatic journeys, learning coping and survival skills, where vulnerabilities connected to the migration and arising from experiences en route can also emerge (Bhabha et al, 2006; Kohli, 2006b; Chase, 2010b; Crawley, 2010). Kohli (2007) suggests the accounts by unaccompanied minors of their lives can often be narrowed down to answering a series of basic questions about who they are – referred to as a 'thin' story. The challenge is to enable the 'thick' story of the young person's life to be told, including their beliefs, values and attitudes, thus creating a much richer narrative. Let's consider Case Study 16.1 of Darius in order to illustrate how important it is for social workers to understand the deeper, 'thick' stories.

CASE STUDY 16.1

Darius was a 14-year-old from Iran when he first came to the UK. Before coming to England, he lived with his mother, father and siblings in an upmarket suburb of Isfahan and had been attending one of the top schools there. He is literate in Farsi (Persian). Darius was a bright student and in addition to getting top marks academically, he excelled in sport, particularly athletics. Darius wanted to succeed in sport, but his main aspirations were to become a doctor. Darius's life had changed overnight following the arrest of his mother for flouting the laws on female behaviour. Darius wanted to support his mother and he had been involved in passing on information, both electronically and through leaflets, about demonstrations being held in response to the arrest of his mother and some other women. His father found out that his name had come to the attention of the authorities and, overnight, sent him on a plane to the UK to apply for asylum.

Darius was subdued and in shock when he arrived. It was October and he was in Year 10. He was placed with a foster family.

Questions

1. What are your initial thoughts on Darius's story and why?
2. Are there any other aspects of his account that you would like to know and why?
3. If you were working with Darius, what are your initial thoughts on how he could be supported?
4. Darius was a high achiever while living at home with his family. What can you do in your role to promote Darius's continued development, so he has the best chance possible to continue his achievements in the UK?

Discussion

In Darius's situation, he flew to the UK; however, most young people travel over land, which takes several months and often more than a year to reach the UK. In addition to difficult experiences prompting the leaving of their countries of origin, they often encounter abuse at the hands of agents and others on their journeys. It can therefore take time for some young people to provide a fuller version of their experiences. A young person's silence, or limited account of their experiences, could be a survival strategy (Kohli, 2007). Viewing their silence suspiciously is likely to undermine building a relationship of trust. This, then, in turn, can impact on the quality of the support provided as the young people may not share their thoughts and feelings, and care plans are therefore not tailored as effectively to their individual needs. As a social worker, you will be learning and practising ways of forming rapport and working relationships with the people you work with (see Chapter 4 in Part I of the companion volume for more on relational social work). Assessment, which is a central part of social work practice, is most beneficial when conducted alongside and with the person and when you are actively engaged with their story rather than completing a routine task.

In addition to ensuring that young people are physically well and their basic needs for nutrition and rest are met, professionals' minds should look for signs that the young person may be a victim of modern-day slavery, including human trafficking, slavery, servitude and forced or compulsory labour for the purpose of exploitation. Trafficking is defined within article 4 of the European Convention against Trafficking in Human Beings: 'Any child who is recruited, transported, transferred, harboured or received for the purposes of exploitation is considered to be a trafficking victim, whether or not they have been forced or deceived' (Department for Education, 2017, p 3) These experiences are likely to have a tremendous impact on the person's development through the life course.

The internationally-defined definition of trafficking is sometimes referred to as the Palermo Protocol (2000) and was ratified by the UK in 2006 (Simon et al, 2016). Darius had not been trafficked. His father made the arrangements for him to come to the UK, the journey was quick, and he was not subjected to any ongoing coercion and control. The next Case Study, 16.2, that of Tuan, provides a picture of how someone who has been trafficked may present and then considers what active steps might be taken to work with him.

CASE STUDY 16.2

Tuan, thought to be aged 15, from Vietnam, was referred to the local authority by the police. He was picked up when the police raided a house having received a tip off from a member of the public that there seemed to be many visitors to a property over recent weeks. Given Tuan's nationality, and intelligence information from the police, it appeared that Tuan might have been trafficked for the purpose of sexual exploitation.

Tuan needed to be protected immediately. The social worker spoke to him about the situation he had been in, but Tuan remained silent.

Questions

1. Given that Tuan has been 'rescued' from this situation, but could be subject to ongoing threats or intimidation by the traffickers, what are your initial thoughts about how you could support him?
2. Trafficked young people are at high risk of going missing within the first 24 to 48 hours of coming to the attention of local authorities. What can you do to prevent this?

Discussion

Trafficked children may be difficult to identify because they might not want to talk about what has happened. This could be for a number of reasons, including that traffickers may hurt them or their families, and anxiety about how they will be treated if their families know they have been sexually exploited, for instance (ILPA, 2006, cited in Hek et al, 2012). It is to be expected that young people may not talk about their experience: most will not know what 'trafficking' is, even if it is something that has happened to them (Finch, 2016). Secondly, young people may not be able to speak of these experiences until they have the language and means to express them. In this context, it is feasible that, at times, interpreters may belong to the same communities as the traffickers or that young people might be frightened that this could be a possibility. The use of telephone interpreting or highly-reputable interpreters would mitigate this risk. The London Safeguarding Trafficking Toolkit provides a framework for the identification of trafficked children and a risk assessment matrix for children who may have been trafficked (London Safeguarding Children's Board, 2011).

For professionals, alarm bells need to be rung when young people present from specific countries such as Vietnam, China and Albania, which are already known for the high numbers of child victims of trafficking. Young people who present at immigration on false passports or with adults who appear not to be relatives may or may not have been trafficked, but until further assessment has taken place, this will not become clear, and such checks can also take some time. Immediate protective action should be taken. The new draft statutory guidance (see Department for Education, 2017) identifies some of these measures:

- temporarily removing mobile phones to prevent traffickers making contact with the child and putting in place other methods for the child to stay in touch with friends or family if required;
- checking clothes for phone numbers which may have been sewn into them;
- encouraging the child to memorise a phone number so that, if they do go missing from care, they can contact the local authority or carer;
- allowing access to the internet only in group settings and monitoring the use of social media;
- providing 24-hour supervision whenever the child leaves their care setting for the first four to 12 weeks in care; and
- providing appropriate training to previously trafficked children so that they can talk to trafficked children newly taken into care about the risks they face.

Such measures may seem restrictive, but failure to keep children and young people safe has profound consequences: it is highly likely that the young people will go missing within the first few days of encountering a statutory agency. It is essential that local authorities hold records of the individual noting their name, stated date of birth and biometric data, including fingerprints and photographs. It is also vital that a referral is made to the National Referral Mechanism – the system by which the Modern Slavery and Human Trafficking Unit collect data and monitor victims of modern slavery in the UK, accessed through the National Crime Agency website.

The 'Every Child Protected Against Trafficking' (ECPAT) UK's report 'Heading back to harm' is the result of a year-long study which reported children either not being believed or missed indications of being trafficked. Variance was found between local authorities in terms of identifying trafficked children, resulting in a series of recommendations, including: creating cultures of trust with professionals and carers to help identify and protect trafficked children; ensuring safe and appropriate accommodation and placements; timely and responsive risk assessments; identifying individuals as trafficked as holding a 'high-risk status'; and taking a coordinated approach to improve data recording and reporting, along with national, regional and local coordination ensuring that statutory and voluntary agencies work together (Simon et al, 2016).

In line with the recommendations overleaf, the following actions were taken in relation to Tuan, whose story is continued in Case Study 16.3.

CASE STUDY 16.3

The police had removed Tuan's phone and money and the social worker explained that these would be looked after for a short period of time. Tuan was placed in a specialist placement for children who might have been trafficked. This meant that, for the first few weeks, Tuan had very little freedom and was not allowed out on his own. As Tuan began to feel safe, he gradually, with the aid of a telephone interpreter and some English, began to talk about his experiences. It became evident during those early weeks that Tuan was fearful of the reprisals towards his family. Tuan's development had been severely affected by these experiences and he would need ongoing sensitive support to work through this, including specialist support services.

Questions

1. In light of your reading on supporting unaccompanied migrant children and young people who have been trafficked, is there anything you would reconsider in answering questions 1 and 2 in Case Study 16.2?
2. Given Tuan's past experiences, what do you think he would need to help him recover and move forward from these?

Discussion

The stories that Tuan is beginning to tell you show the need to take things slowly and to ensure that depth is gained rather than speed. This is where a tension may arise in your practice setting. Social work agencies will often have targets to meet, and in work with unaccompanied children there is guidance to follow. This may mean your agency is pressing you for work to be completed and you may feel you have to rush. However, it is important to build trust and to resist demands that could put at risk the person you are working with. This is not easy, and requires effort to develop. However, treading a thin line between agency and the person you're working with represents an important social work role.

Age assessment

When considering the social policy context of working with unaccompanied migrant children and young people, a second challenge for professionals is the 'age assessment'. There is a wealth of research, guidance and case law in relation to this issue (Crawley and Rowlands, 2007; Cemlyn and Nye, 2012; Association of Directors of Children's Services, 2015; Sauer et al, 2016). Initial case law detailing how local authorities carried out age assessment was contained in the Merton Judgment 2003: this stated that assessments needed to be carried out by two experienced and trained social workers, with the child receiving the benefit of the doubt, and where they had the right to be accompanied by an appropriate adult (*R (B) v. Merton London Borough Council* [2003] EWHC 1689). Early findings indicated a lack of understanding by local authorities concerning their role in age disputes. Indeed, social workers should not be undertaking age assessments at screening units and ports as these are inappropriate to holistic assessments (Crawley and Rowlands, 2007). Additionally, some social work managers may place pressure on workers to assess children as older due to resource implications (Crawley and Rowlands, 2007).

The issue of age assessment has remained, with most unaccompanied migrant children and young people arriving undocumented from many countries where a systematic register of birth does not exist. Dorling (2013, p 6) warns that a 'culture of disbelief' had developed over the past decade, whereby 'the default position taken by immigration officials and social care professionals is that the young person either does not know their age or is lying'. Good practice guidance has now been developed for social service staff in undertaking age assessment, with the intent to support professionals to understand the issues faced by unaccompanied minors, which include trafficking, additional needs and vulnerabilities (for example, the trauma on memory), and how to ensure that assessments are case-law compliant (Association of Directors of Children's Services, 2015). Currently, such 'good practice guidance' does not have a statutory footing.

National Transfer Scheme

One of the ways in which an unaccompanied migrant child or young person may be referred to local authorities is through the National Transfer Scheme. Several unaccompanied migrant children and young people have been transferred to the UK under the provisions of Dublin III, EU Regulation 604/2013. The regulation applies to asylum claims made after 1 January 2014 and provides opportunities for family members to be transferred to other member states and have their asylum claims dealt with by the same authority. This is sometimes referred to as 'family reunification'. This provision applies to children as well as adults, where some of the unaccompanied children transferred from Calais to the UK between 2016 and 2017 have done so under Dublin III. The Refugee

Council recommends the establishment of a mechanism for assessing the best interests of a child whose family members live in a different signatory state (Refugee Council, 2015).

Prior to 1 July 2016, an unaccompanied migrant child or young person who came into contact with a statutory agency, such as the Home Office, Police or Children's Social Work Services, became a 'child in need' in the area where they were found – then becoming the responsibility of that area for the duration that they were a child in care and a care leaver. In 2015, however, Kent County Council received over 1,000 new arrivals into the care of the local authority, which placed disproportionate pressure on their resources in assessing and supporting the needs of these young people. While these were unprecedented numbers, it sparked the call for other local authorities to provide assistance, and led to the inclusion under Part 5 of the Immigration Act 2016 of the transfer of unaccompanied migrant children and young people between local authorities (BBC, 2015). The government identified a formula that unaccompanied migrant children and young people should amount to no more than 0.07 per cent of the total child population within a local authority. Once a local authority has reached their ceiling, they can ask for the child to be transferred.

The Care Planning, Placement and Case Review (England) Regulations 2010, the Looked After Children (Scotland) Regulations 2009, the Care Planning, Placement and Case Review (Wales) Regulations 2015 and the Children (Northern Ireland) Order 1995 all set out local authorities' duties with regard to providing for looked-after children, and these apply equally to unaccompanied minors as they do to any other child within the care of the local authority (Department for Education, 2015b). Early research (Wade et al, 2012, cited in Luckock and Lefevre, 2008) into the needs of this group of children suggested that unaccompanied migrant children and young people needed four key things to assist them to settle:

- a safe and supportive place to live;
- continuity with the past, including customs and cultures, while having opportunities to create new ones;
- accessing purposeful education and training;
- opportunities to re-centre their lives and find purpose in everyday routines and activities.

Rutter (2006) identified that, for unaccompanied minors, the 'relationship web' (including friends, family, food, language, community of worship and education) is lost, and this needs to be rebuilt, which Kohli (2006a) described as regenerating the ordinary rhythm of life. He also stated that many unaccompanied migrant children and young people deal with their situations in very practical ways – dealing with the present first, the future next and the past last.

Much can be done by carers of unaccompanied migrant children and young people to help with the process of resettlement (Wade et al, 2012). These include markers of welcome to help the young person to feel at home – for example, sharing activities in place of language and discovering likes and interests. The quality and style of foster relationships can vary; some may be 'family-type relationships', creating family-like connections that endure beyond the placement. Others are 'temporary home bases' – signalling a good relation, but not expected to last beyond the end of the placement, and 'lodgings'-type placements, whereby the young person is treated more like a lodger in someone else's house (Wade et al, 2012). Clearly, the care afforded to young people can have a significant impact on their experience in the UK. The new statutory guidance makes it clear that any decision with regard to the placement of an unaccompanied migrant child or young person needs to be made following an assessment of risk, including any specific vulnerability, before an appropriate placement is identified (Department for Education, 2017).

In more recent research, factors aiding the educational attainment and social connectedness of unaccompanied migrant children and young people have been explored – for example, building networks with supportive adults and friends, and links with home culture and religion (Farmbrough, 2014). Providing a sense of continuity and structure is important, alongside the potential offered by education and the young person's own adaptive coping mechanisms. Rather than being solely about protection from harm, having a sense of certainty and a trajectory where they could envisage a positive future is a significant factor in a young person's ability to cope, but this becomes even more difficult as a young person approaches adulthood (Chase, 2010b, 2013).

The process of becoming a looked-after child and claiming asylum can contradict and undermine what is known about resettlement. Assessment requires unaccompanied migrant children and young people to provide very detailed accounts of their past, at a time when, as new arrivals, young people do not necessarily know who to trust. Providing a partial or an official version of their life histories can mean they have their credibility undermined, leading to the negative outcome of their asylum claim (Dorling and Children's Legal Centre, 2011). In 2016, the majority of unaccompanied migrant children and young people were granted UASC leave, introduced a few years earlier, with the reason for granting leave being that the young person cannot safely be returned to their country of origin. The number of young people receiving a grant of refugee status was 31 per cent. Refugee status means that a young person's asylum claim is upheld and, in the first instance, they are granted five years' leave to remain. Following this period, young people can make applications for indefinite leave to remain and apply for citizenship. However, in November 2016, the UK government announced that there would be active review of cases where refugee status had been granted. Indeed, 'country of origin' had a significant impact on the grant of refugee status, with only 1 per cent of Albanian applicants qualifying, compared to approximately 45 per cent of Eritrean applicants (Refugee Council, 2017b). This is likely to compound difficulties in 'resettlement' and perhaps highlights the government's intention to deploy tougher policies, adding to the anti-asylum narrative debated earlier in the chapter. It also takes on more significance for unaccompanied minors as they approach adulthood.

REFLECTION POINT 16.2

Considering what you have read so far in this chapter, review your answers with regard to how you would support Darius and Tuan. Is there anything else you would add to your responses or is there anything that you would now do differently?

Preparing young people for adulthood and beyond

So far, we have focused on considerations for professionals when making an initial assessment and subsequent intervention, but this only represents part of the journey of unaccompanied minors. There is also the question of longer-term considerations as they enter and go beyond adulthood. Attention is now being given to what happens as unaccompanied young people approach adulthood (Robinson and Williams, 2014; Wright, 2014; Wade, 2011; Sigona, 2012; Humphris and Sigona, 2016). Young people often live in a protracted state of limbo, unable to envisage a positive future for themselves and living with the constant anxiety that they may have to return to their country of origin (Sigona, 2012; Allsopp et al, 2014). Very little has been known about what happens post-deportation with this specific group. With regard to social workers, Masocha and Simpson note that they 'are required to exclude the very people they are supposed to protect and care for on the basis of their immigration status' (2011, p 15). Government policy not only fails to promote human rights, but in reality dehumanises, marginalises further and leaves many young people feeling that they have no choice but to 'disappear' – surviving in networks, but very susceptible to exploitation.

Pathway planning is the mechanism by which social workers have a duty to prepare young people for their transition to adulthood (Department for Education, 2015b). For all young people, particularly those who have been in the care of the local authority, this can be a difficult time – even more so for those who arrived in the country as children. Young people whose asylum claims are upheld and who are granted refugee status and or humanitarian protection may be able to envisage a future in the UK, and planning may be able to take place accordingly. For many young people, there is no such certainty. Unaccompanied migrant children and young people granted discretionary UASC leave can apply for variation of that leave, and while waiting for the outcome of these claims do continue to have rights and entitlements to access state support. However, if these 'extension' applications and appeals are unsuccessful, a young person technically becomes 'unlawfully in the UK' and should make plans for return to their country of origin. Young people can often find themselves unable to access legal aid to fund appeals and therefore either depend on some financial support from the local authority or are effectively unable to go down this route (Connolly, 2015). Social workers and personal advisers (as defined by the Children (Leaving Care) Act 2000) are supposed to help support and prepare a young person for these multiple options. Read Case Study 16.4 in light of these responsibilities.

CASE STUDY 16.4

Nabi arrived in the UK from Afghanistan aged 15. He was determined to make the most of the opportunities he had, and when he first went to live in foster care, he had aspirations to be an engineer. Nabi settled well in foster care, his carers describing him as respectful, hard-working and a pleasure to be part of their family. In relation to his asylum claim, he was granted UASC leave until he was 17-and-a-half years old. At the time, Nabi did not worry about this too much because he was safe, able to go to school and meet his friends. He achieved seven GCSEs within two years – enough to be able to access the A-level courses he needed to study engineering. Shortly after starting his A levels, Nabi needed to submit an application for further leave to the Home Office. He was beginning to struggle to concentrate. However, being able to do his A levels and work towards his goal gave him a sense of purpose. Nabi received an outright refusal on his application and submitted an appeal. During this time, he was experiencing high levels of anxiety and questioned what his life was about. He was prescribed anti-depressants. Despite the adversity, Nabi still achieved three A levels. He would have been able to access a university course, but his immigration status meant that he could not access university funding. At the same time, the 'staying put' arrangement with his foster carers came to an end and he had to live in shared accommodation with other young people in a similar situation to himself.

Nabi felt stuck. He had plans and felt he was halfway on the path to achieving them; however, the path had fallen away beneath his feet. He couldn't work, he couldn't go forward with the education he wanted and he had no control over where he lived. He was at a loss to find meaning and purpose to his life. He knew for certain that he could not be returned to Afghanistan, as there was no life there for him.

Questions
1. If you were working with Nabi, is there anything that you could have done to help him to prepare for this possibility?
2. Now Nabi is in this situation, what do you think his options are? How can you support him during this period and to prepare for what might happen next?

Discussion

Some universities offer a limited number of places to people who may be seeking asylum or who have refugee status, known as article 26 funding, so it is worth visiting individual university websites to determine their criteria in relation to this. The more likely outcome for Nabi, though, is that he could be in a state of uncertainty for a prolonged period, with the threat of deportation hanging over him. The following section provides some ideas in respect of his situation and what you may do to help.

The Children Act 1989 Guidance and Regulations: Volume 3 details the role of local authorities in planning transition to adulthood for young people leaving care, specifying that care leavers should be afforded the same level of care as others (Department for Education, 2015a). There is a short section within this guidance (2015a, pp 51–53) referring to unaccompanied minors and the complexity of assessing care needs in the context of immigration status. The recommendation proposes a series of short-term goals as appropriate until entitlement to be in the UK is resolved. The document refers to the necessity of dual or triple planning, considering:

- a transitional plan during the period of uncertainty when the young person is in the UK without permanent immigration status;
- longer-term perspective plan in the UK should the young person be granted long-term permission to stay (for example, through the grant of refugee status); or
- a return to their country of origin at any appropriate point or at the end of the immigration consideration process, should that be necessary because the young person decides to leave the UK or is required to do so.

Some local authorities have taken the view that all young people who are unaccompanied migrant children and young people, having been in the care of the local authority for more than 13 weeks, are 'former relevant' care leavers, as defined by the Children (Leaving Care) Act 2000, and are therefore entitled to support. Others have completed Human Rights Assessments to determine whether withdrawing support (accommodation and subsistence) would breach a young person's human rights (No Recourse to Public Funds Network, 2016), which may or may not result in termination of services.

This has led to a disparity from one local authority to another, in terms of levels of support. Some authorities continue to support all former unaccompanied young people, whether 'Appeal Rights Exhausted' or not until the age of 21, or until they fail to comply with removal directions (Coram Children's Legal Centre, 2013). Others cease support when young people become 'Appeal Rights Exhausted', which should follow a Human Rights Assessment. In some ways, the Immigration Act 2016 seeks to clarify and resolve this issue; however, the impact on young people will be even more stark. Former looked-after children with no immigration status will be excluded from receiving accommodation, financial support, contact, a personal adviser, a pathway plan, funding for education or training, 'staying put' with foster carers and any other assistance under Leaving Care Provisions. To date, these provisions contained within the Immigration Act 2016 have not been enacted.

Nabi's situation is not uncommon. Many unaccompanied migrant young people receive some temporary leave to remain, then face difficulties in not being able to access the education, employment opportunities and other services they had become used to as minors. Potentially having conversations with Nabi about his limited options may have enabled him to take a different approach or have different ambitions that he might be able to achieve. Very little has actually been written regarding how social workers should undertake triple planning, how effective this is and the impact on social workers and young people. In 2006, Save the Children published some practice guidance for social workers and other professionals on *Unaccompanied Children Turning 18* (Free, 2006). In it, Free suggested that triple planning had many advantages, including ensuring that the young person is prepared for the most likely possible scenarios, which in itself would relieve some of their anxieties about their future and 'may improve their emotional health' (2006, p 4). She argued that undertaking triple planning would be advantageous to social workers as they would be empowered by providing more practical and comprehensive support, and this may in itself increase job satisfaction and retention. She suggested this might ensure that young people would receive the services to which they are entitled. These statements were written as factual; however, they seem to be based on assumptions and very little, if any, empirical evidence.

Free suggested that triple planning is often put off because very few young people are returned to their countries of origin and professionals avoid upsetting people unnecessarily. This is reinforced by Home Office Statistics detailing 2,766 enforced returns of people and 1,542 voluntary returns in 2016, when over 32,000 people had made a claim for asylum that year (Home Office, 2017). The 'deportation gap' remains wide and the reality is that only a minority of those who have made a claim for asylum, which has been refused, have been returned to a country of origin. Indeed, a recent report suggests that many refused asylum seekers cannot be returned to countries of origin because there are no direct flight routes, or they are stateless and some cannot obtain travel documents (Blanchard and Joy, 2017). Likewise, many young people actually know, from their own networks, that a period of being underground might give them opportunity to gather fresh evidence for a new asylum claim which could result in a grant of refugee status, and they will know or know of other young people where this has been the case.

Free also asserts that triple planning should begin as soon as the young person begins to receive social work support, which would seem to contradict the process of resettlement discussed earlier. Making a claim for asylum and trying to establish a life within a new, unfamiliar country at the same time as beginning triple planning seems fraught with difficulties. This could potentially prevent the young person from adapting to their new environment, a new language and culture, and limit their opportunity to achieve their potential at least for the duration that they are in the UK. It is hard to see how this could be in the young person's best interest, unless the timescale for reaching the age of 18 is so short that planning for that transition cannot be avoided.

In 2014, a social worker from Leeds, Frances Wright, sought to explore this issue by considering social work practice with young people facing removal (Wright, 2014). Wright argued that since 2010, social workers began to see a difference in decisions made by the Home Office regarding extensions of leave to remain and there had been a tightening of immigration control. At the stage young people have exhausted all appeal rights, Wright argues, there are two choices – forced removal or voluntary return – and she explored how workers might respond to these. She cites research by Chase (2010a) suggesting that the way information is given can have a large impact on how the young person perceives the social worker's opinion that providing information about voluntary return 'could lead young people to believe that social workers are monitoring them, taking a role in surveillance and supporting the Home Office to successfully return them to their countries of origin against their will' (Chase, 2010b, cited in Wright, 2014, p 1031).

Wright discusses some of the complexities of the social work role, including how preparing a young person for potential return could be in conflict with social work values because the young person may have fears of being detained or killed on return.

There is a clear tension in what social workers are and are not able to discuss with young people. Discussing what they often view as their only option of 'going underground' could be considered as indeed crucial in order to try and protect them from exploitation, provide them with information about how and where to get help should 'things go wrong' and enable them to think through the risks they are taking.

What Wright's article does achieve is clearly setting out the context for social work practice in this area. She appears to write it from a perspective that seeks to reduce distress felt by young people, in that if young people are prepared for return they are more likely to be able to cope with that eventuality. The report *After Return* and associated practice guidance for professionals has also sought to provide some insight as to the experiences of unaccompanied migrant children and young people post deportation and practical steps professionals might consider in supporting and preparing them for this potential (Gladwell et al, 2016).

Conclusion

There is nothing new about the phenomenon of refugees – indeed, the history of humanity has been defined from time immemorial by the fact of people leaving their countries of origin and seeking new places to call home, whether that be due to being refugees or moving for a different reason. However, each epoch of human history manifests the plight of refugees in particular ways. The moral philosopher Hannah Arendt (1986) noted that the emergence of refugees across during the first half of 20th-century Europe symbolised the triumph of the nation-state, where national, racial and ethnic criteria were deployed to determine who did and did not belong, where, as she puts it, they were simply rendered 'the scum of the earth' (Arendt, 1986, p 269, cited in Gibney, 2004). The post-war period, in the aftermath of the war and the establishment of the United Nations, offered the hope that nationalist parochialism could be overcome by a shared commitment to international human rights by individual states. Although governments across the world freely claim a discourse of human rights and global responsibility, we are living through an era in which populist ethno-nationalism has returned with a vengeance, and this has a huge significance on construction of 'common-sense' discourse through which asylum and immigration are understood.

In this chapter, we have sought to provide an insight into the complex legislative and social policy context and its impact on the lived experiences of unaccompanied migrant children and young people. The accounts of Darius, Tuan and Nabi are all based on realistic situations faced by unaccompanied migrant young people when they come to the UK, and those through which social workers and other professionals have to help them navigate. While it has not been possible to cover every issue in detail, it is hoped that enough information has been provided to assist professionals in their approaches to unaccompanied migrant children and young people and to understand the context and issues which affect their lives. The often precarious lives of this group can be mirrored by elevated levels of uncertainty within which social workers have to operate, and, for this reason, their commitments to humanitarian values and anti-oppressive practice can be tested to the limit.

Reflective questions

1 How is the issue of unaccompanied minors represented in public discourse and how might this influence service-users and professionals?

2 What challenges do professionals face in understanding the experiences and histories of unaccompanied minors?

3 What challenges might these young people face while in care, and how might they be overcome?

4 Consider how you would talk to a young person aged 17 who was granted UASC leave as an unaccompanied minor, regarding their future options.

Further reading

- Kohli, R.K.S. (2007) *Social Work with Unaccompanied Asylum-Seeking Children.* Houndmills: Palgrave Macmillan.
  This book provides a wealth of information about working with unaccompanied minors. Policy and legislation changes quickly and you will need to keep updated about this. However, Kohli introduces some key principles for social workers that remain very useful.

- Humphris, R. and Sigona, N. (2016) *Mapping Unaccompanied Asylum Seeking Children in England*. Becoming Adult Research Brief Series no. 1. July. London: UCL.

  This research document provides you with some of the data relating to unaccompanied asylum-seeking children which is important in ensuring you are aware of the context and situations in which people are coming to social workers for assistance.

- Wright, F. (2014) Social work practice with unaccompanied asylum-seeking young people facing removal, *British Journal of Social Work*, 44(4): 1027–1044.

  It is important to take a critical and reflective approach to social work in this area and Wright's paper provides you with information that is likely to make you angry with the current system for dealing with unaccompanied minors. This is part of social work and anger can be healthy in pursuing our role to 'speak truth to power' and to advocate for change.

References

Allsopp, J., Chase, E. and Mitchell, M. (2014) The tactics of time and status: Young people's experiences of building futures while subject to immigration control in Britain. *Journal of Refugee Studies*, 28(2): 163–182.

Arendt, H. (1986) *The Origins of Totalitarianism*, London: André Deutsch

Association of Directors of Children's Services (2015) *Age Assessment Guidance: Guidance to Assist Social Workers and their Managers in Undertaking Age Assessments in England*. October. London: ADCS.

BBC (2015) Kent sees 'unprecedented' increase in lone asylum-seeker children, 3 September. Available from: http://www.bbc.co.uk/news/uk-england-kent-34139364

BBC (2016) Dentists condemn call for child migrants' teeth to be tested, 19 October. Available from: https://www.bbc.co.uk/news/uk-37700074

Betts, A. and Collier, P. (2017) *Refuge: Transforming a Broken Refugee System*. London: Penguin.

Bhabha, J., Finch, N. and Ward, B. (2006) *Seeking Asylum Alone: United Kingdom*. London and Cambridge, MA: Garden Court Chambers and Harvard University Committee on Human Rights Studies.

Blanchard, C. and Joy, S. (2017) *Can't Stay, Can't Go: Refused Asylum Seekers Who Cannot Be Returned*. London: British Red Cross.

Cemlyn, S.J. and Nye, M. (2012) Asylum seeker young people: Social work value conflicts in negotiating age assessment in the UK, *International Social Work*, 55(5): 675–688.

Chase, E. (2010a) Agency and silence: Young people seeking asylum alone in the UK, *British Journal of Social Work*, 40(7): 2050–2068.

Chase, E. (2010b) In search of security: Young people's experiences of seeking asylum alone in the UK. PhD thesis, University of London, Institute of Education.

Chase, E. (2013) Security and subjective wellbeing: The experiences of unaccompanied young people seeking asylum in the UK, *Sociology of Health & Illness*, 35(6): 858–872.

Chase, E. (2017) Health and wellbeing. Becoming Adult Research Brief no. 5. London: UCL. Available from: http://www.becomingadult.net

Connolly, H. (2015) Cut off from justice: The impact of excluding separated migrant children from legal aid. June. The Children's Society.

Coram Children's Legal Centre (2013) Migrant children's project factsheet: The impact of a young person's immigration status on their eligibility for leaving care support. April. London: Coram Children's Legal Centre.

Crawley, H. (2010) 'No one gives you a chance to say what you are thinking': Finding space for children's agency in the UK asylum system, *Area*, 42(2): 162–169.

Crawley, H. (2016) Unravelling the Mediterranean migration crisis. February. Sound Cloud Podcast.

Crawley, H. (2017) Migration: Refugee economics, *Nature*, 544(7648): 26–27.

Crawley, H. and Rowlands, S. (2007) When is a child not a child? Asylum, age disputes and the process of age assessment: ILPA agency in the UK asylum system, *Area*, 42(2): 162–169.

Department for Education (2014) *Care of Unaccompanied and Trafficked Children: Statutory Guidance for Local Authorities on the Care of Unaccompanied Asylum Seeking and Trafficked Children*. July. London: DfE.

Department for Education (2015a) *The Children Act 1989 Guidance and Regulations*, Vol. 2: *Care Planning, Placement and Case Review*. June. London: DfE.

Department for Education (2015b) *The Children Act 1989 Guidance and Regulations*, Vol. 3: *Planning Transition to Adulthood for Care Leavers*. January. London: DfE.

Department for Education (2017) *Care of Unaccompanied Migration Children and Child Victims of Modern Slavery*. March. London: DfE.

Dorling, K. (2013) *Happy Birthday? Disputing the Age of Children in the Immigration System*. May. London: Coram Children's Legal Centre.

Dorling, K. and Children's Legal Centre (2011) *Seeking Support: A Guide to the Rights and Entitlements of Separated Refugee and Asylum Seeking Children* (4th edn). Colchester: Coram Children's Legal Centre.

Electronic Immigration Network (2015) British Dental Association says x-rays should not be used to establish age of young asylum seekers. 1 December. Available from: https://www.ein.org.uk/news/british-dental-association-says-x-rays-should-not-be-used-establish-age-young-asylum-seekers

Farmbrough, J. (2014) Factors that contribute to the emotional wellbeing, educational success and social connectedness of those arriving in one local authority as unaccompanied asylum seeking children. D.Ed.Psych. thesis/dissertation, University of Birmingham.

Finch, N. (2016) *Better Support, Better Protection: Steps Guardians and Lawyers Can Take to Better Identify and Protect Trafficked Children*. November. London: ECPAT UK.

Free, E. (2006) *Unaccompanied Refugees and Asylum Seekers Turning 18: A Guide for Social Workers and Other Professionals.* London: Save the Children.

Gibney, M.J. (2004) *The Ethics and Politics of Asylum: Liberal Democracy and the Response to Refugees.* Cambridge: Cambridge University Press.

Gladwell, C., Bowerman, E., Norman, B., Dickson, S. and Ghafoor, A. (2016) After return: Documenting the experiences of young people forcibly removed to Afghanistan. April. Refugee Support Network.

Goodman, S., Sirriyeh, A. and McMahon, S. (2017) The evolving (re)categorisations of refugees throughout the 'refugee/migrant crisis', *Journal of Community & Applied Social Psychology,* 27(2): 105–114.

Hall, S. and O'Shea, A. (2015) Common sense neoliberalism. In S. Hall, D. Massey and M. Rustin (eds), *After Neoliberalism? The Kilburn Manifesto Project.* London: Lawrence & Wishart.

Hek, R., Hughes, N. and Ozman, R. (2012) Safeguarding the needs of children and young people seeking asylum in the UK: Addressing past failings and meeting future challenges, *Child Abuse Review,* 21(5): 335–348.

Home Office (2007) Planning better outcomes and support for unaccompanied asylum seeking children. Available from: http://dera.ioe.ac.uk/229/1/1505-3790.pdf

Home Office (2017) National statistics asylum. 23 February. Available from: https://www.gov.uk/government/publications/immigration-statistics-october-to-december-2016/asylum#unaccompanied-asylum-seeking-children

Humphris, R. and Sigona, N. (2016) *Mapping Unaccompanied Asylum Seeking Children in England.* Becoming Adult Research Brief Series no. 1. July. London: UCL.

ILPA (2006) ILPA Annual Report 2005–2006, available from https://www.ilpa.org.uk/resources.php/4098/ilpa-annual-report-2005-2006

Kohli, R.K.S. (2006a) The comfort of strangers: Social work practice with unaccompanied asylum-seeking children and young people in the UK, *Child & Family Social Work,* 11(1): 1–10.

Kohli, R.K.S. (2006b) The sound of silence: Listening to what unaccompanied asylum-seeking children say and do not say, *British Journal of Social Work,* 36(5): 707–721.

Kohli, R.K.S. (2007) *Social Work with Unaccompanied Asylum-Seeking Children.* Houndmills: Palgrave Macmillan.

London Safeguarding Children's Board (2011) *London Safeguarding Trafficked Children Toolkit.* London: Safeguarding Children's Board.

Luckock, B. and Lefevre, M. (eds) (2008) *Direct Work: Social Work with Children and Young People in Care.* London: BAAF.

Masocha, S. and Simpson, M.K. (2011) Xenoracism: Towards a critical understanding of the construction of asylum seekers and its implications for social work practice, *Practice,* 23(1): 5–18.

Matthews, A. (2014) *'What's Going to Happen Tomorrow?' Unaccompanied Children Refused Asylum.* London: Office of the Children's Commissioner.

No Recourse to Public Funds Network (2016) Immigration Bill 2015–16: Local authority support to care leavers with no immigration status (England) factsheet. 23 March. London: NRPF Network.

Perraudin, F. and Mason, R. (2016) Corbyn's migration policy would make Calais more of a magnet, says Cameron, *The Guardian*, 25 January. Available from: https://www.theguardian.com/uk-news/2016/jan/25/jeremy-corbyn-calais-migration-magnet-david-cameron

Refugee Council (2015) The 'Dublin' Regulation and family unity: Policy briefing. November.

Refugee Council (2017a) Children in the asylum system. February. Available from: https://eur02.safelinks.protection.outlook.com/?url=https%3A%2F%2Fwww.refugeecouncil.org.uk%2Fwp-content%2Fuploads%2F2019%2F12%2FChildren-in-the-Asylum-System-Nov-2019.pdf&data=02%7C01%7Cparkerj%40bournemouth.ac.uk%7C1d961e50897c42d1f21608d792d05cb2%7Cede296 55d09742e4bbb5f38d427fbfb8%7C0%7C1%7C637139295918071103& sdata=pCz7mQBnDyZwjG9fAbTkyCpAVKy3Wvd2qA0fNF2Sp64%3D &reserved=0

Refugee Council (2017b) Tell it like it is: The truth about refugees and asylum seekers. April. Available from: https://eur02.safelinks.protection.outlook.com/? url=https%3A%2F%2Fwww.refugeecouncil.org.uk%2Finformation%2Frefugee-asylum-facts%2Fthe-truth-about-asylum%2F&data=02%7C01%7Cparkerj %40bournemouth.ac.uk%7C1d961e50897c42d1f21608d792d05cb2%7Cede 29655d09742e4bbb5f38d427fbfb8%7C0%7C1%7C637139295918071103& amp;sdata=ML3wGncNIF%2FPu5NBxmEIbUm1o%2BPdc7gm2OaawbMa6 KE%3D&reserved=0

Robinson, K. and Williams, L. (2014) Positive futures – a pilot project to develop and test a model to assist appeal rights exhausted care leavers to consider assisted voluntary return. Evaluation report. July. Available from: https://www. secouncils.gov.uk/wp-content/uploads/2012/04/Positive-Futures-Evaluation-Report-Final-18-Aug.pdf

Rutter, J. (2006) *Refugee Children in the UK*. Maidenhead: McGraw-Hill.

Sauer, P.J.J., Nicholson, A. and Neubauer, D. (2016) Age determination in asylum seekers: Physicians should not be implicated, *European Journal of Pediatrics*, 175(3): 299–303.

Sigona, N. (2012) Life in limbo for UK's irregular migrant children and families, *openDemocracy*, 24 June. Available from: https://nandosigona.info/2012/06/

Simon, A., Setter, C. and Holmes, L. (2016) *Heading Back to Harm: A Study on Trafficked and Unaccompanied Children Going Missing from Care in the UK.* November. London: ECPAT UK and Missing People.

Singh, G. and Cowden, S. (2015) The intensification of neoliberalism and the commodification of human need – a social work perspective, *Critical and Radical Social Work*, 3(3): 375–387.

Travis, A. (2016) Home Office rules out 'unethical' dental checks for Calais refugees, *The Guardian*, 19 October. Available from: https://www.theguardian.com/world/2016/oct/19/home-office-rules-out-unethical-dental-checks-for-calais-refugees

UK Rants (2016) UK should NOT accept 3,000 additional migrant children, we have done our bit already. 16 January. Available from: http://ukrants.co.uk/uk-should-not-accept-3000-additional-migrant-kids-we-have-done-our-bit-already/

UNICEF (2016) Uprooted: The growing crisis for refugee and migrant children. Available from: https://www.unicef.org/publications/index_92710.html

Wade, J. (2011) Preparation and transition planning for unaccompanied asylum-seeking and refugee young people: A review of evidence in England, *Children & Youth Services Review*, 33(12): 2424–2430.

Wade, J., Sirriyeh, A., Kohli, R. and Simmonds, J. (2012) *'Fostering Unaccompanied Asylum-Seeking Young People': Creating a Family Life across a 'World of Difference'*. London: BAAF Adoption & Fostering.

Wright, F. (2014) Social work practice with unaccompanied asylum-seeking young people facing removal, *British Journal of Social Work*, 44(4): 1027–1044.

Yeo, C. (2016) Tribunal makes order requiring dental age assessment of young asylum seeker. 20 December. Available from: https://www.freemovement.org.uk/tribunal-makes-order-requiring-dental-age-assessment-of-young-asylum-seeker/

Index

Hesse, E. 254
high-risk *see* risk-taking behaviours
higher education 155, 209, 210
Hinshelwood, R. 33
Hirschi, T. 181–2
Hodges, C.E.M. 277
holding 41
holistic approach 15, 73
Homel, R. 187
homosexuality
    decriminalisation of 177
    see also lesbian, gay, bisexual and
        transsexual (LGBT)
Honneth, A. 298
'honour-based violence' 218–19
hormonal changes 16
'hour glass' economy 156
Hugman, R. 98
human rights 98, 276–7
Human Rights Assessments 326
human trafficking 318–20
Humphris, R. 330
Hyde, B. 122

I

ICD (International Statistical Classification of
    Diseases and Related Health Problems)
    143
identity
    bereavement and loss of 193
    concept of 76–7, 81
    and disability 274
    and individualism 165
    and needs assessment 78
    and Prevent policy 80
    role of peers 161–2
    role of social media 159, 162
    theory in practice 80–1
    and transition to adulthood 155–6
    see also self
ideographic perspectives 71
IFSW (International Federation of Social
    Workers) 92, 98–9
illness
    and spirituality 117-18, 124
    see also mental health disorders
imitative learning 23–6, 57
immigration
    discourses 310–11, 329
    see also unaccompanied migrant children
Immigration Act (2016) 310, 315, 322, 326
imprinting 134
individual responsibility 17, 97, 155, 234
individualism 153–4, 165
individuative-reflective faith 113
inequality 158, 215–16, 275–6

infant-carer relationships 36, 41–4
    see also attachment theory
information technology 154, 159
    see also social media
injuries 229
insecure avoidant attachment 141, 254
instrumental conditioning 20–3
intellectual development 115
intelligence 53
inter-professional collaboration (IPC) 290,
    293, 296–7, 301
inter-professional education (IPE) 290
inter-professional learning (IPL) 290
internal working models 136, 253
International Federation of Social Workers
    (IFSW) 92, 98–9
International Statistical Classification of
    Diseases and Related Health Problems
    (ICD) 143
intersectionality 97, 167
intimacy 43–4
intuitive-projective faith 112
involvement *see* participation; service-user
    involvement
IPC (inter-professional collaboration)290
    293, 296–7, 301
IPE (inter-professional education) 290
IPL (inter-professional learning) 290
Irigaray, L. 37, 43
Irigaray, T.Q. 230, 233
Irish Childhood Bereavement Network *200,
    201*
Irish, L. 229
ISIS (Islamic State of Iraq and Syria) 216
Islam
    and cultural variation 220
    family in 209–10
    gender norms in 209, 217–19
    and morality 111
    piety in 214–15
    see also Muslims
Islamic State 216
Islamist Groups 216
Islamophobia 210–11, 216–17

J

James, A. 68, 82
James, A.L. 68, 82
James, W. 111
Jay, A. 221
Journal of Social Work Practice 44
Judaism, and morality 111

K

Kagan, J. 145–6
Keenan, T. 27

transference 38, 44–5
transition to adulthood 153
  applying knowledge to practice 165–7,
    282–3
  background 153–5
  case studies 157, 166–7
  in complex world 153–4, 155–7, 165
  and crime 185–6
  and culture 211–12, 217–18, 219–20
  of disabled young people 282–3, 284
  further reading 168
  of looked-after children 166, 262–3
  reflection on 156, 159, 163, 167, 168
  and social constructions 79
  theories and theorists
    friends and relationships 161–3
    gender, sex and sexuality 159–61
    living contexts 157–9
    mental health 164–5
    social media 163–4
    young people 155–7
  of unaccompanied migrants 324–8
  see also adolescence; puberty
transracial placements 258–60, 261
trauma 71–2, 118
Trevarthen, C. 34
triple planning 326, 327
truanting 183
true attachment 135
Trump, D. 217
'turning points' 158, 212

U
UKIP 217
UN Convention on the Rights of the Child
  (CRC) 290
UN Convention on the Rights of Persons
  with Disabilities 276–7
unaccompanied asylum-seeking children
  (UASC) 312
unaccompanied migrant children 309
  age assessment 312, 313, 321
  asylum discourses 310–11, 313–14
  background 310–11, 328–9
  case studies 317, 318–19, 320, 325–6
  definition 311–12
  further reading 329–30
  legislation and policy 310, 311, 314–15,
    323–6, 328
  National Transfer Scheme 321–4
  needs assessment 315–20
  reflection on 314, 324, 329
  transition to adulthood 324–8
unconscious 31, 32, 38
undifferentiated faith 112
Universal Credit 88

universalism 98
universalizing faith 113
university education 155, 209, 210

V
values 98–9, 279
Venables, Jon 172–3, 182, 183,
  184
vicarious learning see modelling
violence 58, 63, 91, 218–19
virtual space 43–4
  see also social media
Vis, S.A. 296, 302
von Bertalanffy, L. 17, 91
Vygotsky, L.S. 55–6, 118

W
Waddell, M. 38
Wade, J. 315
Walker, J. 12, 27
Walsh, A. 182
Ward, H. 243-4
Wass, H. 193
Wastell, D. 238, 239–40, 244
Waterhouse inquiry 260
Watson, J.B. 18
Watts, M. 153
weaning 40
Weisz, J.R. 292, 304
welfare benefits 88
Welfare Reform Act (2012) 88
well-being 160, 164–5
White, J. 35
White, S. 238, 239-40, 244
Widom, C.S. 230
Wijedasa, D. 259
Willumsen, E. 289, 294, 297, 304
Wilson, G.L. 185
Wilson, K. 264
Winnicott, D. 35, 36, 37, 40, 41, 44
Wittig, B.A. 139, 148
Wolfgang, M. 179
World Health Organization (WHO) 134,
  227–8, 272, 290, 291
Wright, F. 328, 330

Y
Yip, K.-S. 95
young offenders 180, 196–7

Z
zone of proximal development 55–6

Printed and bound by CPI Group (UK) Ltd, Croydon, CR0 4YY

09/06/2025

14685900-0004